THE MOST TRUSTED NAME IN TRAVEL: **FROMMER'S**

FROMMER'S EasyGuide to
NEW ORLEANS

8th Edition

W9-AQW-677

By Diana K. Schwam
& Lavinia Spalding

FrommerMedia LLC

FROMMER'S STAR RATINGS SYSTEM

Every hotel, restaurant, and attraction listed in this guide has been ranked for quality and value. Here's what the stars mean:

★ Recommended
★★ Highly Recommended
★★★ A must! Don't miss!

AN IMPORTANT NOTE

The world is a dynamic place. Hotels change ownership, restaurants hike their prices, museums alter their opening hours, and buses and trains change their routings. And all of this can occur in the several months after our authors have visited, inspected, and written about these hotels, restaurants, museums, and transportation services. Though we have made valiant efforts to keep all our information fresh and up-to-date, some few changes can inevitably occur in the periods before a revised edition of this guidebook is published. So please bear with us if a tiny number of the details in this book have changed. Please also note that we have no responsibility or liability for any inaccuracy or errors or omissions, or for inconvenience, loss, damage, or expenses suffered by anyone as a result of assertions in this guide.

PREVIOUS PAGE: The Lagniappe Brass Band entertains passersby in Jackson Square. THIS PAGE: It's not just tourist kitsch—a display of Voodoo masks explores the religion's roots in West Africa.

CONTENTS

Bourbon and Orleans streets meet at the heart of the fabled French Quarter.

A LOOK AT NEW ORLEANS

Tennessee Williams famously wrote "America has only three cities: New York, San Francisco, and New Orleans. Everything else is Cleveland." And while that may be an extreme viewpoint (and one that reflects an outdated view of Cleveland!), it's undeniable that NOLA, Crescent City, Nawlins, The Big Easy, or whatever other nickname you want to give it has a joie de vivre that's unmatched in the United States, if not the world. This is a city that raises the pursuit of pleasure to an art form—in its food, its music scene, its festivals, its embrace of culture, and the exquisite architecture that graces its streets. What follow in this section is a brief peek at just some of the scintillating sights and experience that await you on your own trip.

—Pauline Frommer

Summertime blossoms of crape myrtle accentuate colorfully painted houses in the aptly named Garden District.

FRENCH QUARTER

A second-line band leads its traveling street party past the elegant 19th-century Pontalba Buildings, rows of townhouses facing onto Jackson Square at the heart of the French Quarter. For a look inside, visit the 1850 House (p. 158).

The oldest active cathedral in the United States, St. Louis Cathedral (p. 156) presides over the French Quarter from the top of Jackson Square, with museums on either side in the historic Cabildo (p. 160) and Presbytère (p. 163).

The cutting-edge Audubon Aquarium of the Americas (p. 154) houses marine life from across the globe, with an emphasis on the Gulf of Mexico and the Mississippi River.

With an interesting history and an enviable French Quarter location, the Bourbon Orleans Hotel (p. 65) is a reliable choice for those who want to combine culture, comfort, and nightlife.

The small New Orleans Historic Voodoo Museum (p. 163) is packed with displays of intriguing Voodoo objects from around the world.

Running along the Mississippi River past the Audubon Aquarium to Jackson Square, Woldenberg Riverfront Park (p. 157) is a wide-open promenade graced with lawns, trees, public artworks, even a splash fountain.

Definitely the oldest bar, and possibly the oldest building, in the French Quarter, the atmospheric Lafitte's Blacksmith Shop (p. 224) is a popular place to down a brewskie and make new friends.

The famous (and infamous) Bourbon Street strip is known for live music, free-flowing booze, and a let-your-hair-down vibe. You should see it at least once, preferably at dusk, before it gets wild; see Chapter 8 for tips on which bars and clubs are most worth a stop.

A signature taste of New Orleans: the toasted muffuletta and Pimm's Cup at the historic Napoleon House bar (p. 225) on Chartres Street.

At elegant Arnaud's restaurant (p. 97), a century-old Quarter institution, the café brûlot cocktail is made with flaming brandy, spices, and citrus peel.

Expect to get dusted in powdered sugar when you indulge in a hot fried beignet and café au lait at the perennially popular Café du Monde (p. 146).

Pull up a stool to one of the food counters at the lively colonnaded French Market (p. 233), on Decatur Street. Dirty rice and gator burger, anyone?

MARDI GRAS & JAZZ FEST

Carnival season in New Orleans is always better if you plan ahead. Follow our advice in Chapter 4 (p. 49) to grab the best sidewalk views of the many parades, each with its own flavor and distinctive elaborate floats.

With a little strategy and even more luck, you may score a sighting of one of the elusive Mardi Gras Indians (p. 53) in their intricate hand-beaded and -feathered ceremonial garb.

Even spectators join the spectacle on Fat Tuesday by donning costumes and glittering masks. To get yours, check out one of the costume shops on p. 240.

Roving Mardi Gras celebrations in the Cajun countryside (p. 277) call for colorful patchwork costumes, pointy hats, traditional music, and a gumbo feast.

Everything from jazz and rock to zydeco, Delta blues, and folk music is played on 14 stages at the Fair Grounds during the New Orleans Jazz and Heritage Festival. See p. 59.

And this being New Orleans, the "heritage" part of the Jazz and Heritage Festival (p. 59) must include a wide array of food booths featuring local delicacies.

Clang clang! The historic green streetcars of the St. Charles Avenue line clatter uptown, a scenic way to escape the French Quarter and take in the beautiful Victorian and Greek Revival houses of the Garden District. Once you're there, hop off and take our walking tour on p. 257.

Bicycles are a great way to get around this relatively flat city—see p. 291 for rental options. A particularly nice path loops around under the live oaks uptown in Audubon Park (p. 180).

Exploring New Orleans also means exploring the Mississippi River. Docked along the riverfront, paddlewheel steamboats like the *Creole Queen* (p. 197) get you out on the water in style.

The National World War II Museum (p. 168) is one of the finest history museums in the United States. Descriptions don't do justice to its incredibly moving, interactive exhibits, which illuminate the personal side of war.

Some 40,000 works are owned by the New Orleans Museum of Art (p. 170), everything from pre-Columbian sculptures to paintings by European masters to the world's biggest collection of decorative glass.

Restored to its early-19th-century Creole glory overlooking Bayou St. John, Pitot House (p. 171) was originally a plantation home, before the city expanded outward and surrounded the bayou.

A Garden District walking tour pauses in front of the house used in the film *The Curious Case of Benjamin Button*. See p. 190 for a list of knowledgeable walking tour guides.

Aboveground tombs at Lafayette Cemetery No. 1 (p. 186). New Orleans' unusual cities of the dead are a characteristic feature of the city's landscape.

Antiques, boutiques, and galleries line Magazine Street (p. 234), the Garden District's premier shopping drag.

A New Orleans success story, colorful Dat Dog (p. 143)—now with three locations around the city—gives the hot dog stand a delightful upgrade.

The lobby bar of the Ace Hotel (p. 78). Set in a converted Art Deco building in the CBD, this hipster haven sports photo booths, in-room turntables and vintage vinyl, plus three bars and two restaurants.

There's no better place to while away an evening than on Frenchmen Street in the Marigny, especially at the always-hopping Spotted Cat Music Club (p. 218).

Meals are an event in the Crescent City, and that's certainly the case at the Warehouse District's Compère Lapin (p. 124), helmed by Nina Compton, a runner-up on TV's *Top Chef*.

A slave cabin at Laura: A Creole Plantation (p. 275). The tour here offers a window into daily life on an 18th- and 19th-century sugar plantation and a cultural history of the Creole clan who owned it.

The splendid white "big house" at Oak Alley Plantation (p. 275) is complemented by re-created slave quarters that illuminate the other side of 19th-century plantation life.

The Evangeline Oak in St. Martinville (p. 286) commemorates the arrival of the Nova Scotian Acadians from whom modern Cajuns claim their descent.

Tours of the stunning, primeval Atchafalaya swamp (p. 285), near Lafayette, usually include encountering alligators in their native sloshing grounds.

Crawfish boils, andouille and boudin sausage, étouffée stew, pig-fat cracklings—welcome to the down-home tastes of Cajun food. See p. 94 for a list of Cajun eateries in New Orleans.

Kayaking through the mysterious swamps outside New Orleans is vital to understanding the city's Mississippi Delta identity. See p. 194 for tours.

THE BEST OF NEW ORLEANS

By Diana K. Schwam

New Orleans should come with a warning label. No, no, not about hurricanes (or Covid, for that matter). That's like solely identifying Hawaii with erupting volcanoes. No, this is about the city itself. See, there's this group of residents known as the "never lefts." They are the people who first came to New Orleans as tourists, and the city worked its magic on them.

They become spellbound by the beauty of the French Quarter and the Garden District and marvel that history is alive right beneath their feet. They listen to music flowing from random doorways and street corners—jazz, soul, blues, whatever—and find themselves moving to a languorous rhythm. They kiss beneath flickering gas lamps and groove to a brass band in a crowded club long past their usual bedtimes.

They eat sumptuous, indulgent meals and indulge yet again hours later, with beignets at 3 a.m., when the city's beguiling, sexy spookiness is cresting. They catch the scent of jasmine and sweet olive (with a whiff of the Caribbean, and a garlic top note, perhaps) wafting through the moist, honeyed air.

The air . . . aah, the New Orleans air. People say romance is in the air here. It's true, of course, because the air is dreamy. It's the dewy ingénue who grows up fast in the first act, softly whispering your name. And if you're meant to be together, you'll feel that undeniable flutter, the high-voltage spark that says you're in my heart forever.

That's what happens to the never lefts. They came for Mardi Gras, for a festival, conference, tryst, wedding, weekend—just came—and fell hard. New Orleans does that to people.

What is it about this place? Well, New Orleans is where cultures and centuries commingle, perhaps not effortlessly but nowhere more captivatingly. It's where a barstool or a bench becomes the opening salvo in a conversation you may never forget—raconteurship thrives here. It's a living masquerade party of old masters, modernists, and bohemian street artists. It's a city that actually has an official cocktail—which speaks volumes to its state of mind. It's where gumbo—the savory stew that is often (over-) used in describing the city's multicultural tableau—is actually an apt metaphor: for a place that's deep, mysterious, rich with flavor, spiked with spice—and so much more than the hot, heady sum of its disparate parts.

Many a tourist leaves here heart-struck with this unicorn city—this magical, joyful, rare place. It's imperfect, yes, but when you're falling in love it's easy to overlook flaws. There was, however, no ignoring the toll that Covid-19 and Hurricane Ida recently took—in lives and livelihoods lost, in spirits dampened. For many, that remains true.

After a history full of gut punches, New Orleans' storied resilience is a bit of a trope. And yet, it's proven true again. It's back. We're back. Or more likely, never left. Step by step, mask by mask, doors re-opened, parades began rolling, visitors began venturing into town, and now the music again reverberates from river to lake. Dinner is served, y'all . . . c'mon down.

That said, some things have changed: Do bring your vaccine cards and masks, as those may be required at any time (or not—who knows what the future shall bring). Do check the requirements of places or events on your must-do list, and prepare accordingly.

Then, let the ineffable essence of New Orleans enchant you. But don't take our word for it. Go. See, hear, and taste for yourself. The best way to get inside New Orleans is to plunge right in. Don't just go for the obvious. Sure, we've met people who never left Bourbon Street and had a terrific time, but the city has so much more to offer. Look over the advice that follows, and if New Orleans envelops you in its ineffable essence, perhaps you'll come to understand the never lefts. Perhaps you'll even come to be one.

THE most authentic NEW ORLEANS EXPERIENCES

- **Do Festivals, Big or Small:** Yes to Jazz Fest, Mardi Gras, or French Quarter Fest, but also the smaller fests in New Orleans and nearby towns. If one is on while you're visiting, seek it out. See p. 49.

- **Dress Up. Or Down:** At better restaurants, men wear jackets—including seersucker when in season—and un-ironic hats. Women can and do wear dresses (not just LBDs) and heels. It's required at the finest spots, optional but common at more moderate bistros (where jeans are also okay). Dressing down might mean wacky wigs, cosplay, whatever. You can get away with it here, where every day is Halloween.

- **Frequent Dive Bars and Corner-Grocery Back Counters:** If that's your thang, that is. For those whose thang it is, this town is siiick with deeply divey drinkeries (see p. 227), and tasty tucked-away eateries (see p. 107).

- **Tour the Swamps:** Don't discount this because you think it's too touristy (New Yorkers still go to Broadway, right?). It's an absolutely authentic, ecologically and historically fascinating, unique-to-the-region experience. See p. 194.

- **Ride a Bike:** New Orleans is flat and compact, and you can see a lot on two wheels that you might otherwise miss. See p. 291 for rentals and p. 199 for tours.

- **Cheer the Saints:** In the Dome, if possible—ain't nothing like it, nowhere. Or at least from a barstool, like everyone who ain't in the Dome. See p. 178.
- **Look Around:** Pocket the phone for a spell. Walk, look, take it in. The architecture, flora, remnants of Spain, France, Haiti, street tableaus weird and wonderful . . . as New Orleans swirls around you like stars in a new galaxy, let your eyes be your camera.
- **Argue About the Best Po' Boy:** Which requires trying a few (see p. 112). Discussing the next meal during the current meal also counts.
- **Go to Church:** Despite the reputation for decadence, this is a pretty pious city. Going to church is a wonderful way to get some faith on, hear some astounding gospel, and mingle with the welcoming locals. See p. 175.
- **Check Out a Freebie Concert:** Grab a chair or blanket and join the locals. See what's up in **Armstrong Park, City Park,** the **French Market,** or at **Lafayette Square** in the CBD for music, food booths, and an all-around chill scene. Schedule varies, but check www.wednesdayatthesquare.com for regular events.
- **Stroll the Galleries:** Look for openings with low-key revelry and flowing wine the first Saturday evening of each month on Julia Street, and the loosely organized second Saturdays on St. Claude Avenue. But any time will do. See p. 235.
- **Eat Indulgent, Unhurried, Fancy Lunches:** Especially on Friday.
- **Chat:** Discuss. Debate. Banter. In restaurants, bars, or shops. With people you've just met. We'll give you locals' topics: football and city politics/ineptitude. Barring your expertise in those arenas, trading anecdotes about your observations as a tourist, discussing a recent activity or meal, or asking for recommendations for your next will get the convo started.
- **Eat with Your Hands:** Specifically, peel shrimp and crawfish (in season), best done outdoors; and slurp oysters, best done standing at a bar and jiving with the shucker.
- **Loosen Up:** If a wailing trumpet catches your ear, follow the sound 'til you find it. If the swing band playing in the middle of Royal Street moves you, give your partner a whirl (and drop a fiver in their hat). If you track every calorie and swear by the Fitbit, lose count for a few days. And if you're lucky enough to happen upon a second-line parade passing by, don't even think of watching from the sidewalk. Jump in, and high-step it down the street. In other words, if there's something you wouldn't dare do elsewhere, now is your opportunity. You needn't lose *all* sense of propriety—but do lose *some.* It's New Orleans—it's what you do.

Impressions

We dance even if there's no radio. We drink at funerals. We talk too much and laugh too loud and live too large and, frankly, we're suspicious of others who don't.

—*Chris Rose*

1 | THE best PLACES TO EAT IN NEW ORLEANS

o **Best All-Around Dining Experience You Can Have in New Orleans:** No surprises here, they're world-famous for good reason: **Commander's Palace** (p. 135), hands down. At the other end of the spectrum, **Café du Monde** (p. 146). Somewhere in the middle: **Brigtsen's** (p. 134) and **Mosquito Supper Club** (p. 137).

o **Best Classic New Orleans Restaurant:** Three old-line, fine-dining mainstays have been enjoyed for generations. **Arnaud's** (p. 97) is my choice for food; **Galatoire's** (p. 103) for the overall experience; and **Antoine's** (p. 97) for room after amazing room full of history.

o **Best Contemporary Creole or French:** An old favorite and a new one, both well-deserved: the still lovely **Coquette** (p. 136) and the sensational **St. John** (p. 106).

o **Best Contemporary Cajun:** Popular vote goes to pork-centric **Cochon** (p. 128), where you won't find yo mama's Cajun, but my vote goes to **Toups' Meatery** on the casual end (p. 120), and **Gabrielle** (p. 117) for highly refined rustic fare.

o **Best Italian:** We've fallen hard for the *nuovo* take by Uptown's sexy **Avo** (p. 132) and seafood specialist **San Lorenzo** (p. 138). **Irene's Cuisine** (p. 108) and **Italian Barrel** (p. 104) represent New Orleans' traditional Creole Italian; nods to **Arabella Casa di Pasta** (p. 116) for casual.

o **Best Neighborhood Restaurants:** New Orleans tucks away some shockingly good restaurants on unassuming residential streets. **Clancy's** (p. 134), **High Hat** (p. 145), **Bywater Bakery** (p. 116), **Gabrielle** (p. 117), and **Liuzza's by the Track** (p. 122) show the range.

o **Best Neighbahood Restaurants:** In contrast to those above, these are old-school joints, where locals still ask, "Hey, dahwlin', wheah y'at?" We've gotta go wit da fishies and Creole Italian oldies at **Mandina's** (p. 119) and sizzling steak and sass at **Charlie's** (p. 134).

o **Most Innovative Restaurants:** Menu magic is made when talented chefs fuse traditional Creole ingredients and flavors with those of divergent lands: **Maypop** (p. 126) mixes in Southeast Asian concepts with stellar results. **Marjie's** (p. 120) blends heretofore uncommon ideas and essences, and the details make the difference at delicious **Palm & Pine** (p. 109).

o **Best Expense- or Savings-Account Blowouts: Restaurant R'evolution** (p. 105), **Emeril's** (p. 125), or the Chef's Table at **Commander's Palace** (p. 135) will do the job. The 5-course menu and wine pairing at lovely, novel **Saint-Germain** (p. 113) also works just fine.

o **Best Bistro:** Tough choice given the richness of this category, but **La Petite Grocery** (p. 137) and **Sylvain** (p. 109) figure highly. **Zasu** (p. 118) and **Lilette** (p. 137) may rise above the bistro category but deserve mention.

- **Best Outdoor Dining:** The already-full category exploded during the pandemic: the pretty courtyards at **Bayona** (p. 100), **N7** (p. 116), **Jewel of the South** (p. 223), **The Chloe** (p. 139), and **Café Amelie** (p. 107) on starry nights or balmy afternoons; the funky front- and backyard vibes at **Bacchanal** (p. 113) or **Seafood Sally's** (p. 142); or sexy side yards at **Cane & Table** (p. 222). The second-floor galleries at **Tableau** (p. 106), **Gris Gris** (p. 139), and **Dat Dog** (p. 143) overlook the entertaining extremes of Jackson Square, Magazine St., and Frenchmen St. respectively; while **The Delachaise** (p. 139) brings the Parisian along rue due Magazine.

- **Best Rooftop Bars:** They've sprung up nearly everywhere, but we're partial to **Hot Tin**, at the Pontchartrain Hotel (p. 87), and **Alto**, atop the Ace Hotel (p. 78).

- **Best for Kids:** The no-brainers are **Café du Monde** (p. 146), for powdered-sugar mess and mania; the counter at **Camellia Grill** (p. 142); **Joey K's** (p. 145) for tolerance and a something-for-everyone menu; and a **snoball** (p. 148). **Antoine's** (p. 97) offers a fine-dining intro, lots to see between courses, and baked Alaska. Don't skip **Acorn** when visiting the Children's Museum (p. 202) or the **breweries** (p. 229), most of which are family-friendly.

- **Best Slightly Offbeat but Utterly New Orleanian Restaurants:** Definitely **Bacchanal** (p. 113). The fancier **Justine** (p. 104) and decidedly unfancy **Piece of Meat** (p. 120) also fit the category.

- **Best Seafood:** Upscale **GW Fins** sets a high bar (p. 103), though **Pêche** (p. 127) is a strong contender; Mid-City's **Bevi** (p. 121) covers the low-key, boiled-seafood angle. For oysters, **Casamento's** (p. 143).

- **Best Desserts:** A meal at **Emeril's** (p. 125) is incomplete without banana cream pie; ditto **Commander's Palace**'s (p. 135) bread pudding soufflé, **Arnaud's** bananas Foster flambé (p. 97), and **Antoine's** (p. 97) baked Alaska. The pastry chefs at **Lilette** (p. 137) and **Coquette** (p. 136) excel, as do the pie people at **High Hat** (p. 145) or **Gris Gris** (p. 139). Or head to a dessert specialist (p. 146).

- **Best Brunch:** Breakfast at **Brennan's** is rightly famed (p. 100). **Café Degas** (p. 118) or **Patois** (p. 138) can't miss, while the fancy jazz brunch at **Arnaud's** (p. 97) and **Commander's Palace** (p. 135) are great fun—as is the unfancy one at **Buffa's** (p. 216). Gotta give love to the drag brunch at **Country Club** (p. 114) and **Effervescence** for the bubbly (p. 223).

- **Restaurants with the Best Cocktail Programs:** From a looong list, we'll go with **Latitude 29** (p. 108), **Revel** (p. 120), **Compère Lapin** (p. 124), **Cane & Table** (p. 222), and **Zasu** (p. 118), with a nod to wacky **Turkey & the Wolf** (p. 146).

- **Best Wine Lists:** The extensive collections at **Emeril's** (p. 125), **Arnaud's** (p. 97), **Commander's Palace** (p. 135), and **Antoine's** (p. 97) cover every base. The lists are smaller but smart at **Bayona** (p. 100), **Saint-Germain** (p. 113), and **Elysian Bar** (p. 115), and well-curated at **Bacchanal** (p. 113) and **Saffron** (p. 141).

THE best PLACES TO STAY IN NEW ORLEANS

This is a little like deciding on a scoop of ice cream—so many tasty options to choose from, and different people like different flavors. We've tried to narrow down the selections based on specific criteria.

o **Best Moderately Priced Lodging:** In general, you'll get the biggest bang in the off-season (including the heat of summer), when even luxury properties feature enticingly lower rates. In the French Quarter, the **Olivier House** (p. 70) is fun, funky, and very fairly priced. In the CBD, the **Drury Plaza** (p. 81) is surprisingly reasonable and an easy hop to the Quarter. In the B&B category, the **Chimes** (p. 88), a delightful family-owned guesthouse in the Garden District, has generated legions of loyal return guests. And in the hostel department, **HI New Orleans** (p. 83) is a great budget option.

o **Best Luxury Hotel:** At the intimate **Audubon Cottages** (p. 65), luxury commences when your 24-hour butler greets you at the private, unmarked entrance. For classic opulence, attention to your every need, and vast expanses of room, it's the **Windsor Court** (p. 80). A Club Level suite, of course. The new **Four Seasons** (p. 78) adds views-for-days to luxe detail; while boutique **Maison de la Luz** (p. 79) brings understated extravagance

o **Best Service:** All those in the "Luxury" category above excel in the service category, as do the new **Virgin Hotel** (p. 80) and **Hotel Saint Vincent** (p. 86). We're also continually impressed by the attentive **NOPSI Hotel** (p. 82). Of the more modest accommodations, congeniality and overall graciousness awards go to Uptown's **Maison Perrier** (p. 87), the **Chimes** (p. 88) in the Garden District, and Mid-City's **1896 O'Malley House** (p. 75).

o **Most Romantic:** Romance is wherever you make it, but **Ashton's** (p. 76) encourages long, languid mornings. No one will find you in the secluded **Audubon Cottages** (p. 65), and the luxe **Maison de la Luz** (p. 79) prizes privacy and soaking tubs. The rooms in two new hotels, the **Hotel Saint Vincent** (p. 86) and **The Chloe** (p. 139), are swoony enough for you to stay in bed all day.

o **Best for Families:** The safest bet for travelers with kids is often a chain hotel (two-room suites, amenities, freebie meals, pools, cribs, relative anonymity during meltdowns), and chains abound here. However, we haven't listed many of them; we favor charming locally owned businesses. The most family-pleasing of those include, in the luxury category, the **Roosevelt Hotel** (p. 79), where kids always feel extra-special (in Dec, the hotel's a magical wonderland), and the **Hotel Monteleone** (p. 65), also a bit of a splurge. Among more moderately priced indies, our top choices are the new **One11 Hotel** (p. 71), for its pool, fire-pit, and great location next to the Audubon Aquarium in the quiet part of the Quarter (BYO crib, though), and the low-key **Olivier House** (p. 70), with its pool, friendly cats, and mysterious stairways to explore. Budget watchers might reconsider multi-bed rooms at newer hostels, like the **HI New Orleans** (p. 83).

o **Best Faaaabulous B&B:** A lot of B&Bs are crammed with over-the-top antiques, but at the **Antebellum** (p. 76), they all come with a story. I love the tawdry over-the-topness, hidden hot tub, and actual bordello bed.

o **Best for Hipness:** The **Hotel Peter & Paul** (p. 73) opened in 2018 to out-hip everything else, till the **Virgin Hotel** (p. 80) and **Hotel Saint Vincent** (p. 86) came to town. For action, it's still the **Ace** (p. 78).

o **Best Funky Spots:** We're fond of the sweetly eccentric **B&W Courtyards** (p. 74), a Marigny gem, and the Frenchmen-adjacent **Royal Street Inn** (p. 74). The hip, mid-cen motel conversion **The Drifter** (p. 77) is altogether different for altogether different reasons.

o **Best Hidden Gem:** The uneventful location of the **Henry Howard** (p. 86) belies its stunningly renovated interior and comfortable, hip vibe. The **Auld Sweet Olive** is a warm, Marigny respite just far enough from the madding crowds (p. 74).

THE best TRIP MEMENTOS

You'll always have your memories and IG posts. And nothing's wrong with T-shirts, caps, Mardi Gras beads, masks, a voodoo doll, chicory coffee, or beignet mix. For something a little extra, consider these alternate ideas.

o **A Book from Faulkner House:** Many an author has tried, with varying success, to capture New Orleans on the page. Their efforts may help you know what it means to miss New Orleans. Pick up some reading material from this charming jewel on little Pirate's Alley, crammed with Louisiana-related tomes (p. 239).

o **A Photo or Art Book from A Gallery for Fine Photography:** The owner calls his impressive shop "the only museum where you can buy the art." A photograph from one of the many famed photographers represented here is a souvenir to relish every day, not to mention a wise investment. If an original isn't feasible, consider a fine photo book. See p. 237.

o **A Southern Scent from Hové:** This classic perfumery creates its own perfumes and soaps. I'm partial to sachet-favorite Vetivert, described as "smelling like the South." Locals also adore the scents made from the indigenous sweet olive, and the fine gentlemanly scents. See p. 244.

o **Local Art:** Take home a singular treasure from one of the many excellent galleries (p. 235), from the vendors around **Jackson Square,** or at a local art market like those at **Marsalis Harmony Park** (p. 232).

o **Tunes:** New Orleans' soundtrack is as essential to your experience as her sights and tastes. Some vinyl or a few CDs purchased (yes, bought) at gigs or a record-shop (p. 245) will keep the good times rolling back home. See my recorded-music recommendations in chapter 2.

- **A Hat from Meyer:** We're mad about **Meyer the Hatter** for the selection, the service, and the 100-year-plus history. You're in the South, *darlin';* you can rock some class headgear. See p. 241.

- **A "BE NICE OR LEAVE" Sign:** Dr. Bob's colorful, bottle-cap-edged signs are true local works of folk art, handmade with found materials. Visiting his one-of-a-kind Bywater studio, **Dr. Bob Art** (p. 236), just adds to the sentimental value.

- **Fleur-de-Lis Jewelry:** Gold, silver, glass, cufflink, nose ring, pendant—the selection is unending. Wear it with pride; share it with a smile. Consider something from **Mignon Faget** (p. 244) or an inexpensive bauble from the flea-market stands at the **French Market** (p. 233).

- **Sazerac Glasses:** If you've taken a shine to the city's official cocktail, the **Roosevelt Hotel** (p. 79) has perfect reproductions of their original glasses.

- **Pralines:** The choice for office gifts. And for home. Maybe one for the plane or car on the way there. (And remember, it's *prah,* not *pray.*) See p. 239.

- **A Custom-Writ Poem:** Why not a sonnet? Street poets set up their crusty, trusty typewriters most nights along Frenchmen Street and elsewhere, ready to plink out a verse or three based on your input.

- **A Forever Souvenir:** Get inked at **Electric Ladyland Tattoo,** 610 Frenchmen St. (electricladylandtattoo.com; ℂ **504/947 8286**), noon to midnight daily. If you can think it (and you should), they can ink it.

THE best OF OUTDOOR NEW ORLEANS

Not exactly what you think of when you think Big Easy—it's not Yellowstone, after all. But there are some surprisingly wonderful outdoorsy things to do here that will only enhance the vacation you envisioned. Besides, it can't all be about dark bars and decadent meals. Oh wait, it's New Orleans. Yes, it can. Still . . . these experiences provide a fine counterpoint and a different perspective.

- **Kayak Bayou St. John:** A guided kayak tour of placid, pretty Bayou St. John is an entrancing way to see this historically significant waterway—and maybe work off a few bites of fried shrimp po' boy. See p. 196.

- **City Park It:** Whatever your outdoor thing, it's probably doable somewhere in the glorious, 1,300-acre **City Park** (p. 181), from pedal-boating to picnicking, birding to bicycling, golfing (mini or big) to art-gazing. It's great for a morning run, as is Uptown's **Audubon Park** (p. 180). **Lafitte Greenway** (p. 182) and **Crescent Park** (p. 182), two newer, smaller parks, offer interesting and different perspectives of the city.

- **Tour the Swamps:** The swamps are eerie, serene, and fascinating. The gators are spellbinding, and most guides are knowledgeable naturalists who will open your eyes to this unique ecoculture. See p. 194.

- **Ferry Cross the Mississippi:** It's not quite Huck Finn, but a brief "cruise" on the ferry to the historic Algiers neighborhood is an easy way to roll on the river and take in a different view. See p. 292.
- **See the City from Two Wheels (or Three):** Whether you rent a bike (p. 291), take a guided bike tour (p. 199), or zip around on a motorscooter (p. 292), seeing the flat, compact city via two wheels makes for a sweet ride.
- **Dine Alfresco:** I didn't say the best of *active* outdoor New Orleans, did I? A languid, courtyard dinner under the southern stars (or lunch under an umbrella) is an experience to be savored. See p. 5.
- **Do Yoga in the Besthoff Sculpture Garden:** There may be no more sublime way to start a Saturday—especially when it's followed by beignets and coffee (just steps away at **Café du Monde**). A little yin, a little yang. It's Saturdays at 8am in City Park (© **504/482-4888;** p. 171).
- **Twerk in the Park:** New Orleans music accompanies the super fun **Move Ya Brass** (p. 294) twerk, bounce, and stretch classes, open to the community and held in public locales. Check the schedule at moveyabrass.com.
- **Walk. Walk. And Walk Some More:** This city is made for walking. It's truly the best way to take in the captivating sights, appreciate the silken air, and ogle (or join) the goings-on you will undoubtedly encounter. I won't bring up the c-word benefits (calories—oops, drat . . . sorry). No texting while walking, though—these buckling old sidewalks require your full attention.

NEW ORLEANS' best MUSEUMS

New York, Chicago, Paris, Rome . . . great museum cities, all. New Orleans isn't included in that list, but it's a surprisingly excellent museum city. Museums also make stellar retreats when the elements become overbearing.

- **Historic New Orleans Collection:** A tech-forward, 2019 update has vaulted this treasured complex to the best museum list. See p. 161.
- **Louisiana Children's Museum:** Better than ever in its new City Park location, it offers so much hands-on, interactive fun (for all ages) you don't even realize you're also learning. See p. 202.
- **Le Musée de f.p.c.:** The history, plight and stunning accomplishments of Free People of Color (fpc) are not widely enough recognized. A guided tour of this house museum will do a fine job of changing that. See p. 173.
- **National World War II Museum:** It's the best museum of its kind. Period. Do. Not. Miss. Its world-class collection and interactive displays. See p. 168.
- **New Orleans Jazz Museum:** Try to time your visit to see the worthy collection along with a live performance. See p. 163.
- **New Orleans Museum of Art:** Consistently well-curated exhibits and an excellent permanent collection of all forms of fine art, housed in a stunning, neoclassical-meets-modernist building in beautiful City Park. See p. 170.

- **Ogden Museum of Southern Art:** A splendid collection of the art of the American South in a modern atrium between historic buildings. See p. 169.
- **New Orleans Historical Pharmacy Museum:** Leeches and opium and Voodoo spells, oh my. A mightily worthwhile, off-the-wall diversion. See p. 162.
- **The Presbytère:** The excellent exhibit on hurricanes captures their impact from all aspects; other rotating exhibits are consistently good. See p. 163.

NEW ORLEANS IN CONTEXT

By Lavinia Spalding

New Orleans has long been known for its jazz-infused joie de vivre; it's a place where life is lived fully and out loud. But the visitors who truly "get" the city are those who arrive eager to hear the *whole* story. New Orleans is complicated: Its joyful, high-stepping spirit emerged from centuries of struggle; it was built by enslaved people and rebuilt (and is still rebuilding) after multiple catastrophes. Learning the city's past is a path to touching its soul.

Louisiana's largest city (pop. 390,000) and one of the chief urban centers of the South, New Orleans—the ancient ancestral grounds of the Chitimacha, Choctaw, and Houma Indigenous people—lies nearly 100 miles above the mouth of the Mississippi River system, stretching along a low-lying strip of land 5 to 8 miles wide, between the Mississippi and Lake Pontchartrain. New Orleans, which celebrated the 300th anniversary of its founding in 2018, is an old city with untold layers of history. Yet it also upholds the "new" in its name, because while preserving its past, it's forever reinventing itself.

In this chapter, we briefly recount the area's rich history, to help explain how New Orleanians got their resilient, life-affirming "yatitude" (as in "Where y'at?"—the local version of "How ya doin'?"). Think of this chapter as more than just a history lesson; it's an invitation to know New Orleans, so you too can be part of its story.

NEW ORLEANS TODAY

New Orleans has earned its reputation as a hub of glorious music and food and beauty, a nonstop party with friendly locals, and a culture so deep that diving in might permanently alter you. But it's important to note that the city itself has been altered in recent years. New Orleans lies largely below sea level—its highest natural point, in City Park, is a whopping 35 feet above sea level—and that fact has indelibly impacted its history.

New Orleanians will forever mark time as "Before Katrina" or "After Katrina." While the city has rebounded palpably since then, the grim images that focused the world's eyes on New Orleans in August 2005 are not easily erased—nor should they be. Hurricane Katrina, a Category 5 hurricane, was downgraded to a Category 3 when it hit New Orleans, but the surge was too much for the city's federal levee system. The failure flooded 80% of the city, causing 1,836 recorded deaths and all forms of astounding, horrifying loss. Some 28,000 people took refuge in the Superdome, the unplanned refuge of last resort, and hundreds of thousands of locals were permanently displaced. The devastated city mourned, then began the work of cleaning up and restoring.

In 2006, 6 months later, New Orleans still celebrated Mardi Gras (albeit a smaller version). Jazz Fest returned that year, too, with one of the most meaningful musical events in the city's history. For many, participating wasn't just about upholding tradition or reveling or even proving to the world that New Orleans' spirit was alive. It was a respite from despair.

In 2010, four and a half years after Katrina, the Dome's home football team, the New Orleans Saints, at long last came marching in with their first-ever Super Bowl victory. The long-derided 'Aints restored what billions in rebuilding funds couldn't: civic pride. It may seem trivial, even disrespectful, to cite a football game as a turning point in the city's rebirth—but it isn't. The effects of this victory reached far beyond the ecstatic, extended celebrations, and they cannot be overstated.

That year saw more high points: Mitch Landrieu won the mayoral race with 66% of the vote, a resounding response to the previous administration's fumbling, inertia, and corruption; and massive crowds poured into the city again for festival after festival. HBO premiered its series *Tremé,* which portrayed authentic New Orleans with a (mostly) spot-on eye and a killer soundtrack. The good times were rolling again. And then, the whammy. One. More. Time. The Deepwater Horizon oil spill hit in April 2010. Though New Orleans was 150 miles from the spill, the disaster had great ramifications for the economy and the lives of many residents.

But if anything's true about this city, it's that it keeps on keeping on. The unprecedented development that followed Hurricane Katrina brought an influx of new residents and a massive tourism boom. The annual number of visitors to Louisiana set records year after year, and the hotel market grew like kudzu (and is growing still). In the decimated Lower 9th Ward, redevelopment chugs along slowly but proudly, with some significant new developments. Other areas have also repopulated, redeveloped, and gentrified rapidly (threatening, many longtime locals believe, the very character that attracted the gentrifiers in the first place).

Yes, crime and the hobbled criminal-justice system remain problems here, and the city struggles to maintain and update an ancient pumping system and prevent (too-common) street flooding. And like so many American cities, New Orleans has unresolved issues with the racial divide, which flared up for the world to see in 2017, when four of the city's prominent confederate monuments were removed. Yet the next year, 2018, as New Orleans celebrated its

Call it New OR'linz. Call it New AW'linz. Call it New OR-lee-uhns, with four syllables. Call it New Or-LEENZ'. Or NOLA (in print). Even locals can't decide—you'll hear any of the above. But no one, save a true rube, calls it NAW-linz. Don't be a rube.

300th anniversary, LaToya Cantrell, a woman of color, was elected the city's first female mayor. Markers went up around town, finally memorializing the city's shameful history as the center of the domestic slave trade and recognizing the colossal influence of the enslaved on the region's development. Some 37 street names and a handful of parks are in the process of being renamed, mostly because they were formerly named after white supremacists.

In 2019, the dazzling $1-billion new terminal at Louis Armstrong International Airport was completed. And then came . . . 2020.

New Orleans, with its economy so reliant on tourism, was hit hard by the Covid-19 virus. In true form, locals responded with resilience, community, and creativity. **The Krewe of Red Beans** (p. 51), a beloved Mardi Gras walking krewe, organized four grassroots campaigns that raised more than $2 million to feed local healthcare workers and culture bearers and to support struggling restaurants, musicians, artists, and bars. And when Mardi Gras and Jazz Fest were canceled, two new traditions, house floats (p. 51) and "Festing in Place" (p. 60) lifted spirits and delivered hope.

The one-two punch came on August 29, 2021 (the 16th anniversary of Katrina), when Hurricane Ida made landfall as a Category 4 hurricane and barreled through Louisiana, causing an estimated $900 million in damages. The levees held this time (even if the power grid failed). Still, the storm took down many trees and roofs, destroyed a few historic sites, and caused catastrophic damage to the nearby river parishes. Many local businesses still await new roofs and other repairs, but most have reopened, and hopeful times are ahead. At the time of this writing, Covid-19 numbers are improving, parades are rolling, festivals are being green-lit, and music venues are selling out.

The Crescent City has sprung back to life, much like the resurrection fern that covers the branches of its live oak trees. The restaurant scene thrives, continuing to win top awards, as dynamic and diverse as it is delicious. Once-untouristed streets like Oak, Freret, St. Claude Avenue, and Oretha Castle Haley Boulevard are hot spots. Stunning new hotels are cropping up all over the city. And we say good luck finding a better street than Frenchmen for music, people-watching, and sheer exhilaration.

New Orleans' indomitable spirit is intact. The oysters are still sweet, the jasmine-infused air still sultry. Bands still play in Jackson Square, and parades erupt at random. New Orleans is still the best city in America, and the *bons temps*—like those beloved Saints of field and song—go marching in and on. We're right there with them. You should be, too. Go, and be in that number.

HISTORY 101

New Orleans was originally called Bulbancha, a Choctaw word meaning "place of many tongues." Long before the French and Spanish arrived, the area was home to Indigenous peoples, with settlements in the present-day French Quarter, the Lower Garden District, and at the mouth of Bayou St. John. The French Market was once the site of a thriving intertribal trading grounds. Historians estimate that before European colonization, Louisiana was home to 13,000 to 15,000 Indigenous people.

The first explorer to claim the region for France was René-Robert Cavelier, Sieur de la Salle, in 1682; he named it Louisiana, in honor of his monarch, Louis XIV. (Just 5 years later, La Salle's navigational and leadership failures in other explorations resulted in his mutinous murder by his own party.) In 1699, French-Canadian brothers Pierre Le Moyne, Sieur d'Iberville, and Jean Baptiste Le Moyne, Sieur de Bienville, staked a claim at a dramatic bend in the Mississippi River, near where La Salle had stopped 17 years earlier. Iberville also established a fort at Biloxi. Brother Bienville stayed on there, becoming commanding officer of the territory while harboring thoughts of returning to the upriver spot to establish a new capital city.

Finally, Bienville got his chance. In 1718, the French monarch—eager to develop, populate, and garner the riches that Louisiana promised—charged Bienville with finding a suitable location for a settlement, one that would also protect France's New World holdings from British expansion. Bienville chose the easily defended high ground at the bend in the river. Although it was some 100 miles inland from the Gulf of Mexico, the site was near Bayou St. John, a waterway into Lake Pontchartrain. This "back door" was convenient for a military defense or escape, and as a trade route (as the Choctaw people had long known)—allowing relatively easy access to the Gulf while bypassing a perilous section of the Mississippi. The Choctaw people called it Bayouk Choupic, and they shared this and other knowledge with the colonists (who would later enslave many of them).

The next year, in 1719, the first two ships carrying captive Africans arrived in Louisiana.

The new town was named La Nouvelle-Orléans in honor of the duc d'Orléans, then the regent of France. Following the plan of a late French medieval town, a central square (the Place d'Armes) was laid out with streets forming a grid around it. A church, government office, priest's house, and official residences fronted the square, and earthen ramparts dotted with forts were built around the perimeter. A tiny wooden levee was raised against the river, which still periodically turned the streets into rivers of mud. Today this area of original settlement is known as the Vieux Carré (old square) and the Place d'Armes as Jackson Square.

A Melting Pot

In its first few years, New Orleans was a community of French officials, adventurers, merchants, soldiers, prostitutes, convicts from French prisons,

Greater New Orleans

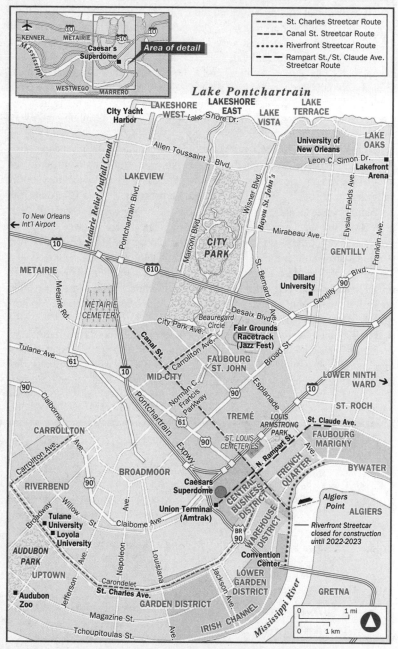

and the enslaved, all living in crude huts of cypress, moss, and clay. These were the first ingredients of the city's population gumbo. Commerce was mainly a matter of trading with Indigenous tribes and launching agricultural production. "Property development" was entrusted to John Law's Company of the West, which marketed the city as Heaven on Earth, full of boundless opportunities for wealth and luxury. Real estate values soared, and rich Europeans, merchants, exiles, soldiers, and a large contingent of German farmers arrived—to find only mosquitoes, a raw frontier existence, and swampy land. The scheme nearly bankrupted the French nation, but by 1721 the region was the most densely populated in the Gulf South. Half of its inhabitants were enslaved Africans.

In 1723, New Orleans replaced Biloxi as the capital of the Louisiana territory. In 1724, Bienville adopted the Code Noir, a set of laws controlling the lives of enslaved Africans and establishing Catholicism as the territory's official religion. While it codified slavery and banished Jews from Louisiana, the code did give enslaved people recognition and a very slight degree of legal protection, unusual in the South at that time. They were allowed to rest on Sundays and holidays, were given food and clothing allowances, and could petition a prosecutor if they were mistreated. Manumission was legalized, and young children could not be taken away from their mothers. The laws were meant to ensure the well-being of the enslaved (while simultaneously severely controlling them), but many enslavers ignored the laws and continued to horribly mistreat the enslaved.

By 1726, there were 1,385 enslaved Africans and 159 enslaved Indigenous people in New Orleans. They built the city's infrastructure, raising levees, digging drainage canals, and working as blacksmiths, carpenters, cooks, and farmers. They cleared swampland, tended livestock, and cared for their

DATELINE

1682 La Salle stops near the present site after traveling down the Mississippi River from the Great Lakes. He plants a cross claiming the territory for Louis XIV.

1699 Pierre Le Moyne, Sieur d'Iberville, rediscovers and secures the mouth of the Mississippi on Mardi Gras day.

1718 Iberville's brother, Jean-Baptiste Le Moyne, Sieur de Bienville, founds New Orleans.

1719 First ships carrying enslaved people arrive in New Orleans.

1723 New Orleans replaces Biloxi as the capital of Louisiana.

1724 The Code Noir is established.

1752 Ursuline Convent completed.

1762 Louis XV secretly cedes New Orleans and all of Louisiana west of the Mississippi to Spain.

1768 French residents in New Orleans banish Spanish commissioner Don Antonio de Ulloa, proclaiming independence from Spain.

1769 The Spanish return. A Spanish code replaces the Code Noir,

enslavers' children. By 1741, enslaved Africans outnumbered white people in the colony nearly four to one.

One significant barrier to the colony's population growth was a lack of potential wives. In 1727, a small contingent of Ursuline nuns established a convent, and while the nuns themselves weren't eligible, they did provide shelter and education for many subsequent shiploads of *les filles à la cassette*. These "cassette girls" or "casket girls"—named for the government-issue casketlike trunks in which they carried their possessions—were virtuous young women sent to Louisiana by the French government to be courted and married by colonists. (If we're to believe current city residents, the plan was remarkably successful: Nearly everyone in New Orleans claims descent from the casket girls or from Spanish or French nobility rather than from the colony's motley initial population of convicts and "fallen women," who therefore must have been wholly infertile. Hmm. . . .)

John Law's company relinquished its governance of Louisiana in 1731, and the French monarch regained control of the territory. In the following decades, planters established estates up and down the river. In the city, the upper crust began to develop a courtly atmosphere on the French model. Alongside their rough-and-tumble plantation existence, families competed to see who could throw the most opulent parties in their city town houses.

During the 18th century, colonization of a different sort began along the Gulf of Mexico. There, many French colonists, displaced by British rule from Acadia, Nova Scotia, made their way south from Canada and formed a rural outpost, where their descendants still live, farm, trap, and speak their unique brand of French to this day. The Acadians' name has been Anglicized, and we know them today as Cajuns.

giving the enslaved the right to buy their own freedom. Native American slavery is outlawed.

1788–94 Fires destroy much of the city; brick buildings replace wood.

1794 Planter Etienne de Boré granulates sugar from cane for the first time, spawning a boom in the industry.

1800 Louisiana again becomes a French possession.

1803 United States purchases Louisiana and takes possession.

1805 New Orleans incorporates as a city; first elections are held.

1808 International slave trade banned; New Orleans becomes center of domestic slave trade.

1809–10 10,000 Haitians arrive, doubling the city's population.

1812 The *New Orleans*, the first steam vessel to travel the Mississippi, arrives from Pittsburgh. Louisiana admitted as a U.S. state.

1815 Battle of New Orleans.

1817 City restricts gatherings of enslaved people to Congo Square only.

continues

New Orleans' commercial development, however, was stymied by French restrictions requiring the colony to trade only with the mother country. To subvert these restrictions, smugglers and pirates provided alternative markets and transportation for local crops, furs, bricks, and tar. As the French saw it, their return on investment wasn't paying off, and so in 1762, Louis XV traded the city and all of Louisiana west of the Mississippi to his cousin Charles III of Spain in the secret Treaty of Fontainebleau. It took 2 years for the news to reach a shocked New Orleans, and 2 more for Spain to send a governor, Don Antonio de Ulloa—who made few friends among local residents and was eventually sent packing. Some proposed the formation of a Louisiana republic. For a time, New Orleans and Louisiana were effectively independent of any foreign power. That came to a crashing end in 1769 when the Spanish sent forth Don Alejandro "Bloody" O'Reilly and 2,000 soldiers. Local leaders of the relatively peaceful rebellion were executed, and Spanish rule was imposed again. With a Gallic shrug, French aristocracy mingled with Spanish nobility, intermarried, and helped to create a mingled "Creole" culture.

Thousands more enslaved Africans arrived. The Code Noir was replaced by a more liberal Spanish system that allowed the enslaved to earn money, to buy their own freedom, and to own property. This gave rise to an extensive population of free people of color, who enjoyed a number of privileges. Many were artisans, musicians, and scholars who contributed enormously to the city's culture. The new code also outlawed the enslavement of Indigenous people.

A devastating 1788 fire destroyed more than 850 buildings; another in 1794 interrupted the rebuilding. From the ashes emerged a new architecture dominated by Spanish-style brick-and-plaster buildings designed with arches, courtyards, and cast-iron balconies (and, of course, attached slave quarters). Today you'll still see tile markers giving Spanish street names on French Quarter corners.

1832–33 Yellow fever and cholera epidemics kill 10,000 people in 2 years.

1837 First newspaper coverage of Mardi Gras parade.

1840 Antoine Alciatore, founder of Antoine's restaurant, arrives from Marseille.

1850 Booming commerce totals $200 million; cotton accounts for 45% of total trade. City becomes largest slave market in the country.

1853 Yellow fever epidemic kills 12% of population in roughly 2 months.

1861–62 Louisiana secedes from the Union; city captured by Admiral Farragut.

1865–77 Reconstruction; city swarmed by "carpetbaggers."

1884–85 Cotton Centennial Exposition (World's Fair) held at present-day site of Audubon Park.

1890 Jelly Roll Morton born.

1890 Creole of color Homer Plessy arrested on a train recently segregated by Jim Crow laws. He sues the state, culminating in the landmark U.S. Supreme Court decision *Plessy v. Ferguson*.

Meanwhile, imperial conflict intensified among the Spanish, French, English, and Americans. There were more trade restrictions and more good times for pirates like the infamous brothers Pierre and Jean Lafitte. Spain had allowed some American revolutionaries to trade through the city in support of the colonists' fight against Britain, but in 1800 France regained possession of the territory with a surprisingly quiet transfer of ownership. The French held on for 3 years while Napoleon negotiated the Louisiana Purchase with the United States for the paltry sum of $15 million. (Not a lot of money, when you consider that the purchase doubled the size of the U.S.)

By this time, there were 2,773 enslaved Africans and 1,335 free people of color in New Orleans. Together, they comprised 51% of the city's total population. In 1808, the international slave trade was abolished, and New Orleans became the center of the domestic slave trade. Human beings were bought and sold all over the city. From 1809 to 1810, some 10,000 Haitians—both enslaved and free—arrived, fleeing the Saint-Domingue Revolution in their country. They approximately doubled the city's population.

For Creole society, a return to financially strapped French rule had been unpleasant enough, but a sale to uncouth America was anathema. To their minds, it meant the end of a European lifestyle in the Vieux Carré. Feeling shunned, the American upper classes installed their showy new settlements across Canal Street (so named because a drainage canal was once planned along its route)—away from the old city and its insulated Creole society.

So it was that New Orleans came to be two parallel cities. The American Sector spread outward from Canal Street along St. Charles Avenue; business and cultural institutions centered in the Central Business District; and mansions rose in what is now the Garden District, which was a separate incorporated city until 1852. French and Creole society dominated the Quarter, extending toward Lake Pontchartrain along Esplanade Avenue. Soon,

1892 First electric streetcar operates along St. Charles Avenue.

1897 Sidney Bechet born. Storyville established.

1901 Louis Armstrong born.

1911 Razzy Dazzy Spasm Band performs in New York; another band takes its name, adjusts it to Razzy Dazzy Jazzy Band—first use of the word "jazz."

1917 Original Dixieland Jazz Band attains height of popularity.

1921 Inner-Harbor Navigational Canal built, connecting Lake Pontchartrain and the Mississippi.

1928 Huey P. Long elected governor of Louisiana; 4 years later he is elected to U.S. Senate. Three years after that, he is shot dead.

1939 French Quarter Residents Association formed as an agent for preservation.

1956 Lake Pontchartrain Causeway, world's longest over-water bridge, completed.

1960 New Orleans' public schools integrated.

1973 Parades banned in the Vieux Carré, changing the character of Mardi Gras celebrations.

continues

however, the Americans brought commercial success to the city, which quickly warmed relations. The Americans sought the vitality of downtown society, and the Creoles sought the profit of American business. They also had occasion to join forces against hurricanes, yellow-fever epidemics, and floods.

2 From the Battle of New Orleans to the Civil War

The great turning point in Creole-American relations was the Battle of New Orleans during the War of 1812. To save the city, Andrew Jackson set aside his disdain for the pirate Jean Lafitte (and the Choctaw people and Black soldiers) to create a ragtag army, and Lafitte supplied the Americans with cannons and ammunition that helped swing the battle in their favor. When Jackson called for volunteers, some 5,000 citizens from both sides of Canal Street responded. During the battle on January 8, 1815, at Chalmette Battlefield (p. 181), a few miles downriver from the city, some 2,000 British troops and 20 Americans were killed or wounded. The course of history was changed, Louisiana was incorporated into the Union, and Jackson became a national hero—despite the treaty concluding the war having been signed a full 2 weeks before. Who knew?

In 1817, a city ordinance was put in place restricting enslaved people to a single gathering place: an open area on Rampart Street that would become known as Congo Square. On Sundays, the enslaved freely worshipped, sang, played instruments, danced, and sold food and wares there. Such gatherings were generally not allowed in the south, and not only did these gatherings shape New Orleans' diverse culture and jazz—they shaped all American music.

Colonial trade restrictions had evaporated with the Louisiana Purchase, and with the advent of steam-powered river travel, commerce burgeoned. By the 1840s, New Orleans' port was on par with New York's. Cotton and sugar made

1975 Superdome opens.

1976 Anne Rice publishes best-selling *Interview with the Vampire*, set in New Orleans.

1977 Ernest N. "Dutch" Morial becomes first African-American mayor.

1984 Louisiana World Expo spurs redevelopment of the riverside area.

2005 More than three-quarters of the city floods when levees fail following Hurricane Katrina.

2010 Saints win NFL Super Bowl for first time. HBO's *Tremé* debut.

BP Deepwater Horizon has worst offshore spill in U.S. history.

2018 City of New Orleans' 300th anniversary. LaToya Cantrell elected city's first female mayor. Site-specific slave trade markers posted.

2019 Jazz and Heritage Festival celebrates 50th anniversary.

2020 Covid-19 pandemic begins. Jazz Fest canceled; WWOZ creates "Jazz Festing in Place."

2021 Mardi Gras celebrations canceled; Covid-19 cases surge; Hurricane Ida causes widespread damage.

many local fortunes on the backs of enslaved people's labor; wealthy planters joined city merchants in building luxurious town houses and attending opera, theater, banquets, parades, and spectacular balls (including "Quadroon Balls," where beautiful biracial girls were peddled to the male gentry as possible mistresses). As always, politics and gambling were dominant pastimes.

By the middle of the 19th century, there were 17,000 enslaved people in New Orleans. Cotton-related business was responsible for nearly half of the total commerce in New Orleans, and the city housed the largest slave market in the U.S., where more than 130,000 humans were ultimately bought and sold. Paradoxically, by this time New Orleans also had one of the largest populations of free people of color in the south. Racial distinctions within the city became increasingly difficult to determine; people could often trace their ancestry back to two or even three different continents. Adding to the diversity were waves of Irish and German immigrants, vital labor sources supporting the city's growth. The only major setbacks to the city's development were occasional mosquito-borne yellow fever epidemics, which killed thousands of residents and visitors, and persisted until late in the 19th century.

Reconstruction & Beyond

The boom era ended rather abruptly with the Civil War. Louisiana seceded from the United States in 1861; Federal troops marched into the city in 1862 and stayed until 1877, through the bitter Reconstruction period. All over the South, this period saw violent clashes between armed white groups and the state's Reconstruction forces.

After the war, the city went about the business of rebuilding its economic life—without slavery. Lacking a free labor base, some fortunes crashed, but the city persevered. By 1880, annexations had fleshed out the city limits, port activity had picked up, and railroads were establishing their economic importance. A new group of immigrants, Sicilians, arrived and put their unique mark on the city. Gambling thrived; there were hundreds of saloons and scores of "bawdy houses" engaged in prostitution (illegal, but largely unenforced). New Orleans was earning an international reputation for open vice, much to the chagrin of the city's polite society.

In 1897, seeking to improve the city's tarnished image, Alderman Sidney Story moved all illegal (but highly profitable) activities into a restricted area along Basin Street next to the French Quarter. Quickly nicknamed Storyville, the district boasted "sporting palaces" with elaborate decor, entertainment, and all variety of ladies of pleasure. The *Blue Book* directory listed the names, addresses, and races of more than 700 prostitutes working everywhere from the "palaces" down to decrepit "cribs." Black musicians such as Jelly Roll Morton played in the more ornate bordellos, popularizing early forms of jazz. When the Secretary of the Navy decreed in 1917 that armed forces should not be exposed to such open vice, Storyville closed down and disappeared—with nary a trace beyond its immense cultural impact.

The 20th Century

In the early 20th century, New Orleans' port became the largest in the United States and the second-busiest in the world (after Amsterdam), with goods coming in by barge and rail. Electrification and other modern technology kept the port whirring. Drainage problems were conquered by means of high levees, canals, pumping stations, and great spillways, which directed floodwater away from the city. Bridges were built across the Mississippi River, including the Huey P. Long Bridge, named after Louisiana's infamous politician and demagogue. New Orleans' emergence as a regional financial center, with more than 50 commercial banks, led to the construction of soaring office buildings, mostly in the Central Business District. World War II spawned a thriving shipbuilding industry, which was replaced by expanded oil, gas, and petrochemical businesses after the war. Later in the 20th century, tourism became another primary economic driver.

As in most other American cities, the population spread outward, filling suburbs and nearby municipalities. A thriving community in New Orleans East was developed by Vietnamese refugees, who immigrated here in the 1970s. Unlike other cities, however, New Orleans was able to preserve its original town center and much of its historic architecture. And fortunately, it has also preserved the blend of cultures, races, and traditions that makes the city unique, always honoring its history—while welcoming whatever comes next.

NEW ORLEANS IN POPULAR CULTURE

Books

You can fill many bookcases with New Orleans literature and authors, so consider the following list as just a jumping-off point. Get more recommendations at the fine bookshops listed in chapter 9.

GENERAL FICTION

Many early fiction works provide a taste of old-time New Orleans life. George Washington Cable's stories are revealing and colorful, as in *Old Creole Days* (1879). Kate Chopin's works, including *The Awakening* (1899), are set in Louisiana and discuss the earliest Creoles. Frances Parkinson Keyes, who lived on Chartres Street from 1945 to 1970, depicts life in the city at that time in her most famous work, *Dinner at Antoine's*.

Ellen Gilchrist's contemporary short-story collection *In the Land of Dreamy Dreams* portrays life in wealthy uptown New Orleans. Sheila Bosworth's tragicomedies perfectly sum up the city and its collection of characters—check out favorites *Almost Innocent* or *Slow Poison*. Michael Ondaatje's controversial *Coming Through Slaughter* is a wonderful fictionalized account of Buddy Bolden and the early New Orleans jazz era.

Newer favorites include Moira Crone's sci-fi thriller *The Not Yet*, set in a future even stranger than the present; Michael Zell's challenging but satisfying thriller *Errata;* and *King Xeno* by Nathaniel Rich, in which an ax murderer meets a Mafia kingpin in the early jazz age, and fiction meets fact. In the perennially popular series by James Lee Burke, misfit Cajun detective Dave Robicheaux keeps the bad guys running and the pages turning.

And then there is the cottage industry known as Anne Rice, who undeniably ignited current pop vampire culture (bow to the master, *True Blood, Twilight,* and *Vampire Diaries*). Her now-classic *Vampire Chronicles* expertly capture the city's elegant, otherworldly essence.

HISTORY

Lyle Saxon, director of the writer's program under the WPA, wrote *Fabulous New Orleans*—a charming place to start learning about the city's past—and coauthored the folk-tale collection *Gumbo Ya-Ya.* Mark Twain visited the city often in his riverboat days, and his *Life on the Mississippi* has a number of tales about New Orleans and its riverfront life. *The WPA Guide to New Orleans* also contains excellent social and historical background and provides a fascinating picture of the city in 1938. *Beautiful Crescent,* by Joan Garvey and Mary Lou Widmer, is a solid reference book on the city's history. *Gangs of New York*'s author Herbert Asbury gave the same highly entertaining—if not terribly factual—treatment to New Orleans in *The French Quarter: An Informal History of the New Orleans Underworld.* New Orleans's favorite patroness, the Baroness de Pontalba, gets the biography treatment in Christina Vella's *Intimate Enemies.* In *The Last Madam: A Life in the New Orleans Underworld,* Christine Wiltz reveals a bawdy bygone era, conveyed through brothel owner Norma Wallace, who recorded her memoirs before her 1974 suicide. Before there was *Frommer's,* there was *The Bachelor in New Orleans,* a 1942 guide (reissued in 2017) for the coolest of visiting cats—charming, if anachronistic, and surprisingly informative.

Three eminently readable recent histories are Ned Sublette's *The World That Made New Orleans,* which focuses on the cultural influences of European, African, and Caribbean settlers; Lawrence Powell's *Accidental City,* a look back at the city's scrappy evolution; and the elegantly entangled *Unfathomable City,* a coffee-table atlas with essays by Rebecca Solnit and Rebecca Snedecker. Local historian Richard Campanella's works, including his essay collection *Cityscapes of New Orleans* (2017), are eminently worthy.

Of the many guides to Mardi Gras, Henri Schindler's *Mardi Gras New Orleans* account is that of a historian and a long-term producer of balls and parades. *Mardi Gras in New Orleans: An Illustrated History,* by *Mardi Gras Guide* publisher Arthur Hardy, describes the celebration's evolution. *I Wanna Do That!* by Echo Olander and Yoni Goldstein captures the extraordinary spirit of marching krewes.

Lovers of the lurid will enjoy *Madame LaLaurie,* a biography of the notorious high-society murderess. Sara Roahen's charming *Gumbo Tales: Finding*

My Place at the New Orleans Table discovers the culture through its distinctive food and drink. Kim Marie Vaz's *The "Baby Dolls"* tells the story of the Baby Dolls, from Storyville brothels to their post-Katrina re-emergence. In *The Fish That Ate the Whale: The Life and Times of America's Banana King,* Rich Cohen recounts the rags-to-riches tale of fruit magnate Sam Zemurray. John Churchill Chase's *Frenchmen, Desire, Good Children . . . and Other Streets of New Orleans* is an intriguing tour of the city's street names. Emma Fick's brilliantly illustrated *Snippets of New Orleans* explores all sorts of insider secrets. Finally, ex-Mayor Mitch Landrieu's 2017 memoir *In the Shadow of Statues: A White Southerner Confronts History* is a provocative read.

LITERATURE

William Faulkner penned *Soldiers' Pay* while living on Pirate's Alley, and several other Faulkner novels and short stories are set in New Orleans. Tennessee Williams, who lived in New Orleans on and off for many years, was inspired by the city to write *A Streetcar Named Desire,* one of the best-known New Orleans tales; he also set *The Rose Tattoo* here. Robert Penn Warren's classic 1946 novel *All the King's Men,* an exceedingly loose telling of the story of Huey P. Long, portrays the performance art known as Louisiana politics. Walker Percy's novels, notably *The Moviegoer,* are classic portrayals of the idiosyncrasies of New Orleans and its residents. Shirley Grau's *The Keepers of the House* won the Pulitzer Prize in 1964. At the time of his suicide in 1969, John Kennedy Toole was an unknown author, but his posthumously published Pulitzer-winning *A Confederacy of Dunces* is a timeless New Orleans tragicomedy and probably the city's most beloved novel.

New Orleans' Vietnamese community is the setting for Robert Olen Butler's 1993 Pulitzer Prize–winning collection, *A Good Scent from a Strange Mountain.* Maurice Carlos Ruffin's excellent *The Ones Who Don't Say They Love You* (2021) is a bracing collection of short stories about local characters.

POST-KATRINA LITERATURE

From great tragedy comes great art, and the following books help shape an image of pre- and post-flood New Orleans. Tom Piazza's *Why New Orleans Matters* is a love letter to the city and the number-one choice for people trying to "get" New Orleans. His novel *City of Refuge* bisects Katrina through the experiences of two families. *My New Orleans,* edited by Rosemary James, collects essays by locals, from writers to restaurateurs and raconteurs, attempting to pin down what it is about this place that keeps them here. Historian Douglas Brinkley's meticulous *The Great Deluge* may be the definitive postmortem examination of Katrina. *Times-Picayune* columnist Chris Rose collected his heartbreaking personal essays, written as he and his colleagues covered their flooded city, in *1 Dead in Attic.* Pulitzer Prize–winning journalist Sherri Fink recounts the crisis in her harrowing *Five Days at Memorial. Letters from New Orleans* by Rob Walker is packed with poignant just-moved-to-town observations. Sarah Broom won the National Book Award for *The Yellow House,* a stunning memoir about her relationship with the city. For young kids, Janet Wyman Coleman's *Eight Dolphins of Katrina* (set in Gulfport, Mississippi) is a relatable, pictorial tale of disaster and survival. *Zeitoun,* Dave Eggers' gripping narrative nonfiction, recounts the tale of one man's horror and a nation's injustice, while *New Yorker* columnist Dan Baum weaves together differing perspectives to illustrate the multihued city in *Nine Lives.* Finally, fans of football and motivational memoirs may enjoy *Home Team* by Saints coach Sean Payton or Drew Brees' *Coming Back Stronger.*

BOOKS ABOUT MUSIC

For a look at specific time periods, people, and places in the history of New Orleans jazz, you have a number of choices. They include William Carter's *Preservation Hall;* John Chilton's *Sidney Bechet: The Wizard of Jazz;* Gunther Schuller's *Early Jazz: Its Roots and Musical Development;* the excellent *A Trumpet Around the Corner: The Story of New Orleans Jazz,* by Samuel Charters; *New Orleans Jazz: Images of America,* by Edward Branley; and *New Orleans Style,* by Bill Russell. Al Rose's *Storyville, New Orleans* is an excellent source of information about the very beginnings of jazz; while *Up from the Cradle of Jazz* tells its story post-WWII. *Songs of My Fathers* is Tom Sancton's fine retelling of his boyhood at the feet of the great Preservation Hall musicians. If you prefer primary sources, read Sidney Bechet's autobiography *Treat It Gentle,* or Louis Armstrong's *Satchmo: My Life in New Orleans,* or *Satchmo: The Wonderful World and Art of Louis Armstrong,* a bio by way of his own artworks.

Ann Allen Savoy's *Cajun Music Vol. 1,* a combination songbook and oral history, features previously untranscribed Cajun music with lyrics in French and English—a definitive work and an invaluable resource. *The Kingdom of Zydeco* by Michael Tisserand delves into Black Creole music with equal parts depth and delight. Ben Sandmel's exhaustively researched *Ernie K-Doe: The R&B Emperor of New Orleans* can't help but be entertaining, given the subject. Mac Rebennack (aka Dr. John) recounts his wild life in the New Orleans music scene in *Under a Hoodoo Moon.*

Film & Television

With atmosphere and mystery to spare, not to mention generous tax incentives, film and TV production abound here in "Hollywood South." The city isn't a character in all of them, but it's the heart of the HBO series *Tremé.* Don't miss the stellar, hard-to-find series *Frank's Place* (1987–88). *True Blood* was filmed mostly in Baton Rouge, but important scenes were set in the gorgeous Marigny Opera House, among other New Orleans locations. The popular *NCIS New Orleans,* filmed on location, does what it can to catch the city's lightning-in-a-bottle aura and tricky accents—with equally mixed results. Depending on your perspective, the raunchy *Girls Trip* (2017) did a better job. The creepy FX series *American Horror Story: Coven* was filmed in some of the city's oldest mansions, a notorious haunted house, and a possible fountain of youth in City Park. The most affecting recent filmwork came from Beyoncé, in her thought- (and tweet-) provoking, long-form video "Lemonade."

Consider these for some pre- or post-visit flavor: classics like Marlon Brando in *A Streetcar Named Desire* (1951); Bette Davis in *Jezebel* (1938); the certified best Elvis film *King Creole* (1958); and counterculture Mardi Gras freakout *Easy Rider.* Tom Waits bums around the city, the countryside, and jail in the indie *Down by Law* (1986); and a young Brooke Shields navigates a Storyville childhood in Louis Malle's *Pretty Baby* (1978). Then there's the steamy but flawed (and locally derided) *The Big Easy* (1986). Brad Pitt ages backwards in *The Curious Case of Benjamin Button* (2008) and goes fang to fang with Tom Cruise in *Interview with the Vampire* (1994). The Oscar-nominated *Beasts of the Southern Wild* (2012) set its powerful magic realism in the Louisiana bayous. Lastly, for kids, Disney's animated *The Princess and the Frog* (2009) is based on the late chef Leah Chase; and when *Abbott & Costello Go to Mars* (1953), they end up at Mardi Gras.

All of the late, very great Les Blank's documentaries on Louisiana are worthy, but start with *Always for Pleasure* (1978). *Bayou Maharajah,* the excellent 2013 biodoc of noted pianist James Booker, also explains much about the New Orleans music scene in his day (and now). Documentaries about the Katrina experience notably include Spike Lee's *When the Levees Broke;* the remarkable, Oscar-nominated *Trouble the Water;* and the superb prize-winning *Faubourg Tremé: The Untold Story of Black New Orleans.* A few more documentaries of note: *Bury the Hatchet, Tchoupitoulas, A Tuba to Cuba, The Whole Gritty City, Tootie's Last Suit,* and *Up from the Streets.*

Recordings

Oh, boy. Well, the selections listed below should give you a good start, though we could fill pages more. We're barely even touching on the many fine pop, rock, or folky contributions (but we can't not mention the Revivalists, Lost Bayou Ramblers, and Hurray for the Riff Raff). Also check out the names listed in the Nightlife chapter (p. 206), and for more advice, consult the uber-helpful know-it-alls at **Louisiana Music Factory** and the other stores on p. 245.

CROSS-GENRE ANTHOLOGIES

There are many collections and anthologies of New Orleans and Louisiana music available, including the 1990s Alligator Stomp series by Rhino Records. The most comprehensive is 2004's acclaimed four-disc package *Doctors, Professors, Kings & Queens: The Big Ol' Box of New Orleans,* which touches all the bases of the diverse musical gumbo that is the Crescent City. The *Tremé, Season 1* soundtrack covers a bit of the same fertile, funky ground from recent years. Lovers of live music should grab Smithsonian Folkways' *Jazz Fest: The New Orleans Jazz & Heritage Festival,* a gorgeous box set that focuses on Louisiana-rooted live performances from Fests going all the way back.

JAZZ

A classic New Orleans jazz collection starts with the originators: King Oliver, Kid Ory, Sidney Bechet, Original Dixieland Jazz Band, and Jelly Roll Morton. Add early Louis Armstrong, with his Hot Five and Hot Seven bands.

Ken Burns' Jazz box covers the originators and more from New Orleans and beyond, and the anthologies *New Orleans* (Atlantic Jazz), *Recorded in New Orleans Volumes 1 and 2* (Good Time Jazz), and *New Orleans Jazz* (Arhoolie) are good choices. Baby Dodds Trio's *Jazz A La Creole* and Preservation Hall's *Preservation* cover classic territory; Pete Fountain, Al Hirt (try *Honey in the Horn*), and Louis Prima (*The Wildest*) all swing things in new directions.

Wynton Marsalis, Terrance Blanchard, and Harry Connick, Jr., build on those traditions, and trumpeters Irvin Mayfield and Nicolas Payton push them forward. Terrific old-time revivalists like the New Orleans Jazz Vipers, Panorama Jazz Band, Meschiya Lake (check out *Lucky Devil*), the Smoking Time Jazz Club, Tuba Skinny, and Aurora Nealand are well worth the cost of a disc or a download. Pianist Jon Cleary is killing it on his Grammy-winning *Go Go Juice. American Tunes,* Allen Toussaint's final collection, is not at all a sentimental choice. Okay, it is. But it's also excellent, as are Jon Batiste's *Hollywood Africans* and *We Are.*

BRASS BANDS

The age-old tradition of brass-oriented street bands underwent a spectacular revival in the 1980s and 1990s with the revitalization of such long-term presences as the Olympia Brass Band and the arrival of newcomers like the Dirty Dozen Brass Band (try their monster anthology, *This Is the Dirty Dozen Brass Band*). They inspired a younger and funkier generation, including Grammy winners Rebirth Brass Band and New Orleans Nightcrawlers, plus New Birth, the Hot 8, the Stooges, up-and-comers TBC, hybridists the Brass-a-Holics, the Soul Rebels, and the Soul Brass Band, among the best of the crowd. 2019's *Bonerama Plays Zeppelin* is just plain fun, and 2013's *I Am a Brass-a-Holic* is irresistibly bumping. It's all better live, so get ye to the clubs or try *The Main Event: Live at the Maple Leaf,* or the loose, bumping *Rock with the Hot 8.*

RHYTHM, BLUES & SOUL

First things first: Get your Fats on with *My Blue Heaven.* Then get Dr. John's *Gumbo* or *Mos Scocious: The Dr. John Anthology.* Round out your legends collection with Professor Longhair's *'Fess: The Professor Longhair Anthology* and fellow keyboard wizard James Booker's *Classified: Remixed.* Go down funk road with The Meters' eponymous debut and *Rejuvenation,* Lee Dorsey's *Yes We Can,* and then *The Wild Tchoupitoulas* and *The Wild Magnolias* for Mardi Gras Indian funk. Ivan Neville's Dumpstaphunk band is keeping the funk alive, while Galactic might be funk, might be jazz, could be rock or jam—but is never uninteresting. Trombone Shorty rocks jazz, R&B, funk, and hip hop into his own thang, as on *Say That to Say This.* We're true to hometown heroes the Neville Brothers' *Yellow Moon* and *Treacherous: A History of the Neville Brothers, 1955–1985. Southern Nights* and *Songbook* shows why producer/writer Allen Toussaint, who passed away in 2016 to tremendous shock and sadness, remains a true icon and son of the city. Also get some soul crooners in, like Soul Queen Irma Thomas's *Time Is on My Side* and Johnny Adams' *Heart & Soul*. Worthwhile anthologies include *The Best of New Orleans Rhythm & Blues Volumes 1 and 2; Sehorn's Soul Farm;* and *The Mardi Gras Indians Super Sunday Showdown.* Bring it all current with multi-Grammy-winning P J Morton or Tank and the Bangas' infectious, genre-busting *Green Balloon* (which could also fit in the next paragraph).

HIP HOP, BEATS & BOUNCE

New Orleans's distinctive hip hop and rap scene has produced numerous stars and a home-grown subgenre: booty-dropping, second-line-influenced, twerk-propagating bounce. It busted out with Big Freedia, who must be experienced live, but *Just Be Free* will do. Breakout dirty Southerner Juvenile's *400* is a classic, while rebounding hip-hop star Lil Wayne's breakout flow on *Tha Carter III* still holds up massively (really, any Hot Boyz cuts will do). The risqué rhymes on Mystikal's eponymous debut broke musical ground before jail time sidelined his career; he's out and back now. Also back is Choppa's infectious *Choppa Style,* which has fans shakety-shaking wid it years after its initial release on the album *Straight from the N.O.*

EATING & DRINKING

Where to start? Is there any other American city so revered, so identified with the glory of gluttony and the joy of the juice than New Orleans? Perhaps, but none with a truly indigenous cuisine (or two), none that lay claim (rightly or not) to inventing the cocktail, and surely none that goes about it with such unbridled gusto. As the oft-repeated homily goes: In most places, people eat to live; in New Orleans, people live to eat. Seriously, you're only visiting, so convince your tortured psyche that you can resume a sensible diet when you get home. Immerse yourself in the local culture and *indulge.* It's so very worth it. A strident vegan friend gave it up for a few days while here to go pork-wild (yes, really), though most chefs, and certainly those in the better restaurants, are adept at adapting to any dietary restriction. The single most important thing to know? *Make reservations.* Another important thing to know: Restaurants are short-staffed and struggling to recover from Covid-19 and Hurricane Ida; be patient and be kind and tip your server and bartender well.

Chapter 11 has much more about Cajun and Creole food. Chapter 8 has cocktailing info. And chapter 6 points you to the top troughs.

WHEN TO GO

With the possible exception of muggy July and August, just about any time is the right time to go to New Orleans. We love the jasmine-infused nights and warmer days of mid-fall and spring best, and even relish the occasional high drama of a good summer thunderstorm. Winter can be chilly, and New

Hot Time in the City

If you can stand it, brave the city in summer. The tourist business slows down a tad, leading to hotel bargains. On a recent July visit, high-end hotels were offering rooms from $89 to $129 (way below regular rates), sometimes with additional perks. A lot of hotels have great pools (and poolside bars), and you can often get upgrades to fancy suites for a song—ask when you check in. From mid-July to early September, local restaurants run prix-fixe "COOLinary" specials (www.coolinary neworleans.com), and some restaurants offer "temperature lunches" (if it's 96 out, your lunch is $9.60). Yeah, it's hot and humid, but there are always plenty of air-conditioned respites and, as you'll see below, fantastic festivals to distract you from the heat.

Orleans isn't particularly known as a holiday destination, but in December it's gussied up with decorations, and special seasonal events abound. Eager hotels have good deals, and many restaurants offer prix-fixe "Réveillon" specials.

It's important to know *what's* going on *when,* since the city's landscape, hotel availability, and rates can change dramatically depending on events. Mardi Gras is, of course, the hardest time to get a hotel room, but it can also be difficult during major festivals (French Quarter Fest, Jazz & Heritage Festival, Essence) and sporting events (BCS, Sugar Bowl, Saints and LSU Superdome games).

The Weather

The average mean temperature in New Orleans is an inviting 70°F (21°C), but it can drop or rise considerably in a single day. (It can be 40°F/4°C and rain one day, 80°F/27°C and low humidity the next.) Conditions depend primarily on whether it rains and whether there is direct sunlight or cloud cover. Rain can provide slight and temporary relief on a hot day; it tends to hit in sudden (and sometimes dramatically heavy) showers, which disappear as quickly as they arrive. In unimpeded sun it gets much warmer. The high humidity can intensify even mild warms and colds. Still, the semitropical climate is part of New Orleans' appeal—the slight moistness makes for lush, sensual air.

New Orleans is pleasant most of the year. During the sweltering summer months, follow the locals' example: Stay out of the midday sun, seek shade, and duck from one air-conditioned locale to another. August is a great time to visit museums, as the city offers "museum month" deals. June and September are still hot and humid; early spring and mid-fall are glorious. Winter is mild by American standards (just don't expect Florida warmth), punctuated by an occasional freeze-level cold snap. But *unpredictable* and *flexible* are the watchwords. The whims of the weather gods are at play, so be ready to adjust accordingly.

Hurricane season runs June 1 to November 30. There are no guarantees, but severe storms are fairly rare. In the height of summer, T-shirts, shorts, and tissue-weight fabrics are acceptable everywhere except the finest restaurants.

New Orleans's Average Temperatures & Rainfall

	JAN	FEB	MAR	APR	MAY	JUNE	JULY	AUG	SEPT	OCT	NOV	DEC
HIGH (°F)	62	65	71	78	85	89	91	90	87	80	71	65
HIGH (°C)	17	18	22	26	29	32	33	32	31	27	22	18
LOW (°F)	43	46	52	58	66	71	73	73	70	60	50	45
LOW (°C)	6	8	11	14	19	22	23	23	21	16	10	7
DAYS OF RAINFALL	10	9	9	7	8	11	14	13	10	6	7	10

In the spring and fall, something a little warmer is in order; in the winter, carry a mid-weight coat or jacket and pack a folding umbrella (though they're available everywhere, as are cheap rain ponchos for unexpected downpours). The biggest summertime climate problem can be the air-conditioning overcompensation that chills rooms—especially restaurants—to meat-locker-like temps, so bring those light wraps along even on warm nights.

New Orleans Calendar of Events

There's lots more on **Mardi Gras** and **Jazz Fest** in chapter 4. For other Louisiana festivals (more than 400 total!), see www.laffnet.org. Times and dates are always subject to change. Due to Covid concerns, some event dates, times, and ticket prices weren't finalized at press time; they may be canceled, postponed, or limited. Check the event websites to be safe. For general information, contact **New Orleans & Company,** 2020 St. Charles Ave., New Orleans, LA 70130 (www.neworleansonline.com; ℂ **800/672-6124** or 504/566-5011).

JANUARY

Allstate Sugar Bowl Classic. New Orleans' oldest yearly sporting occasion dates to 1934. The football game in the Superdome is the main event, but in the preceding days look for a kickoff second-line parade and a massive Fan Fest in the French Quarter. allstatesugarbowl.org. ℂ **504/828-2440.** January 1.

FEBRUARY

Lundi Gras. This tradition brings a free outdoor music-and-food celebration to Spanish Plaza (Poydras St. at the river), with the big event at 6pm: the ceremonial waterfront arrival of the Kings of Rex and Zulu, marking the start of Mardi Gras. They're welcomed by the mayor, fireworks, and much whoop-de-doo. www.lundigrasfestival.com. See p. 52. Monday before Mardi Gras.

Mardi Gras. The culmination of the 2-month-long carnival season, Mardi Gras is the centuries-old annual blowout. Each year the eyes of the world are on New Orleans, as the entire city stops working and starts partying, and the streets are taken over by awe-inspiring parades. See chapter 4. Day before Ash Wednesday.

MARCH

St. Patrick's Day Parades. There are several, with dates (like the paraders) usually staggered. Instead of Mardi Gras beads, watchers are pelted with veggies, including coveted cabbages. **Molly's at the Market** usually hosts a black-tie limo pub crawl and a parade (www.mollysatthemarket.net; ℂ **504/525-5169**). On the preceding Sunday and on St. Patrick's Day, the party tends to go on all day between Tracey's and Parasol's bars in the Lower Garden District. On St. Patrick's Day (Mar 17), the downtown parade typically begins at 6pm at Burgundy and Piety in Bywater and stumbles to Bourbon Street. www.stpatricksdayneworleans.com.

St. Joseph's Day Parade. A fascinating, less well-known fete. Sicilians venerate St. Joseph, patron saint of families and working men, on his saint's day (Mar 19) with a parade and the creation of devotional altars, elaborate works of art featuring food, candles, and statues. They can be viewed at various churches, Italian restaurants, and private homes (where you might also get fed), and at the **American Italian Cultural**

Center (537 S. Peters St.; americanitalian culturalcenter.com; *©* **504/522-7294**). Locations are listed in the *Times-Picayune* classifieds and on www.nola.com prior to the event. March 19.

Buku Music + Art Project. This packed millennial party of hip hop, EDM, acrobats, and visual artists is New Orleans' answer to Electric Daisy or Movement. Sellout crowds of anything-goes attendees fill six stages overlooking the Mississippi River and floats at Mardi Gras World. Unsurprising, given artists like SZA, Migos, Kid Kudi, Flaming Lips, and Kendrick. Weekend passes for the 2022 10-year anniversary started at around $200, VIP packages way more. www.thebukuproject.com. Late March.

Super Sunday. At these annual Mardi Gras Indians gatherings, tribes garbed in full feathered regalia preen, parade, and engage in ritualized showdowns with traditional chants. The Uptown event takes place on the Sunday nearest St. Joseph's Day at A.L. Davis Park (Washington Ave. and LaSalle St.), from noon till late afternoon, with music and food booths. The looser Downtown street meeting is usually a few weeks later on Bayou St. John at Orleans Avenue. For details, check with the **Backstreet Cultural Museum** (p. 173) or www.wwoz.org/inthestreet. Mid-March–mid-April. More on p. 53.

Tennessee Williams/New Orleans Literary Festival. This 5-day series celebrates New Orleans' rich literary heritage with theatrical performances, readings, discussions, master classes, musical events, walking tours, and the ever-popular Stella Shouting Contest. It's not exclusive to Williams, and the roster of writers and publishers participating is impressive. www.tennesseewilliams.net. *©* **504/581-1144.** Late March.

APRIL

The Crescent City Classic. This scenic 10K race from the Superdome through the French Quarter to City Park brings in an international field of top (and lesser) runners. ccc10k.com. *©* **504/861-8686.** Easter Saturday.

Easter Sunday. Expect posh restaurant brunches and three fabulous parades: The

bonneted one proceeds to St. Louis Cathedral in mule-drawn carriages and convertibles; then family-friendly floats (led by an ex-stripper) roll down Bourbon Street; and lastly, drama and drag overrule decorum in the untraditional gay parade. Easter Sunday.

French Quarter Festival. This 4-day festival, the world's largest showcase of Louisiana music and food, has become wildly popular, attracting an estimated 825,000 in 2019. Scores of free outdoor concerts, food booths, art shows, children's activities, tours, and seminars are set throughout the Quarter, making it easy to return to your hotel for a rest. Book travel early; this good time is becoming a victim of its own success. www.frenchquarterfest.org. *©* **800/673-5725** or 504/522-5730. Late April.

Festival International de Louisiane. Some people split their festing between Jazz Fest and the popular Festival International in Lafayette, which focuses on French music and culture. The free 5-day street fair, held on the first weekend of Jazz Fest, dovetails nicely with the opening events of the bigger fest. www.festivalinternational.org. *©* **337/232-8086.** Late April.

New Orleans Jazz & Heritage Festival. An 8-day event that draws musicians, cooks, and craftspeople and their fans to celebrate music and life, Jazz Fest rivals Mardi Gras in popularity. Get a full description in chapter 4. See www.nojazzfest.com or call *©* **504/410-4100.** Late April-early May.

MAY

Mid-City Bayou Boogaloo. Another weekend, another laid-back New Orleans music, art, and food fest. This one's themeless, with the pretty location along Bayou St. John (and the rubber-ducky derby) the draw for the largely local crowd. Bring a blanket, a parasol, and cash for snacks and brews, and go now before it gets too huge. www.thebayouboogaloo.com. *©* **504/488-3865.** Mid-May.

JUNE

Oyster Festival. Aw shucks, it's a weekend dedicated to slurping delicious Gulf oysters and listening to live music while overlooking the Mississippi River at Woldenberg Park. Local restaurants serve up their best bivalve recipes and pro shuckers compete, all to promote the centuries-old local oyster fishing industry. It's still free (VIP $75), with a mostly local crowd. www.nolaoysterfest.org. ✆ **504/888-7608.** Early June.

New Orleans Wine & Food Experience. About 10,000 people attend this 3-day epicurean pleasure. Some 150 vintners and 75 restaurants feature wines and wares via tastings, seminars, and vintner dinners. The culmination is a grand tasting held at the Sugar Mill, but the party really hits its stride with the Royal Street Stroll, where revelers indulge their way from one tasting station to the next. www.nowfe.com. ✆ **504/655-5158.** Early June.

Creole Tomato Festival. This sweet, smallish, free fest set in the French Market celebrates the humble tomato with cooking demos, tastings, a Tomato Parade, local music . . . and all manner of Bloody Marys. www.frenchmarket.org. ✆ **504/522-2621.** Mid-June.

Louisiana Cajun-Zydeco Festival. This free fest sponsored by Jazz Fest brings plenty of two-stepping, a few waltzes, and lessons for both at Armstrong Park in the Tremé. It also has art markets, kids' activities, and yes, food booths with a seafood focus. ✆ **504/558-6100.** Late June-early July.

JULY

Essence Music Festival. This massive 3-day event sponsored by *Essence* magazine consistently presents a stellar lineup of first-name-only R&B, soul, and hip-hop musicians (like Mary J., Kendrick, Nas, Usher, Beyoncé, Kanye, Prince [RIP], and Janet) in evening concerts on a main stage and clublike "Super Lounges." During the day, this "party with a purpose" has educational and empowerment seminars featuring A-list speakers (Michelle Obama! Oprah! Deepak!!), plus crafts, merchandise, and trade fairs. In 2019 tickets ranged from $75 for a single day to $4,800 for a VIP weekend package (some events are free). www.essence.com/festival. Early July.

Go Fourth on the River. The Independence Day celebration culminates with a spectacular fireworks display from dueling barges in the Mississippi River at 9pm. www.go4thontheriver.com. ✆ **800/672-6124.** July 4.

Running of the Bulls. In perfectly imperfect New Orleans logic, Bastille Day, the famed Pamplona event, and the city's mixed French-Spanish heritage are celebrated with a reenactment of the manic dash, except the bulls are roller-skating **Big Easy Rollergirls** (p. 204) and other roller derby clubs using plastic bats as horns. Pomp, parties, and hilarity accompany what is now the centerpiece of a 3-day **San Fermin in Nueva Orleans** fiesta. nolabulls.com. ✆ **800/672-6124.** Mid-July.

Tales of the Cocktail. This 20-year-old 6-day mixtravaganza celebrates all things liquor. Based at the Monteleone Hotel but pouring over into other venues, it's a serious, sometimes scholarly gathering of upwards of 20,000 professional mixologists, brand ambassadors, and admirers of cocktail culture. (If you make your own bitters and take 10 min. to mix a drink, this might be for you.) The seminars, tastings, and popular "Spirited Dinners" (food and cocktail pairings at top restaurants) fill up fast. www.talesofthecocktail.com. ✆ **504/948-0511.** Late July.

AUGUST

Satchmo Summerfest. Louis Armstrong, hometown boy made very good, is celebrated with his own festival, held around his real birthday (he claimed to be born on July 4, but records say Aug). There's food, music, kids' activities, and seminars, with the emphasis on jazz entertainment and education to ensure Satchmo lives on. The token $5 to $7 admission is worth it. www.satchmosummerfest.org. ✆ **504/522-5730.** Early August.

SEPTEMBER

Southern Decadence. In 2019, this multi-day, multi-night dance/party/raunchfest attracted 275,000 gay, lesbian, bisexual and transgender participants who proved that even NOLA in September was not too hot for leather. The annual "Gay Mardi Gras" peaks during a frenzied, bar-studded parade. Book rooms early. www.southerndecadence.net. Labor Day weekend.

OCTOBER

Festivals Acadiens & Creoles. This small Lafayette event combines the Bayou Food Festival, the Festival de Musique Acadienne, and the Louisiana Native Crafts Festival. Players, bring your instruments—there's a jam tent. It's fun, easygoing, tasty, and free. www.festivalsacadiens.com. ℭ **800/346-1958** in the U.S., 800/543-5340 in Canada, or 337/232-3737. Early October.

Crescent City Blues & BBQ Festival. A recent rash of credible BBQ restaurants might finally be changing the city's low profile in the pantheon of great BBQ destinations. 'Cue teams strut their stuff at this free fest, located in Lafayette Park in the CBD. Add two stages for blues tunes, a good lineup, and consider our folding chairs strapped on. Go soon, this one is set to blow up. www.bluesfest.jazzandheritage. org. ℭ **504/558-6100.** Mid-October.

Prospect.5. This contemporary art triennial features the works of leading and emerging international artists, interpreting New Orleans' expansive history and diverse culture in traditional and site-specific venues citywide. www.prospectneworleans.org. October 23, 2023–January 23, 2024.

Halloween. Halloween is celebrated especially grandly in this haunted city, rivaling Mardi Gras for costume outrageousness. The French Quarter is Halloween central (especially for the LGBTQIA+ crowd), where the **Krewe of Boo** parade rolls a week or so before Halloween (www.kreweofboo.com); another parade leaves **Molly's at the Market** (p. 224) on Halloween night. Other ghoulish action includes **Boo-at-the-Zoo** (last 2 weekends in Oct) for kids; the truly scary **Mortuary Haunted House** (www.themortuary.net); and City Park's interactive **Scout Island Scream Park.** October 31 and surrounding days.

Voodoo Music + Arts Experience. The monstrous 3-day Voodoo Fest draws 180,000 music fans to the City Park festival grounds, where some 70 acts fill four live stages. The diverse lineup features major stars from Post Malone, Ozzy, Travis Scott, and Jason Isbell to the Killers, Skrillex, Beck, and Snoop Dogg, plus up-and-comers and a solid crop of locals. Eclectic art, exotic performances, a huge EDM space, costumed people-watching, and food and drink round out the diversions. Tickets start around $150 and go way up. www.voodoofestival.com. Late October.

NOVEMBER

Po-Boy Festival. You *could* just go to the participating restaurants any other day of the year, but you'd have to go 60 times to try each sandwich. And you'd miss the blessing of the po' boy. This Oak Street fest gets crazy crowded, but it's got some dang delish sandwiches, tunes, and a fun locals' scene. www. facebook.com/poboyfest. Mid-November.

Celebration in the Oaks. More than a million holiday lights bedeck about 2 miles of City Park, and a walking and mini-train tour lets you take in the charm and grandeur at your leisure. It's nostalgic winter wonderment for the whole fam. Plus, ice skating and amusement-park rides. www.neworleans citypark.com. ℭ **504/482-4888.** Day after Thanksgiving–January 2.

DECEMBER

LUNA Fête. This free, multi-day, multi-location "Light Up" festival uses lighting, music, and video projections to transform architecturally significant buildings around Lafayette Square, creating artistic awesomeness. In 2019, it drew 100,000 fans. www.artsnew orleans.org/event/luna-fete. Late November–early December.

Christmas, New Orleans Style. The ever-celebratory New Orleanians do Christmas really well. The town is decorated to a fare-thee-well, with nightly concerts in St. Louis Cathedral and candlelit caroling in Jackson Square (the Sun before Christmas, Dec 20). Bonfires line the levees along River Road on Christmas Eve (to guide Papa Noël, in his alligator-drawn sled), and house tours offer glimpses of stunningly turned-out residences. The Running of the Santas adds hilarity whether you're a runner or watcher. www.neworleansonline.com/christmas. ℭ **504/522-5730.** Throughout December.

New Year's Eve. The countdown party takes place in Jackson Square and, in the New Orleans equivalent of Times Square, revelers watch a lighted fleur-de-lis drop from the top of Jackson Brewery. Fantastic fireworks ensue. December 31.

RESPONSIBLE TOURISM

Given the tribulations that New Orleans and Louisiana have undergone, one of the most important acts of responsible travel may simply be going, spending locally, tipping generously, behaving respectfully, and encouraging others to do the same. Responsible tourism in New Orleans may start as you tip the brass band playing in the airport and continue as you leave the airport in a hybrid shuttle van. The next day, ride one of the city's new fleet of biodiesel/electric hybrid buses. Many attractions are easily accessed by foot, streetcar, tour bus, pedicab, or bike. Renting a **Blue Bike** (p. 292) is where convenience marries sustainability.

Many dining establishments embrace the lake-, river-, Gulf-, bayou-, and farm-to-table movement, sourcing from local ingredients and purveyors; some even have their own farms and gardens. We love supporting restaurants that participate in the oyster shell recycling program by the **Coalition to Restore Coastal Louisiana** (www.crcl.org/restaurant-guide).

You can learn about Louisiana's shrinking coastline and restoration efforts on a tour with **Lost Land** (p. 196) or **The Great Delta** (p. 195). Then do your part and haul your empty bottles to **Glass Half Full** (www.glasshalffullnola.com) where they'll become sand for coastal restoration and disaster relief.

Infrastructure, fragility, and landmark regulations can make green improvements difficult and expensive, especially in the French Quarter. Many properties that suffered damages in Katrina's flooding expended their rebuilding resources just to get back on their feet, forsaking going green. That said, nearly every property has instituted programs like recycling and on-demand linen replacement. The new **Virgin Hotel** (p. 80) is LEED-silver certified, with a goal of eventually making the hotel "net zero," net zero carbon and net zero waste. **Hotel Monteleone** has also implemented a host of eco-friendly initiatives (and we love that they donate leftover food to a local nonprofit organization). And although our preferences lean away from major hotel chains, those with corporate-supported sustainability programs, like **Hyatt, Sheraton, Marriott,** and **Loews,** are doing some of the better work in this arena. **HI Hostels** is a great choice for responsible budget travelers.

In the wake of Hurricane Katrina, the Deepwater oil spill, Covid, and Hurricane Ida, New Orleanians have become much more focused on the need to support locally owned businesses, as a means of economic rebuilding and cultural preservation. The Urban Conservancy's **Stay Local** program (www.staylocal.org) has a directory of locally owned and Black-owned businesses to patronize. Along those lines, be sure you understand the consequences when considering a short-term rental (p. 72).

Donating to local causes is a significant way to make a difference (and feel more connected to the city). **Voluntourism** is popular, especially with groups; start at www.neworleans.com/meeting-planners/planning-tools/voluntourism. The respected organization **Habitat for Humanity,** which created the Musicians Village for artists who lost their homes in the flood, offers many volunteer opportunities (www.habitat-nola.org; © **504/861-2077**). Or try **Common Ground** (www.commongroundrelief.org; © **504/312-1729**) or the **United Saints Recovery Project** (www.unitedsaints.org; © **504/233-8883**). **Youth Rebuilding New Orleans,** which rehabs homes primarily for teachers, is geared toward teens and even younger kids—service hours, anyone? (www. yrno.com; © **504/264-3344**). **Groundwork New Orleans,** which builds rain gardens and other ecological improvements, sometimes has volunteer activities (www.groundworknola.org; © **504/383-4035**). **Green Light New Orleans** (www.greenlightneworleans.org; © **504/324-2429**) helps homeowners make their properties more sustainable. Larger groups can also work through **Projects with Purpose** (www.projectswithpurpose.com; © **504/934-1000;** allow 2 weeks to complete applications and paperwork, volunteers may be responsible for expenses, equipment, and accommodations). If you can't give time, you can always give money: All of these worthy organizations gratefully accept donations.

SUGGESTED ITINERARIES

By Lavinia Spalding

3

I t's easy to wander aimlessly through New Orleans with your eyes wide, your mouth agape, and your hand holding someone else's (or your *Frommer's* guide). It's truly unlike any other place in the United States, so nearly everything you happen upon will be new and wondrous. It's equally easy to duck into a restaurant or watering hole, or take a meditative rest on a bench in Jackson Square or along the Mississippi River....and end up there for hours. Nothing wrong with that (we encourage it, in fact). But New Orleans has gobs of locales and historic sites that can't be missed and countless curious little nooks that shouldn't be.

The following itineraries are designed to help you make the most of your visit as you navigate the city. If you have the time, take our **walking tours** (see chapter 10) or sign up for a **guided tour**—see our recommendations on p. 190.

ORIENTATION & NEIGHBORHOODS

"Where y'at?" goes the traditional local greeting, in place of "How's it going?" "Where" is straightforward in the French Quarter, a 13-block-long grid between Canal Street and Esplanade Avenue, running from the Mississippi River to North Rampart Street.

After that, fuggedaboutit. Because of the bend in the river (the "crescent" in the "Crescent City" moniker), streets are laid out at angles and curves that render directions useless. Readjust your thinking to New Orleans' compass points: *lakeside, riverside, uptown,* and *downtown.* You'll catch on quickly if you keep in mind that North Rampart Street is the *lakeside* boundary of the Quarter, and Canal Street is its *uptown* border. And by all means, use the maps provided—you'll need them.

Note that street names change when they cross Canal Street: Bourbon Street becomes Carondelet, and Royal becomes St. Charles Avenue, for example.

City Layout

The French Quarter (FQ) Made up of about 90 short square blocks in a 1-mile-square footprint, this section is also known as the Vieux Carré (Old Square). It's bordered by Canal Street, North Rampart Street, the Mississippi River, and Esplanade Avenue, with Jackson Square at its heart. Packed with hotels, restaurants, clubs, bars, stores, residences, and museums, the Quarter is the city's most historic and best-preserved area, and the natural starting point for most first-time visitors. Use our French Quarter walking tour (p. 248) to explore the neighborhood in detail.

Faubourg Marigny Bordering the French Quarter on the east, across Esplanade Avenue, the Marigny boasts the city's premier nightlife center: famed Frenchmen Street. Named for six French dudes who were hanged here for rebelling against colonial government (in 1768—8 years before the Declaration of Independence), Frenchmen Street is a must-visit haunt for music lovers and anyone seeking a scene. This small Creole suburb is populated by old-time residents, young urban dwellers who've moved in recently, and a thriving LGBTQIA+ community.

Bywater A hotbed of gentrification, this riverside neighborhood downriver from the Faubourg Marigny still has several modest homes set amid sparkling renovations and artily rehabbed shotgun–style homes. Historically, the area was home to immigrants, free people of color, tradesmen, and artisans. Today, studios and old-school corner groceries still dot the area, alongside hipster bars, art galleries, upscale restaurants, many, many moustaches, and peaceful, scenic **Crescent Park** (p. 182).

Mid-City/Esplanade Ridge Stretching north from the French Quarter to City Park, Esplanade Ridge hugs either side of Esplanade Avenue (once the grand avenue of New Orleans' Creole society). Bisecting Esplanade is the historic **Bayou St. John** waterway, adjacent to the lovely **Faubourg St. John** neighborhood. Booming, popular **Mid-City** also encompasses **City Park;** its

residential neighborhoods stretch upward toward Lake Pontchartrain and include the BioDistrict research zone along Tulane Avenue.

Faubourg Tremé Directly across Rampart Street from the French Quarter, this dense 19th-century Creole community is the oldest African-American neighborhood in the country and the birthplace of jazz. Home for generations to many of the city's best and best-known musicians, the Tremé remains a massively productive musical incubator. Despite creeping gentrification, especially closer to Rampart Street and Esplanade Ave., it continues to be a dynamic, organic residential community with a fierce heritage (as highlighted in the eponymous HBO series). Once considered unsafe for tourists, it's much more welcoming now, including **Armstrong Park** (home to **Congo Square**). Still, some sections have their share of crime, so as you explore, go with a pal and heed your Spidey sense.

Central Business District (CBD) In the 19th century, **Canal Street** divided the French and American sections of the city. Historically New Orleans' main street, today it's a far cry from its peak as an upscale shopping district, but several fine hotels, restaurants, and renovated theaters demonstrate Canal's ongoing renewal. Uptown of Canal Street is the **CBD,** roughly bounded by the elevated Pontchartrain Expressway (Business Rte. U.S. I-90) between Loyola Avenue and the Mississippi River. Here you'll find major business and government offices, along with some of the city's coolest and most elegant hotels, best restaurants, and the **Caesars Superdome.** Within the CBD, the **Warehouse District,** which was just a heap of abandoned warehouses 20-ish years ago, has evolved into a thriving residential and commercial neighborhood that includes the city's lively **arts district,** with major museums and myriad galleries along **Julia Street** (see p. 234). **Note:** The CBD area is still growing; before booking a room, check with the hotel to see if any nearby construction might impact your rest or the view.

The City at a Glance

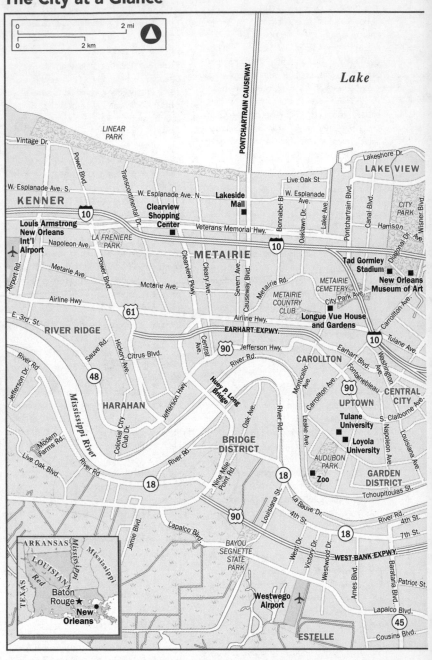

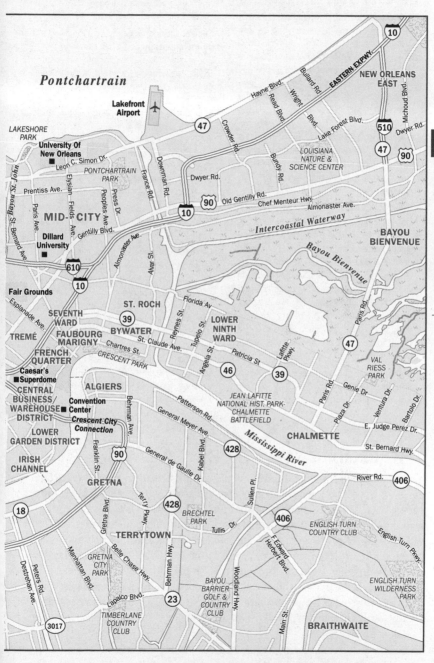

Uptown/The Garden District (GD) Bounded by St. Charles Avenue (lakeside) and Magazine Street (riverside) between Jackson and Louisiana avenues, the **Garden District** remains one of the city's most picturesque areas. Originally the site of a plantation, it was developed as a residential neighborhood for wealthy Americans, who built elaborate homes and gardens here. (See the walking tour on p. 257.) While the Garden District is *located* uptown, the neighborhood west of the Garden District is also *called* **Uptown**. There's also the **Lower Garden District (LGD),** which lies between the Pontchartrain Expressway (I-90) and Jackson Avenue.

The Irish Channel The area bounded by Magazine Street and the Mississippi River, between Jackson and Louisiana Avenues, got its name during the 1800s when more than 100,000 Irish immigrated to New Orleans, mostly to work blue-collar jobs. In this quiet residential neighborhood, the rundown mixes comfortably with the fixed-up, along streets dotted with amazing churches, some good local restaurants, cute shops, a whole lotta dive bars, and the occasional cobblestone street.

Algiers Point Directly across the Mississippi River and connected by ferry (p. 178), quaint Algiers Point is another original Creole suburb, largely unchanged (if a little less lively now) since the boom days of the railroad and dry-docking industries.

Central City This sleepy neighborhood of shotgun houses was the city center for Irish, German, and Jewish immigrants in the early 1800s, as well as working-class African Americans (including jazz legends Jelly Roll Morton, Buddy Bolden, and Professor Longhair). But hard times fell, blight set in, and while it's still home to many, it's long been avoided by tourists. That's changing with creeping redevelopment, including the blossoming of **Oretha Castle Haley Boulevard** (aka O.C. Haley), which is now dotted with worthy eateries and attractions. It's an easy walk from the St. Charles Streetcar (Euterpe St. stop), but to play it safe, don't stray far from O.C. Haley after dark.

Carrollton/Riverbend Once a resort destination for French Quarter denizens (a whopping 5 miles away—or an overnight train ride in the mid-1800s), this is now a charming, solidly middle- and upper-middle-class bedroom neighborhood. The St. Charles streetcar makes the big turn here, as does the entire neighborhood, following the arching Mississippi River. The **Maple Street** and **Oak Street** stops both lead to sweet stretches for shopping, noshing, and hanging with the locals.

THE ICONIC QUARTER IN 1 DAY

You could spend days, weeks even, in the glorious, historic **French Quarter,** but even if you only have 1 day to explore, you can't go wrong here. This very full day includes all the requisites for an ideal New Orleans visit: eating, walking, drinking, soaking in some history, eating more, listening to music, and dancing. *Tip:* As you stroll the neighborhood, check out the building exteriors: Apart from the ironwork (mostly made by the enslaved, originally; and in the Spanish style, not French), they're actually on the plain side. The Creoles saved the embellishments for their indoor living quarters. Many current residents outfit their courtyards with lush landscaping, so do peek discreetly through gates and down alleyways. *Start: Along the riverfront at St. Louis Street.*

Hour 1: A Riverfront Stroll in Woldenberg Park ★

Rise with the riverboats and take a walk along the **Moonwalk** pedestrian walkway (named for former Mayor Moon Landrieu, not a dance step), which parallels the river on one side and grassy, sculpture-dotted **Woldenberg Park** on the other. Stop to notice some of the curious public art installations and take in the sight of the vessels rounding the curving crescent in Ol' Man River, much as they have for centuries. **Oscar Dunn Park** (formerly Washington Artillery Park), the platform above the steps just across from **Jackson Square** (named for General/President Andrew, not Michael or Janet), provides a perfect picture-taking perch.

Hour 2: Café du Monde ★★★

Downing a cup of creamy, chicory-laced café au lait (coffee with milk) and savoring beignets heaped with powdered sugar is the ideal way to start a New Orleans day. Watch this city come to lazy life as carriage drivers queue up across the street. Or take your order to go and enjoy it from a park bench in Jackson Square or along the river. *Hint:* Dark clothing and powdered sugar don't mix. More hints on p. 146.

Hour 3: St. Louis Cathedral ★

It's not the most inspiring ecclesiastical building, but it is the center of spiritual life for a town that is surprisingly devoutly Catholic (it's always a shock to note how many foreheads bear ashes the day after Mardi Gras' frantic antics). Legend has it that the serene garden in the back was a favorite haunt of good Catholic Marie Laveau—better known as the Voodoo Queen. Not even the infamous Pere Antoine, sent to New Orleans by the Office of the Inquisition, could convince Madame Laveau to forsake Voodoo. The imposing statue of Jesus lost a thumb and finger to Katrina; at night, its shadow is otherworldly. See p. 156.

Hour 4: The Presbytère & the Cabildo ★★★

The former home of the priests who worked at St. Louis Cathedral has been turned into a museum housing a terrific "Living with Hurricanes" exhibit (p. 164). It's well worth an hour. If you still have time, the **Cabildo** museum (on the other side of St. Louis Cathedral; p. 160) is where the Louisiana Purchase was signed. Its exhibits illustrate New Orleans and Louisiana history and culture—including Mardi Gras and Napoleon Bonaparte's death mask. For real. See p. 163.

Hour 5: Muffuletta at Central Grocery ★★★

Ya gotta do it. Get a muffuletta from **Central Grocery,** whose version of the celebrated Italian sandwich—filled with olive salad, Italian cold cuts, and cheese—is ginormous; half is more than enough for one hungry person. Eat in at the tiny tables in back or thread your way through the buildings across the street to chow down along the banks of the Mississippi (p. 111). If you're olive averse (or if Central Grocery isn't open

New Orleans Itineraries

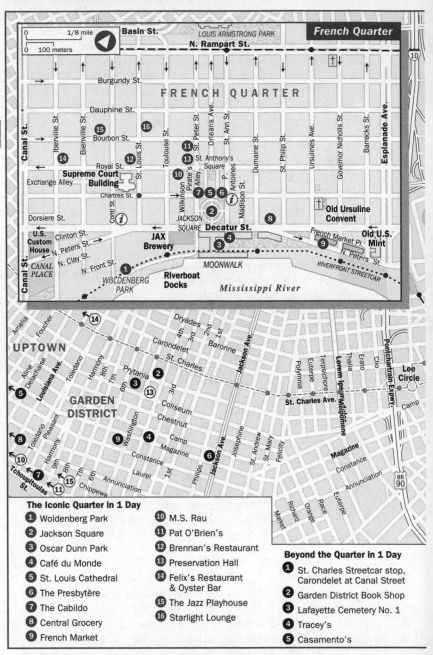

The Iconic Quarter in 1 Day

1. Woldenberg Park
2. Jackson Square
3. Oscar Dunn Park
4. Café du Monde
5. St. Louis Cathedral
6. The Presbytère
7. The Cabildo
8. Central Grocery
9. French Market
10. M.S. Rau
11. Pat O'Brien's
12. Brennan's Restaurant
13. Preservation Hall
14. Felix's Restaurant & Oyster Bar
15. The Jazz Playhouse
16. Starlight Lounge

Beyond the Quarter in 1 Day

1. St. Charles Streetcar stop, Carondelet at Canal Street
2. Garden District Book Shop
3. Lafayette Cemetery No. 1
4. Tracey's
5. Casamento's

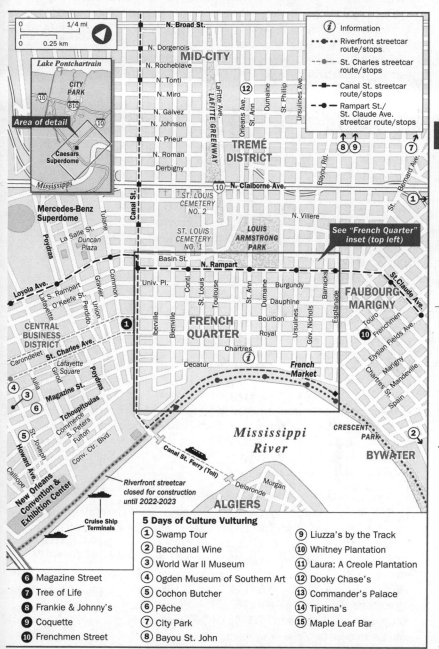

0   1/4 mi
0   0.25 km

N. Broad St.

N. Dorgenois
N. Rocheblave
N. Tonti
N. Miro
N. Galvez
N. Johnson
N. Prieur
N. Roman
Derbigny

MID-CITY

LAFITTE GREENWAY
LaFitte Ave.

Orleans Ave.
St. Ann
Dumaine
St. Phillip
Ursulines Ave.

TREMÉ DISTRICT

Information

•••●••• Riverfront streetcar route/stops

–––●–– St. Charles streetcar route/stops

–■–■– Canal St. streetcar route/stops

–●– Rampart St./ St. Claude Ave. streetcar route/stops

8 9   7

Lake Pontchartrain

CITY PARK

Area of detail

Caesars Superdome

Mississippi

N. Claiborne Ave.

Bayou Rd.

Bernard Ave.

1

ST. LOUIS CEMETERY NO. 2

ST. LOUIS CEMETERY NO. 1

N. Villere

LOUIS ARMSTRONG PARK

See "French Quarter" inset (top left)

St.

Mercedes-Benz Superdome

Poydras

La Salle St.
Duncan Plaza

Tulane

Canal St.

Basin St.

N. Rampart

FAUBOURG MARIGNY

St. Claude Ave.

Loyola Ave.
S. Rampart
Lafayette
O'Keefe St.
Perdido
Union
Gravier
Common

Univ. Pl.

Conti
St. Louis
Toulouse

St. Ann
Dumaine
Burgundy
Dauphine
Bourbon
Royal

Barracks
Esplanade
Gov. Nichols
Ursulines

Touro
Frenchmen

10

CENTRAL BUSINESS DISTRICT

St. Charles Ave.
Carondelet

Lafayette Square
Girod

Poydras

1

Iberville
Bienville

FRENCH QUARTER

Elysian Fields Ave.

Marigny
Chartres St.
Mandeville
Spain

4
3
6

Julia

Magazine St.

Tchoupitoulas
Commerce
S. Peters
Fulton

Chartres

Decatur

i

French Market

5

St. Joseph

Howard Ave.

Calliope

Conv. Ctr. Blvd.

CRESCENT PARK

2

BYWATER

Mississippi River

Canal St. Ferry (Toll)

Riverfront streetcar closed for construction until 2022-2023

Cruise Ship Terminals

New Orleans Convention & Exhibition Center

Delaronde
Morgan

ALGIERS

5 Days of Culture Vulturing

① Swamp Tour	⑨ Liuzza's by the Track
② Bacchanal Wine	⑩ Whitney Plantation
③ World War II Museum	⑪ Laura: A Creole Plantation
④ Ogden Museum of Southern Art	⑫ Dooky Chase's
⑤ Cochon Butcher	⑬ Commander's Palace
⑥ Pêche	⑭ Tipitina's
⑦ City Park	⑮ Maple Leaf Bar
⑧ Bayou St. John	

⑥ Magazine Street
⑦ Tree of Life
⑧ Frankie & Johnny's
⑨ Coquette
⑩ Frenchmen Street

yet—the building sustained damages in Hurricane Ida and was closed at press time), we got you: Hit **Verti Marte** (p. 107) for a cult-favorite po'boy—yes, dressed, yes, to go—or head to **Coop's Place** (p. 111) where the atmosphere is divey and the grub is solid. We usually go for the rabbit and sausage jambalaya. If you'd rather shop than eat, take a detour to the **French Market** (p. 233), 2 blocks down and across the street. (**Meals from the Heart** [p. 233] is a consistently great lunch option.)

Hour 6: Strolling Royal & Chartres Streets ★★★

Royal Street is lined with swanky antiques, art, and clothing shops and has loads of pre-war architectural eye candy. Be sure to browse the sublime collection at **M. S. Rau,** at 622 Royal (p. 235)—the 100+-year-old antiques store welcomes gawkers. Several blocks of Royal are usually closed to vehicles from 11am to 4pm, and myriad street performers, from the talented to the tawdry, entertain for tips. On **Chartres Street,** sniff out **Hové Parfumeur** (p. 244) and the **Pharmacy Museum** (p. 162) before enjoying a Pimm's Cup at **Napoleon House** (p. 225).

Hour 7: Bourbon Street ★

Sure, Bourbon Street is gaudy, loud, and, truth be told, pretty gross and seedy nowadays. For our money, the best time to do Bourbon is dusk, when it's neither too tame nor too rowdy—when music pours out the doors and dancers and barmen hawk their wares, it can be exhilarating. Everyone gets a pass to do it at least once. If you're ready to party it up, drink a legendary Hurricane on the always-lively patio at **Pat O'Brien's** (p. 222).

Hour 8: Brennan's Restaurant ★★★

Food is an intensely important part of your time in New Orleans, and you must dine well, several times daily. For your iconic French Quarter dinner, hit **Brennan's,** which is named for the famed first family of New Orleans restaurants and lives up to the mantle (p. 100). You've planned ahead and made reservations, right?

Hour 9: Let the Good Times Roll ★★★

Nightlife is essential to your day. Do not miss **Preservation Hall** (p. 213)—it's affordable, and it's the real, traditional jazz McCoy. Late-night munchies? Head for **Felix's Restaurant & Oyster Bar** (p. 111) for a dozen raw. Still going? Slink into the swanky **Jazz Playhouse** (p. 212), for the city's finest jazz or a bit of burlesque, or the atmospheric **Starlight Lounge** (p. 213) for jazz or blues. A nightcap at **Cane & Table** (p. 222) or **Jewel of the South** (p. 223) will never disappoint. And if you skipped **Café du Monde** (p. 146) earlier because the line was bonkers, now's an even better beignet-binging hour.

BEYOND THE QUARTER IN 1 DAY

You've had your day of exploring the Quarter. Now get out of the Quarter, *get out of the Quarter,* **get out of the Quarter!** Today we send you to the other side of the city for a completely different perspective. It's another full day of exploring, packed with great stuff to see and do. And eat. *Start: St. Charles streetcar line, Carondelet at Canal Street stop.*

Hour 1: St. Charles Avenue Streetcar ★★★

Hop on the oldest continuously operating wooden streetcar in the country. Expect breezes through open windows, *not* air-conditioning, so doing this in the cool of the morning is a good idea. Admire the gorgeous homes and sprawling oaks dripping with Mardi Gras beads along the way, and remember which side of the car you sat on, so you can enjoy the other side on the ride back. (*Tip:* Get a **JazzyPass,** good for a full day of streetcar/bus transportation. See p. 292.)

Hours 2–3: The Garden District ★★★

Aside from its historical significance, this neighborhood of fabulous, meticulously preserved houses and lush greenery is just plain beautiful. Contrast the plain exteriors of the "French" Quarter with these grand, ornamented "American district" spectacles. Follow the walking tour on p. 257 or take a guided tour from **Historic New Orleans Tours** (p. 192). Start at the **Garden District Book Shop** (p. 239), 2727 Prytania St. at Washington Ave. Be sure to stop by **Lafayette Cemetery.** At press time, it was closed for repairs—and had been for 2 years—but it's well worth at least peeking through the gates. These "little cities of the dead" are part of the iconic landscape of New Orleans, and this is one of its prettiest. The city's first planned cemetery, it catered to Uptown folks, and has more foliage and room than others. If you do gain entry (fingers crossed!), notice the tombs with French or German writing, and the four matching mausoleums in the far-left corner—they belong to four boyhood friends (one a Civil War vet) who played together here. See p. 186.

Hour 4: Magazine Street Lunch Break ★

Two surefire lunch options are on nearby Magazine Street. For a cold beer and a very respectable roast beef po' boy, hit up **Tracey's,** just 2 blocks away on 2604 Magazine St. About a mile up, **Casamento's** (p. 143) at 4330 Magazine is about as classic as an oyster bar gets, and its bivalves are sublime. A cab or the no. 11 bus will get you there. Call ahead to make sure they'll be open; lunch is served Thursday through Saturday September through May.

Hour 5: Magazine Street Shopping ★★★

Explore the fab boutiques, antiques, and galleries along **Magazine Street** (p. 234), where even nonshoppers can enjoy the quirky mix of upscale-downscale, old-meets-new. The souvenir options trounce those of the Bourbon Street T-shirt shops. Use that JazzyPass to hop on and off the no. 11 bus (it runs about every 20 min.); cabs or feet also work.

Hour 6: The Tree of Life ★★★

One of the sweetest spots of shade in town is the magnificent **Tree of Life** (officially named the Étienne de Boray Oak). Take the no. 11 bus to the Magazine & Exposition stop, then walk 6 minutes. Countless couples get engaged and wed beneath this 300-year-old giant. Nuptials aside, it's a serene place to rest your body and mind, snap some tree-hugging photos, and perhaps even spot a giraffe poking its head over the zoo fence.

Hour 7: Dinner at Frankie & Johnny's or Coquette ★★★

Your choice: lowbrow or highbrow. No wrong answer here; we love both. At nearby **Frankie & Johnny's** (321 Arabella St.), local families have devoured boiled seafood, gumbo, and oyster po'boys since 1942. For a fine-dining experience, **Coquette** (p. 136), though it's a bit farther (a 10-min. Lyft or Uber). Why are we so positively smitten with Coquette? Because it's perfect. Do make a reservation; don't skip dessert.

Hour 8: Frenchmen Street ★★★

Hit up the clubs and bars of **Frenchmen Street** in the Quarter-adjacent Faubourg Marigny. Wander, mingle, people-watch, heed the music pouring forth, and then pick a club or three in which to work your mojo. See p. 213.

5 DAYS OF CULTURE VULTURING

A trip to New Orleans is not just about eating, drinking, dancing, and admiring fancy houses (although that's a big part of it, *huge*). The city and environs are dripping with cultural coolness and historic eye-openers. Each of these five itineraries combines an enlightening or entertaining activity, plus suggestions for nearby dining (and maybe another suggestion or two that we can't resist planting)—leaving time to discover the city as it's meant to be discovered—in serendipitous fashion. Do them all, or choose a couple of faves.

Day 1: Swamp Tour & Bacchanal ★★★

We scoff at those who scoff at swamp tours because they're too "touristy." Unless you're from Florida, you need to do this. Everyone knows about the gators, and they're cool enough. But the swamps themselves are mystical and otherworldly, and their ecological, cultural, historic, and economic relevance is fascinating. Get an early start so you have time for afternoon activities. Most tour companies can arrange round-trip transportation from your hotel. See p. 194.

Since you're already steeped in nature, we'll keep you outside for your afternoon-into-evening entertainment. Take a cab or Uber out to **Bacchanal** (p. 113) in the Lower 9th Ward to hang with locals under the stars, enjoy a lovely meal, sip fine wine, and soak up great live jazz. Get dropped off and picked up right at the front door—the immediate area's seen a lot of crime lately, but the restaurant itself is magical.

Day 2: National World War II Museum ★★★

This remarkable historical jewel (p. 168) sprawls across a complex of buildings, each jam-packed with thought-provoking exhibits. Make sure to listen to some of the potent, personal oral histories, and if you see a veteran, volunteering or visiting, say thank you for us, please.

You could spend hours here, and you should. But you could also split your time appreciating the premier collection of Southern art in the country, traditional and modern, at the stylish, airy **Ogden Museum of Southern Art,** just a block away (p. 169).

Have lunch at **Cochon Butcher** (p. 132), an upscale, Cajun-inflected deli 2 blocks from the museum. The cured meats stand out, but just about everything is stellar (including the marinated brussels sprouts). If you liked the muffuletta from Central Grocery, you can taste-test the version here. It's debatable, but Butcher's might just be the best in town. If it's impeccably prepared seafood you require, reserve a table at **Pêche** (p. 127).

Day 3: City Park & Bayou St. John ★★★

Full of nature's glories, City Park's 1,300 acres are also full of activities, from the splendid **New Orleans Museum of Art** (p. 170) to the outstanding **Besthoff Sculpture Garden** (p. 171). If you have kids in tow, visit the stellar **Louisiana Children's Museum** (p. 202), followed by a ride in a pedal boat in the lake, or a visit to the kids' amusement park and **Storybook Land.** The lush **Botanical Gardens** include the **Train Gardens,** a sort of melted Dr. Seuss replica of the city in miniature, complete with model trains (not to mention enormous lily pads). See p. 181.

Just outside the main entrance to City Park is **Bayou St. John,** a former bustling canal turned scenic body of water, and the site of the city's origins. If you're up for more footwork, a stroll here is one of the lesser-known, more peaceful delights of the city. (See the walking tour on p. 264.) Alternately, plan your timing to coincide with a **kayak tour** along this mellow waterway (p. 195). Or just point yourself down Esplanade Avenue and turn left on Lopez for shivering-cold schooners of Abita and one of the city's best gumbos at **Liuzza's by the Track** (p. 122). Also, get the garlic oyster po' boy. You're welcome.

Day 4: River Road ★★★

To see an altogether different but vitally important side of the city's history, visit the **Whitney** and **Laura plantations** (p. 276 and p. 275). The extraordinary Whitney focuses entirely on the lives of the enslaved, and nearby Laura has long endeavored to include this history (as opposed to that of only the plantation owner). You'll need a car or tour company for this outing, a very worthwhile look at the pre– and post–Civil War eras, slavery, and Reconstruction.

For dinner back in the city, make a beeline for legendary **Dooky Chase's** (p. 118). You'll not only enjoy a classic, casual meal, you'll pay homage to New Orleans' Creole cuisine queen, the late Leah Chase, who fed everyone from Martin Luther King Jr. and presidents George W. Bush and Barack Obama to Ray Charles, James Baldwin, and Beyonce. (Chase was also the inspiration for Disney's first African American princess.) Get the gumbo. Get the fried chicken. Get a reservation. (And though casual attire is fine, do heed the dress code on the website—it's enforced.)

Day 5: Do It Up & Get on Down ★★★

Your iconic cultural event today is a meal at **Commander's Palace** (p. 135). Choose a long, luxurious dinner or a languid, martini-laden lunch. *When* you fit this into your schedule is up to you; just do it in a leisurely fashion and savor the experience, one cocktail or course at a time. The world-famous establishment never rests on its laurels but continues to push Creole cuisine in new and exciting directions, while honoring its origins. It's fine dining done the New Orleans way: with a side of fun. (Wear your Sunday best; don't hold back!)

Later, check out **Tipitina's** (p. 220) or the **Maple Leaf Bar** (p. 220), both pillars of stellar NOLA tuneage (yes, you can wear your fancy-pants clothes to a club; you won't be alone, and besides, no one cares). This represents our perfect day in New Orleans: mixing high-society dining with down-and-dirty dancing, going from an elegant manse to an every-man's dive. There isn't any *one* way to do New Orleans, but we can say with some degree of certainty that if you end your night at Tip's (or the Maple Leaf), you've done something right.

MARDI GRAS & JAZZ FEST

By Lavinia Spalding

For many people, what they know about New Orleans begins and ends with its parties: Mardi Gras—the biggest street blowout in America—or Jazz Fest, the grand-père of all other music fests and still the best music event in the country. Here, where anything is an excuse for a celebration (there are festivals in Louisiana for swamps, gumbo, crawfish, frogs, tomatoes, daiquiris, hexes, pork, cracklins, burlesque, and on it goes), all you need to bring is a rollicking, party-ready attitude. New Orleans pretty much does the rest.

While **French Quarter Fest** (p. 31) and **Essence Fest** (p. 32) attract nearly as many (or more) visitors, they're somewhat more straightforward to navigate. This chapter, therefore, gives you some background, foreground, and tips to get you on your good foot for the two other biggies: Mardi Gras and Jazz Fest.

MARDI GRAS

The granddaddy of all New Orleans celebrations is Mardi Gras. This massive, weeks-long street party rejoices in traditions new and old. It's the rare citywide event that's still remarkably, gloriously unsponsored and free of charge.

Thanks to sensationalized media accounts that zero in on the salacious aspects of this Carnival, its reputation persists as a Bourbon Street "Girls Gone Wild"–style spring break, drawing masses of wannabes for decadent, X-rated action rather than tradition. If that's your thang, by all means go forth and par-tay (just remember, the Internet is *eternal*).

But there is so much more to Carnival than media-hyped wanton action. Truth is, Mardi Gras remains one of the most exciting times to visit New Orleans, for people from all walks of life. Yes, you can hang in the Bourbon Street fratmosphere 'til you're falling down, but you can also spend days admiring and reveling in the city's rich traditions, or have a fun, memorable family vacation beyond what any mouse could offer.

Knowing some of its long and fascinating history helps put matters in perspective. First of all, Mardi Gras is just 1 day: French for "Fat Tuesday," Mardi Gras is the day before Ash Wednesday, when Lent begins. Though many people *call* it Mardi Gras, "Carnival" is the correct term for the 5- to 8-week "season" stretching from Twelfth Night (Jan 6) to Fat Tuesday. The idea was that good Christians would massively indulge while they still could, before their impending self-denial during Lent.

The party's origins can be traced to the Roman **Lupercalia** festival: 2 days when all sexual and social order disappeared, cross-dressing was mandatory, and the population ran riot (sound familiar?). The early Christian Church was naturally appalled by this, but unable to stop it. So Lupercalia was grafted onto the beginning of Lent, as a compromise to bribe everyone into observance.

Carnival (from a Latin word roughly meaning "farewell to flesh") and its lavish masked balls and other festivities became popular in Italy and France, and the tradition followed the French to New Orleans, where the first Carnival balls occurred in 1743.

The Birth of the Krewes

By the mid-1800s, Mardi Gras mischief had grown so ugly (the harmless habit of tossing flour on partiers gradually turned into throwing bricks at them) that everyone predicted the end of the tradition. Everything changed in 1856. Tired of being left out of the Creoles' Mardi Gras, a group of Americans who belonged to a secret society called Cowbellians formed the Mystick Krewe of Comus (named after the hero of a John Milton poem). On Mardi Gras evening, they presented a breathtakingly imaginative, torch-lit parade. And so a new tradition was born, with new rituals established. Mardi Gras marked the height of the social season for **"krewes,"** groups comprised of prominent society and business types. After the Civil War put a temporary halt to things, two new enduring customs were added. Members threw trinkets to onlookers, and a queen reigned over their lavish balls.

As an elite Old South institution, Mardi Gras eschewed racial equality or harmony. African Americans participated in parades only by carrying torches to illuminate the route (the atmospheric if controversial *flambeaux*, as the torches are known). In 1909, a Black man named William Storey mocked the elaborately garbed Rex (aka King of Carnival) by prancing after his float wearing a lard can for a crown. Storey was promptly dubbed "King Zulu." Thus begat the Krewe of Zulu, which parodied the high-minded Rex krewe while mockingly condemning racial stereotypes. The Zulu parade quickly became one of the most popular aspects of Mardi Gras, famously crowning jazz legend Louis Armstrong as King Zulu in 1949.

Unfortunately, even as recently as the early 1990s, many krewes still excluded Blacks, Jews, and women. Anti-discrimination sentiment and laws (tied to parade permits) finally forced the issue. In a move that many old-liners still feel marked the beginning of the end of classic Mardi Gras, the mighty

Comus canceled its parade in 1992 rather than integrate. Proteus and Momus followed. Proteus later relented and now parades again; Momus parties but no longer parades. Zulu itself—which was founded in response to racism—has seen a resurgent review of its controversial tradition of masking in blackface.

The krewes of Mardi Gras change. Today there are dozens of unofficial krewes and "sub-krewe" spinoffs, and more crop up like roadside wildflowers (or weeds), some with hilarious or subversive themes. New "superkrewes" have emerged, like **Orpheus** (founded by local musical royalty and lifelong Mardi Gras enthusiast Harry Connick, Jr.), **Bacchus,** and **Endymion,** with nonexclusive memberships and block-long floats. Also keep a watch out for offbeat krewes and marching clubs like the sci-fi **Krewe of Chewbacchus,** the legume-adorned **Krewe of Red Beans,** or the severely spangled and side-burned, scooter-based **Krewe of Rolling Elvi.** Some of the best march early in Carnival season, including **Joan of Arc** and the stunning **Krewe Boheme.** (See "Parade Watch," p. 58.)

Parade Traditions

Parades were always things of spectacle and beauty, but as time passed, they grew bigger than the narrow French Quarter streets could accommodate and moved to various other sections of the city (see the map on p. 57). The largest parades might have dozens of floats, celebrity guests, marching bands, dance troupes, motorcycle or scooter squads, and thousands of participants. Hilarity, irony, political and social commentary, and New Orleans–based inside jokes are often on blatant display on the floats and among the spectator costumes.

Traditionally, trinkets known as **throws** fly thick and fast from the floats, to the traditional cry of "Throw me something, Mister!" The ubiquitous strings of beads are mostly plastic nowadays, though they were originally glass, often from Czechoslovakia. **Doubloons**—oversize aluminum coins stamped with the year and the krewe's coat of arms—are collector's items for locals. Other throws include toys, T-shirts, plastic krewe cups, stuffed animals, and blingy things. Many krewes have signature throws such as the cherished **Zulu coconuts,** glittery **Muses shoes, Nyx purses, Iris Sunglasses,** even **Tucks toilet plungers.**

New traditions also emerge. In 2021, after festivities were canceled due to the pandemic, thousands of residents decorated their homes instead, coining the term "house floats." The Krewe of Red Beans spearheaded the hiring of local artists to create custom designs and raised more than $300,000 for the arts community.

Impressions

It has been said that a Scotchman has not seen the world until he has seen Edinburgh; and I think that I may say that an American has not seen the United States until he has seen Mardi Gras in New Orleans.

—*Mark Twain*

Some deep-pocketed residents hired **Kern Studios** (p. 167) to create giant, papier-mâché creations. Most folks just got crafty and DIY'd. The house-float movement soothed the soul of many a mournful local and gave us one more reason to love Carnival. The celebrations started up again in 2022, but with limited parade routes, and it's anybody's guess what form they'll take in 2023. Check **www.mardigrasguide.com** for up-to-date news.

Kickin' Up Your Heels: Mardi Gras Activities

Mardi Gras can be whatever you want. The entire city shuts down (including schools and many businesses) so that every citizen can join in the celebrations. Families and friends gather on the streets, on their stoops, or on balconies. They barbecue on the neutral ground (median strip) along the route and throw elaborate house parties. Bourbon Street is a parade of exhibitionism and drunkenness. Canal Street is a hotbed of bead lust. Royal and Frenchmen streets are a dance of costumed free spirits and fantasies come to life.

THE SEASON The date of Fat Tuesday is different each year, but Carnival season always starts on **Twelfth Night,** January 6, when the Phunny Phorty Phellows kick things off with a streetcar party cruise. Over the following weeks, the city celebrates, often with round purple, green, and gold **king cakes.** Each has a tiny plastic baby (representing the Baby Jesus) baked right in. Getting the slice with the baby is a good omen, and traditionally means you have to throw the next King Cake party. For the high-society crowd, the season brings parties and **masked balls,** where krewes introduce their royal courts.

Two or 3 weeks before Mardi Gras itself, the parading (and parodying) begins. Adorable canines parade in the **Mystick Krewe of Barkus,** often with their humans in matching costumes. The riotous **Krewe du Vieux** outrages with un-family-friendly decadence. Sweetly insubordinate **'tit Rəx** features itsy-bitsy insurrectionary floats, shoebox-size stabs at the more established traditions (like those of *grande* Rex—'tit being an abbreviation of the French *petit,* meaning "wee"). To dip your toe into Mardi Gras, come for Mini Gras, the weekend 10 days before Fat Tuesday. You can count on at least 10 small-to-midsize parades, more manageable crowds, and better hotel rates.

The following weekend the parades and the crowds are *way* bigger—the massive party is *on.* Saturday's biggie is **Endymion;** Sunday's day-long action is capped with the spectacular **Bacchus.**

LUNDI GRAS In a tradition going back to 1874, King Zulu arrives by boat (or train, sometimes) to meet King Rex on the Monday before Fat Tuesday. With the mayor presiding, this officially welcomes Mardi Gras day. Nowadays, there's (surprise!) an all-day music and food fest along the riverfront to celebrate the grand event (www.lundigrasfestival.com). Events start by noon (Feb 20, 2023; Feb 12, 2024); the kings meet around 5pm; major fireworks follow. That night, **Proteus** and the **Krewe of Orpheus** hold their parades, and a good portion of the city pulls an all-nighter.

pay respect TO THE MARDI GRAS INDIANS

On Mardi Gras day, keep an eye out for the elusive **Mardi Gras Indians,** small communities of African Americans and Black Creoles (some of whom have Native American ancestors). The tribes have an established hierarchy and deep-seated traditions. They don enormous, elaborate beaded and feathered costumes made entirely by hand, each attempting to outlandish-do the next. The men work on them all year in preparation for rituals and parades on Mardi Gras and St. Joseph's Day (see below); they're a great source of pride, and the designs usually have deep personal meaning. Timing and locations of Indian gatherings are intentionally discreet, but traditionally tribes converge throughout the day at St. Augustine Church in the Tremé, and at main intersections along the Claiborne Avenue median (underneath the interstate). Crowds of locals mill around to see the spectacle: When two tribes meet, they'll stage a mock confrontation, resettling their territory. After marching in various parades, they reconvene around mid-afternoon on Claiborne, where a party gets going. Play it cool, however—this is not your neighborhood, nor a sideshow act. It is a ritual deserving of respect. Also, Indian suits are copyrighted works of art; photos of them can't be sold without permission. To find the Indians, ask locals, check **www.wwoz.org/inthestreet**, or head to Claiborne and Orleans avenues and listen for drums. You can also try to catch these fantastic cultural confrontations at **Super Sunday** near St. Joseph's Day, at parties, and at Jazz Fest.

MARDI GRAS DAY   The two biggest parades, **Zulu** and **Rex,** run back-to-back to kick things off. Zulu starts at 8:30am; Rex starts at 10am. Across town, the bohemian **Societé of St. Anne** musters around 9am. This fantastical walking club (no floats) is known for incredibly creative, madcap, and occasionally risqué costumes. In between the parades, you can see other elaborately costumed Mardi Gras **walking** or **marching clubs,** such as the Jefferson City Buzzards, the Pete Fountain Half-Fast, and Mondo Kayo (identifiable by their tropical/banana theme). They walk (or stumble), accompanied by marching bands, along St. Charles Avenue.

The last parade each day (on both weekends) is loosely scheduled to end around 9:30pm but can run way later, and most krewes hold balls or parties after they parade. Some are members-only, but those of Bacchus, Endymion, Zulu, and Orpheus sell tickets to the public. Endymion's massive Extravaganza doubles as a concert—in 2020, Tim McGraw, Styx, and Train played to around 20,000 formally attired party people. (Diana Ross and Maroon Five were booked as headliners for 2022.) At day's end (or the start of the next), expect exhaustion. If you're in the Quarter at midnight, you'll see another traditional marvel: The police come en masse, on foot and horseback, and efficiently, effectively, shoo the crowds off—officially ending Mardi Gras. If you're tucked in, tune in to WYES (Channel 12) for live coverage of the Rex Ball—it's serious pomp.

Doing Carnival & Mardi Gras Day

LODGING During Carnival season, accommodations in the city and the nearby suburbs are booked solid, *so book a room as early as possible*—a year in advance is quite common. Price-spike, minimum-stay requirements, and "no cancellation" policies often apply. Some hotels along the parade routes offer popular but pricey packages that include bleacher or balcony seats.

DINING If you're planning to take time off from parade watching to dine out, be aware that some restaurants close on Mardi Gras day, so check ahead, and make reservations as early as possible. *Pay attention to those parade routes* (see the map on p. 57), because if there is one between you and your restaurant, you may not be able to drive or park nearby, or even cross the street, and you can kiss your dinner goodbye. This can also work to your advantage, however: Restaurants often have a high no-show rate during Mardi Gras, so a well-timed drop-in may unexpectedly snag you a table. You'll find food trucks, barbecue rigs, and enterprising homeowners-turned-delis along the parade routes.

CLOTHING For the parades before Mardi Gras day, dress comfortably (especially thy feets) and prepare for whatever weather is forecast (which can vary widely). You'll see lots of glitter, wigs, and masks, but most spectators don't dress up. Fat Tuesday is a different story. A **costume** and **mask** automatically make you a participant, which is absolutely the way to go. You needn't do anything fancy (though you certainly *can*). See p. 240 for costume shops or try the secondhand stores along Magazine Street or Decatur Street, and in the Bywater.

DRIVING & PARKING Don't. Navigating traffic during Mardi Gras is horrendous. Take a cab, walk, or pedal (arrange well in advance for bike-rental reservations; see p. 291). Parking along parade routes is not allowed 2 hours before and after the parade. Parking on the neutral ground (median strip) is illegal (despite what you may see), and you'll likely be towed. Streets in "the box" (the square blocks around parade routes) are blocked off. *Note:* Taxis and rideshares are hideously busy—surge pricing can cause sticker shock; and streetcar and bus schedules will be radically altered (none run on St. Charles Ave.). For more, go to the **Regional Transit Authority (RTA)** website (www.norta.com) or call ✆ **504/248-3900.**

FACILITIES Restrooms are notoriously scant along the parade routes. The city brings in ever-popular Port-o-Lets; their **routewise.nola.gov** site shows locations. Most restaurants, bars, and hotels only allow paying guests to enter, and security is tight, but some establishments (and entrepreneurial homeowners) offer pay-to-pee passes. Bring tissues and take advantage of any facilities you come across. *Note: The vast majority of arrests on Mardi Gras day are for public urination. Just **don't**.*

THE DAY (OR MULTI-DAY) PLAN It's not necessary to make a plan for the big day (or for the entirety of your Carnival season visit), but it might help.

MARDI GRAS & JAZZ FEST | Mardi Gras

Get your hands on the latest edition of *Arthur Hardy's Mardi Gras Guide* through **www.mardigras guide.com** or at nearly any store. Download the app, since schedules and routes occasionally change at the last minute. Also download the real-time **parade-tracker app** from WWLTV.com or WDSU and cue up the city's helpful **routewise.**

nola.gov. Because we're thorough, we also check **WWOZ.org** and **Gambit** (www.bestofneworleans.com) for coverage of some of the smaller and newer marching krewes. Resolve that you'll probably adjust the plan, or throw it out altogether, and that you'll chill and go with it. The fun is everywhere—but with limited transportation and facilities available, unless you're an old hand with a well-set routine, you'll have to make some choices about what to do in advance *and* on the fly. Read the rest of this section and check the route maps. Then decide if you want to head uptown, downtown, to the Quarter, the Bywater, Claiborne Avenue, or some combination of the above, as your shoes and stamina dictate.

SAFETY Many, many police officers are out, making the walk from uptown to downtown safer than at other times of year. All in all, it's a joyous occasion, but pickpockets come out at Mardi Gras, and rowdy revelers are known to go too far. Stay ever-aware, calm, cautious, and reasonably sober.

SEATING Some visitors buy cheap folding chairs at local drugstores, which typically don't make it home; others just bring a blanket or tarp. You might (*might*) find a spot to use them on the Uptown routes (especially if you stake a spot in the morning); downtown, you'll probably be standing. The longest parades can last 3-plus hours, so plan according to your staying power. A limited number of bleachers are erected along the downtown parade route, with seats sold to the public, which are actually not as pricey as you might expect (from $10 per person for the smaller, first-weekend parades; $65-ish for Mardi Gras day). Bleacher seats do sell out, though, so start checking **www.neworleansparadetickets.com** in September. Bleacher seats are general admission, so you still need to arrive early to stake out your turf. Most of these reserved areas come with designated Porta Potties. On Bourbon Street, some bars sell VIP access to their balconies.

KIDS It may seem contrary to the common stereotype, but Mardi Gras *is* a family affair, and you can bring the kids (especially if you stick to the Uptown locales, where hundreds of local kids sit atop custom-rigged ladders . . . the better to catch throws). NOLA youngsters prefer Mardi Gras to Halloween. Why? The treats include frisbees, nerf footballs, plastic swords, hula-hoops, stuffed animals, tiaras, and light sabers (pack extra bags to hold all their loot). Do bring supplies and diversions for between parades, however. It's worth all the schlepping involved, because the children's delight multiplies everyone's enjoyment. Just be sure to keep kids on the curb, safe from rolling floats and easily spooked horses.

WHAT ELSE TO BRING The usual dilemma applies: You'll want to stay unencumbered but well-supplied. Much depends on whether you plan to stay in one place or make tracks. A starter set of beverages and snacks is called for, or a full picnic if you desire. Toilet tissue and hand sanitizer are good ideas; don't forget a bag or backpack for those beads. Locals often stake a spot in or near a favorite bar along Magazine Street or St. Charles Avenue, for drinks and restroom use.

How to Spend the Big Day

Your Carnival experience will depend on where you go and whom you hang out with. Here are three ways to do it: nice, naughty, and nasty. Us? We prefer the first two, traversed on two wheels.

NICE Hang out exclusively Uptown with the families. Find a spot on St. Charles Avenue (which is closed to traffic that day) between Napoleon Avenue and Lee Circle and set up camp with a blanket and a picnic lunch for **Rex,** the walking clubs, and truck parades. Dressed-up families are all around. One side of St. Charles is for the parades and the other is open only to foot traffic, so you can wander about, admire the scene, and angle for an invitation to a barbecue or balcony party. The one downside is that you may miss **Zulu,** which traditionally marches downriver; staking out a spot downtown is another option, but the crowds there are a bit thicker and rowdier. For an utterly different experience, head to Claiborne Avenue around 9am and look for the **Mardi Gras Indian** tribes' meeting (p. 53). It's a hit-or-miss proposition; the Indians themselves may not know in advance when or where the gatherings occur. But running across them on their own turf is one of the great sights and experiences of Mardi Gras.

NAUGHTY Around mid-morning, track down the **Krewe of Kosmic Debris** and the **Societé of St. Anne:** no floats, just wildly creative, costumed revelers. At noon, try to be near the corner of Burgundy and St. Ann streets for the **Bourbon Street** awards. You may not get close enough to actually see the judging, but participants sporting all form of human expression (and sexuality) are everywhere, so you can gawk at their inventive, sometimes R- and X-rated costumes. It's boisterous and enthusiastic, but not (for the most part) obnoxious. Afterward, head to **Frenchmen Street,** where dancing and drum circles celebrate Carnival well into the night.

NASTY Despite the popular impression of Mardi Gras, the parades don't even go down **Bourbon Street,** but it has its own trademark action—and yep, it's every bit as crowded, booze-soaked, and vulgar as you've heard. There are no fabulous floats. Instead, every square of street and overhanging balcony is packed with partiers. Those balcony dwellers pack piles of beads (some with X-rated anatomical features) ready to toss down in exchange for a glimpse of

Major Mardi Gras Parade Routes

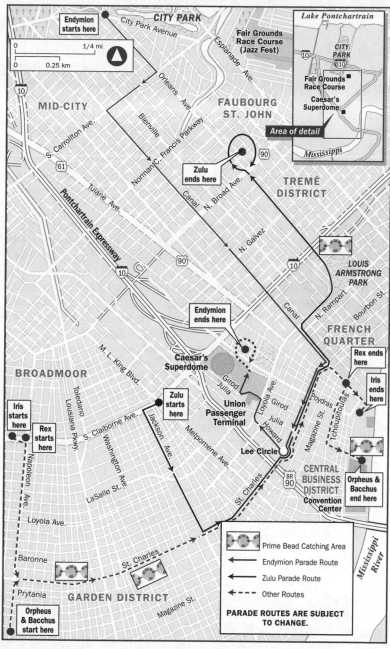

flesh (flashing is technically illegal). It's anything goes, which works for this crowd. (It can also grow old fast; try starting with semi-madness on the parade route in the Central Business District and migrating later to the full madness of Bourbon St., or vice-versa.)

Parade Watch

A Mardi Gras parade works a spell on people. There's no other way to explain why thousands of otherwise rational men and women scream, plead, jostle, and sometimes (again, mostly just on Bourbon St.) expose themselves for a plastic trinket. Nobody goes home empty-handed (even the trees end up laden with glittery goods), so don't forget to actually look at the amazing floats. At night, when lit by flambeaux torchbearers, it is easy to envision a time when Mardi Gras meant mystery and magic. It still does, if you let it.

Below are just some of the major parades of the last days of Carnival. See the route map on p. 57, and check **www.mardigrasguide.com** for updated information on schedule and route changes.

- o **Muses** (founded 2000): This popular all-gals krewe honors New Orleans' artistic community—and shoes. Its glittery, decorated pumps are highly sought throws, and its floats are superb. Thursday evening before Mardi Gras.
- o **Krewe d'Etat** (founded 1996): Social satire is its specialty. No current event is left unscathed, and its hilarious float designs can fuel water-cooler and barstool discussions for weeks. Friday evening before Mardi Gras.
- o **Iris** (founded 1917): This women's krewe follows traditional Carnival rules of costume and behavior. Its bedazzled sunglasses are a coveted throw, and its pastel-colored beads are lovely. Saturday afternoon before Mardi Gras.
- o **Endymion** (founded 1967): One of the early 1970s "superkrewes," it features a glut of floats, millions of throws, 3,200 riders, and celebrity guests such as Anderson Cooper, Kelly Clarkson, Dolly Parton, and John Goodman. It concludes with an enormous, black-tie party, usually in the Superdome (but sometimes in the convention center). Saturday evening.
- o **Bacchus** (founded 1968): The original "superkrewe," it was the first to host international celebrities. Traditionally Bacchus runs from Uptown to the Convention Center. Sunday before Mardi Gras.
- o **Orpheus** (founded 1993): Another youngish krewe, it was founded by a group that includes Harry Connick, Jr., and adheres to classic krewe traditions. Popular for its many stunning floats and generous throws. Lundi Gras evening.
- o **Zulu** (founded 1916): The city's first African American club to parade, Zulu's lively float riders are decked out in woolly wigs and blackface. Riders carry the most prized Mardi Gras souvenirs: glittery hand-painted coconuts. These status symbols must be placed in your hands, not tossed, so go right up to the float and do your best begging. Mardi Gras morning.
- o **Rex** (founded 1872): Rex follows Zulu and various walking clubs down St. Charles. It features the King of Carnival and classic floats. Mardi Gras day.

Cajun Mardi Gras

For an entirely different experience, take the 2½- to 3-hour drive out to Cajun Country, where Mardi Gras traditions are just as strong but considerably more, er, traditional. **Lafayette** celebrates Carnival in a manner that reflects the Cajun heritage and spirit. The 3-day event is second in size only to New Orleans', with parades and floats and beads a-plenty, but the final pageant and ball are open to the general public. Don your formal wear and join right in!

MASKED MEN & A BIG GUMBO   In towns like Eunice and Mamou in the Cajun countryside, the Courir de Mardi Gras celebration is tied to the traditional French rural lifestyle. Bands of masked men (and women, now) dressed in raggedy patchwork costumes and peaked *capichon* hats set off on Mardi Gras morning on horseback, led by their *capitaine*. They ride from farm to farm, asking at each, *"Voulez-vous reçevoir le Mardi Gras?"* ("Will you receive the Mardi Gras?"). *"Oui,"* comes the invariable reply. Each farmyard then becomes a miniature festival of song, dance, antics, and much beer. As payment for their pageantry, they get "a fat little chicken to make a big gumbo" (or sometimes a bag of rice or other ingredients).

All meet back in town, where cooking, dancing, storytelling, and general merriment continue into the wee hours, and yes, there is indeed a very big pot of gumbo. Some are private events, but your best bet for particulars comes from the **Lafayette Convention & Visitors Commission** (www.lafayette travel.com; ℭ **800/346-1958** in the U.S., 800/543-5340 in Canada, or 337/232-3737).

NEW ORLEANS JAZZ & HERITAGE FESTIVAL

What began in 1970 as a small gathering in Congo Square to celebrate the music and culture of New Orleans now ranks as one of the best attended, most respected, and most musically comprehensive festivals in the world. Although people call it Jazz Fest (or just "Fest"), the full name is **New Orleans Jazz & Heritage Festival.** The "Jazz" part hardly represents the scope of the musical fare. Each of the dozen or so stages spread around the mile-long Fair Grounds' horse-racing track showcases a musical genre or three. The "Heritage" part is why this fest rises above all those that have tried to claim its crown: 50+ years on, other music festivals may be more glam, more hip, more swank . . . but they don't, can't, and never will be able to bring the NOLA.

Jazz Fest encompasses everything the city has to offer, in terms of music, food, and culture. That, and it's a hell of a party (even for kids and grandparents, since it takes place from 11am to 7pm). While headliners such as Dave Matthews, Katy Perry, Jimmy Buffet, Diana Ross, Van Morrison, Santana, Pitbull, Al Green, Bonnie Raitt, Gladys Knight, Alanis Morissette, Chris Stapleton, and Galactic (just a handful of performers in 2019) draw huge crowds, serious Festers also savor the lesser-known acts, about 85% of which are Louisianan. They range from the avant-garde, old-time Delta bluesmen, and African artists making rare U.S. appearances to bohemian street folkies, top zydeco players, and gospel mass choirs. And, of course, jazz in its many forms.

Filling the infield and outlying areas of the Fair Grounds' horse racing track near City Park, the festival covers 2 long weekends, the last in April and the first in May. While Jazz Fest doesn't release the exact dates until closer to each Festival, the 2023 dates are suspected to be April 28 through May 7, and for 2024, April 26 through May 4. It's set up as well as a large event can be. When the crowds get thick, though (especially on the popular second Sat), it can be tough to move around, more so if the grounds are muddy from rain (Elton John caused a massive human traffic jam in 2015). But folks are friendly, and spirits stay high. And the music doesn't stop when the gates close; there are *hundreds* of stellar nighttime shows, all over town, all night long. Be it a hotspot or hole-in-the-wall, you never know what legendary artist might sit in with a musician pal and rock your world.

Musical and emotional epiphanies abound here. In 2006, after Shell Oil sponsored Jazz Fest's uncertain return after Katrina, a triumphant set by Bruce Springsteen sealed its resurrection. And even in 2020, when the pandemic caused Jazz Fest to be canceled for the first time in half a century, the music didn't stop. WWOZ, the beloved local community radio station, instituted "Festing in Place," airing past Jazz Fest shows that could be heard from open windows and doors in every neighborhood.

As for the **nonmusical aspects of Jazz Fest,** they're plentiful and exceptional. Hundreds of local craftspeople and juried artisans fill a huge area with artwork and products for show, demonstration, and purchase. Most vendors will pack and ship goods to your home (and there's a U.S. post office on-site, too). Some of the coolest experiences on the Jazz Fest grounds involve digging into New Orleans' heritage. In the **Louisiana Folklife Village,** artisans showcase their gorgeous work; in **Congo Square** there's music, art, and culture from the African diaspora; in the **Native American Village,** indigenous heritage is celebrated through dance, music, and food; and the **Cultural Exchange Pavilion** features bands from around the world. Meanwhile, experienced fest-goers know to duck into the **Grandstand** for art and folklore exhibits, cooking demonstrations, air-conditioning, a hideaway music stage, and (wait for it) **real bathrooms.** The upstairs **Allison Miner Music Heritage Stage** features interviews and short performances by top acts in a much more intimate setting.

And as always in New Orleans, there's food. Expect local standbys—not burgers and pizza but red beans and rice, jambalaya, étouffée, and gumbo. A few favorites are *cochon de lait* (a mouthwatering roast-pig sandwich); a fried softshell crab po' boy; quail and pheasant gumbo; buttery, crab-topped trout Bacquet; and all manner of oysters and crawfish—not to mention the various ethnic or vegetarian dishes, or the desserts. Food ranges from about $6 to $13. The terrific kids' area has PB&J, mac 'n' cheese, and other kid-pleasers. Try at least one new thing daily, and share, so you can sample more variety and decide which booths to revisit. At peak times, lines at the most popular of the 75-ish food booths look long, but it's all civil; lines move quickly, and it's invariably worth any wait. *Tip #1:* There's copious cold beer, but those lines can get long, too. Smaller stages = shorter lines, and it's often worth it to trek there. *Tip #2:* Many hours of sun + many beers = premature crash.

Attending Jazz Fest means making some tough decisions. Hotels, restaurants, and flights fill up months (if not a year) in advance, but the schedule is not announced until a couple of months before the event. So reserving travel requires a leap of faith in the talent bookings. Truth be told, every day at Jazz Fest is a good day regardless of who's playing. (Avoid the dilemma by attending both weekends.) The Thursday before the second weekend traditionally has more locals, on stage and in the audience, and smaller crowds. It's a great time to hit the most popular food booths and check out crafts areas.

Jazz Fest Pointers

"It's a marathon, not a sprint," as the saying goes. With music in every direction, you can plot out your day or just wander from stage to stage, catching a few songs by various acts—some of the best Jazz Fest experiences come from stumbling across an undiscovered musical gem. Or you can set up camp at one stage—from the big ones with famous headliners to the gospel tent, where musical miracles are pretty much a given. Everyone except perhaps serious Zen practitioners experiences *some* FOMO, so stage-hopping is standard. The decision is akin to sit-down dining versus a buffet: Both have advantages, but the offerings are incredible so you really can't lose.

At your hotel, or as you're walking to Fest, grab a free *Offbeat, Gambit,* or *Where Y'at* magazine (they're dispensed everywhere). You'll need the schedule "cubes" and performer descriptions. Also download the Jazz Fest and Offbeat apps. For $10, the official Fest program (available on-site) also has the schedule, plus food coupons.

On a typical Jazz Fest day, arrive sometime after the gates open at 11am and stay until you are pooped or when they close at 7pm. The whole thing usually runs as efficiently as a Swiss train. After you leave, get some dinner and hit the clubs. (See chapter 8 for details.) Every venue in the city has top-notch bookings—of note are the late-night blow-outs at **Tipitina's** and intimate sets at **Preservation Hall.** Also, **Piano Night** at the House of Blues, the jam-heavy shows produced by **NolaFunk** (nolafunk.com), **Winter Circle** (wintercircle productions.com), and **Backbeat** (backbeatfoundation.org). The **Jazz Fest Grids** (jazzfestgrids.com) is a very handy aggregate of the evening music options.

Wear and bring as little as possible; you'll want to be comfy and unencumbered. Do pack sun protection, something that tells time, a poncho if rain is forecast (they sell them there, but at twice what you'll pay at a souvenir store), and moolah (it's mostly cash-only for food; cards are okay for crafts; there are ATMs, but you'll want to be doing anything other than waiting in line for one).

Wear comfy, supportive, well-broken-in shoes that you're willing to sacrifice to dirt or mud. If serious rain or mud is forecast, waterproof boots are your saviors (needless to say, this is *not* one of those fashion-forward fests). Flip-flops + mud = fail. The only beverage you can bring in is water, in an unopened bottle (one liter bottle per person maximum).

There are seats in the tented stages. Outside, a few of the bigger stages have a small VIP pit area; behind that is a standing-only (no-chair) zone; then grass. The two largest stages have bleachers way back. Generally, people stand or sit on the ground, a blanket, or a folding chair where allowed. When left vacant, these become annoying space hogs. Kind Fest-goers invite others to use their space when they leave temporarily, but don't be shy about asking. VIPs also get covered, raised seating areas.

TICKETS Purchase tickets right when they go on sale (generally after the start of the new year, when the lineup is announced); they're cheapest then. Tickets are available through www.nojazzfest.com or usually at the gate on festival days. Daily admission for adults ranges from around $75 to $90 (ages 2–10 get in for $5); buy in advance online to get the best deals. Three-day weekend passes run $200 to $225. A lot of locals pony up for a $800 Brass Pass (available on www.wwoz.org), which not only covers admission for all 6 days of the festival but also generously supports beloved local radio station WWOZ. Various VIP packages, purchased by weekend, also come with a range of swanky seating, access, and amenities, from the $800 Krewe of Jazz Fest package to the $1,600 Big Chief VIP pass. All sell out, so order early. For details, contact **New Orleans Jazz & Heritage Festival** (www.nojazzfest. com; ✆ **504/410-4100**).

PARKING & TRANSPORTATION The only parking *at* the Fair Grounds is for VIP ticket holders to purchase or for people with disabilities, at $50 a day, first-come, first-served. E-mail access@nojazzfest.com or contact ✆ **504/410-6104**. Enterprising neighbors and nearby schools and businesses provide parking in their driveways or lots at $25 a day and up. Most people take public transportation or a shuttle. The **Regional Transit Authority** operates bus routes to the Fair Grounds from various pickup points; for schedules, contact ✆ **504/248-3900** (www.norta.com). Taxis, though busy, charge a special-event rate of $7 per person or the meter reading, whichever is higher (see p. 290). Uber and Lyft are also in operation; expect surge rates, but if split among a few passengers it may even out. Gray Line's **Jazz Fest Express** (www.graylinenewworleans.com; ✆ **800/233-2628** or 504/569-1401) operates shuttles from the steamboat *Natchez* dock in the French Quarter, the Sheraton at 500 Canal Street, on Poydras Street near Loyola Avenue, and City Park. You must have a Jazz Fest ticket to ride; shuttle tickets cost $22 round-trip. *Note:* The **Canal Street streetcar line** will be packed, but it's an option from the Quarter. Take cars destined for "City Park"—not "Cemeteries." Fare is $1.25 or use your multi-day **JazzyPass** (p. 292). All of these options have designated drop-off and pick-up locations outside the Fair Grounds. **Bicycling** is a great way to get to Fest (see p. 291 for rental info). Bike parking lots are located near the Gentilly and Sauvage Streets entrances.

PACKAGE DEALS Check the "Travel" section of the Jazz Fest website for package deals that include airfare, hotel accommodations, Fest tickets, and shuttle tickets to get you there. **Festival Tours International** (www.festivaltours.com; © **310/749-2035**) offers a tour that includes accommodations and tickets for Jazz Fest, plus a midweek visit to Cajun Country for unique personal encounters with leading local musicians. A crawfish boil with the Savoys (reigning first family of Cajun music) and a barbecue at zydeco master Geno Delafose's ranch are regular outings. The company has been around since 1982. Their "nontours," which are filled with music lovers, are positively stellar. Tours start at around $2,300 but deliver a lot for the price.

WHERE TO STAY

By Lavinia Spalding

Accommodations in New Orleans range from your basic lodger to over-the-top luxurious: Like the city itself, there's something for every preference. Prices also vary widely. Summer and winter are great times to snag deals (and avoid 2- to 3-night minimum stays), especially when you purchase in advance (no canceling allowed). *Note: Rates shown here don't reflect spikes during high season or discounts during low season.* (And remember that festival weekends can easily triple or quadruple regular rates. Book super early for those.)

In the New Orleans market, inexpensive hotels price most rooms $150 and under, moderate up to $249, and expensive, $250 and up, on average.

Hotel taxes are 14.45%, plus an assessment of 1.75% and a per-night occupancy fee of $1 to $3. Parking rates shown may not reflect tax or rates for oversized vehicles. Be aware that parking can up your day rate considerably and may not include ins-and-outs. If you're budget-conscious, consider staying outside the French Quarter, where street parking will be easier. By law, all hotels are now nonsmoking, although some provide an outdoor smoking area. *Note:* During the pandemic, many food and beverage programs (including room service) were limited or canceled; however, things change quickly, so if food and drink are paramount to your lodging experience, we recommend making a phone call to ask what's available. Why not just check the website? Because in these ever-fluctuating times, many local businesses aren't keeping websites updated. Best to chat with a real human!

FRENCH QUARTER

Called the Vieux Carré (old square), this is the picturesque soul of the city that most people envision—visitors walk out of their hotels and feel wholly transported to the late 17th and early 18th centuries, when the Quarter was built. In the French Quarter, you are ensconced in the total N.O. experience—from the serene to the sybaritic. (That said, there's some construction in the Quarter nowadays, so before you book, do call to ask if you'll be in the middle of it.)

Best for: First-time visitors; short-term visitors; historians; architecture buffs; photographers; shoppers; foodies; partiers; everyone in the entire world.

Drawbacks: It can be bustling with tourists and goings-on. It's generally pricier than other areas, and parking can add to the wallop.

Expensive

Audubon Cottages ★★★   Liz Taylor was a guest here, but it feels like you're staying at her home (if she had lived in a sublime warren of 18th-c. apartments). A subtly marked gate and leaf-canopied pathway lead to seven ultra-private one- and two-bedroom cottages with large courtyards (some private, some shared). Each is gracefully but not overly antiqued amid gorgeous brick walls and gleaming hardwood floors. The cottages surround a brick-lined heated swimming pool, and it's all attended to by an onsite butler. It's easy to imagine naturalist John James Audubon watching birds alight from his studio here (he did), inspiring him to capture their images in his historic paintings. If you prefer seclusion to services (since it's akin to a private home), by all means stay here. Some cottages sleep up to four, including children.

509 Dauphine St. www.auduboncottages.com. © **504/586-1516.** 7 units. $259–$399 single, $369–$1,000 suite. Rates include bottled water, soda, coffee/tea. Parking nearby $36. **Amenities:** Butler service; outdoor pool; free Wi-Fi.

Bourbon Orleans Hotel ★★   In a word, location. You can't ask for a better one, smack in the middle of the French Quarter. And a big pool. This large, bustling property has those, plus good service, and even better history (it was an opera house *and* a convent). The formal lobby makes an impressive first impression. Under new ownership, rooms were just renovated with hardwood floors and updated furnishings; bathrooms are sexied-up in black marble. The smallest rooms are a tad tight; bi-level loft suites with Bourbon-facing balconies are ideal for party people but may be too noisy for others (nearby bars tend to blare tunes). Long hallways mean you might be walking your muffuletta off—for some that's a plus (otherwise, request elevator proximity). **Bourbon O** bar has live jazz Thursday through Sunday nights and a super cocktail list.

717 Orleans St. www.bourbonorleans.com. © **800/935-8740** or 504/523-2222. 218 units. $139–$499 double, $199–$1,230 suite. Valet parking $42. **Amenities:** Restaurant (breakfast only); bar; fitness room; outdoor saltwater pool; free Wi-Fi.

Hotel Monteleone ★★★   There is almost nothing modest about the venerable Monteleone, family-owned since 1886. Not the ornate lobby, not the hallowed literary tradition (Faulkner, Hemingway, Capote, Tennessee Williams, and Eudora Welty are just a few of the scribes who slept, drank, and/or wrote here), not the happy-hour scene or stellar view from the rooftop pool. And certainly not the fancifully sublime, legendary **Carousel Bar** (p. 222). Okay *maaay*be the traditional, gilt-y room decor, which leans toward the mumsy side of formal (though a recent renovation modernized somewhat). Suites offer roomy, classic gentility. Floors 7 and up have city views; those below have next-door-building views (but #56 and #59 are bigger and

New Orleans Hotels

Ace Hotel **13**

Antebellum Guest House **25**

Ashton's Bed & Breakfast **24**

Auberge NOLA Hostel **3**

Auld Sweet Olive Bed & Breakfast **31**

B&W Courtyards Bed & Breakfast **32**

The Burgundy Bed and Breakfast **31**

Cambria & Suites **7**

The Drifter **21**

Drury Plaza **16**

1896 O'Malley House **22**

Eliza Jane **11**

Four Seasons Hotel **9**

Henry Howard Hotel **2**

HI New Orleans **19**

Hotel Peter & Paul **30**

Hotel St. Vincent **5**

Hotel Storyville **26**

India House Hostel **22**

The Inn at the Old Jail **23**

Madame Isabelle's House in New Orleans **27**

Maison de Luz **14**

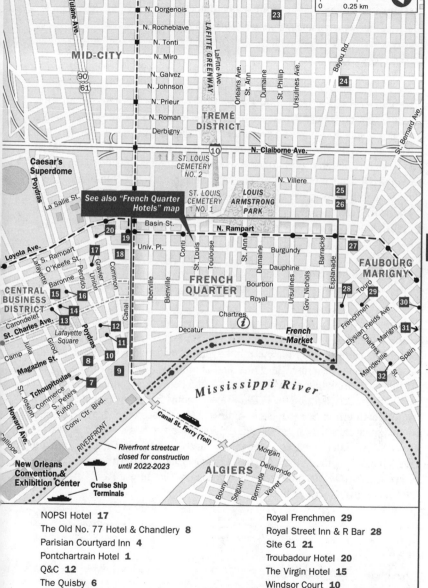

NOPSI Hotel **17**

The Old No. 77 Hotel & Chandlery **8**

Parisian Courtyard Inn **4**

Pontchartrain Hotel **1**

Q&C **12**

The Quisby **6**

The Roosevelt **18**

Royal Frenchmen **29**

Royal Street Inn & R Bar **28**

Site 61 **21**

Troubadour Hotel **20**

The Virgin Hotel **15**

Windsor Court **10**

high-ceilinged). The family ownership is reflected in gracious service—gentlemen should spring for a proper hot-towel, straight-razor shave in the barbershop, and everyone should spring for something from the pricy but so soothing full-service spa. The fitness equipment is notably good, and **Criollo Restaurant** is a big step up from standard hotel fare.

214 Royal St. www.hotelmonteleone.com. ℂ **800/535-9595** or 504/523-3341. 522 units. $152–$499 double, $345 and up suite. Children 17 and under stay free in parents' room. Valet parking $40. Pets allowed ($100 + $25/night). **Amenities:** Restaurant (breakfast/brunch only); bar (lunch/dinner); concierge; fitness center; rooftop pool and bar; live entertainment; room service (breakfast); spa; free Wi-Fi.

Ritz-Carlton New Orleans ★★★　It may not be the ritziest of all Ritz-Carltons, but do expect Ritz-level luxury, service, and amenities, including a stellar spa and the soignée **Davenport Lounge.** It's all quite gracious and stately, as was its previous incarnation as the landmark department store Maison Blanche (though the repurposed space can be a bit confusing to navigate). Room decor leans toward traditional, with posh purple and gold fabrics; bedding is superb even in the smaller rooms. Try for a larger room on the 12th, 14th, or 15th floor, or better yet, the updated Maison Orleans club level. With its plush lounge, handsome library, concierge, and food and beverage service, it's among the best VIP sleeps in town.

921 Canal St. www.ritzcarlton.com/neworleans. ℂ **800/522-8780** or 504/524-1331. 527 units. $269–$599 double, $699 and up suite. Valet parking $46. Pets allowed ($150). **Amenities:** Restaurant; bar; concierge; live music; complimentary access to spa and fitness center; 24-hr. room service; shops; indoor pool; free Wi-Fi.

Royal Sonesta ★★★　You might forget you're right on Bourbon Street, what with all the graciousness inside. The Sonesta is large, busy, and classy, with outstanding service for the mix of tourists and business guests. Rooms are handsomely decorated in white and shimmery blue; bathrooms, on the smaller side, are white-on-white. Some of the better suite options are here or opt for the added perks on the R Club floor. Rooms facing the inside courtyard avoid the Bourbon Street racket—unless that's what you're here for; some rooms open onto the large courtyard pool, which is convenient but can get crowded. All amenity bases are covered; almost everything you could need is here, including the so-so **Desire Oyster Bar,** the terrific **Restaurant R'evolution** (p. 105), and the very good **Jazz Playhouse** (p. 212)—which adds to the luster and liveliness.

300 Bourbon St. www.sonesta.com/royalneworleans. ℂ **800/766-3782** or 504/586-0300. 483 units. $199–$429 double, $400–$2,500 suite. Parking $45. **Amenities:** 3 restaurants; 4 bars; cafe; concierge; fitness center; outdoor pool/terrace; room service; free Wi-Fi.

Moderate

Grenoble House ★　This midrange property has a lot of pluses that add up to a good choice. A heated pool, hot tub, and spacious courtyards link three 19th-century buildings with 17 big, apartment-style suites with full kitchens

French Quarter Hotels

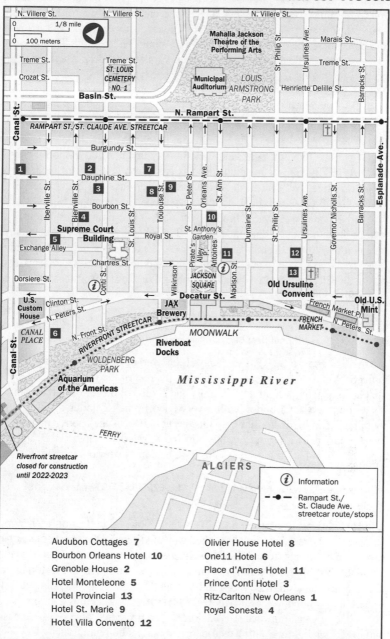

Audubon Cottages **7**
Bourbon Orleans Hotel **10**
Grenoble House **2**
Hotel Monteleone **5**
Hotel Provincial **13**
Hotel St. Marie **9**
Hotel Villa Convento **12**

Olivier House Hotel **8**
One11 Hotel **6**
Place d'Armes Hotel **11**
Prince Conti Hotel **3**
Ritz-Carlton New Orleans **1**
Royal Sonesta **4**

(if you're cereal eaters and leftover snackers, the dining-out savings add up). Decor is comfy, if a bit tired. Room sizes and configurations vary (some work well for families or small groups). Street noise can be an issue for front-facing rooms; third-floor rooms are cheaper for a reason: no elevators. But it's near Bourbon Street, the AC rocks, and staff is friendly and helpful. The property uses a secure key-hold system (guests check keys at front desk when leaving).

323 Dauphine St. www.grenoblehouse.com. © **800/722-1834** or 504/522-1331. 17 units. $199–$399 suite (advance payment may be required). Parking garage 1 block away, $30. **Amenities:** Pool; hot tub; free Wi-Fi. No children under 13; no pets; no smoking.

Hotel Provincial ★★

This family-run hotel has a healthy dose of character, from the flickering gas lamps and jumbly layout to the rumored ghosts (it's a former Civil War hospital). Rooms are quiet, ceilings are high; those facing the street get a bit of noise but nothing serious. The better ones have nonworking fireplaces or huge windows; the best—on the upper floors, accessible only by stairs—reward climbers with peek-a-boo river views. We're also fond of those that open onto the small courtyard and fountain; another courtyard is mostly pool. Rooms are regularly spruced, with a nod to modernity added to the mix of antiques, reproductions, and hotel traditional; rooms also have a sweetly sequestered bar. The lobby's **Ice House Bar** feels like your own private space.

1024 Chartres St. www.hotelprovincial.com. © **800/535-7922** or 504/581-4995. 92 units. $132–$349 double, $179–$559 suite. Valet parking (onsite, secure, with in-and-out privileges) $32. **Amenities:** Bar; pool; restaurant; free Wi-Fi.

Hotel St. Marie ★

We've always been fond of **Vacherie,** the restaurant in the St. Marie. After a recent renovation, the rest of the property has caught up. Given its Bourbon Street proximity and choice of on- or off-street rooms, it's a good mid-level option with a very good French Quarter location, and room rates can be downright bargains during low season. There's nothing to knock your socks off here, but the staff has a friendly, helpful vibe, and we especially like that 80% of the rooms have balconies overlooking the street or the modest pool.

827 Toulouse St. www.hotelstmarie.com. © **888/626-4812.** 103 units. $99–$189 double, $159–$329 suite. Valet parking $34. **Amenities:** Bar; concierge; pool; free Wi-Fi.

Olivier House Hotel ★★★

This family-owned collection of historic 1839 Creole houses is seriously packed with old French Quarter character. No two of the 42 rooms (former kitchens, liveries, laundry rooms, nurseries, etc.) are alike, but all feature funky architectural elements and unfussy antique decor. Some have high ceilings and wrought-iron staircases leading to loft beds. Others (tall folks take heed!) have absurdly low ceilings. Many have your Granny's taste in linens. We adore the arched brick doorways, damask tapestries, gas lighting, unfinished barge wood, peeling paint, teeny-tiny elevator, hidden staircases, and three hotel cats. It's a block off Bourbon, so request an interior-facing room for quietude. Service is warm, casual, and excellent. Imagine a quirky B&B run by pals who offer free coffee, tea, and snacks all day; add a peaceful courtyard and small swimming pool, and it's a splendid, unique stay for a great price.

828 Toulouse St. www.olivierhouse.com. ℂ **504/525-8456.** 42 units. $116–$259 double, $179–$600 deluxe. Valet parking $38 ($55 during special events). **Amenities:** Free coffee, tea, hot chocolate, and snacks all day; 24-hr. front desk; free Wi-Fi.

One11 Hotel ★★ A former sugar refinery, this is the first new French Quarter hotel to open in 50 years, and we're sweet on it. The boutique eight-story restoration is exceptionally clean and contemporary, with stunning old faded brick and massive wood and metal beams. Next to the **Audubon Aquarium** (p. 154), it's a primo spot. Extra swoonworthy are the swimming pool, outdoor fireplace, and guests-only rooftop deck for chillaxing with a go-cup of sangria from onsite bistro/bar **Batture.** (Cheers to daily happy hour!) Rooms have a serene spa vibe, with natural light and sugary hues (think caramel and white). We prefer the rooms and suites—called "sweets," naturally—in the historic wing, but the modern wing's no slouch. Either way, views from riverfront rooms dazzle. One caveat: Passing trains may disrupt your slumber. Be a pro and pack earplugs.

111 Iberville St. www.one11hotel.com. ℂ **504/699-8100.** 83 units. $144–$400 double, $419–$900 suites. In-and-out self-parking $48. **Amenities:** Pool; bar; bistro; concierge; complimentary access to fitness center across street, free Wi-Fi.

Inexpensive

Hotel Villa Convento ★★ It belonged to the Ursuline nuns; it became a brothel; it's rumored to be the original House of the Rising Sun; Jimmy Buffett lived in room #305. But even without all that incredible history, the location can't be beat (a quiet Quarter spot 1½ blocks to Bourbon and 4 blocks to the French Market). It's an old charmer that's been spiffed up, and the hospitality is so warm it's almost familial. Prices are also among the best in the area, with multiple options for budget travelers, but if you can, snag a balcony room with exposed brick and a balcony table. (And if you're feeling splurgy, suite #401 is a quiet, spacious beauty with a superb view.) One proviso: Must love ghosts.

616 Ursuline St. www.villaconvento.com. ℂ **504/491-7374.** 25 units. $69–$175 double, $125–$215 suite. Free garage parking (limited spaces). **Amenities:** Free coffee; microwave/refrigerator in lobby; free Wi-Fi.

Place d'Armes Hotel ★★ If you plan to spend a lot of time sightseeing, this historic landmark (the site of Louisiana's first French Colonial school) is a good choice for decently priced French Quarter lodging. You're a hop-skip from Jackson Square and Café du Monde, and it's hard to have a care when you're lounging around an amoeba-shaped pool shaded by palm trees, listening to the bells of St. Louis Cathedral. If, however, your vacation fantasies include much lolling about in plush rooms, or you live for light-filled mornings, this may not be for you. Several buildings are knit together by brick hallways and awfully pretty, awfully *vieux* courtyards. Rooms and bathrooms, while perfectly serviceable, are showing their age. Some rooms are dark or windowless, even, but a few splendid ones have terraces with a Jackson Square corner view.

625 St. Ann St. www.placedarmes.com. ℂ **800/626-5917** or 504/636-1023. 84 units. $99–$399 double, $159–$479 suite. Valet parking $34. **Amenities:** Pool; free Wi-Fi.

Prince Conti Hotel ★ Bourbon-Street bound? Then convenience is the draw here—along with friendly, accommodating staff and prices in the $100 range during nonfestival weeks. Set in a historic building with some rooms renovated in 2018, this isn't a chain experience. Some rooms are quite small, but they're comfy, with old-school décor and icy AC. If you aren't spending tons of time in the room, this heart-of-the-Quarter lodging delivers. Though a block from Bourbon, it's quiet (aside from some thin guest-room walls), and all your needs are met nearby, from booze to beer to beignets. The leafy courtyard offers serenity; the **Bombay Club** offers live piano music, decent dinners, and 100+ martinis; and the morning after all those martinis, **Café Conti** offers sustenance.

830 Conti St. www.princecontihotel.com. ℂ **504/529-4172.** 84 units. $85–$249 double, $189–$479 suite. Parking $34. **Amenities:** Bar; 24-hour concierge; free Wi-Fi.

MARIGNY & BYWATER

A few inns and a slew of B&Bs (many newly minted) dot this gentrified-meets-working-class area. Artists' workshops, galleries, dive bars, and a fresh crop of fantastic restaurants are scattered throughout.

Best for: Artists and art appreciators; bohemians and alternative scenesters; B&B fans; people seeking a less-bustling neighborhood experience;

LGBTQIA+; music lovers and street partiers who want to fall out of bed and onto Frenchmen Street.

Drawbacks: Some parts are walking distance to the French Quarter; others are too far from the action or from public transportation, warranting a car or bike. Dicey, rundown shotgun homes commingle with cool renovations.

Expensive

Hotel Peter & Paul ★★ This spectacular conversion, a former church, vies for the title of hippest hotel in New Orleans. Given its Faubourg Marigny location, it may have the edge. Add the "Marie Antoinette's private picnic" design aesthetic, and all doubts dissolve. A stunning double wood staircase greets guests in the schoolhouse building, which houses most of the 71 rooms. Gingham, antiques, and church relics miraculously blend into a vibrant look, aided by high ceilings and huge windows on the second and third floors. The fourth floor, the former attic, features skylights and original beams. Each room differs; some are pretty petite. But dashes of whimsy, like hand-painted armoires and "Cleanliness is Next to Godliness" hankies (as "Housekeeping, Please" door hangers), tamp down any self-serious tendencies. In the convent's Mother Superior room, a huge tub set right in the shower made us guffaw (others have tubs in the bedroom). Firm-mattress people will be happy; those who like to sink into cushy loungers may go longing—those sexy antiques aren't always made for comfort. Frenchmen Street is a short stroll and the hotel's **Elysian Bar** and restaurant (p. 115), sweet courtyard, ice cream shop, and coffee cafe are stellar. Decorous but friendly service sets a genial tone. If there's Pilates, a play, or anything else going on in the exquisite 1860's church building, do go.

2317 Burgundy St. www.hotelpeterandpaul.com. © **504/356-5200.** 71 units. $93–$319 room, $309–$708 suite. Parking $10. Dogs allowed ($25). **Amenities:** Bar; restaurant; coffee bar; ice cream shop Wed–Sun; free Wi-Fi.

Royal Frenchmen ★★ If your plans include extensive Frenchmen Street nightclubbing (p. 213), this is a good option. The freshly renovated historic building (previously a Boys and Girls Club) is a moderately sophisticated respite from the street scene, yet within stumbling distance of the action. The building facing Frenchmen houses 13 rooms with double queens or kings; those upstairs have French doors leading to small balconies where you can check out the street scene (and vice versa). Three suites are in a quieter back building, on the far side of a pleasant brick courtyard. Guest-room character comes from original or reproduced architectural touches like fireplaces (nonworking), crown moldings, and window shutters, which complement simple faux-antique furnishings and small but nicely updated bathrooms. The handsome white-marble-laden lobby features dramatic paintings by surrealist artist Vladimir Kush. A complimentary fruit, yogurt, and bagel breakfast is a nice plus. The calm, cozy **bar** serves unexpectedly tasty small plates, daily happy hours, and occasional live music; service throughout is casual and friendly.

Soundproofing is decent, but expect some street noise. For many visitors, that's a plus—but if you're not in that number, march on.

700 Frenchmen St. www.royalfrenchmenhotel.com. © **504/619-9660.** 16 units. $160–$299 double, $239–$399 suite. On-site parking $30. **Amenities:** Bar; free Wi-Fi.

Moderate

Auld Sweet Olive Bed & Breakfast ★★

Sweet is the operative word for this newly spiffed butter-yellow Creole cottage, from the laziness-inducing wicker porch chairs to the lovingly prepared hot breakfast to the four clean, airy rooms (and one separate kitchenette suite) custom-painted with pretty botanical patterns. It's genuine and unfussy, just like innkeeper Jessica, whose regard for NOLA shows through her hospitality and great local recommendations.

2460 N. Rampart St. www.sweetolive.com. © **877/470-5323** or 504/947-4332. 5 units. $137–$300 double and suite. Kids ages 13 and up. Rates include buffet breakfast. Street parking. **Amenities:** Free Wi-Fi.

B&W Courtyards Bed & Breakfast ★★

The simple exterior masks a serene courtyard, a soothing hot tub, and a charming B&B compound, 3 blocks and a world away from the Frenchmen crowd. The building was originally owned by a Sicilian family who ran a grocery store out front. The décor is mix-and-match fun, a blend of tropical West Indies hues with French antiques and Asian touches, and each clever space is unique (sometimes even strange—you enter one through the bathroom; saloon-style swinging doors lead from the bathroom to the bedroom). One unit is a three-bedroom cottage that sleeps up to seven. New owners have updated rooms. The hosts are music lovers who freely share insider club tips and occasionally jam with guests.

2425 Chartres St. www.bandwcourtyards.com. © **504/322-0474.** 4 units. $155–$223 double. Street parking. **Amenities:** Hot tub; free Wi-Fi.

Royal Street Inn & R Bar ★

The fact that the name of this all-suite guesthouse includes the name of the attached bar is not incidental. You're welcomed with complimentary drink tokens, and you should count on participating in the bar action (here or elsewhere) late into the night—lest you become its victim. As long as you know this is part of the experience here (music, billiards, cigarette smoke), it's all good—including the actual rooms. They're a clever mix of platform bedding, Pottery Barn–ish leather seating, mood lighting, and pops of color within the existing wood-and-brick vibe—all comfortable and worn-in but hip, like torn jeans. It's the free-spirited, decidedly Marigny attitude at play—which also describes the service and the clientele—but it's Quarter- and Frenchmen-close. Location and atmosphere help you feel a bit like a local (free crawfish boil on Fri during crawfish season; on Mon evenings, dudes can get a $10 shot and a haircut).

1431 Royal St. www.royalstreetinn.com. © **504/948-7499.** 5 units. $169–$499. Rates include bar beverage. Limited street parking. **Amenities:** Bar; free Wi-Fi.

Inexpensive

The Burgundy Bed and Breakfast ★ What do you get when you cross four cheerful guest rooms with four private baths, add a great breakfast (eggs to order, yes, please), a clothing-optional hot tub, and two convivial hosts named Joe and Federico? You get a superb selection for a budget-minded traveler. The convenient location (close enough to the Quarter and Frenchmen St. to walk; distant enough to easily escape the madness) is another huge bonus.

2513 Burgundy St. www.theburgundy.com. © **504/261-9477.** 4 units. $110–$220. Rates include breakfast. Free self-parking. **Amenities:** Garden, laundry, hot tub; free Wi-Fi.

Madame Isabelle's House in New Orleans ★ The fact that it's within easy walking distance of the Quarter and Frenchmen Street is sufficient to make this youth hostel attractive, but it's also a lovely, historic home run by friendly folks. With dorm rooms, a hot tub, loaner guitars, and social events (pub crawls, yoga, beer pong), it's party-positive but not (always) party central, thanks to private rooms, secure vibes, and a peaceful back yard (not to mention a cute house cat). Breakfast is included.

1021 Kerlerec St. www.isabellenola.com. © **504/509-4422.** 7 units. $43 and up dorm (guests under age 40 only), $70–$132 private double. Rates include breakfast. Street parking. **Amenities:** Lockers, hot tub; shared kitchen, self-serve laundry; luggage storage; free Wi-Fi.

MID-CITY/ESPLANADE/TREMÉ

This thriving area encompasses diverse socio-economies and architectural styles amid quiet neighborhood streets and busy commercial corridors. It includes a number of B&Bs along sometimes grand, sometimes shabby Esplanade Avenue.

Best for: Repeat visitors seeking to experience the city more like a resident; those who prefer B&Bs; Jazz Fest and Voodoo Experience goers; bike riders.

Drawbacks: You'll rely on a car, bikes, taxis, rideshares, or public transportation. It's a large area with some altogether lovely sections; other neighborhoods are more ramshackle.

Expensive

1896 O'Malley House ★★ A quiet, nondescript Mid-City neighborhood unexpectedly houses this splendid B&B, antiqued but not frilly, steps from the Canal Street streetcar line. Stunning woodwork and a gorgeous fireplace add architectural flair. A tasty full breakfast is in the formal dining room, or you can take your homemade muffin to the pleasant but unexceptional courtyard. The largest rooms are on the second floor, where the impressive decor ends at the bathroom door (though most have Jacuzzi tubs, so we'll deal). The smaller, garretlike rooms on the third floor make clever use of their odd shapes. Ghost hunters should request the haunted room. Host Larry and the family's golden retrievers add a pleasantly personal touch.

120 S. Pierce St. www.1896omalleyhouse.com. ℭ **866/226-1896** or 504/488-5896. 8 units. $155–$199. Rates include breakfast. Limited free off-street parking. **Amenities:** In-room iPads; free snacks and beverages, free Wi-Fi.

Ashton's Bed & Breakfast ★★★

Ashton's stops just short of lavish, remaining comfortable rather than over-the-top. We might even call it homey—if home were a genteel Esplanade Avenue mansion. Once you sink into your comfy bed, you may not want to leave the romantic, pastel-walled, antiques-filled room. But you will, for stellar breakfasts like eggs *cochon de lait*. The main-house rooms are plenty spacious; ceilings are ridiculously high, sheets silky. Room #4 has a half-tester bed and an extravagant rain shower; #7 has a claw-foot whirlpool tub. It's all light and bright, from the wide front gallery to the oak-shaded backyard, and the on-site hosts are most congenial. Excellence is in the details, and the owners have carefully attended to them.

2023 Esplanade Ave. www.ashtonsbb.com. ℭ **504/942-7048.** 8 units. $178–$284 double. Rates include breakfast. On-site free parking. **Amenities:** Free snacks and beverages; free Wi-Fi.

The Inn at the Old Jail ★★★

It's exactly what the name implies—only better. Built as a police jail and patrol station in 1902, this Queen Anne-style inn in the Tremé is a gem of a restoration, all old brick and wood and attention to detail. With a baby grand piano in the library, vintage police memorabilia, and old black-and-white photos, it feels just like a night at the (very comfortable, very hospitable) museum. Hosts Liz and Raul are generous with their time and knowledge, and the shared commercial kitchen rocks. (But **Gabrielle, Dooky Chase,** and **Willie Mae's Scotch House** are all nearby; you won't go hungry.)

2552 St. Philip St. innattheoldjail.com. ℭ **504/301-5743.** 9 units. $189–$350 double. Street parking. **Amenities:** Rooftop deck; free coffee and tea; shared kitchen; free Wi-Fi.

Moderate

Antebellum Guest House ★★★

The name's problematic; the lodging is not. Grandiosity, check. Antiques everywhere. High ceilings. Elaborate breakfast. Check, check, check. The real difference is the experience, and the hosts. You could spend your entire visit chatting with them about New Orleans, art, travel, history, and whatever far-flung topics arise. They're interesting and interested, which describes much of New Orleans' population, but now you're at home with them—home being a tarted-up 1830s Esplanade Avenue glamour gal. Quibblers (Instagram posters of scuffed baseboard shots—who probably shouldn't come to a 300-year-old city) may find things to complain about. The anachronistic, 1970s bathrooms are ho-hum, for starters. But when you step into the moss-hung backyard, with its hot tub and secret garden, magic begins.

1333 Esplanade Ave. www.antebellumguesthouse.com. ℭ **504/943-1900.** 3 units. $150–$185 double, $260–$365 suite. Rates include full breakfast. Street parking. **Amenities:** Hot tub; bicycles; free Wi-Fi.

The Drifter ★★★ The pool-centric Drifter is on a whole other hipness plane. It's just barely removed from its previous life as a boxy mid-century modern, no-tell motel on an as-yet-untrammeled stretch of Tulane Avenue (5–15 Lyft minutes to the Warehouse or Marigny). Yet it's eons beyond that blah existence. Beds have Casper mattresses and Frette linens, and while the smallish cement-walled rooms have no TVs and few amenities beyond a mini-fridge, a couple of swank magazines, and a Tivoli radio/speaker, it's deliberate . . . because life here revolves around the ample bar and spacious, "toptional" (topless-optional) pool area, where parties large and small happen year-round (in winter, they spark up the fire pits and set the water heater at 95°F/35°C; occasionally a custom catwalk spans the pool). The understated high design engages without engulfing, from the lobby's wall-size crawling ivy sculpture and '60s furniture to the so-new-yet-looks-so-old tiled floor and outdoor mirror balls. Naturally, there's a good coffee bar. Let the fun begin.

3522 Tulane Ave. www.thedrifterhotel.com. © **504/605-4644.** 20 units, some w/ bunk beds. $90–$250 double queen or king, $150–$400 bunk (4 full beds). Free street parking. **Amenities:** Coffee bar; cocktail bar; pool; free Wi-Fi. Not appropriate for kids.

Hotel Storyville ★★ Great location (especially for Jazz Fest–goers), clean and unfussy rooms with full kitchens: all good. The exterior looks fittingly New Orleanian, with tall columns and wide double galleries, and its aqua color hints at the hotel's laid-back beachy vibe. Rooms vary in size and configuration, from a tiny single to a multi-bedroom. The gorgeous back courtyard is event-ready, which may or may not work to your benefit (if a crawfish boil is on, you're probably invited; if a wedding is on—which is often—there's a party in your yard). Other amenities are scant, so don't expect to be doted on, but the on-site innkeeper is terrific, the rooms are apartment-like, and the price is surely right.

1261 Esplanade Ave. www.hotelstoryville.net. © **504/948-4800.** 8 suites, 1 studio. $89–$299. Off-street parking $10, limited free on-street parking. **Amenities:** Courtyard; free Wi-Fi.

Inexpensive

India House Hostel ★ Foreign travelers and students over 18 (passport or student ID required) looking for budget lodging and an instant party, welcome home. The four buildings house private rooms (some with their own bathrooms), standard bunk-bed dorms, and a usable kitchen that also serves good, cheap meals. A pool, deck stage, and outdoor bar make for a ready-made social scene and frequent events. It's close to buses and the Canal Street streetcar, and tour companies pick up here regularly. It's funky but not filthy, friendly, and backpacker-ready. Book directly for the best rates.

124 S. Lopez St. www.indiahousehostel.com. © **504/821-1904.** 168 beds. $17–$100. Street parking. **Amenities:** Kitchen use; pool; restaurant; courtyard; BBQ; free Wi-Fi.

Site 61 ★ Sci-fi buffs: The mothership is calling you home. Eco-conscious backpackers will also be psyched. But really, anyone with a healthy sense of fun should enjoy this quirky hostel; it's friendly and family-run, in a spiffy historic rooming house. Guest rooms offer six, four, or two beds (occupancy was limited during the pandemic, so check ahead), some with en suite bathrooms. (Private bathrooms can be reserved, as well.) There's also a shared kitchen and, oh yeah, a time machine. Beam me there, Scotty!

3701 Tulane Ave. www.site61nola.com. ℂ **504/304-9974.** 9 rooms. $32–$156. Street parking. **Amenities:** Kitchen use; free coffee and tea; free Wi-Fi.

CENTRAL BUSINESS DISTRICT

The "CBD" abuts the French Quarter along Canal Street and extends west to include the Warehouse District, with loft-conversion hotels, a thriving club scene, and the arts district. As the city's commerce center, it's a mix of modernity and history, where tourists and businesspeople mingle. Many of the city's finest restaurants and hotels are here, as are some good deals (especially on weekends and off-season). Most of it is still walking distance to the French Quarter action.

Best for: Hipsters; foodies; conventioneers; Superdome attendees; museumgoers; art enthusiasts; families (lots of suite and chain hotels are here).

Drawbacks: It's not New York, but this is a city center, with people working and view-obstructing office buildings (and nonstop construction—ask what's nearby when making reservations). Parking is pricey; do without a car or save a few bucks and minutes by using a nearby private lot rather than the valet.

Expensive

Ace Hotel ★★ If a hotel could have a soul patch, the Ace would. Every hipster-bait amenity is attended to. Situated in a converted Art Deco building, this outpost of the Portland-based chain sports photo booths, in-room turntables and vintage vinyl, and room snacks of ramen and Bulleit bourbon. It all works. The chocolate-and-charcoal rooms look great, with their nominal, angular furnishings and custom painted armoires, but they aren't built for deep comfort. No worry, cuz you be chillin with the <30 crowd in the action-packed lobby bar, excellent **Josephine Estelle** restaurant (p. 126), stellar rooftop pool and bar **Alto, Three Keys** club, and terrif **Seaworthy** oyster bar. The **Lovage Coffee** shop, **Parker Barber,** and **Freda** boutique and Local DNO further augment the hipness. Bring the swag and you'll fit right in.

600 Carondolet St. www.acehotel.com/neworleans. ℂ **504/900-1180.** 235 units. $189–$414, $369–$1,600 suite. Pets under 25 lb. allowed ($25/night). Valet parking $39. **Amenities:** 2 restaurants; 3 bars; coffee cafe; music/performance venue; gym; rooftop pool; room service; free Wi-Fi.

Four Seasons Hotel ★★★ Transforming the World Trade Center into a five-star hotel (and private residences) was a 3-year, $530 million project. This is New Orleans, so it tracks that the hotel doors open into the bar. And it's a Four Seasons, so it also tracks that above that bar hangs a fairytalelike chandelier of 15,000 hand-strung crystals from the Czech Republic. No expense was spared in this property, and we appreciate the made-in-Louisiana touches: All art is local or locally inspired, and the food and beverage stars revered locals. There's **Miss River,** Alon Shaya's flawless ode to N.O. classic dishes; **Chemin de la Mer,** Donald Link's spin on modern French cuisine, complete with oyster bar; and **Chandelier Bar,** featuring libations by expert mixologist Hadi Ktiri. The fifth floor boasts a 75-foot infinity pool overlooking the Mississippi River, a state-of-the-art fitness center, and an extensive spa with groovy treatments like rye whisky oil massages and hypnotherapy. (It's still New Orleans, y'all.) A 34th-floor observation deck (admission charged) offers 360-degree city views. The rooms are sizeable with smart layouts, refined mid-century modern furnishings, sedate colors, and thoughtful *lagniappes* such as customized lighting and iPads for in-room controls—but the scene stealers are the floor-to-ceiling windows, many with glorious river and city views. Bathrooms are lovely, too: white Carrara marble with modern soaking tubs. It's a bevy of sophisticated gorgeousness.

2 Canal St. www.fourseasons.com/neworleans. ℰ **800/819-5053** or 504/434-5100. 341 units. $400–$950 room, $700–$2,100 and up suite. Valet parking $48. **Amenities:** 2 restaurants; bar/lounge; concierge; indoor pool; live music; gym; spa; room service; babysitting; free Wi-Fi.

Maison de la Luz ★★★ Opened in 2019, MdlL has quickly staked its claim as one of NOLA's utmost luxury accommodations. Celeb fave designer Pamela Shamshiri artfully styled this stately former City Hall annex, built in 1908, for Atelier Ace, the Ace Hotel's (p. 78) luxury marque; its sister property is across the street, but miles away in spirit. (MdlL guests can access its pool, gym, eateries, and nightclub, while the Maison maintains its own more serene vibe and intimate guesthouse scale.) It's an enclave of care, comfort, and discretion, where finery is at your fingertips before you know you're reaching for it. The lobby honor bar, tiny speakeasy, and petite natty dining room are exclusive to Maison guests; only chic **Bar Marilou** (p. 226) welcomes outsiders—by separate entryway. Second-floor ceilings soar to 18 feet, while the third through sixth floors are still lofty, at 14 feet. Fabrics in midnight and ochre complement warm woods, pale lilac walls, hand-painted cabinetry, and local art. A regal embroidered crest crowns the velvet platform bed, where sumptuous sheets and spring-less mattresses define extravagance, as do the huge bathrooms with deep soaking tubs and multicolored marble floors. Chromecast, digital sound systems, stocked bars, and top-of-the-line, top-to-bottom service underscore the experience. Fresh morning coffee is silently delivered; concierges pay subdued attention and act accordingly. New Orleans awaits, but you might have trouble leaving such splendid, satiating repose.

546 Carondolet St. www.maisondelaluz.com. ℰ **504/814-7720.** 67 units. $288 and up double, $468 and up suite. Rates include breakfast. Self-parking $25. Pets under 25 lb. allowed ($125). **Amenities:** Restaurant; bar; concierge; access to nearby pool and gym; afternoon wine reception; room service; free Wi-Fi.

The Roosevelt ★★ This grandiose Waldorf property is regal throughout, but the movie-star-glamorous, block-long lobby is positively magnificent, and the history and pedigree equally impressive. Sizes and views in the well-appointed, traditional rooms vary: Luxury suites are more than ample, but the smallest rooms are simply too small for what you're probably paying, even if the upholstery is striped silks and/or deeply tufted. Some have tubs (even claw-foot); others on the upper floors overlook the city or the fourth-floor pool. All have luscious beds. But guest rooms really take a back seat to the exceptional lobby and other common areas: the sumptuous **Waldorf Astoria Spa, Domenica** restaurant (p. 128), **Sazerac Bar** (p. 228), the historic **Blue Room** club, and the **Fountain Lounge,** where on Monday nights Chef Carl serves his famous spicy fried chicken. The pool gets packed, and service can sometimes feel stretched. Check for occasional good package deals and seasonal rates. Holiday season here is dreamlike.

130 Roosevelt Way. www.therooseveltneworleans.com. ⓒ **800/925-3673** or 504/648-1200. 504 units, including 125 suites. $200–$599 double, $329–$999 suite. Valet parking $49. Pets under 25 lb. allowed ($175). **Amenities:** 2 restaurants; coffee shop; bar; spa; concierge; fitness room; indoor pool and spa; room service; Wi-Fi (free in lobby and cafe; $15/day in-room; free for Hilton Honors members).

Virgin Hotel ★★★ We love a hotel that's stylish yet whimsical, so the fact that what you see first is a life-sized, realistic (but not real) dude in a head-to-toe bunny suit playing chess may tip you off: We *love* it. Freshly opened in 2021, this boutique from Sir Richard Branson is high-design but cheerful and easygoing, with living room–like public spaces and intimate nooks. The "Shag Room" has shag carpet and a fireplace; the "Funny Library" stocks books, sketching supplies, and board games (plus the aforementioned "Bunny Man") and a good cafe. We dig the local- and Matisse-inspired artwork and the breezy, tropical motif that pervades—including in the **Commons Club** restaurant. You get killer city views from the 13th-floor rooftop's **Pool Club** (bar and pool) and **Dreamboat Lounge** (air-conditioned club with wrap-around deck), or from the 14th-floor rooms, including two penthouses. Rooms are a nice size (not huge but big enough, with separate dressing rooms), and nine have terraces. The ergonomically designed red lounge beds are, um, perfection. The location's also spitting distance from loads of restaurants and museums. And finally, it's LEED-gold certified, making it one of the city's most eco-friendly stays. Say hi to Bunny Man for us.

550 Baronne St. virginhotels.com/new-orleans. ⓒ **504/603-8000.** 238 units. $160–$400 double, $464–$1019 and up suite. Pets allowed free. Valet parking $43 (or nearby lots). **Amenities:** Restaurant; cafe; 2 lounges; poolside bar; concierge; fitness center; pool; room service, free Wi-Fi.

Windsor Court ★★★ There's a kind of hush at this ultra-fine hotel, for decades the center of New Orleans high society. Everything is tranquil and mannerly, from the proper high tea and mind-blowing hallway galleries of original 17th- to 19th-century fine art, to the restaurant—the highest-end **Grill Room.** The property completed a $15 million upgrade in 2018, and it looks and feels spiffier than ever. The spacious, handsome accommodations are traditional European in style but not at all stodgy in serene pale aqua, cream, and silver (you can feel the luxe upon entry—those carpets have extra cush). Marble-laden bathrooms are roomy; suites are large-windowed, light-filled, and enormous. Those with balconies and river views are exceptional (though some "view" rooms are only partial views); a ritzy club level adds 24/7 concierge service. It has indisputably the city's best hotel spa. The outstanding rooftop pool is one of several superb places to enjoy a smart beverage, along with the chichi **Polo Club** (p. 228). We've never loved the odd, 1980s exterior, but once inside we want to wrap ourselves in the Windsor Court and stay and stay and stay.

300 Gravier St. www.windsorcourthotel.com. © **888/596-0955** or 504/523-6000. 316 units. $295–$459 double, $309–$529 suite, $579–$899 club level. Children 17 and under stay free in parent's room. Pets allowed ($150). Valet parking $48. **Amenities:** 2 restaurants; coffee bar; 2 lounges; poolside cafe and bar; concierge; fitness center; pool; room service; spa; free Wi-Fi.

Moderate

Cambria & Suites ★★ The Cambria, Choice Hotels' upscale imprint, reels you in with a good location and selfie-inviting design. Although new in late 2017, its worn brick and exposed piping help the boxy seven-story building fit the artsy Warehouse District. Even before you see your room, you'll surely post from the oversize wing chairs under the blue neon THE BIG EASY sign. Art glorifies local and pop culture (famed New Orleanian Ellen DeGeneres is painted in Renaissance wear). Hallways are a sleek, deep plum; skulls are woven into the damask wallpaper pattern; upholstery is metallic or faux gator. Design is paramount, but the subway-tiled bathrooms are well-sized, and rooms are perfectly practical, with plenty of outlets, a Roomio streaming device, bougie chaise lounges, and thick mattresses. Warehouse nods come from the rooms' floor-to-cement-ceiling windows: The best have a bridge view; some look at neighboring buildings. The main entrance around back off Commerce Street lends a private-entry feel (drivers take note: It's unsafe to pull over at the Tchoupitoulas St. address). A restaurant, bar, and grab-and-go shop offer convenience in a neighborhood flush with activity. Great deals can be had here.

632 Tchoupitoulas St. www.cambrianeworleans.com. © **504/524-7770.** 152 units. $102–$462 double, $179–$479 suite. Valet parking $40. **Amenities:** Restaurant; bar; fitness room; free Wi-Fi.

The Drury Plaza ★ Don't judge by the looming, generic exterior, cavernous brown lobby, or ho-hum hallways, lest you call it the Dreary Inn. Here lies a ton of amenities and spacious rooms. Guest rooms are somewhat monochrome with pops of local art, and many have high ceilings (avoid the darker ones on the lower floors and shorter ones on floors 4 and 5). Suites, though not luxurious, are downright huge. A free hot breakfast buffet and generous evening drinks and snacks aren't fancy but add big value. Staff is invariably friendly and helpful, and the serviceable fitness room looks onto a good-size pool and whirlpool spa. All that, a good location, and very reasonable rates make this one of the best deals in town.

820 Poydras St. www.druryhotels.com. © **800/378-7946** or 504/529-7800. 214 units. $125–$289 double, $152–$309 suite. Rates include breakfast. Valet parking $30. **Amenities:** Fitness room; pool and spa; afternoon drinks reception; free Wi-Fi.

Eliza Jane ★★   We love a place with a good story to tell, and they ooze from the walls of the Eliza Jane's seven conjoined warehouses. Once home to the Peychaud's Bitters factory (essential to the Sazerac cocktail), a munitions factory, and the *Daily Picayune* newspaper, it's named for Eliza Jane Nicholson. a poet who was also the first female publisher of said newspaper. The guest rooms vary widely in configuration, natural light (those facing Magazine St. have huge windows; others are windowless), and size (first-floor rooms are small; fifth-floor ceilings are low). Decor is a goodly step above generic thanks to original exposed beams, joists, and brick, and rooms are well-appointed (except for those nonclosets . . . aka wardrobe racks), with Keurig coffeemakers, robe and slippers, fluffy feather pillows. Check out those shower curtains—yes, there are beignets hidden in that custom toile pattern. Yet it's the Jane's common spaces that make it a good option, for Hyatt point collectors in particular (it's part of their individualized Unbound Collection): the Press Room lobby bar; a large, comfy sitting room with decorative nods to its newspaper heritage; terrific restaurant **Couvant;** and a charming brick courtyard (whose fireplace was the original privy!).

315 Magazine St. www.theelizajane.com. *(C)* **504/882-1234.** 196 units. $150–$327 double, $190–$432 suite. Service pets only. Valet parking $42. **Amenities:** Restaurant; bar; fitness center; free Wi-Fi.

NOPSI Hotel ★★   Ninety years after it first opened, this 1927 building got a massive renovation, transforming it into the NOPSI Hotel. Fortunately, the grandiose lobby—boasting 20-foot vaulted ceilings and stunning moldings—remains, reminding many locals of the electric services, bus passes, and appliances they once bought here (NOPSI stands for New Orleans Public Service Inc.). In contrast, the spacious, comfortable, well-appointed rooms are staid, with a yacht-y navy-white-and-tan scheme (this is a good thing). Perhaps marking NOPSI as a woman-owned property, the bathrooms rock: They're big, with double sinks, an enormous shower, and a separate lighted vanity tucked just outside the oft-steamy space. The well-thought-out spaces also have plenty of mirrors and storage space. The central CBD location is a big plus, and **Above the Grid** rooftop pool and bar has impressive Superdome views. All-around pro service is the capper. *Note:* A $19-per-night "destination fee" is added to your room rate, ostensibly to cover amenities.

317 Baronne St. www.nopsihotel.com. *(C)* **844/439-1463** or 504/962-6500. 217 units. $113–$269 double, $259–$339 suite. Valet parking $47. Dogs allowed ($25). **Amenities:** Restaurant; 2 bars; concierge; fitness room; pool; free coffee; free Wi-Fi.

The Old No. 77 Hotel & Chandlery ★   Set in an 1854 warehouse formerly called the Old No. 77—a name borrowed from the former warehouse's I.D. number—this Warehouse Arts District hotel dishes history with original hardwood floors, exposed brick walls, and interesting ghost signs uncovered during the hotel's renovation. Several rooms are windowless and priced accordingly, but in general the sleep space is comfortable and oozes local charm. This 167-room hotel is all about local art and products from New

Orleans makers, including New Orleans Center for the Creative Arts and Where Y'art Gallery, for exhibits and artist-curated loft suites. Hotel service can be spotty at times. But chef Nina Compton's superb **Compère Lapin** restaurant (p. 124) is on site . . . which might be the hotel's best feature.

535 Tchoupitoulas St. www.old77hotel.com. ℭ **504/527-5271.** 167 units. $97–$313 double, $367–$550 suite. Pets allowed ($25). Self-parking $30. **Amenities:** Coffee shop; restaurant/bar; in-room fitness kit; free Wi-Fi.

Q&C ★ Housed in a renovated national historic building, Marriott's Q&C is one of the better millennial-targeting hotels. It's got the requisite distressed leather sofas in the living-room–style lobby, industrial lighting and hardware bits, scratchy blues tunes playing, and communal tables to collectively stare at screens. But there's also a vintage shuffleboard table, a terrific selection of art and music coffee-table books for perusing in stylized nooks, and wink-wink cameo silhouettes of Fats Domino and Duke Ellington. The decent, small-scale bar actually does kinda feel like a home den, and the pizza and pub food are just about right. Rooms are in two buildings split by a narrow street. They're small but stylish in muted grays, browns, whites, and brick; metal barn doors shield the subway-tiled, single-sink bathrooms. In Building A, the third-floor rooms have huge windows; floors 8–12 have views. In Building B, snag #14 or #23. Rooms down low can face other buildings or suffer from street noise. Service-wise, it's not the Ritz, but staff is cute, friendly, and generally on top of things.

344 Camp St. www.qandc.com. ℭ **504/587-9700.** 196 units. $118–$409 double. Self-parking $29. Pets allowed ($75). **Amenities:** Restaurant; bar; fitness room; free Wi-Fi.

Troubadour Hotel ★ As tempted as you'll be to ooh and aah over the eye-popping art and sleek, contemporary design in the Troubadour lobby, first you need to take the elevator to the 17th floor and prepare to be gobsmacked. New Orleans unfurls in every direction from the spectacular 360-degree views at the **Monkey Board** rooftop bar, which has date night written all over it. That's probably the hotel's best feature, but some other reasons to check in to the 184-room boutique hotel are the crisp, comfy guest rooms (each has a cocktail station complete with go-cups, a retro Igloo mini fridge, and a code to scan on your phone for room-service orders) with lots of handy bathroom storage space. The location is within strolling distance of the French Quarter, the Superdome, and the lively dining and entertainment scene in the Warehouse District.

1111 Gravier St. thetroubadour.com. ℭ **888/858-6652** or 504/518-5800. 184 units. $127–$279 double, $243–$849 suite. Self-parking $35. **Amenities:** Rooftop bar; fitness center; room service; free Wi-Fi.

Inexpensive

HI New Orleans ★★★ If you're not familiar with HI Hostels, this terrific, feature-laden lodging option might surprise you. Although it's still largely the purview of young travelers, all ages, families, and groups are welcome. Built in 1900, the fully converted 5-story building retains some original architectural features (high ceilings on the fourth floor, wood floors where they've lasted) and is centrally located and clean. It has dorm, quad, and 24 private queen-bed rooms (with TVs and en suite baths; #414 has killer old windows); request an off-street room if you're sensitive to street hubbub. Sturdy, built-in bunk beds don't shift; they're extra-long and pretty comfy. Each has a curtain, bed light, charger station, and ample, locked storage. There's also a gorgeous guest-use kitchen, a cafe, and well-decorated areas for hanging out or working. (BTW, no, that's not a giant whiskey barrel in the lobby near the custom mural—it's a cistern!) Individual, all-gender restrooms abound; it's eco-friendly; Wi-Fi is good throughout; and activities and helpful, friendly folk are plentiful.

1028 Canal St. www.hiusa.org/new-orleans. (*) **504/603-3850.** 122 beds; 24 private rooms. Dorms $23–$65; private rooms $110–$220. HI membership $18; nonmember charged additional $4/night. Parking lots nearby, about $20/day. **Amenities:** Restaurant, free coffee and tea; laundry facilities; bike storage; luggage storage; free Wi-Fi.

UPTOWN/GARDEN DISTRICT

The residential Garden District and Lower Garden District offer iconic Southern charm, complete with moss-laden greenery and palatial, columned homes. Not all of Uptown is as grandiose as the name might suggest—there are many more modest, no less charming properties—but the best sections are both spacious and gracious. Public transportation is easy, and street parking is usually free and easy to find. *Note:* Lower Garden District hotels can be found on the map on p. 66.

Best for: Repeat visitors; romantics; history buffs; claustrophobes; garden lovers; Tulane parents, style-seeking shoppers (for nearby Magazine St.).

Drawbacks: Allow a little extra time to get around—it's sure pretty, but you're not in the thick of the action or near the city's top attractions (though there are some exceptional music venues, restaurants, and clubs). You'll likely be close to inexpensive public transportation but may prefer a car or bike.

Expensive

The Chloe ★★ This new boutique hotel might initially remind you of that older, cooler cousin you had growing up—the moody, brooding one. The Chloe is impressively decked, with its dark teal paint, red and purple furniture, provocative art, hidden nooks—but belly up to the bar for a welcome beverage and you'll find it's also friendly. Built in 1891, the once-private mansion has 14 elegant guest rooms with nice natural light and hipster touches like turntables, vinyls from **Peaches** (p. 245), and Marshall speakers. Toss in Italian Bellino sheets, covetable bird-shaped lamps, and local Piety & Desire chocolates, and we're sold. (Narnia fans, please report to one of the Uptown King rooms or the Picard suite, where you enter the bathroom *through the wardrobe.*) The only drag is the off-limits balconies. Sigh: I suppose we'll adjourn to the pristine pool, where guests enjoy priority all-day and all-night access

Uptown Hotels

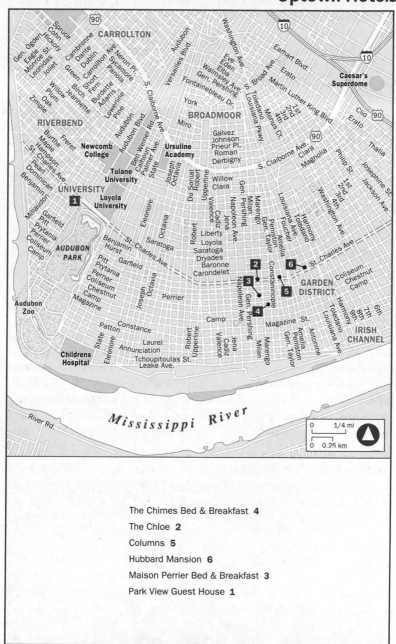

The Chimes Bed & Breakfast **4**

The Chloe **2**

Columns **5**

Hubbard Mansion **6**

Maison Perrier Bed & Breakfast **3**

Park View Guest House **1**

(and mixed-to-perfection cocktails at the pool bar), or the restaurant—led by inimitable chef Todd Pulsinelli—with its exceptional modern Creole fare and dizzying wine list. Bonus: The streetcar stops by the front door.

4125 St. Charles Ave. www.thechloenola.com. ⓒ **504/541-5500.** 14 units. $287–$659 double. Discounts on extended stays. Rates include grab-n-go breakfast. Street parking. **Amenities:** Restaurant; bar; pool; free Wi-Fi.

Columns ★★   We'd be remiss to not point you to the newly revamped version of an old classic—and not just because we've spent countless afternoons on its patio, sipping Sazeracs. The Columns of yesteryear was beleaguered, but the new *Columns?* Blammo. It's back, baby. Built in 1884, the mansion hotel changed hands in 2019 and got spruced up, complete with rooftop sundeck and new cocktail bar. Some modern-meets-antique rooms have dainty toile wallpaper; others are brightly painted. All are equipped with custom beds and Parachute linens. Fifteen-foot ceilings in the second-floor rooms heighten the experience. The kitchen is run by the **Coquette** (p. 136) team. With a streetcar rumbling by, like you're on a movie set, you're bound to be charmed.

3811 St. Charles St. www.thecolumns.com. ⓒ **504/899-9308.** 5 units. $250–$500 double. Rates include breakfast. Street parking. **Amenities:** Bar/restaurant; free Wi-Fi.

Henry Howard Hotel ★★★   This stunning 1867 townhouse with classic columns and soaring ceilings is a drop-dead gorgeous, super-stylish choice, where crisp white-black-blue decor and sleek custom touches meet classy antiques. Second-line instruments as artwork and (limited) amenities like a small, butler-style bar in the polished parlor keep it friendly; the wide front gallery, complete with dawdle-ready wicker rockers, keeps it welcoming. Second-floor rooms with private balcony spaces feel positively Southern-chic, and a few hours on that front porch are very well spent. The Lower Garden District is a nice central locale and convenient to the streetcar line.

2041 Prytania St. www.henryhowardhotel.com. ⓒ **504/313-1577.** 18 units. $149–$519 double. Street parking. **Amenities:** Concierge; parlor bar; free Wi-Fi.

Hotel Saint Vincent ★★★   Built in 1878, this property was originally The Saint Vincent's Infant Asylum, an historic orphanage. In 2021 the building was fully reimagined with a distinctly posh European girlcation vibe. (The design inspiration was "The kids inherited a castle." Nailed it!) It's filled with vintage glass and groovy art and dreamy, lush velvety furniture (custom-made art deco, mid-century modern, and 20th-c. imported Italian). Rooms are next-level stylish, with muted grey paint against bright tile and marbled wallpaper (think trippy hot pinks and bold teals). About a third have outside patios. Bathrooms are appointed with gorgeous tubs. Mattresses are Wink, robes are silk, phones are vintage. We kinda wish they'd sourced more locally for design and food, but aside from that, it's *divine*. The neighborhood is great, too, on a sweet stretch of Magazine Street across from Mojo Coffee and steps from Coliseum Square, a two-fountained dog-friendly park that often has great live music on Sundays. (In fact, bring your pup, since this is that rare swanky hotel that's also kid- and canine-friendly.) Adult humans will appreciate very pretty sunken pool with bar and courtyard, and solid drinking and dining options: two inside bars: gorgeous (and guests-only) **Chapel Club** and cheerful **Paradise Lounge,** plus two restaurants, **San Lorenzo** (upscale coastal Italian) and casual **Elizabeth Street Café** (French Vietnamese). Chef's kiss to this new glamour gal.

1507 Magazine St. www.saintvincentnola.com. © 504/350-2450. 75 units. $254–$612 double; $425–$1530 suite. Pet allowed free. On-site self-parking free. **Amenities:** 2 restaurants; 2 bars; pool; concierge; room service; free Wi-Fi.

Hubbard Mansion ★★★ Wait, who says we could never be royals? This stunner of a Greek Revival mansion on St. Charles Avenue makes us feel otherwise. Five gracefully decorated, immaculate suites are filled (but not overfilled, thank you), with museum-quality furnishings and heirloom antiques. There are velvety settees and clawfoot tubs, marble-topped dressers and canopy beds. The treatment is royal, too. Sheila & Don are the consummate hosts, and the uptown location is convenient and peaceful, right on the streetcar line, one block from a large grocery store, 2 blocks from **The Columns** (p. 86), where we never tire of cocktail-sipping on the porch, and across from **The Delachaise,** a must-visit wine bar. Lovely courtyard and continental breakfast included.

3535 St. Charles St. www.hubbardmansion.com. © 504/897-3535. 5 suites. $180–$340 double. 2-night minimum. Rates include breakfast. Street parking. **Amenities:** Free Wi-Fi.

Maison Perrier Bed & Breakfast ★★★ The impressive exterior of this former house of ill repute is frillier than inside, though there is still plenty to impress here. Antiques abound, and a smattering of country touches help create genuine, warm comfort. The beds are deep and piled with soft linens, and room configurations are amenable to couples, families, and friends (two- or four-legged). Nearly all the well-appointed bathrooms have whirlpool tubs—some big enough for two. There's a full breakfast with Southern specialties like puffed pancakes, and weekend wine and cheese parties. A complimentary nonalcoholic bar, an ample supply of homemade sweets, and gracious hosts round out the very pleasing experience here. Check the website for excellent seasonal deals. *Bonus:* The leafy, quiet residential neighborhood is only 2 blocks from Constantinople Stage, where you can often catch terrific low-key weekend porch concerts.

4117 Perrier St. www.maisonperrier.com. © 888/610-1807 or 504/897-1807. 9 units. $149–$380 double. Seasonal and weekend minimum stays apply. Rates include breakfast. Limited free on-site parking or street parking. **Amenities:** Concierge; free Wi-Fi.

Ponchartrain Hotel ★★ This 1920s apartment building was reborn in the '40s as a high-end hotel, hosting presidents, movie stars, and Tennessee Williams (who wrote parts of *A Streetcar Named Desire* here) and throwing storied parties for the likes of the Doors and many a well-heeled local. The latest post-slump redo, a $10-million job, is splendid. Guest-room decor maintains a throwback feel with traditional furnishings, crystal chandeliers, and luxe fabrics (leather, velvet); patterns and accessories evoke the tropics.

Modern needs are well met with the expected comforts and conveniences and spaciousness (even more so in the impressive suites). The busy St. Charles Avenue location, outside more touristed areas and a pleasant walk from some stunning manses, is part of the experience. But it's the common areas that really reel us in, from the foyer forward: the sweet **Silver Whistle** cafe, gentlemanly **Bayou Bar** (where Sinatra and Capote imbibed *and* where the deal to create the Saints was signed—who dat!), and the swank **Living Room** lounge outside **Jack Rose** restaurant, where a wall of campy floral still-lifes surround an enormous Ashley Longshore painting of Lil' Wayne chowing a slice of the hotel's legendary Mile High Pie. And then there's **Hot Tin** on floor #11, arguably the city's most see-and-be-seen rooftop bar, is styled after a 1940s writer's salon. If only these walls could talk. (Ok, we'll talk, though: A family member once ran into Katy Perry here.)

2031 St. Charles Ave. thepontchartrainhotel.com. © **800/708-6652.** 106 units. $169–$569 double, $211–$799 suite. Valet parking $39. **Amenities:** Restaurant/lounge; bar; cafe; access to nearby fitness center; rooftop bar; concierge; free Wi-Fi.

Moderate

The Chimes Bed & Breakfast ★★★
Reasons why this is a perennial favorite: constant upgrades and upkeep to the rooms, grounds, and common spaces; the tasteful, unfussy, unpretentious mix of antiques, modernity, creature comforts, and thoughtful amenities; the fresh-baked breakfast pastries (even tastier in the pretty courtyard); and the striking black-and-white photographs of local musicians decorating the rooms (the work of one of many repeat guests). But mainly it's because there are no grand airs, just pure charm and contentment in a true neighborhood setting. You'd be hard-pressed to find hosts who are more gracious, friendly, welcoming, and helpful—their 35+ years of hospitality experience (they built the Chimes themselves) shows in the details. (Also, on weekends, top local bands often play on the porch across the street, delivering true New Orleans spirit and soul to an otherwise quiet street.)

1146 Constantinople St. www.chimesneworleans.com. © **504/899-2621** or 504/453-2183. 5 units. $144–$200 double. Rates include breakfast. Street parking. **Amenities:** Free Wi-Fi.

Parisian Courtyard Inn ★★
Hospitality and location are the key words here, though the accommodations in this converted 1846 mansion are by no means slouchy. The Lower Garden District locale is far enough from the name-brand action to merit slightly lower rates, but close enough to access it all by foot or nearby streetcar. In the soignée parlor, elaborate ceiling details and porcelain chandeliers are among many fab fixtures. Rooms have plenty of carved antiques; sizes vary from liberal to slight (we like the second-floor balcony suites; the third and fourth floors have angled ceilings). But if you're one of those vacationers who seeks the best in rest(rooms), these teensy tubless ones won't cut it. The courtyards are sweetly pleasant, and the hot breakfast is, too.

1726 Prytania St. www.theparisiancourtyardinn.com. © **504/581-4540.** 10 units. $104–$269 double. No children under 12. Street parking. **Amenities:** Free Wi-Fi.

NOT YOUR MOTHER'S room & board

Wherever you stay in New Orleans, good food is close by. But if that's just not close enough—if you're one of those who selects your accommodations based on its culinary offerings—here are a few hotels with outstanding restaurants:

- **Chemin à la Mer** (p. 127) in the Four Seasons (CBD)
- **Compère Lapin** (p. 124) in Old No. 77 Hotel & Chandlery (CBD)
- **The Chloe Restaurant** (p. 139) in the Chloe (Uptown)
- **Couvant** in Eliza Jane (CBD)
- **Domenica** (p. 128) in the Roosevelt Hotel (CBD)
- **Elysian Bar** (p. 115) in the Hotel Peter & Paul (Marigny)
- **The Grill Room** in the Windsor Court (CBD)
- **Jack Rose** in the Ponchartrain Hotel (LGD)
- **Josephine Estelle** (p. 126) in the Ace Hotel (CBD)
- **Latitude 29** (p. 108) in the Bienville House (FQ)
- **Lüke** in the Hilton St. Charles (CBD)
- **Miss River** (p. 127) in the Four Seasons (CBD)
- **Restaurant R'evolution** (p. 105) in the Royal Sonesta (FQ)
- **The Rib Room in the Omni** (FQ)

Park View Guest House ★★ For Tulane and Loyola visitors and others staying far uptown, this late-1800s boardinghouse with easy streetcar access is a splendid choice. Views of verdant Audubon Park from the wide front porch, large breakfast room, or park-facing guest rooms add serenity and spaciousness. Antique-laden decor is Victoriana-meets-reproduction; smaller and nonview rooms can feel cramped, but all have updated bathrooms with deep tubs. The ample breakfast also ranks high. Daily cookies and evening libations add delightfulness; warm, helpful staff multiplies it.

7004 St. Charles Ave. www.parkviewguesthouse.com. ℂ **504/861-7564.** 22 units. $169–$259 double. Rates include breakfast. Street parking. **Amenities:** Free afternoon drinks and snacks; free Wi-Fi.

Inexpensive

Auberge NOLA Hostel ★ This mellow, clean youth hostel has a helpful staff, a decent shared kitchen, and standard-issue metal bunk beds in mixed and female-only dorms. It's not party-central like some hostels in town—just friendly. The big selling point is location: It's a few blocks off the St. Charles streetcar line, and a few blocks the other direction from the heart of the CBD. Another plus: on-site bikes for rent (but not enough of them), a small courtyard, and a bit of old NOLA character in the converted home. A small apartment has a private kitchen and bath and two double-bunk beds. *Note:* Guests must show a foreign passport or out-of-state ID, and proof of travel may be required.

1628 Carondelet St. www.aubergenola.com. ℂ **504/524-5980.** 60 beds. $17–$60 bunk bed; $75–$150 private room. Rates include linens. Street parking. **Amenities:** Shared kitchen and TV room; concierge; lockers; rental bicycles; free Wi-Fi.

The Quisby ★★   The newer youth hostels are, as they say, lit. Unlike the derelict dives of yore, some are super-sleek and even—yes—clean. The Quisby is one of the best. Opened in 2017 after a gut-rehab of a long-shuttered historic building, the Quisby and its techno lobby area—sleek bar, sculpted industrial lighting, and graphical mural—sets the poppin' social scene. There, $2.50 well drinks rule at happy hour, and trivia nights on Thursday are—as they also say—legion. The beds offer the best evidence that the Quisby is something special: no rickety Ikea-style pole kits, but handsome, sturdy, XL beech bunks built by a noted local wood craftsman, with memory-foam mattresses. Each has an adjacent book light, charging outlet, accessory cubby, and oversize storage locker. Most of the 30 coed or female-only en suite rooms have four beds (two bunks); a few have two or six beds; there are six private queen beds. Perhaps the Quisby's single best feature is its streetcar-adjacent St. Charles Avenue location (to snag a window-laden room overlooking the avenue during Mardi Gras, book 8–12 months ahead). All ages welcome; guests under 18 must stay in a private room with a parent.

1225 St. Charles Ave. www.thequisby.com. ✆ **504/208-4881.** 120 beds. $23–$40/bed, $60–$100 during events; private rooms $70–$300. Rates include breakfast. Street parking. **Amenities:** 24-hr. bar with snacks; on-site laundry room; free Wi-Fi.

WHERE TO EAT

By Diana K. Schwam

The late New Orleans restaurant matriarch Miss Ella Brennan once said that whereas in other places, one eats to live, "In New Orleans, we live to eat." It seems that as soon as you step foot in this city, your appetite for just about everything somehow increases: adventure, romance, joy . . . and food food food.

Here, we don't call a friend and ask, "How are you?" Instead, it's either the colloquial "Where y'at?" or, more often, "What're you eatin'?" Here, cuisine is community, cuisine is culture, cuisine is practically church (literally and figuratively—except for the fact that Church is church). Food forms the crucial threads of the city's multicolored fabric: It weaves through the people, the music, the history, the parties, the traditions. A style of gumbo can define a neighborhood. A roux technique can unite (or divide) generations of families.

New Orleans has always been recognized by food lovers, but with the advent of the foodie movement, the restaurant scene has positively erupted, and the city is undeniably a foodie destination. The post-Katrina population fell to three quarters of the pre-K population, but the number of restaurants doubled. Some closed during the coronavirus pandemic, but more opened. So there's goodness in every direction and on every level: in centuries-old grande-dame restaurants and the corner po' boy shops, in a gas station with shockingly good steam-table food, and in the sleek bistro of a brash, upstart culinary-school grad fusing Grandma's recipes with unpronounceable techniques and ingredients. And that's not even counting the many bars and nightclubs serving stellar snacks. Or the much-anticipated restaurants that are *about* to open as we're turning in this book, including **Chemin a la Mer** in the new Four Seasons Hotel (p. 78) and Mexican prix-fixe **Lengua Madre** (1245 Constance St.; www.lenguamadrenola.com; ℂ **504/655-1338**). Culinary training grounds like **Café Reconcile** (1631 Oretha Castle Haley Blvd.; www.cafereconcile.org; ℂ **504/568-1157**) and **Liberty's Kitchen** (300 N. Broad and 1615 Poydras Sts.; www.libertys kitchen.org; ℂ **504/822-4011**) serve sturdy meals while preparing young people for careers in food service (as well, **New Orleans Culinary and Hospitality Institute** now offers certificate programs in culinary arts and baking and pastry arts class in 2022;

go to www.nochi.org for details). Meanwhile, fourth-generation chefs work backstreet dives whose menus and ingredients haven't varied since, well, forever.

You are going to want to eat a lot here. And you are going to want to eat here a lot. And then you are going to talk about it. You'll probably adopt the local custom of talking about dinner while you're at lunch (and lunch while you're breakfasting). The food here is utterly, unashamedly regional, which isn't to say that (in some cases) it's not also utterly of the moment, sophisticated, and/or redolent of other influences as well. But it's ingredient- and chef-driven, which makes it uniquely New Orleanian: Michelin-style frippery is irrelevant here, and it will never be Tokyo, Oslo, Paris, or New York, nor does it want (or need) to be.

In many restaurants—certainly in the more traditional ones—dishes are based largely on variations of Creole recipes. Others, the innovators, take Creole as a cue and go wildly afield. Creole food was originally based on recipes brought by the French settlers, the herbs and filé (ground sassafras leaves) used by the Native Americans, and saffron and peppers introduced by the Spanish. From the West Indies came new vegetables, spices, and sugar cane, and when slave boats arrived, an African influence was added. Today, the Italian influence runs deep, and even Vietnamese has found its way onto the plate, the gift of a newer wave of immigrants. While nearly all restaurateurs source fresh ingredients from local purveyors, butter phobia has never taken hold here (thankfully). Flavor comes first. If you absolutely can't abandon those healthy habits while here, it's actually not hard to find healthy foods, including vegetarian and vegan options. Consult the NOLA Eat Fit site (www.eatfit nola.com) for suggestions.

So indulge and enjoy. It's what you do here. Try some of everything. We're particularly big on lunching, since many of the best restaurants have terrific prix-fixe lunch deals that include dishes that'd cost twice as much during dinner. Then start planning the next trip, so you can do it again.

Please keep in mind that all prices, hours, and menu items in the following listings are subject to change according to season, availability, or whim. Vaccination and mask requirements may still be in effect and seating may be limited as many of the spots listed are still clawing back from Covid-induced slowdowns or shutdowns. Staffing remains a challenge, so add an extra dollop of patience. Call in advance to ensure the accuracy of anything of import to you.

Make sure to check out our **"Best of"** recommendations in chapter 1.

Of Beignets, Boudin & Dirty Rice

Many of the foods in New Orleans are unique to the region and consequently may be unfamiliar. This list should help you navigate local menus:

> **andouille** (ahn-doo-*we*) A spicy Cajun sausage made with pork.
> **bananas Foster** Bananas sautéed in liqueur, brown sugar, cinnamon, and butter, drenched in rum, set ablaze, served over vanilla ice cream.

barbequed shrimp   Not actually grilled or BBQ-sauced, but a butter-soaked, garlicky, pepper-shot peel-and-eat Gulf specialty.

beignet (bin-*yay*)   A big, puffy, deep-fried, hole-free doughnut, liberally sprinkled with powdered sugar—the more sugar, the better.

boudin (boo-*dan*)   Cajun liver-and-rice sausage of varying spice levels.

café brûlot (cah-*fay* brew-*low*)   Coffee, spices, and liqueurs, served flaming.

crawfish   A tiny, lobster-like creature common locally and eaten in every conceivable way, including boiled whole with spices and peeled by hand.

debris   The rich, juicy bits of meat that fall off during roasting and carving.

dressed   A "dressed" po' boy comes with lettuce, tomato, mayonnaise, and sometimes pickles.

étouffée (ay-too-*fay*)   A Cajun stew (usually containing crawfish or shrimp) served with rice.

filé (*fee*-lay)   Ground sassafras leaves, frequently used to thicken gumbo.

gumbo   A thick, spicy soup of poultry, seafood, and/or sausage, with okra in a roux base, served with rice. Gumbo z'herbes, a Good Friday tradition, eschews meat for greens.

holy trinity   Onions, bell peppers, and celery: the base of much Creole and Cajun cooking.

Hurricane   A local drink of rum and passion-fruit punch.

jambalaya (jum-ba-*lie*-ya)   A simmer of yellow rice, sausage, seafood, poultry, vegetables, and spices.

lagniappe (lan-*yap*)   A little something extra: a bonus freebie.

mirliton (*mur*-li-tone)   A pear-shaped squash, also called chayote.

muffuletta (moo-foo-*let*-ta or moo-fuh-*lot*-ta)   A mountainous sandwich made with Italian deli meats, cheese, and olive salad, piled onto a specially made seeded round bread (see the box on p. 111).

oysters Rockefeller   Oysters on the half shell in a creamy spinach sauce, so called because Rockefeller was the only name rich enough to match the taste.

po' boy, po-boy, poor boy   A sandwich on long French bread, similar to submarines and hoagies (see the box on p. 112).

pralines (*praw*-leens)   A sweet confection of brown sugar and pecans.

rémoulade   A spicy sauce, usually over shrimp, made of mayonnaise, boiled egg yolks, horseradish, Creole mustard, and lemon juice.

roux   A mixture of flour and fat that's slowly cooked over low heat, used to thicken stews, soups, and sauces.

Sazerac   The official cocktail of New Orleans, consisting of rye whiskey (or sometimes cognac), sugar, and bitters.

shrimp Creole   Shrimp in a tomato sauce seasoned with what's known around town as the "holy trinity:" onions, bell peppers, and celery.

RESTAURANTS BY CUISINE

BAKERY (ALSO SEE DESSERTS)

Angelo Brocato's ★★★ ($, p. 146)
Bakery Bar ★★ ($, p. 225)
Bywater Bakery ★★★ ($, p. 116)
Café Beignet ★ ($, p. 110)
Croissant D'Or ★★ ($, p. 148)
District Donuts. Sliders. Brew. ★★ ($, p. 143)
Gracious Bakery ★★ ($, p. 149)
La Boulangerie ★★ ($, p. 149)
Willa Jean ★★★ ($$, p. 130)

BARBEQUE

Blue Oak ★★★ ($$, p. 115)
The Joint ★★★ ($$, p. 115)
Piece of Meat ★★★ ($$, p. 120)

BARS & CLUBS WITH NOTABLE FOOD

Avenue Pub ★★ ($$, p. 225)
Bacchanal ★★★ ($$, p. 113)
Bakery Bar ★★ ($$, p. 225)
Bar Marilou ★★★ ($$, p. 226)
Bombay Club ★ ($$, p. 222)
Cane & Table ★★★ ($, p. 222)
Cure ★★★ ($$, p. 226)
Effervescence ★★ ($$, p. 223)
Erin Rose/Killer Po' Boys ★★★ ($, p. 223)
Hi-Ho ★★ ($, p. 219)
Jewel of the South ★★★ ($$$, p. 223)
Latitude 29 ★★★ ($$, p. 108)
Manolito ★★★ ($$, p. 224)
Napoleon House ★★ ($, p. 225)
Revel ★★ ($$, p. 120)
Snug Harbor ★★★ ($$, p. 216)
Starlight Lounge ★★ ($, p. 213)
Three Muses ★★ ($$, p. 218)

BISTRO

Café Degas ★★★ ($$, p. 118)
Coquette ★★★ ($$$, p. 136)
Delachaise ★★ ($$, p. 139)
Herbsaint ★★★ ($$$, p. 125)
Justine ★★ ($$$, p. 104)

La Petite Grocery ★★★ ($$$, p. 137)
Lilette ★★★ ($$$, p. 137)
Patois ★★★ ($$$, p. 138)
Sylvain ★★★ ($$, p. 109)
Zasu ★★★ ($$$, p. 118)

CAFES/COFFEEHOUSES

Backatown Coffee ★★ ($, p. 147)
Café Beignet ★ ($, p. 110)
Café du Monde ★★★ ($, p. 146)
Café Maspero ★ ($, p. 110)
Coffee Science ★★★ ($, p. 147)
Croissant D'Or ★★ ($, p. 148)
District Donuts & Coffee Bar ★★ ($, p. 144)
District Donuts. Sliders. Brew. ★★ ($, p. 143)
French Truck ★★ ($, p. 147)
Mammoth Espresso ★★ ($, p. 147)
Old Road Coffee ★★★ ($, p. 147)
Orange Couch ★★★ ($, p. 147)
P.J.'s Coffee & Tea Company ★★ ($, p. 149)
Spitfire ★★ ($, p. 147)

CAJUN/CONTEMPORARY CAJUN

Bearcat ★★★ ($, p. 130)
Brigtsen's ★★★ ($$$, p. 134)
Cochon ★★ ($$, p. 128)
Cochon Butcher ★★★ ($, p. 132)
Gabrielle ★★★ ($$$, p. 117)
Mosquito Supper Club ★★★ ($$$, p. 137)
Toups' Meatery ★★ ($$, p. 120)

CASUAL FARE

Acme Oyster House ★★★ ($, p. 110)
Auction House Market ★★ ($, p. 130)
Bearcat ★★★ ($, p. 130)
Bevi Seafood ★★★ ($, p. 121)
Bourree ★★ ($, p. 139)
Café Amelie ★★ ($$, p. 107)
Café Maspero ★ ($, p. 110)
Camellia Grill ★★ ($, p. 142)
Central Grocery ★★★ ($, p. 111)
Cochon Butcher ★★★ ($, p. 132)
Coop's ★ ($, p. 111)

KEY TO ABBREVIATIONS:
$$$** = Expensive   **$$** = Moderate   **$ = Inexpensive

Dat Dog ★ ($, p. 143)
District Donuts. Sliders. Brew. ★★ ($, p. 143)
Domilise's ★★ ($, p. 144)
Frady's ★ ($, p. 107)
Good Bird ★ ($, p. 142)
Johnny's Po-Boys ★ ($, p. 112)
Junction ★★ ($, p. 116)
Killer PoBoys ★★★ ($, p. 223)
Liuzza's by the Track ★★★ ($, p. 122)
McHardy's ★★★ ($, p. 117)
Melba's ★★ ($, p. 121)
Molly's Rise & Shine ★★ ($, p. 146)
Mother's ★ ($$, p. 132)
Parkway Bakery and Tavern ★★★ ($, p. 122)
Piece of Meat ★★★ ($$, p. 120)
QuarterMaster ★ ($, p. 107)
R&O's ★★ ($$, p. 144)
St. Roch Market ★★★ ($, p. 116)
Stanley ★★ ($, p. 112)
Surrey's ★★★ ($, p. 145)
Turkey & the Wolf ★★★ ($, p. 146)
Verti Marte ★★ ($, p. 107)
Wakin' Bakin' ★★ ($, p. 113)
Willa Jean ★★★ ($$, p. 130)

CREOLE/CONTEMPORARY CREOLE/CONTEMPORARY MODERN LOUISIANA

Annunciation ★★ ($$$, p. 124)
Antoine's ★★ ($$$, p. 97)
Arnaud's ★★★ ($$$, p. 97)
Brennan's ★★★ ($$$, p. 100)
Brigtsen's ★★★ ($$$, p. 134)
Café Sbisa ★★★ ($$, p. 108)
Clancy's ★★★ ($$$, p. 134)
Commander's Palace ★★★ ($$$, p. 135)
Coop's ★ ($, p. 111)
Country Club ★★ ($$, p. 114)
Court of Two Sisters ★ ($$$, p. 100)
Dooky Chase ★★ ($$, p. 118)
French Toast ★★★ ($, p. 112)
Elizabeth's ★ ($$, p. 115)
Elysian Bar ★★ ($$, p. 115)
Emeril's ★★★ ($$$, p. 125)
Felix's Restaurant & Oyster Bar ★★ ($, p. 111)
Gabrielle ★★★ ($$$, p. 117)
Jacques-Imo's ★★ ($$, p. 140)

Joey K's ★ ($, p. 145)
Killer PoBoys ★★★ ($, p. 223)
Lil' Dizzy's ★★ ($, p. 122)
Liuzza's by the Track ★★★ ($, p. 122)
Mandina's ★★ ($$, p. 119)
Meril ★★ ($$, p. 130)
Mr. B's Bistro ★★ ($$$, p. 104)
Mother's ★ ($$, p. 132)
Muriel's ★ ($$, p. 104)
Napoleon House ★★ ($, p. 225)
Palace Café ★★ ($$$, p. 105)
Patois ★★★ ($$$, p. 138)
Ralph's on the Park ★★★ ($$$, p. 117)
Restaurant August ★★★ ($$$, p. 127)
Restaurant R'evolution ★★★ ($$$, p. 105)
Stanley ★★ ($$, p. 112)
St. John ★★★ ($$$, p. 106)
Tableau ★★ ($$$, p. 106)
Tujague's ★ ($$$, p. 107)

DESSERT/ICE CREAM/ SNOBALL

Angelo Brocato Ice Cream & Confectionery ★★★ ($, p. 146)
Café du Monde ★★★ ($, p. 146)
Creole Creamery ★★★ ($, p. 147)
Hansen's Sno-Bliz ★★★ ($, p. 148)
Imperial Woodpecker ★★ ($, p. 148)
Pandora's SnoBalls ★★★ ($, p. 148)
Plum St. Snoballs ★★★ ($, p. 148)

DINER

Camellia Grill ★★ ($, p. 142)
Clover Grill ★ ($, p. 110)
Joey K's ★ ($, p. 145)
Port of Call ★★ ($$, p. 109)

FRENCH/CONTEMPORARY FRENCH/CLASSIC CREOLE

Antoine's ★★ ($$$, p. 97)
Arnaud's ★★★ ($$$, p. 97)
Café Degas ★★★ ($$, p. 118)
Delachaise ★★ ($$, p. 139)
Galatoire's ★★ ($$$, p. 103)
Lilette ★★★ ($$$, p. 137)
N7 ★★★ ($$, p. 116)
Restaurant August ★★★ ($$$, p. 127)
Saint-Germain ★★★ ($$$, p. 113)
Tableau ★★ ($$$, p. 106)
Tujague's ★ ($$$, p. 107)

THE FRENCH QUARTER

Expensive

Antoine's ★★ CLASSIC CREOLE We're sentimental about Antoine's, it being one of the first fine-dining restaurants in the New World. It's been owned and operated by the same family (serving generations of patrons' families) for more than 180 amazing years. It's as classic as New Orleans dining gets. Truth be told, the food and presentation can be uneven, but the experience is still well worth it. The best strategy: Go for conviviality, classics, and drama. Request Johnny or Sterling as your server. Befriend neighboring guests. Order the spinach-soaked baked oysters Rockefeller (invented here); buttery, crab-topped trout Pontchartrain; and a side or two of the hallowed soufflé potato puffs. Finish with a *café brûlot* and the frivolous, fabulous football-size baked Alaska. Get the daily featured 25¢ cocktails. Touring some of the 15 memorabilia-packed collections and rooms (can you find Groucho's beret?) and peeking at the astounding wine alley are part of the experience. The seasonal three-course weekday lunch at $20.20 (it goes up one cent a year) is worth every penny. Make dinner reservations well in advance during peak periods.

713 St. Louis St. www.antoines.com. ℭ **504/581-4422.** Entrees $27–$48. Mon–Sat 11:30am–2pm and 5:30–9pm; Sun 11am–2pm. No shorts, sandals, or T-shirts; collared shirts for gentlemen (jackets welcome, not required).

Arnaud's ★★★ CLASSIC CREOLE Arnaud's isn't the best-known of the old New Orleans restaurants, but it tops them in quality, and far exceeds them in the cocktail arena. Arnaud's, which celebrated its centennial in 2018, is classically atmospheric, with white tile floors and dark wood accents, and the recipes are classics as well. Have the signature shrimp Arnaud appetizer (topped with a spicy rémoulade sauce) and the spicy pompano Duarte or the definitive *filet au poivre*. We also love the quail Elzey—petite, elegant fowl stuffed with foie gras mousse, wrapped with bacon, and ensconced in a truffle-wine sauce—and no one should leave without ordering some puffy soufflé potatoes and *café brûlot,* flamed tableside (see the "Anythin' Flamin'" box, p. 102). Our resident crème brûlée expert rates theirs very high. Allow time to visit the impressive Mardi Gras museum upstairs (Count Arnaud's daughter's collection—free to diners and others during restaurant hours). A pre- or post-meal stop in the classic **French 75** (p. 223) bar is required, and a more casual **jazz bistro room** features nighttime entertainment (a $4 cover goes to the band)—all of which makes Arnaud's a good fine-dining introduction for well-behaved children. Reserve in advance during peak periods.

813 Bienville St. www.arnauds restaurant.com. ℭ **866/230-8895** or 504/523-5433. Entrees $27–$42. Daily 6–10pm; Sun jazz brunch 10am–2:30pm. Reservations suggested. Business casual.

Impressions

The Louisiana diet will kill a man as surely as the sword.

—*King of the Hill*

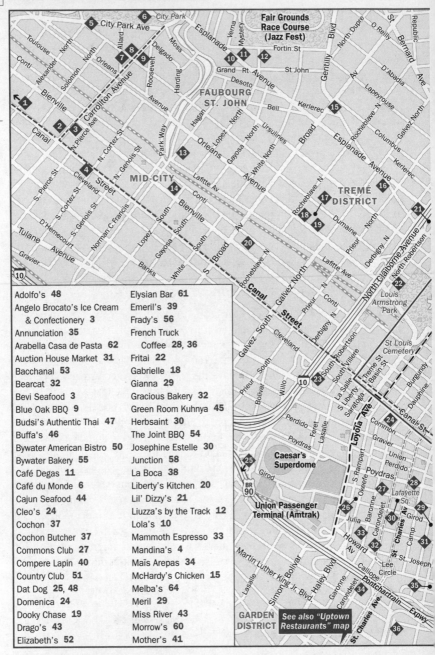

Adolfo's **48**

Angelo Brocato's Ice Cream
& Confectionery **3**

Annunciation **35**

Arabella Casa de Pasta **62**

Auction House Market **31**

Bacchanal **53**

Bearcat **32**

Bevi Seafood **3**

Blue Oak BBQ **9**

Budsi's Authentic Thai **47**

Buffa's **46**

Bywater American Bistro **50**

Bywater Bakery **55**

Café Degas **11**

Café du Monde **6**

Cajun Seafood **44**

Cleo's **24**

Cochon **37**

Cochon Butcher **37**

Commons Club **27**

Compere Lapin **40**

Country Club **51**

Dat Dog **25, 48**

Domenica **24**

Dooky Chase **19**

Drago's **43**

Elizabeth's **52**

Elysian Bar **61**

Emeril's **39**

Frady's **56**

French Truck
Coffee **28, 36**

Fritai **22**

Gabrielle **18**

Gianna **29**

Gracious Bakery **32**

Green Room Kuhnya **45**

Herbsaint **30**

The Joint BBQ **54**

Josephine Estelle **30**

Junction **58**

La Boca **38**

Liberty's Kitchen **20**

Lil' Dizzy's **21**

Liuzza's by the Track **12**

Lola's **10**

Mammoth Espresso **33**

Mandina's **4**

Maïs Arepas **34**

McHardy's Chicken **15**

Melba's **64**

Meril **29**

Miss River **43**

Morrow's **60**

Mother's **41**

See also "Uptown Restaurants" map

98

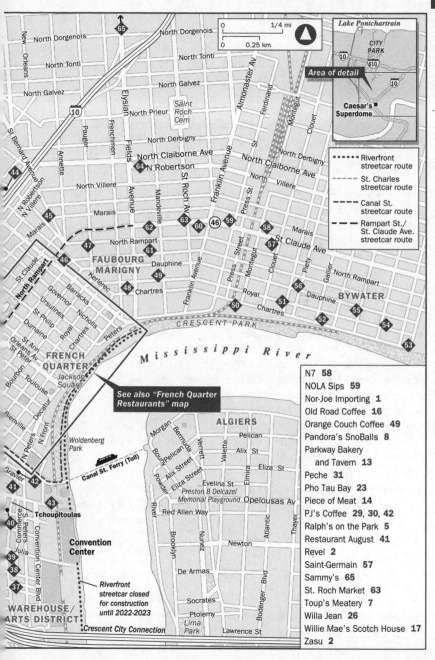

Bayona ★★ CONTEMPORARY SOUTHERN/INTERNATIONAL After celebrating 25+ years, we'll forgive chef/owner Susan Spicer if her modern classic restaurant has slipped a notch. The food, cocktails, and wine list are still thoughtful and inspired. The ambience inside and out is positively lovely, although service can be annoyingly spotty. Begin with the signature cream of garlic soup; and select among extremes of sweetbreads with lemon caper butter, any rabbit preparation, or whatever vegetarian dish is on—ever-changing preparations of the latter are consistently superb. At lunch, the famed smoked duck with cashew butter and pepper jelly is a flavor bomb. Desserts center on seasonal fruits, like the divine mango cheesecake flan with pistachio crust and blackberries. Reservations required for dinner; book early.

430 Dauphine St. www.bayona.com. ✆ **504/525-4455.** Entrees $15–$17 lunch, $28–$34 dinner. Wed–Sat 11:30am–1:45pm; Mon–Thurs 6–9:30pm; Fri–Sat 5:30–9:45pm.

Brennan's ★★★ MODERN CREOLE After a fall to lesser heights, brief closure, ownership change, and $20-million-plus renovation, Brennan's is back in all its pink glory and then some. The look and feel of the elegant dining room and charming courtyard and the attentive service all scream old New Orleans, but there's nothing tired on the plate: Twists on Creole classics turn updated plates into newfound awesome. Breakfast at Brennan's is an automatic celebration. First course: cocktails, as in a rum-spiked milk punch or a Ramos Fizz. They do well with breakfast meats, and the famed egg preparations are pretty perfect, so we choose the house-smoked duck ham or crispy veal cheek grillades. You need a side of the BBQ lobster, slow-roasted in the shell with mild Creole spice. At dinner, the crispy Sazerac-lacquered roast duck is phenomenal; beef Stanley with mushrooms, caramelized banana, and a truffle-infused sauce stands out. The signature turtle soup is well sherried, and we're promised that the turtles living in the fountain won't ever . . . well, you know (kids love 'em, and Brennan's loves good kids; they offer summer manners classes). Bananas Foster, born here in 1951 and prepared tableside, makes for a flaming fun finale. Come back Friday for the 5pm champagne sabering ceremony. *Deal alert:* A two-course breakfast/lunch menu costs $29–$31.

417 Royal St. www.brennansneworleans.com. ✆ **504/525-9711.** Entrees $15–$40 breakfast/lunch, $24–$45 dinner. Mon–Fri 9am–2pm; Sat–Sun 8am–2pm; dinner nightly 6–10pm. Smart casual dress.

Court of Two Sisters ★ CLASSIC CREOLE · No doubt about it, this is one of the prettiest places around, thanks to its huge wisteria-shaded courtyard in a 200-year-old building, and you should soak up that ambience by enjoying a smart cocktail or two. Then you should head elsewhere to

Impressions

In America, there might be better gastronomic destinations than New Orleans, but there is no place more uniquely wonderful. . . . It's a must-see city because there's no explaining it, no describing it. You can't compare it to anything.

—*Anthony Bourdain*

Acme Oyster House **10**
Antoine's **22**
Arnaud's **7**
Backatown Coffee **1**
Bayona **9**
Brennan's **21**
Café Amelie **38**
Café Beignet **8, 18**
Café du Monde **33**
Café Maspero **27**
Café Sbisa **44**
Central Grocery **43**
Clover Grill **37**
Coop's **46**
Court of Two Sisters **25**
Croissant D'Or **42**
Dian Xin **47**

Dickie Brennan's Bourbon
   House Seafood **15**
Doris Metropolitan **29**
Effervescence **36**
Erin Rose/Killer Po'Boys **13**
Felix's Restaurant
   & Oyster Bar **11**
French Toast **45**
French Truck Coffee **17**
Galatoire's **4**
Galatoire's 33 **5**
GW Fins **6**
Irene's **19**
Italian Barrel **47**
Jewel of the South **3**
Johnny's Po-Boys **24**
Latitude 29 **20**

Mr. B's Bistro **14**
Muriel's **31**
Napoleon House **23**
Palace Café **16**
Palm & Pine **2**
PJ's Coffee **24**
Port of Call **40**
QuarterMaster **39**
Restaurant R'evolution **12**
Spitfire **26**
St. John **46**
Stanley **32**
Sylvain **28**
Tableau **30**
Tujague's **34**
Verti Marte **41**
Wakin' Bakin' **35**

Once upon a time, while waiting for **Casamento's** (p. 143) to open and just moments from an oyster loaf, three youngish tourist gals struck up a chat (as happens nearly automatically in New Orleans) with three Uptown ladies-of-a-certain-age ahead of them. They were St. Charles–born and –bred, dined at Casamento's weekly, and offered us NOLA newbies some well-tested tips. The one that still sticks sounds best when read with a high-pitched, breathy lilt: "You simply *must* go to any of the fine old French restaurants, and when you do, why, you just order anythin' flamin'." Meaning, go to **Antoine's** (p. 97), **Arnaud's** (p. 97), **Commander's Palace** (p. 135), or **Galatoire's** (p. 103), and get bananas Foster, baked Alaska, *café brûlot*, or anything prepared tableside and involving conflagration. Naturally, we bought the ladies a round, and to this day we're still living by the "anythin' flamin'" creed: Indulge a bit, relish the fun, and while one needn't embrace drama in all aspects of life, when it comes to dessert, *bring it on.*

eat. Sadly, the food is nothing special. The daily jazz brunch buffet is nonetheless popular, and we do get the attraction: There are plenty of items available, it's kid-friendly and fairly priced, and you get all that jazz and atmosphere; so fill up and enjoy the company. Make brunch reservations in advance.

613 Royal St. www.courtoftwosisters.com. ✆ **504/522-7261.** Dinner entrees $25–$37; brunch buffet $32 adults, $14 children 5–14. Daily 9am–3pm and 5:30–10pm.

Dickie Brennan's Bourbon House Seafood ★★ SEAFOOD

Although it looks a bit sprawling and formulaic from the street, this modern version of a classic New Orleans fish house has much to recommend it. Hang out at the super-fresh raw bar or order the head-turning *fruits du mer* platter. A simple grilled redfish is perfect (top it with fresh lump crabmeat for $15 more, a worthy addition). In a city of good BBQ shrimp dishes (shrimp sautéed in a buttery, garlicky, spicy sauce—bread-sopping heaven), we love their bourbon-finished version. Leave room for a frozen bourbon milk punch, a dreamy booze-shake. (Naturally they're committed to, and knowledgeable about, all things bourbon.) Great happy hour with $1 oysters, $3 Abita Amber, plus a good shucker show. Parking is guaranteed to be available and can be purchased in advance online.

144 Bourbon St. www.bourbonhouse.com. ✆ **504/522-0111.** Entrees $14–$36 lunch, $18–$49 dinner. Sun-Thurs11am–9pm, Fri-Sat 11am–10pm.

Doris Metropolitan ★★ STEAK

Upscale Doris audaciously displays its dry aging beef in the front window like an Amsterdam madam. Besides the distinctive, slightly pungent flavor of dry-aged steaks (sourced from raised-to-specification cattle), the Israeli-based restaurant brings some Middle Eastern touches to its menu, like a delectable charred eggplant appetizer with glossy tahini. Servers are warm and knowledgeable. The room's presentation is indisputably handsome. Locals have embraced the hopping bar with its beguiling wines and open-kitchen view, and a luxe, chill vibe permeates the moneyed air in the comfortable dining rooms. A juicy pan-glazed chicken knocked us over, and the silken tuna tartare is superb, but ultimately it's about the beef. After a couple of initial missteps, in due time we found the carnivorous knowledge we sought in the Butcher's Cut, its crunch of char displaying a perfectly marbled, ultra-flavorful, and densely sensuous mouthful.

620 Chartres St. www.dorismetropolitan.com. ✆ **504/267-3500.** Entrees $32–$86 (Wagyu more). Daily 5:30–10:30pm; Fri noon–2:30pm.

Galatoire's ★★ CLASSIC CREOLE/FRENCH Considered New Orleans' consummate old-line Creole French restaurant, Galatoire's is a time-honored, fine-dining classic beloved by generations—perhaps because their families are beloved by Galatoire's. Or perhaps because Tennessee Williams supped here, as did his characters Stella and Blanche in *A Streetcar Named Desire*. It oozes tradition: Ceiling fans whir, bentwood chairs strain, mirrored walls reflect the civilized frivolity. Things are a tad more somber in the (lesser—but perfectly fine) upstairs dining room. Either way, the drinking commences upon arrival, and doesn't (and shouldn't) let up for a few hours.

No one comes here for great gastronomy, but Galatoire's does know fish (it's had 115 years of practice, after all). Go with a classic shrimp rémoulade, crab maison, or the eggplant fingers. Ask the waiter which fish is best today, get it a la meunière and topped with crabmeat; or order the softshell crab if available and some creamed spinach. We're not fond of the heavy sauces they ladle on the fine fish, but don't scoff at asparagus with spot-on hollandaise. The puffy soufflé potatoes are legally required. Skip the meh desserts; order a glass of port instead. Reservations accepted for upstairs only; reserve well in advance. Worth mentioning: Galatoire's regulars have known for years that these seafood specialists grill a mean steak. That's the specialty at the offshoot next door, **Galatoire's 33** (215 Bourbon St.; ✆ **504/335-3932**), which also corners the Galatoire's bar scene.

209 Bourbon St. www.galatoires.com. ✆ **504/525-2021.** Entrees $21–$42. Tues–Sat 11:30am–10pm; Sun noon–10pm. Get in line 45–60 min. before opening. Jackets required after 5pm and all day Sun.

GW Fins ★★★ SEAFOOD This modern seafood shrine is one of the city's best restaurants, period (and leaders in seafood sustainability education and practices). It is polished from the top down, in service and seafood sourcing, with a shipment of fresh fish arriving straight from the Gulf and beyond at 4pm daily. Stylish preparations include the signature "scalibut" (thin-sliced scallop "scales" atop grilled halibut) on lobster risotto, worthy of its fame. A diverting starter of watermelon and pork belly, or lobster dumplings with a light brush of fennel, are both to be savored. The wine list is thoughtfully complementary, with a good range of mid-priced bottles and an extensive array of finer pours by the glass. Order the pretzel-crusted salty-malty ice cream pie, even if you only have room for a bite. The large, tiered dining room is handsome and high-ceilinged yet conversation conducive. We particularly love those high-backed gangsta booths along the back wall.

808 Bienville St. www.gwfins.com. ☏ **504/581-3467.** Entrees $21–$46. Sun–Thurs 5–10pm; Fri–Sat 5–10:30pm (summer from 5:30pm). Collared shirts for men; no shorts or flip-flops.

Italian Barrel ★★ ITALIAN   If longevity and popularity are solid measures, Italian Barrel shares the banner with Irene's (p. 108) for best Italian food in the French Quarter, covering the downtown end. Northern Italian is the focus, and the menu is full of familiar favorites. We're partial to the veal dishes and scampi, but pastas are generally winners (ask for sauce on the side if you like yours lightly sauced). Its popularity with locals and tourists alike also stems from the excellent wine selection and "friendly white tablecloth" ambiance; sidewalk tables offer a different take on romantic, even if the view faces the scruffier end of the Quarter.

1240 Decatur St. www.theitalianbarrel.com. ☏ **504/569-0198.** Entrees $32–$68. Sun–Thurs 11am–10pm; Fri–Sat 11am–10:30pm.

Justine ★★ BISTRO   This is dining as event and for events, a neo-nod to the Moulin Rouge reset in the French Quarter, just short of raucous and a definite fête for the eyes. This iteration comes with a D.J. and strolling burlesque dancers (the disrobing is tastefully done), where French antiques flirt with color-saturated modern decor (*j'adore* the multimedia murals, which mix historic and current local imagery). The straightforward French bistro cuisine isn't as exuberant, nor is it on par (yet) with proprietors/chef Justin and Mia Devillier's flagship **La Petite Grocery** (p. 137). Still, it's no second thought (and priced accordingly), and a worthy accompaniment to the overall fabulousness that a night here can be. Splurge on a showy seafood platter (plateau des fruits de mer) or play it safe with onion soup, a salad maison, and steak frites. Finish with the Pavlova ('cause passion fruit) and creamy gâteau Basque. The bar is a fun hang and serves food late.

225 Chartres St. www.justinenola.com. ☏ **504/218-8533.** Entrees $15–$42. Mon 5:30–11pm; Tues–Thurs & Sun 11am–11pm; Fri–Sat 11am–1am.

Mr. B's Bistro ★★ CONTEMPORARY CREOLE   The "B is for Butter." BBQ shrimp is the claim to fame here, and that's what you should get. Other dishes tempt as well (the gleaming ginger-glazed pork chop is terrific, for example), but the plump, peppery house special is the standout and indeed the distinguishing feature here. The hunt-club motif draws a businessman's lunch crowd for the strong drinks and attentive service, and the roving-band jazz brunch is a hit with all ages.

201 Royal St. www.mrbsbistro.com. ☏ **504/523-2078.** Entrees $18–$24 lunch, $29–$37 dinner; jazz brunch entrees $22–$34. Mon–Sat 11:30am–2pm; bar menu 2–5:30pm; dinner 5:30–9pm; Sun jazz brunch 10:30am–2pm. Business casual; no shorts or tank tops.

Muriel's ★ CONTEMPORARY CREOLE   The dreaded "fine." That's how we feel about perennially popular Muriel's. We want to fall in love with

YOU GOT cajun IN MY CREOLE!

The murky difference between Cajun and Creole cuisine lies chiefly in distance between city and countryside. Cajun cooking came from the Acadians who settled in the swamps and bayous of rural Louisiana and adapted the recipes of their French heritage to their new location. Their cuisine is like their music: robust and full of flavor (and despite the reputation, not necessarily spicy). They used available ingredients like sausage, seafood, poultry, and rice in single-pot stews that fed large families and farms. Creole dishes, on the other hand, were developed by French and Spanish city dwellers and feature fancier sauces and ingredients. Today, the two cuisines have a happy marriage, often blurring the distinctions and inviting other influences. Our advice? Disregard the classifications, try it all, and decide what *you* prefer.

its romantic, red-walled dining rooms, and pose on the elegant balconies overlooking Jackson Square. We want to *ooh* over the crawfish and goat-cheese crêpes, like others seem to do. But except for the admittedly fab atmosphere, there's just nothing especially inspired or inspiring here, on the plate or working the floor. That said, there's no denying that the table d'hôte menus are good value. So we opt for the safety of the pan-roasted half-chicken or the generous double-cut pork chop. Visit the ghost's table, have your palm read in Jackson Square, and the night is still, well, fine. Muriel's is popular with groups, so reserve in advance during peak periods.

801 Chartres St. (at St. Ann). www.muriels.com. ✆ **504/568-1885.** Entrees $15–$25 lunch/brunch, $21–$39 dinner. Mon–Fri 11:30am–2:30pm and 5:30–10pm; Sat 5–10pm; Sat–Sun brunch 10:30am–2pm (jazz Sun only).

Palace Café ★★ CONTEMPORARY CREOLE A good standby for low-key, non-intimidating Creole dining, this historic two-story restaurant (formerly the famed Werlein's music store) has sidewalk seating for people-watching and a craft rum bar upstairs. It comes with the stamp of New Orleans authenticity that Brennan-family ownership conveys, and the crab-meat cheesecake appetizer makes people pound the table. Andouille-crusted fish is a winner, and the pleasantly familiar rotisserie chicken with truffle-mashed potatoes is done well. White-chocolate bread pudding was invented here, so opt for that (we like coming just for dessert at the streetside tables). Good happy hour deals and small nosh plates. You gotta love the summertime "Temperature Lunch": two courses priced (in cents) at 10 times the prior day's high temperature.

605 Canal St. www.palacecafe.com. ✆ **504/523-1661.** Entrees $15–$34 lunch/brunch, $18–$44 dinner. Mon–Fri 8–10pm; Sat-Sun 10:30am-2:30pm and 5:30–until closing. No tank tops; business casual at dinner.

Restaurant R'evolution ★★★ MODERN LOUISIANA This extravagant spot, helmed by food-world icons John Folse and Rick Tramonto, keys the cuisine to New Orleans' globe-hopping cultural influences. Go big at this big-idea, big-ticket spot in a fanciful but refined setting, with unpretentious service and beautiful plating. Tour the rooms (better yet, book one, like the stunning Storyville Parlor, or come for the festive jazz brunch). Indulge in something marvelous from the wine list, so enormous that only an iPad can contain it; select from the caviar, salumi, cheese, and potted meat sub-menus; and augment your order with sides, sauces, and toppings. Lead with the rich "Death by Gumbo" and gently crisped crab beignets, each with a different rémoulade dollop. Ricotta lobster gnocchi dotted with tarragon is a delight. Gulf shrimp get an Iberian kick with saffron, basil, and chorizo; unctuous braised short ribs are sweet, meaty heaven. A jewelry box of tiny cookies is a darling lagniappe, but get "beignets with coffee" anyway. Service can be a bit casual for a restaurant of this caliber and cost, but it doesn't lag, and we'll take that over snooty. Do relish the luxe bar before or after dining.

777 Bienville St. (in the Royal Sonesta Hotel). www.revolutionnola.com. © **504/553-2277.** Entrees $26–$35 brunch, $29–$65 dinner. Daily 5:30–10pm; Sun 10:30am–2pm. Reserve well in advance for dinner.

St. John ★★★ MODERN CREOLE   We have to admit to being starry-eyed fangirls of Chef Eric Cook, having followed his career for more years than we want to admit. But we knew it was only a matter of time before he helmed two of the best restaurants in the city, **Gris Gris** (p. 139) and now the sleek and energetic St. John, opened in late 2021. "Everyday basic" Creole standards are anything but. Dishes like shrimp etouffee and French-style beef daube (wine-braised short ribs) benefit from the kitchen's skill and modern oomph in technique, composition, and presentation. (Our favorite spot is the raised booths with open-kitchen views; counter seating brings you even closer to the action.) You can't go wrong with anything, but we'll cite the oysters, stuffed crab, whole fish almondine, and aforementioned daube as personal faves. Cocktails rock and the wine selection is fine, if limited; lunch and brunch are great deals for the quality.

1117 Decatur St. www.stjohnnola.com. © **504/581-8120.** Entrees $16–$19 lunch/brunch $17–$38 dinner. Weds-Thurs & Sun 11am–9pm; Fri-Sat 11am–10pm.

Tableau ★★ CLASSIC CREOLE   Tableau's pristine white space, soaring staircase, and high-arched entries are impressive . . . but that balcony view overlooking Jackson Square is peerless. Relish an afternoon there with a well-balanced classic cocktail, slices of the addictive tart bread, and a "Grand Royal" quartet of seafood starters—including sublime garlicky oysters. In cooler weather, opt for a hearty red and the heartier, hopped-up onion soup. The airy main dining room looks onto the gleaming open kitchen and brick courtyard. Things we like there: the broad selection at the oyster bar; brunch every day; the juicy dark and white portions of chicken Tableau in a rich béarnaise sauce; the logo-branded crème brûlée, served in a shallow, wide bowl (as at other Brennan's restaurants) to maximize the crispy-crust-to-silken-custard ratio; summer "Temperature" deals (see Palace Café, p. 105). Service occasionally hits overwhelm, but the overall

BACK-ROOM bites

Long before there were pop-up restaurants, there were back-room deli counters in unassuming corner stores. It's how a lot of French Quarter residents still eat, because it's fast, cheap, diverse, available 'round-the-clock, and often surprisingly good. Take it out or have it delivered, and be sure to ask for utensils. True locals eat while leaning against a wall or seated on someone's front stoop.

o **Frady's** ★ (in the Bywater at 3231 Dauphine St.; *C* **504/949-9688;** Mon–Fri 9am–6pm, Sat 9am–3pm). Best choice: hot sausage or oyster po' boy.

o **QuarterMaster** ★ (1110 Bourbon St.; *C* **504/529-1416;** open 24 hr.). Best choice: basic po' boys, especially the French-fry po' boy, and greasy burgers.

o **Verti Marte** ★★ (1201 Royal St.; *C* **504/525-4757;** open 24 hr.). Best choice: anything in the deli case or from the mother lode of a menu, especially the day's specials, like Grandma's Boardinghouse Meat Loaf or catfish Bienville. Also salads, specialty sandwiches, and loads of veggies.

experience is classic New Orleans, turned up enough to honor gastronomy in 1880 as well as today.

675 St. Peter St. www.tableaufrenchquarter.com. *C* **504/934-3463.** Entrees $13–$26 brunch, $19–$38 dinner. Mon–Fri 11am–late; Sat-Sun 10am–late. Appropriate dress required at dinner (men's jackets not required).

Tujague's ★ CLASSIC CREOLE   Tujague's holds the silver medal for oldest New Orleans restaurant (Antoine's has the gold), and tradition still reigns here, despite a move from its long-held location down the block. Some things changed for the better: Both food and décor are archetypal but spiffed up; others fell victim to the real estate transaction that pre-empted the move (trek to 823 Decatur to check the fab original neon sign and famed wooden bar and mirror—we miss 'em). The bar still makes a perfect Sazerac, as well as Tujague's own invention, the frothy minty Grasshopper (better with brunch). The traditional five-course prix-fixe menu is the way to go; the anti-nouvelle fork-tender brisket, softshell crab meunière (when in season), and off-menu baked garlic chicken Bonne Femme are good choices. You'll enjoy solid, if not earth-shattering, authentic Creole cooking at this true classic, from the sinus-clearing shrimp rémoulade appetizer to the last bite of bread pudding.

429 Decatur St. www.tujaguesrestaurant.com. *C* **504/525-8676.** Entrees $15–$21 brunch; $25–$38 dinner; for 5-course dinner add $31 to entrée price. Weds–Thurs and Sun 5–9pm; Fri-Sat 5–10pm; brunch Fri 11am–2:30pm, Sat-Sun 10:30am–2:30pm.

Moderate

Café Amelie ★★ CONTEMPORARY SOUTHERN/CASUAL FARE
The pretty-as-a-chocolate-box, greenery-laden brick courtyard is Amelie's calling card; it's where Beyoncé & Jay-Z dined quite publicly days after the scandalous Solange elevator, um, incident. Expect cafe standards with

something for everyone. Standouts include crab cakes, goat cheese and beet salad, local fave cochon de lait pork sandwich, and grilled catfish with a kick. The relaxing spot calls out for a lemonade or mint julep and slice of lemon doberge cake. (*Fair warning:* Call ahead, it's frequently closed for weddings.) Reserve in advance for Sunday brunch.

912 Royal St. www.cafeamelie.com. ⓒ **504/412-8965.** Entrees $21–$27 lunch/brunch; $21–$29 dinner. Tues–Sun 11am–3pm and 5–9pm (Fri–Sat until 10pm).

Café Sbisa ★★ CREOLE This atmospheric stunner sashays with original wood, intimate balcony and patio dining, and a staircase that harks back to a golden age. In 2016, Chef Alfred Singleton, who worked his way up from busboy to chef until Katrina devastated the restaurant, took over as partner and chef. His outstanding French-Creole cuisine includes blue crab cakes and an amazing turtle soup laced with sherry, served under the watchful eyes of a bawdy George Dureau mural (which somehow survived the mold that bloomed after the flood). During Sunday brunch, live jazz fills the restaurant, providing a wonderful ambience in which to enjoy Creole classics like crawfish and andouille omelet, cheese grits, and smoked-salmon Benedict. Reserve a table on the balcony for alfresco dining.

1011 Decatur St. www.cafesbisanola.com. ⓒ **504/522-5565.** Entrees $12–$26 brunch, $20–$32 dinner. Wed–Sun 5:30–10pm; Sun 10:30am–2:30pm.

Irene's Cuisine ★★★ ITALIAN If you detect the scent of simmering garlic from blocks away and aren't lured by it, Irene's may not interest you. No worry—that leaves more of the French Provincial and Creole-Italian cooking for the rest of us. Irene (herself a Quarter institution) and her friendly crew create delectable house-made pastas and sauces, but the *secondi* are the real standouts. Locals come on Thursdays for the ginormous osso buco flavor bomb, and someone at the table needs to order Duck St. Phillip (with raspberry-pancetta demi-glace) so that everyone can taste it and wish they had ordered it. The seemingly simple *pollo rosemarino*—marinated, par-cooked, re-marinated, and roasted—is nearly perfect. Smallish, warmly lit rooms (designed to resemble the beloved original location) engender a genial time, and chat between the closely set tables is common. Would that the desserts were a little bit better, but the cheesecake will do.

529 Bienville St. irenesnola.com. ⓒ **504/529-8811.** Entrees $19–$30. Mon–Sat 5:30–10pm. Closed major holidays and week of Labor Day.

Latitude 29 ★★ INTERNATIONAL/POLYNESIAN When rumors first arose that Jeff "Beachbum" Berry was moving to New Orleans and opening up a bar/restaurant, the buzz in the tiki community (yes, there is one) was deafening. After all, Berry literally wrote the book on tiki. That the cocktails would deliver was never in doubt, but Lat 29 succeeds because it's all the tiki you could hope for and less: There's bamboo-wood-and-thatch decor, but it's understated; the fun, made-for-sharing rum bombs in bowls and giant clamshells are nuanced and ingredient-driven. This ratcheted-up Polynesian fare is less cloy, more Cantonese-meets-Creole-meets-craft than the mid-century version (well, there *is* rumaki). But do expect elaborate garnishes, cute umbrellas, and kitschy custom stir sticks. Don't skip the riblets or the light veggie poke with the oddly excellent pistachio froth.

321 N. Peters St. (in the Bienville House hotel). www.latitude29nola.com. © **504/609-3811.** Entrees $15–$21. Sun–Thurs 3–11pm; Fri–Sat 1pm–midnight.

Palm & Pine ★★★ INTERNATIONAL This former pop-up leapt to the top of our "love" list shortly after opening in 2019. We're fond of its often indefinable flavor hybrids that span the menu (and the globe, with elements of Latin, Asian, Southern U.S., and Caribbean) and its easy-going vibe, in line with many other "edge of the quarter" restaurants. Dishes are creative enough for those who want to push their palates beyond the usual, without venturing into bizarre foodie adventures. Plan to share—everyone will want a bite of what you have. Pre-theatre and late menus for those attending nearby shows at the Saenger, Joy, or Orpheum; a winner for brunch, too.

308 N. Rampart St. www.palmandpinenola.com. © **504/814-6200.** Entrees $25–$30. Mon & Thurs 5:30–9pm; Fri–Sat 5:30pm–1am; Sun 10:30am–2pm.

Port of Call ★★ HAMBURGERS For a decade or two before the great national gourmet burger tsunami overtook New Orleans, Port of Call was putting out a product that drew hordes. That hasn't changed. This is not a burger for teeny-patty people: It's a dripping half-pound monster (we like ours with wine-soaked sautéed mushrooms), served with a massive loaded baked potato. You're probably going to wait a good while for it (the fruity signature Monsoon cocktail helps pass the time), and you'll barely be able to see it inside the dark den of a dining room (a good thing since the restaurant has needed a redo for years). There are steaks on the menu, but they're irrelevant. Sometimes you just need a good burger, and even with other serious contenders around town (if the line is hideous, hightail it uptown to **Company Burger;** see p. 142), Port of Call's still holds up.

838 Esplanade Ave. www.portofcallnola.com. © **504/523-0120.** Cheeseburger $12, rib-eye $23. Sun–Thurs 11am–midnight; Fri–Sat 11am–1am. No reservations.

Sylvain ★★★ BISTRO The tradition-bound French Quarter is surprisingly devoid of coolness, save for a few spots including gastropub Sylvain, with its side-alley entrance, resident ghost, Civil-War-meets-Soho vibe, and literary heritage (it was once the home of a tall, feisty Storyville madam who was the inspiration for Miss Reba in Faulkner's *Sanctuary* and *The Reivers*). Fortunately, it's delicious, friendly, and unexpectedly unpretentious, even when packed and loud. The lush chicken liver crostini and the green curry sweetbreads are worthy starters. Try the absurdly tender beef cheeks, signature fried chicken sandwich, or a brightly delightful brussels sprouts salad with bits of wine-brined cherries. Since the menu doesn't skew light, share the chocolate pot du crème. On a nice evening, the discreet back-alley tables have their own cool vibe (a quieter one).

625 Chartres St. www.sylvainnola.com. © **504/265-8123.** Entrees $14–$23 brunch, $15–$29 dinner. Mon–Thurs 5:30–11pm; Fri–Sat 10:30am–2:30pm and 5:30pm–midnight; Sun 10:30am–2:30pm and 5:30–10pm.

Inexpensive

Acme Oyster House ★★★ SEAFOOD/CASUAL FARE   Is it worth the wait, you ask, eyeing the block-long lineup? They're Gulf oysters, people, and this is the oldest oyster bar in the French Quarter. In other words, yes (unless you're famished—then just go across the street to **Felix's;** see below). The oysters are tastiest when you're standing at the bar, talking tourist trash with the shucker, piling up shells to be tallied later, knocking back some oyster shooters (chilled vodka, cocktail sauce, erster, gullet). But if you sit at a checked-cloth-covered table, you can also order a dozen or two of the garlicky chargrilled oysters, which may change your life. Or po' boys served in red plastic baskets, and Creole standbys (jambalaya, gumbo, red beans and sausage) good enough for those who do not slurp oysters. It's boisterous and there's much waiter scurrying, so things do move fast once you're inside.

724 Iberville St. www.acmeoyster.com. ℭ **504/522-5973.** Oysters $16/dozen raw, $21 chargrilled; po' boys & platters $10–$24. Sun–Thurs 10:30am–10pm; Fri–Sat 10:30am–11pm. No reservations.

Café Beignet ★★ CAFE/BAKERY   Some swear the beignets here are better than those at Café du Monde, and we can attest that they're usually fresh out of the deep fryer, though we're true to the CdM for just the right chewiness and puffiness. Still, you won't find insane lines here, and you will find brioche French toast, omelettes, gumbo, sandwiches and salads. All locations except Decatur St. have nice patios; there's even live jazz Thursday through Sunday afternoons and evenings at the Bourbon Street location, a respite from the street's insanity.

334 Royal St.; 714 St. Peter St.; 600 Decatur St. www.cafebeignet.com. ℭ **504/524-5530.** Most items under $15. Daily 8am–10pm (Bourbon St. until midnight).

Café Maspero ★ CAFE/SEAFOOD/CASUAL FARE   Why is it always so crowded here? We'll give you five good reasons: the big menu with something for everyone, decent food, inexpensive prices, convenient location, and a seat for watching the Decatur action go by. It's nothing to post home about, but it's an easy stop for a standard breakfast, a burger, jambalaya, onion soup, or muffuletta (regular or veggie).

601 Decatur St. www.cafemaspero.com. ℭ **504/523-6250.** Entrees $12–$20. No separate checks. Sun–Thurs 8am–10pm; Fri–Sat 8am–11pm;

Clover Grill ★ DINER   The burger here is just a frozen patty thrown on the grill, but it's cooked under a hubcap (the better to seal in the juices), available at 4am, costs $6.49, and is served by a sassy queen in a "Clever Girl" T-shirt, making it so very worthwhile. Basic egg breakfasts and standard diner fare are also available. Bonus points for: excellent '80s jukebox, Formica counter, red vinyl stools you can spin around on, pie. But mostly for aforementioned sass, which they have in spades here, 24/7.

900 Bourbon St. www.clovergrill.com. ℭ **504/598-1010.** All items under $10. Daily 24 hr.

Muffulettas are sandwiches of (pardon the pun) hero-ic proportions, enormous concoctions of round seeded Italian bread, Italian cold cuts, cheeses, and olive salad. One person cannot (or should not) eat a whole one—at least not in one sitting. A half makes a good meal; a quarter is a filling snack. They may not sound like much on paper, but once you try one, you'll be hooked. Vegetarians swear they're delicious done meatless.

Several places in town claim to have invented the muffuletta and also claim to make the best one. You decide: Comparison-shopping can be a rewarding pastime.

The lunchtime line can be daunting but moves fast (and it's part of the aura) at world-famous **Central Grocery ★★★**, 923 Decatur St. ((②) **504/523-1620**). There are a few seats at the back of this crowded, garlic-scented Italian grocery, or you can order to go. Best of all, they ship, so you can satisfy your craving or throw an envy-inducing party back home. Eat it across the street on the banks of the Mississippi for an inexpensive, romantic meal ($27 for a whole, with tax). The impersonal staff at Central Grocery starts making and wrapping their sandwiches early in the day, so they're ready for the rush. Don't worry about freshness; it actually helps when the flavors soak through the layers. It's open daily 9am to 5pm.

Are the hot muffulettas at **Napoleon House ★★** (p. 225) better or blasphemy? It's a heated debate (it's the former if you're a toasted bread fan). Feeling experimental? Drive to **Nor-Joe's Importing Co. ★★**, 505 Friscoe, in Metairie ((②) **504/833-9240**), where the ginormous muffulettas, constructed with iconoclastic ingredients like prosciutto and mortadella, have their own cult following. Feeling fancy? The upcycled version at newcomer **Miss River ★★** (p. 127) is pretty terrific. Then there's **Cochon Butcher ★★★** (p. 132), where house-cured meats top a mini 'letta, which may actually be our favorite. Okay it is. There, we said it.

Coop's Place ★ CREOLE/CASUAL FARE   This divey locals hangout has long since been discovered by tourists, which may mean an unjustifiably long wait: It's good, but not OMG good—except for the well-known rabbit-and-sausage jambalaya, and the fried chicken, both of which really are pretty awesome. Decent food, friendly prices, late hours, and a menu that covers all the bases make this a good fallback if the line isn't crazy prohibitive.

1109 Decatur St. www.coopsplace.net. (②) **504/525-9053.** Entrees $10–$21. Daily 11am–close (at least 10pm, later on weekends). 21 and older only.

Felix's Restaurant & Oyster Bar ★★ SEAFOOD/CREOLE   Seventy-year-old Felix, the friendly across-the-street rival to **Acme Oyster House** (p. 110), has two rooms: the original, a down-home, nuthin'-fancy oyster bar/diner (entrance on Iberville), and a new spiffier spot around the corner (entrance on Bourbon St.). In both locales, oyster dozens come out fresh and bitterly chilled, needing nothing more than a spritz of lemon. You can also have them in stews, soups, pastas, or omelets, broiled, fried, or baked. And if it's crawfish season, order up a spicy pile. It's not nearly as much of a scene as Acme (a big plus), and the shuckers have fast hands and quick wit—even, nay especially, Mr. Paul, in his mid-80s and going strong. *Tip:* If there's a line at the Iberville entrance, check the Bourbon Street entrance. They seat separately. Or, take a drive to the Lakefront location.

739 Iberville St. and 208 Bourbon St. www.felixs.com. ℂ **504/522-4440.** Oysters $18/dozen raw; po' boys $12–$18; entrees $12–$28. Sun–Thurs 11am–10pm; Fri–Sat 11am–11pm. Also at 7400 Lakeshore Dr., ℂ **504/304-4125.**

French Toast ★★★ CASUAL FARE   Breakfast, thy name is French Toast. Lunch, too. This darling French Quarter offshoot of one of our fave uptown spots has rolled omelets, sweet or savory crepes, waffles, and yes, French toast (including a decadent king cake version with cinnamon cream filling). Start with ebelskivers for the table (a pancake-donut hole offspring, sorta; we like 'em with Nutella or lemon sauce) and go from there, as you watch the passing Decatur Street parade through the enormous windows (or sit at the old-fashioned counter). Most everything, including larger entrees like a fried chicken biscuit sandwich or hanger steak, is tasty and generously sized.

1035 Decatur St. www.toastneworleans.com ℂ **504/300-5518.** Everything under $15. Daily 8am–3pm.

Johnny's Po-Boys ★ CASUAL FARE   Johnny's is the standard-bearer for po' boys in the French Quarter—in fact, it's the only proper po' boy joint in the area. They'll put almost anything on that crunchy, fluffy Leidenheimer bread pretty much the way they've done it for 70 years, but they're best known for their roast beef po' boy. We have a soft spot for the fried pork chop version, just because it's hard to find one elsewhere. The line moves fast; don't be discouraged. Little-known insider fact about the family-owned fave: It's also a good, cheap, quick breakfast spot. Other little-known fact: They deliver to French Quarter hotels.

511 St. Louis St. ℂ **504/524-8129.** Most items $8–$18. No credit cards. Daily 8am–4:30pm.

Stanley ★★ CONTEMPORARY CREOLE/CASUAL FARE   It's cute and convenient (Jackson Square–adjacent) and serves well-prepared "regular" food that kids and grown-ups like (pancakes, good burgers, and an

---

The Po'Boy Lowdown

Often filled with fried seafood or roast beef, or famously with French fries and gravy, po'boys can include most anything. The story goes that they were originally a free sustenance offered to striking transit workers, those "poor boys." After decades of apostrophe and hyphen use, some purists are returning to the full "poor boy" name. They're delish in any spelling. Do yourself a favor: Taste and compare the classic po'boys at **Domilise Po'Boys** (p. 144), **Johnny's Po-Boys** (p. 112), **Liuzza's By the Track** (p. 122), and **Parkway Bakery & Tavern** (p. 122).

old-fashioned soda fountain serving homemade ice cream). So naturally it's popular as all get-out; try to go during off-peak hours (early-bird alert: They're open at 7am). If you choose the sit-down restaurant, the cornmeal-crusted oyster po' boy is a good way to go. For breakfast (served all day), those oysters come Benedict style, with poached eggs and hollandaise. Yum.

547 St. Ann St. (corner of Jackson Sq. and St. Ann). www.stanleyrestaurant.com. © 504/587-0093. Everything under $20. Daily 7am–7pm.

Wakin' Bakin' ★★ CASUAL FARE   Headline: "Neighborhood breakfast fave finds new French Quarter home. Tourists approve." We've always loved this quiet bi-level corner space, and it suits Wakin's down-home friendly, familiar fare just fine. Don't come for innovation, do come for pancakes, omelets, shrimp and grits, sammies, and homemade touches (including biscuits and sourdough bread). Well-priced and kid-friendly but BYOB.

900 Dumaine St. www.wakinbakin.com. © 504/233-3877. Everything under $15. Daily 7am–2pm.

THE FAUBOURG MARIGNY & BYWATER

Expensive

Saint-Germain ★★★ CONTEMPORARY FRENCH   Proposing? Whether or not, consider this romantic 16-seat dining room in a converted shotgun house, which transports you from gritty St. Claude Avenue to a country inn outside Lyon, perhaps. The nightly menu is based on availability and chef's whim; you're wise to put yourself in his hands for five courses. At various times here we've enjoyed a lean venison tartare with a rich gorgonzola sauce; our first guodong clam with cantaloupe; and a less exotic but no less lovely salmon, delicately herbed and accompanied by buttered shitakes. There's verve to the cooking, vitality to the components, and a bit of chef madness, yet French roots lurk. If you can't get a dining room reservation, liver pate and a basket of magical frites in the adjacent wine bar are an excellent also-ran. Wines are on point and fair; service is gracious. Alert for vegans and vegetarians: The third week of every month, the menu is meat-free.

3054 Saint Claude Ave. www.saintgermainnola.com. © 504/218-8729. 5-course menu $109, bar snacks $9–$20. Weds-Thurs 5–11pm, Fri-Sat 5–11:30pm, Sun 5–11pm. Dining room reservations essential. No children.

Moderate

Bacchanal ★★★ INTERNATIONAL   It's a ramshackle old building and a big backyard. It's a wine store. It's a bar. It's a jazz club. And now, it's an actual restaurant. Whatever it is, it epitomizes New Orleans, and it's one of our favorite spots anywhere. The unusual, European-leaning wine selection and funky, twinkle-lit outdoor garden with a jazz combo attracts locals kicking back in mismatched chairs, steampunk wine snobs in deep discussion, and out-of-towners enlightening to the "real" New Orleans . . . all tantalized by romantic ambience and Spanish-inspired small plates. Get wine bottles inside, glasses out. Find a table, order at a window, and get a number. Grab your utensils, and a starter of grilled corn with Cotija cheese, crema, and spices (or bacon-wrapped dates with chorizo, or smoked trout crostini with crisp apples) soon arrives. An attic converted to a dining room means it's available even on rainy days, but ahh, that garden. It won't be the best meal you have in New Orleans (the food is two stars), but it's frequently tasty, never boring, and ultra-atmospheric. It all seems thrown together, but it melds into something much greater than the sum of its parts (thus the three stars).

600 Poland Ave. www.bacchanalwine.com. ✆ **504/948-9111.** Tapas and small plates $6–$16, entrees $18–$29. Sun–Thurs 11am–midnight; Fri–Sat 11am–1am. Kitchen closes an hour earlier. 21 and over only. No reservations.

Bywater American Bistro ★★★ INTERNATIONAL/CONTEMPO-RARY SOUTHERN   About a week after opening BABs, as Nina Compton's second New Orleans restaurant is known, she snagged the James Beard award for Best Chef South for **Compère Lapin** (p. 124), her flagship locale. No pressure. And still she persists . . . and rises to meet her own high bar. This more casual spot is no less inventive, featuring flavor profiles that spark the palate in ways both newfound and comforting, taking techniques and ingredients from NOLA and the Caribbean by way of Europe. A crispy fried brick of hearty hog's head boudin sausage balances the rustic side, while tender, sweet duck breast satisfies for sophistication. Flavor-packed crab fat rice and the anything-but-innocuous roasted cabbage round out a fine meal. That said, the biggest hit is the simple spaghetti pomodoro: It's perfection. Desserts don't wow but the bar program is solid, and a seat there is a fun hang. A seat in one of the enclosed outdoor yurts, added during the pandemic, is its own type of fun.

2900 Chartres St. www.bywateramericanbistro.com. ✆ **504/605-3827.** Entrees $20–$26. Wed–Sun 5–10pm; Sun brunch 10am–2pm.

The Country Club ★★ MODERN CREOLE   The Country Club, located in a stunning plantation house in Bywater, has been around for more than 4 decades, but its locally inspired menu, with a nod to Italian-French and Creole-Southern heritages, has been reinvigorated, with dishes from barbecue shrimp and grits to an 18-ounce chateaubriand, jumbo sea scallops, and Louisiana speckled trout. Long known for its free-wheeling backyard pool scene, the Club was spruced up a few years ago with tropical murals inside (and powerful A/C—you've been warned), and lush landscaping and an outdoor kitchen outside, for poolside nibbles (guests pay a day rate for pool access). Drag brunch on Saturdays is a hoot, as gaggles of bachelorette parties digging into truffled mac n' cheese or debris and eggs can attest (it books up months in advance).

634 Louisa St. www.thecountryclubneworleans.com. ✆ **504/945-0742.** Entrees $12–$21 brunch/lunch, $19–$26 dinner. Sun–Thurs 10am–9pm; Fri–Sat 10am–10pm; brunch Sat–Sun 10am–3pm. 21 and over only.

Elizabeth's ★ CREOLE Elizabeth's was driving the bacon truck long before the bandwagon hooked on, and it's rightly famous for its brown-sugar-coated praline bacon. If the quality's dropped a bit since that heyday and service leans toward perfunctory, this is still a solid choice, especially for breakfast or brunch, for bacon and more—like the rarely seen fried chicken livers with pepper jelly or bleu cheese oyster appetizer. The bananas Foster *pain perdu* is a perennial winner. The dinner menu is stacked with solid Southern staples: stuffed catfish (thumbs up), duck breast in cherry wine sauce, an impressive and well-priced smoked rib-eye. Dessert? More praline bacon, please.

601 Gallier St. www.elizabethsrestaurantnola.com. ⓒ **504/944-9272.** Breakfast/lunch everything under $16; brunch $12–$24; dinner $12–$26. Daily 8am–2:30pm; Tues–Sat 5–10pm.

Elysian Bar ★★ CONTEMPORARY It's in a converted church that houses the ultra-hip **Hotel Peter & Paul** (p. 73), so the stage is set for an eclectic vibe and menu. Expectations are met. Fortunately, it's also good. The bar's overgrown cypress tree sculpture (crafted by Mardi Gras float builders) is worth a look, and the two parlor-style rooms are well-suited for sharing a bowl of mussels and bottle of wine. The sunshine yellow "breakfast room" is the most practical for dining. Menus are limited but enticing, veggie-forward, and made for sharing. Heirloom red grits come loaded with mushrooms and crispy shallots, a sumptuous delight. Flaky, lightly smoked gulf fish is heaped high on crisped avocado-slathered bread. Perhaps the amplest plate is a confit of chicken in a hearty braise of white beans, softened apples, and shallots. Desserts aren't much but justify another selection from the wine list's fine curiosities.

2317 Burgundy St. www.theelysianbar.com. ⓒ **504/356-6769.** All items $9–$24. Daily 10:30pm–midnight.

The Joint ★★★ BARBECUE When you think of barbecue, you might conjure up Memphis, St. Louis, Texas, the Carolinas . . . now think Bywater (unless you're in Mid-City—then think **Blue Oak** ★★★, 900 N. Carrollton Ave.; www.blueoakbbq.com; ⓒ **504/822-2583**). The Joint stands up to the best of them. Its location in an old corner store is less joint-like and more modern roadhouse, with picnic tables inside and out and the enormous smoker on ready view. The luscious baby-backs and lean, smoldering brisket are sublime; for something local, try the house-made Cajun sausage. If pastrami is on special, get it. Trust us. Save room for the peanut butter pie.

701 Mazant St. www.alwayssmokin.com. ⓒ **504/949-3232.** Entrees $8–$29. Mon–Sat 11:30am–10pm.

Morrow's ★★ SOUL FOOD/KOREAN Two traditions meet in this mother-son operation. Mom's in charge of Korean dishes; son handles the straight-up New Orleans Creole-meets-soul dishes. There's not much fusion going on, just two-in-one goodness with fair prices, fun vibes, and a warm, cross-cultural welcome. So NOLA. Order the Oysters Morrow immediately.

2438 St. Claude Ave. www.morrowsnola.com. ⓒ **504/827-1519.** Entrees $12–$26. Mon 4–10pm; Tues–Thurs 11am–10pm; Fri–Sat 11am–11pm; Sun 10:30am–4pm.

st. claude **ICONOCLASTS**

There's talent in the clubs *and* the kitchens of St. Claude Avenue, where a burgeoning homegrown, farm-to-hipster restaurant scene is incubating some crushing creativity at bargain prices. Anchoring the avenue is **St. Roch Market ★★★**, a controversial (Google Bywater+gentrification) if stunning food hall showcasing 12 varied vendors (2381 St. Claude Ave.; www.strochmarket.com; *Ⓒ* **504/609-3813;** Sun–Thurs 7am–10pm, Fri–Sat 7am–11pm). Other faves nearby:

○ **Arabella Casa di Pasta ★★**
At the counter, order mixy-matchy style from skillfully house-made pastas and sauces, plus veggie, shrimp, or sausage add-ins. Consulting Italian Grandma Nettie says check YES box next to the meatballs; ditto the filled-to-order cannoli. 2258 St. Claude Ave.; www.arabellanola.com; *Ⓒ* **504/267-6108;** Mon–Thurs noon–10pm, Fri–Sat noon–11pm.

○ **Budsi's Authentic Thai ★★** If this book has the faint aroma of lemongrass, Thai basil and fish sauce it's because much was written while munching on Budsi's when it was a wee pop-up in our neighborhood. Now it's a grown-up brick-and-mortar restaurant, but we still drive there to savor all that flavor and freshness. 1760 Rampart St.; budsisauthentic thai.com; *Ⓒ* **504/381-4636;** Tues–Thurs and Sun 11am–9pm, Fri–Sat 11am–10pm.

○ **Junction ★★** High-quality burgers (beef sourced from a local small-production cattle farm) on soft, sweet brioche buns baked by Dong Phuong (p. 144). Straight up or with specialty toppings plus one of 40 tap craft beers. 3021 St. Claude Ave.; www.junctionnola.com; *Ⓒ* **504/272-0205;** Thurs–Mon 1–11pm.

N7 ★★★ CONTEMPORARY On a balmy eve, there may be no better place than under N7's pergola. This idyllic setting secreted behind an unmarked door in an untrammeled neighborhood feels as if you've dropped into a backyard in Laurel Canyon—or Avignon—circa 1967. The cuisine, however, is assuredly 2020. As we languidly sipped an aromatic viognier at one of the mix-and-match patio tables, while noshing a bacon-studded Alsatian tarte and grilled bok choy with bleu cheese applesauce, it made perfect sense that the couple at the table on our left were practicing card tricks; the well-shod middle-agers at a bottle-laden picnic table were sampling pours; and the scruffy dudes across the room were polishing off tempura escargot and frites between intense chess moves. During more inclement weather, house-made charcuterie and onion soup in the charmant dining room is nearly as dreamy.

1117 Montegut St. www.N7nola.com. Small plates $9–$17; large plates $17–$26. Mon–Thurs 5:30–10pm; Fri–Sat 5:30–11pm.

Inexpensive

Bywater Bakery ★★★ CASUAL FARE The only bad thing about Bywater Bakery is that it closes too early. This casual Bywater breakfast-lunch cafe is a multi-threat, with delicious pastries, scrumptious savories, really cool local art (usually), and local talents tinkling the ivories on the old upright in the center of the room (often, especially on weekends). We're fond of the thick-crusted hand pies with rotating fillings, from fresh fruit to a gumbo-like stew; the ya-ka-mein (a locally beloved noodle soup specialty, chock-a-block with hangover-curing ingredients); and the breakfast-in-a-go-cup options. The dazzling cakes lure us with their good looks and keep us with their good taste.

3624 Dauphine St. www.bywaterbakery.com. ℭ **504/336-3336.** Everything under $10. Daily 7am–3pm.

McHardy's Chicken and Fixin' ★★★ SOUL FOOD Popeye's will do when we're far from New Orleans, but if we're in town, it's gotta be family-owned McHardy's for take-out fried chicken. It's moist, tender, slightly crispy skinned, perfectly seasoned, and cheap. Stellar. We never have a party without it, and often *make* a party *just* to have it. Shrimp and other "fixins" are okay— the mustardy, nearly mashed homemade potato salad is a standout—but the bird is the word here.

1458 N. Broad St. www.facebook.com/pages/McHardys-Chicken-Fixin/176427879083461. ℭ **504/949-0000.** 5-piece box $6; 100-piece $117. Mon–Thurs 10am–7pm, Fri–Sat 11am–8pm, Sun 11am–3pm. Takeout only.

MID-CITY/TREMÉ/BAYOU ST. JOHN

Expensive

Gabrielle ★★★ CONTEMPORARY CAJUN It took 12 years for this charming neighborhood gem to return from its watery (Katrina) demise, and one bite for us to be all in. The warm French blue exterior in the midst of Orleans Avenue in the Tremé is a welcoming beacon to the creative Cajun and Creole riffs within (i.e., why have garlic butter frites when you can have *guava* garlic butter frites with hanger steak?). Regulars table-hop between bowls of smoked quail gumbo, an insanely good concoction coaxed from the delicious depths of a near-black roux. The BBQ shrimp-sweet potato pie appetizer positively works and leads directly to the signature dusky sweet roast duck, or a braised rabbit delicately topped with rose-petal syrup, grapes, and caramelized onions. And then, all the desserts. We mean it. We can't pick.

2441 Orleans Ave. www.gabriellerestaurant.com. ℭ **504/603-2344.** Entrees $27–$42. Tues–Sat 5–10pm.

Ralph's on the Park ★★★ CONTEMPORARY CREOLE Huge picture windows look out on Spanish moss–draped oaks in City Park. Joe Krown's stylish stride piano seeps from the lounge and across the cream-upholstered dining room. You're sipping a French 75, eagerly anticipating the turtle soup and brown-butter sweetbread starters, gazing upon the setting sun, glistening rain, or your sweetheart's baby blues. Whatevs—it's dreamy here. The fare is traditional fine Creole with a pinch of globalization. A polished version of ya-ka-mein, the local ramen-like hangover cure, is a soothing surprise. Roast cobia comes glazed with teriyaki accompanied by popped rice, pea shoots, and grilled eggplant. Shrimp and grits get a curry and yogurt twist. Desserts are crowd-pleasing: Just say chocolate crème brûlée. The whole experience epitomizes Southern elegance—a vacation within a vacation, it's easily reachable by cab or the City Park streetcar, and there are usually multi-course specials. Allow time to hear Mr. Krown at happy hour or brunch.

900 City Park Ave. www.ralphsonthepark.com. (℃ **504/488-1000.** Entrees $18–$29 lunch/brunch, $23–$29 dinner. Tues 5:30–9pm, Weds–Thurs 11:30am-2pm and 5:30–9pm, Fri 11:30am-2pm and 5:30–9:30pm, Sat 10:30-2pm and 5:30–9:30pm; Sun 10:30-2pm and 5:30–9pm.

Zasu ★★★ CONTEMPORARY   One of our favorite newish fine dining restaurants is this petite, sophisticated bistro. Music is low; walls an urbane, asparagus green; service informed and affable; plating striking. Whip-smart preparations are just atypical enough to stretch the palate's expectations yet gentle enough to spotlight the fine ingredients. Proof is in a seared halibut in a graceful mushroom-ginger broth, surrounded by crisp peas and haricot verts—a simple, perfect melding of textures, components, and maker. The sumptuous Korean veal short ribs starter satisfies more robust cravings; delicate pierogis (!) are a "for the table" requisite. Drinks are equally well prepared; wines well selected; desserts, too, are swell (the pretty Pavlova is hard to resist, but we're smitten with the chocolate cake and port-fig ice cream).

127 N. Carrollton Ave. www.zasunola.com. (℃ **504/267-3233.** Entrees $23–$32. Mon–Sat 5:30–10pm. Reservations advised.

Moderate

Café Degas ★★★ BISTRO/FRENCH   Every neighborhood in every city should have a charming, casual French bistro that serves a perfect salad Niçoise and has a tree growing in the middle of the indoor/outdoor dining room. But only Faubourg St. John can claim it. Café Degas is darling, perfectly suited to a romantic dinner or a gals' lunch. Favorites like escargot, hanger steak, and rack of lamb are straightforward, flavorful, and generous; a delicate roast quail starter was tempting to double as an entree. It's a popular spot, particularly for brunch and the $18 two-course prix-fixe weekday lunch, so reserve ahead. Check the website for coupons.

3127 Esplanade Ave. www.cafedegas.com. (℃ **504/945-5635.** Entrees $12–$18 lunch/brunch, $14–$31 dinner. Wed–Sat 11am–3pm and 5:30–10pm; Sun 10:30am–3pm and 5:30–9:30pm. Reserve ahead for peak periods.

Dooky Chase ★★ SOUL FOOD/CREOLE   Our heart aches as we write this, recalling the 2019 passing of Leah Chase, the chef, hostess, art curator, activist, educator, unifier, mother, goddess—and proprietress of Dooky Chase since the 1940s. The quiet powerhouse, wife of founder Dooky, was a visionary who knew that food and grace could unite the divided, impel the immobile, and ultimately, change the world. And it did—*she* did. The Chases created a welcoming place for Rev. Dr. King and other civil rights leaders to dine and work; Dooky's was where Sarah Vaughn, Nat King Cole, Ray Charles, and other musicians hung out at all hours; they hosted Obama, and Bush II. Miss Leah was the model for Tiana in Disney's delightful *The Princess and the Frog.* She won just about every culinary award in existence, and after Katrina decimated the restaurant (they lived in a FEMA trailer across the street for years while rebuilding), after Dooky passed in 2016, after she turned 90, then 95, she persevered, "cooking with love" and making immeasurable contributions to New Orleans and the U.S. She leaves us with so much more than a tasty weekday lunch buffet of Creole standards and a handsome, art-filled dining room (now run by younger Chases who promise to carry on and perhaps expand the hours—check the website for updates). Friday dinner, when the neighbor-saturated atmosphere sizzles like the crisp fried chicken, will only become an even more requisite pilgrimage. So come for the hallowed history and to pay respects, stay for the fried chicken, a contender for the city's best.

2301 Orleans Ave. www.dookychaserestaurants.com. ℂ **504/821-0600.** Lunch buffet $18; dinner entrees $20–$25. Tues–Fri 11am–3pm; Fri-Sat 5:30–9:30pm.

Lola's ★★ INTERNATIONAL/SPANISH   For something very European yet very local—and completely different—try the Spanish fare at Lola's in the Bayou St. John neighborhood. Start with garlic soup (one of several good vegetarian options; another is refreshing gazpacho). Then get a sizzling platter of paella—we prefer the mussel-loaded combination. The teeny interior is cozy in inclement weather; the pretty outdoor tables added during Covid are lovely (especially when a flamenco guitarist is there to lend musical atmo). If there's a wait, relax with a carafe of red or white sangria; if there isn't, relax with a carafe of red or white sangria. Service is prompt, but do allow 30 minutes for cooked-to-order paellas. Close with the silky homemade flan. A very good day can be had by ending here after an afternoon in City Park or at the New Orleans Museum of Art (p. 170). Check the website to see if the restaurant has added its long-hoped-for brunch service.

3312 Esplanade Ave. www.lolasneworleans.com. ℂ **504/488-6946.** Entrees $18–$36; paellas $18–$62. Sun–Thurs 5:30–9:30pm; Fri–Sat 5:30–10pm.

Mandina's ★★ CREOLE/ITALIAN   Dis is da ultimate N'Awlins neighbahood restaurant, owned by the same family since the late 1800s—and largely unchanged—as it should be. Nothing innovative here, just heart, soul, and comfort food the way Maw Maw made it (including canned veggies—skip 'em), served by someone who looks like her. If the daily specials aren't to your liking, get some butter-soaked garlic bread to share, and the right and true seafood gumbo or turtle soup au sherry. Then go for the sweet Italian sausage and spaghetti combo, or the brown-buttery trout meunière. The cocktails are strong here; so is the A/C. Bring a sweater.

3800 Canal St. www.mandinasrestaurant.com. ℂ **504/482-9179.** Entrees $13–$28. Mon–Thurs 11am–9:30pm; Fri–Sat 11am–10pm; Sun noon–9pm.

Marjie's Grill ★★ CONTEMPORARY SOUTHERN/INTERNATIONAL
Oddball menu, off-cuts of meats and poultry, weird location, weirder flavor
mashups. No worry, it mostly works. Adventurous Marjie's fuses Thai, Cam-
bodian, and Filipino ingredients with NOLA standards and, in many cases,
smokes them over coal or wood. It's not all rabbit livers and lamb belly (just
some of it); less-novel options might include a deeply succulent grilled pork
or charred shrimp with lemongrass chili butter. Cool it down with smashed
cucumbers and sticky Thai-style BBQ ribs. A side of roast sweet potatoes is
necessary. Service and space are mismatched-dish-style casual; in good
weather, the outdoor wood deck is a sweet spot here.

320 South Broad St. www.marjiesgrill.com. *©* **504/603-2234.** Entrees $12–$30. Mon–
Fri 11am–2:30pm, 4–10pm; Sat 4–10pm.

Piece of Meat ★★★ CASUAL FARE   Two rebel butchers are smoking
and brining and curing and roasting and slicing and piling the goods high on
breads and boards, and you want them. Whichever you choose, add a side of
the boudin eggrolls. Some of the better spots around town procure from this
Mid-City shop, tucked in a neighborhood that's a mini-hotbed of good casual
food and drink.

3301 Bienville St. www.pieceofmeatbutcher.com. *©* **504/372-2289.** Sandwiches $11–
$15, charcuterie board $22. Mon-Tues & Thurs 11am–7pm; Fri–Sat 11am–8pm; Sun
10am–4pm.

Revel ★★ CONTEMPORARY LOUISIANA   When Chris McMillian,
renowned OG craft bartender and globally revered liquor historian, opens his
own place, we come, and imbibe. There's nothing frou-frou here: Revel is a
regular neighborhood hang, and that's the atmosphere to expect. Although it's a
cocktail mecca (the drinks menu is a great read), the food is no second thought.
The best way to "Revel" is to start at happy hour (or a mixology class, if they're
on) and just keep going. We're hesitant to cite specific dishes since they change
frequently, but the tempura-battered Creole crawfish corndog is a staple for a
good reason. Chef plays well with Mediterranean, Asian, and African flavors
and lets his culinary freak flag fly, so we tend to trust the extensive menu's oddities and ask to pair drinks. Desserts are good, but in a classic case of New
Orleans' embarrassment of riches, Angelo Brocato's (p. 146) is steps away.

133 N. Carrolton Ave. www.revelcafeandbar.com. *©* **504/309-6122.** Snacks and small
plates $6–$14, large plates $16–$29. Tues–Thurs 4–11pm; Fri–Sat 11am–11pm.

Toups' Meatery ★★ CONTEMPORARY CAJUN   Just another neighborhood spot with killer food that speaks our oinky language. As you are
being seated, order some crunchy porkalicious cracklins to munch on while
you're deciding what to eat. As the name implies, one should order the charcuterie plate here. Another should get the cheese board, just to even things out.
We're actually more a fan of lunch here than dinner (and the hearty brunch is
a fabulous new addition), but we'll happily eat the short ribs or lamb neck if
they're on the oft-changing menu. And despite this meat-centric advice, the

LATE-NIGHT bites

When in New Orleans, no appetite should be denied, regardless of circumstance or hour. These places will salve the savage tummy at any hour, or nearly so. Also see the full listings for **Buffa's** (p. 216), **Clover Grill** (p. 110), **Avenue Pub** (p. 225), and **Verti Marte** (p. 107).

o **Bouligny Tavern:** If your late-night desires lean toward caviar, smoked salmon, and French wines, this is your jam. 3641 St. Charles Ave., www.bouligny tavern.com, Ⓒ **504/891-1810;** Mon-Wed 4pm-midnight, Thurs-Sat 4pm-1am.

o **Cleo's:** Far better than average Mediterranean fare, extensive candy counter, good soda selection. 941 Canal St.;

www.facebook.com/cleosnola; Ⓒ **504/522-4504;** open 24/7; $6.50–$25.

o **Crepe a la Carte:** We get it. The Nutella hankering can hit hard. This walk-up window satisfies that and other sweet or savory crepe cravings. 1039 Broadway St., www.crepesala cartenola.com, Ⓒ **504/866-2362;** Mon-Thurs 6pm-midnight; Fri-Sun noon-midnight.

o **Melba's:** Po' boys, hot plates, wings, and occasional book signings (!) worth the short ride from the Marigny. 1525 Elysian Fields Ave.; www.eatatmelbas.com; Ⓒ **504/267-7765;** open 24 hr.; $6.50–$13.

---

sky-high chicken sandwich and a rich confit of chicken thighs are also worthy. Absolutely get whatever variety of multi-layered Debbie Does Doberge cake is available.

845 N. Carrollton Ave. www.toupsmeatery.com. Ⓒ**504/252-4999.** Entrees $14–$34 lunch, $18–$34 dinner. Tues–Sat 11am–2:30pm and 5–10pm (Fri–Sat to 11); Sun 10am–3pm.

Inexpensive

Bevi Seafood ★★★ SEAFOOD/CASUAL FARE   Bevi is a smidge more proper and pricey than a divey corner seafood shack, but make no mistake, these folks know how to berl (boil) and fry up a downright fine batch of shrimp, oysters, crab, or crawfish. The seafood is fresh, seasonal, and local—and the spice is right, even in the tangy slaw. Carnivores have excellent options, too. Consider making your last meal the Messi Swine po' boy (pork belly, cochon, ham, and—for good measure—bacon fat mayo). It's counter service with just a few tables, but don't get fried stuff to go: A concise fryer-plate-mouth interval is essential. **Bonus:** It's a few doors from **Angelo Brocato's** (p. 146), thus amortizing the Mid-City Lyft ride.

236 N. Carrollton Ave. www.beviseafoodco.com. Ⓒ **504/488-7503.** Everything under $20. Tues–Sat 11am–8pm; Sun–Mon 11am–4pm.

Cajun Seafood ★★ SEAFOOD   Those intrepid travelers who ask, "Where can I eat like the locals do?" will find their just rewards at Cajun Seafood, which is where to go if you like substantial spice—in your food and in your urban travel adventures. Order at the counter and take it to go or sit at one of the rudimentary tables. If it's crawfish season (roughly mid-Feb to mid-May), that's what everyone comes for. First-timers can order a starter pound or two per person, though you might get some side-eye—experienced Louisianans can inhale the weight of a small child in crawfish. If the nearby table heaped with 10 times your order stares at your timid pile, admit you're a newbie and ask them for a crawfish eating lesson. For sides, add some potatoes, sausage, and corn, and be warned: Corn and taters soak up the heat. Peel-and-eat boiled shrimp, grilled or fried catfish, or trout work any time of year, or try whatever else strikes your fancy from the extensive menu. Don't come for wings, salads, or pastas, although they are available if you want some familiar with your unfamiliar. There are even Chinese standards at the Claiborne location, but we're true to the boiled goods here. You want plenty of cold drinks and paper towels: This ain't for the dainty. Now dig in.

1749 N. Claiborne Ave. www.cajunseafoodnola.com © **504/948-6000.** Boiled seafood market price, platters and po'boys mostly under $16. Mon-Sat 10:30am-9pm, Sun 11am-8:30pm. Also at 2730 S. Broad Ave. (Uptown); © **504/821-4722.**

Lil' Dizzy's ★★ CREOLE/SOUL FOOD   This Tremé mainstay is another quintessential family-owned neighborhood restaurant. It's warm and lively with locals at the mostly average breakfast (the homemade hot sausages are slightly above that, and the catfish and eggs are a winner) and lunch buffet. For that, come hungry and early to dig into the terrific fried chicken, okay gumbo, red beans, and a few other soul-food standards. Better yet, order a la carte: The aforementioned chicken or our favorite, the standout trout Baquet, a delicate fillet topped with garlic-butter sauce and lump crabmeat.

1500 Esplanade Ave. www.lildizzyscafe.com. © **504/569-8997.** Lunch buffet $16 ($7 kids 8 and under), a la carte items under $16, Sun brunch buffet $18. Mon–Sat 7am–2pm; Sun 8am–2pm.

Liuzza's by the Track ★★★ CREOLE/CASUAL FARE   When friends fly in for a visit, we stop here on the way home to get them in the gumbo groove. Liuzza's by the Track has one of the best in town. The BBQ-shrimp po' boy is its signature, overstuffed with peppery butter-soaked shrimp, but we're partial to the garlic oyster sammie. When we're feeling feisty, we switch to the drippy garlic-stuffed roast beef, with a pinch of horseradish in the mayo (we'll often get the cup of gumbo and half po' boy deal). Specials can be pretty special, so check the board. The veggie-deprived should opt for the Portobello salad, and everyone here should strike up a conversation with whoever's nearby. It's that sort of place. Avoid prime weekday lunch hours if you can.

1518 N. Lopez St. www.liuzzasnola.com. © **504/218-7888.** Everything under $20. Mon–Sat 11am–7:30pm.

Parkway Bakery and Tavern ★★★ CASUAL FARE   This corner shop began life as a bakery more than a century ago; was shuttered for decades; reopened; and was underwater in 2005. Now, after heaps of love from magazines and travel- and food-channel shows (plus a visit from the Obamas), people come by the literal busload. Try to sit inside or on the original deck; either has more charm than the massive picnic area now required to accommodate its fame. What matters is that the po' boys are still terrific. Claims to fame are the fried shrimp and NOLA-style roast beef (our favorite in the city)—slow roasted to the point of nothing beyond a juicy, shredded heap of beefy deliciousness. We like ours naked, with Swiss and a horseradish shmear, and use a fork and knife. We're fond of the Reuben or lighter caprese, and oysters (Mon and Wed only; just say yes to adding bacon). Don't neglect the excellent sides (killer potato salad, chili and sweet potato fries). Do hit the sauce bar (across from the pick-up window) and squeeze in the lip-smacking, old-skool banana pudding. Round it all out with a bottled Barq's and a stroll along nearby Bayou St. John. There may be a line. It may be daunting. Try to go at off-peak hours, but if you're hungry, have a snack before you go. (Don't scoff. It's New Orleans. Eating before eating is what you do.) The line actually moves pretty fast, more so with a beer in hand, so hit up the bar. *Pro tip:* If you can score a stool at the teensy bar, do. Order your po'boy from the bartender, thereby skipping the food line.

538 Hagan Ave. www.parkwaypoorboys.com. © **504/482-3047.** Everything under $20. Wed–Mon 11am–10pm; closed Tues.

PeeWee's Crab Cakes ★★ SEAFOOD   Tourists do not often venture to this part of town (with good reason), but parts of town like this, and down-home diners such as this, are often where the good local eats can be found. (PeeWee's now has four locations, but this is the closest to most tourist sections.) The namesake crab cakes come in several varieties, so choose your pleasure. We'll also throw down for a dozen garlicky grilled oysters and have a hard time resisting crispy catfish or, in season, creamy linguini with fried soft-shell crab.

2908 Martin Luther King Jr. Blvd. www.peeweescrabcakes.com. © **504/264-7330.** Most items $11-$21. Wed–Sat 10:30am–7:30pm, Sun 10am–5pm.

Willie Mae's Scotch House ★★ SOUL FOOD   Since the 1970s, this humble chicken shack in a not-great part of the Tremé neighborhood was known mainly to locals, the foodie community, and a few enterprising tourists. In 2005, octogenarian Willie Mae and her secret-recipe fried chicken were designated "American classics" by the James Beard Foundation, and the world came knocking. Weeks later, her home and restaurant were 8 feet under water. A remarkable volunteer-driven recovery began quickly, with hands-on help from local restaurateurs—a testament to New Orleans' supportive food community. Nowadays, the matriarch's family helms the fryers. The chicken is still beautifully spiced and crisped—on a good day (consistency can be an issue). So go on what you hope is a good day, and because it's a classic Southern cultural icon, definitely get the creamy butterbeans (which don't get *near* the attention the chicken does but should). Make a reservation or plan to wait in line for the fried-to-order bird.

2401 St. Ann St. www.williemaesnola.com. © **504/822-9503.** Everything under $15. Mon–Sat 10am–8pm. Also a stall in the Pythian Market (234 Loyola Ave.).

CENTRAL BUSINESS DISTRICT & WAREHOUSE DISTRICT

Expensive

Annunciation ★★★ CONTEMPORARY CREOLE It doesn't get near the accolades it should, but Annunciation mines the classic bentwood-chair, white-tablecloth décor, and "good time was had by all" tone we love so well in New Orleans. Time-honored recipes prepped by some of the city's best chefs are attentively served. Fried oysters with spinach and brie, and buttery crispy chicken Bonne Femme au jus, two signature dishes, both belong on the table. A salad of abundant crab and a creamy herb dressing is delicious; and the tender veal with crawfish and andouille cornbread dressing is a little bit Southern, a little bit city, and a lot of flavor. A stunning softshell-crab special we had here was enough for two, but too good to share. Despite the cool brick, jet-black stained floors, and angular black-and-white abstract artwork, there's a warmth to the room that sets the mood on genial, owing largely to Richard Williams, the perpetually bow-tied maître d'. Good moods mean wine and dessert, and while the wine list is the more interesting of the two, a simple tawny Port with budino and the requisite lemon icebox pie will lengthen a lovely night of lingering.

1016 Annunciation St. www.annunciationrestaurant.com. ☏ **504/568-0245**. Entrees $24–$34. Daily 5:30–10pm.

Commons Club ★★★ CONTEMPORARY SOUTHERN Part of the fun of dining at the Commons Club is in visiting the Instagram-ready Virgin Hotels New Orleans—a fun-suffused eyebomb that stops just short of overkill. Each eating and drinking space here has a singular ambiance: One is literally named the "Funny Library," and definitely check out the Shag Room. But Sir Richard knows when to get serious, and at the Commons Club, exec chef Alex Harrell brings his sophisticated hand to inevitably fresh, ingredient-forward, and fully approachable modern Southern cuisine. We're long-time Harrell fans, and without hesitation trust his pastas (especially gnocchis) and seafoods (a bluefin crudo stood out). The potato croquettes are a requisite starter, and a hearty pork chop rich with roast mushrooms and a sweetly tangy bourbon mustard was pleasure on a plate. Cocktails deliver (it's New Orleans), and the wine options in the $60-$80 range are equally satisfying. We're partial to tables in the anachronistic but delightful "springtime on the verandah" window-lined lane, but with kitchen counter and community picnic table seating, any mood can be met.

550 Barronne St. www.virginhotels.com/new-orleans. ☏ **833/791-7700**. Entrees $25-$34. Mon-Fri 5-10pm; Sat-Sun 9am-2pm and 5-10pm.

Compère Lapin ★★★ CONTEMPORARY SOUTHERN/INTERNATIONAL *Top Chef* alumnus and St. Lucia native Nina Compton has some tasty culinary tricks up her sleeve, blending Caribbean, French, Italian, and

Creole influences into James Beard award–winning dishes that are just exotic enough for adventurous diners: deeply flavored, wonderfully textured curried goat with sweet plantain gnocchi, perfectly jerked crisped local drum with caramelized sunchokes, or island-inflected hot fried chicken. At the commodious bar, munch on seasoned corn and pig's ears with spiked aioli (c'mon, try 'em) while sipping shimmery, beautifully balanced drinks. Stellar lighting, blue highlights, and the dotted bunny logo help update the lively room's warehouse-y bones (huge windows, weathered wood, and brick), though it suffers on the noise front, thanks to all that liveliness and hard surfaces (and its shared space with the lobby of the Old No. 77 Hotel; see p. 82).

535 Tchoupitoulas St., in Old No. 77 Hotel. www.comperelapin.com. © **504/599-2119.** Entrees $16–$30 lunch, $28–$34 dinner. Mon–Fri 11:30am–2:30pm and 5:30–10pm; Sat–Sun 10:30am–2pm and 5:30–10pm.

Emeril's ★★★ CREOLE/MODERN LOUISIANA He heads an empire and pioneered New Orleans' modern restaurant scene, but Emeril's flagship restaurant has never flagged. Menu and décor underwent major overhauls during the pandemic shutdown, and it's still exciting high-quality (and high-priced) dining, with a clear commitment to first-rate locally sourced ingredients. Dishes build meaningfully on local traditions with global touches that never overwhelm the finery. The wine list is intelligent and broad; service is helpful and professional but unstuffy; and noise is well managed in the buoyant room. If you're able, go for one of the splendidly composed multi-course tasting menus. A salmon tartare appetizer benefits from mango, plantain crisps, and a wisp of spice; grilled pork chops, done perfectly despite their girth, are artfully glazed with tamarind and tomatillo molé sauces; and Meyer lemon crème elevates brandied lobster bucatini. Order chocolate soufflé with your entrée but get the banana cream pie, too, a new deconstructed version that might top the original version of this legendary menu staple. *Tip:* The open-kitchen bar seating is perfect for single diners.

800 Tchoupitoulas St. www.emerils.com. © **504/528-9393.** 5-course tasting menu $130-$150, a la carte entrees $32–$70. Tues-Thurs 5pm-9pm, Sat-Sun 5pm-10pm.

Herbsaint ★★★ BISTRO Donald Link may not be a Food Channel staple like Emeril, but he's right up there in terms of modern New Orleans restaurant royalty. His sweet window-lined bistro, rooted in French, Italian, and Creole traditions, earned a Best Chef South award (under Rebecca Wilcomb, now helming Link's Gianna; see p. 129), and it remains one of New Orleans' best restaurants. It's usually packed and always lacks elbow room, but it's uphill from there. Herbsaint dishes superb gumbos, including, occasionally, a meatless, herb-based gumbo z'herbes version we crave. The winning signature starter of housemade spaghetti with a creamy guanciale-spiked sauce is topped with a batter-fried poached egg (yes, you can—and should—double it as an entree); Herbsaint's version of ceviche has a Creole spice kick and crunchy pepitas, a refreshing cup of summer. For heartier fare, lately we're partial to a grilled chicken entrée with crawfish curry, an unlikely combo that works. Desserts here are terrific—try whatever they put in a tart shell. A bistro menu served from 1:30 to 5:30pm features light entrees from both the lunch and dinner menus. Reserve well in advance.

701 St. Charles Ave. www.herbsaint.com. © **504/524-4114.** Entrees $16–$34. Mon–Fri 11:30am–10pm; Sat 5:30–10pm.

Josephine Estelle ★★ ITALIAN Though it's located in the über-hip Ace Hotel, this restaurant is not at all too hip for regular people. It's surprisingly sprawling, high-ceilinged, and bright in a rather uncool way (although those dark-green velvet booths are v. cool). While the hipness mostly happens in the Ace bar (with some spillover), at Josephine Estelle it's about the food (though the drinks are darn good, too). Highlights include any of the crudo starters—the snapper melts in the mouth. Also get a generous order of meatballs, and then do your best to work your way through the pasta selection—the entrees pale in comparison to, say, a delicate agnolotti with creamy sweetbreads and rustic wild mushrooms, or the very tasty, very traditional mafalde "with maw maw's gravy," a.k.a. marinara sauce. You could also make a meal of the tasty veggie sides. Save room for the delectable peanut butter budino. We'll caveat all this by noting that a new chef—one we know and love—was recently installed. He can only improve on a good thing.

1600 Carondelet St. www.josephineestelle.com. © **504/930-3070.** Entrees $12–$21 lunch, $22–$40 dinner. Sun–Thurs 7am–10pm; Fri–Sat 7am–11pm.

La Boca ★★★ STEAK One might not think of New Orleans as a steak town, but it's yet another tradition that runs deep here—this is the city that gave us Ruth's Chris, after all. You choose your cut and your knife at this Argentinean steakhouse in a commodious loft-like room where aged brick mingles with contemporary fixtures—and regardless of what else you order, you should get the transcendent 3-day fries. For the best-flavored beefiness, we suggest the *entraña fina* skirt steak (which can also be had skin-on, interesting but unnecessary) or the *centro de entraña* hanger steak. Temperatures are proper; a trio of chimichurri sauces adds zip. Servers know their meats and are helpful about the (accordingly Argentinian) wines but aren't particularly sociable.

870 Tchoupitoulas St. www.labocasteaks.com. © **504/525-8205.** Entrees $29–$54. Mon–Wed 5:30–10pm; Thurs–Sat 5:30pm–midnight.

Maypop ★★★ INTERNATIONAL Possibly our all-around favorite newish spot in the city; hands-down our favorite spot for Asian Italian Indian Southern-American cuisine (sometimes all in one dish). The inventive, flavor-packed cooking surprises rather than stuns, satisfying both the serious foodie and the food-shy (especially at the more affordable lunch and, on weekend mornings, for envelope-pushing dim sum). Don't skip the standard-sounding bibb lettuce salad; the hot chicken in vindaloo curry sauce is fire, literally and figuratively. You'll do well with any handmade pasta, like an uproarious recent variation with blue crab, Laotian sausage, tofu, and fermented tomatoes. Servings aren't huge, thus everyone should get a slice of Maypop pie.

It's all beautifully plated, in keeping with the room's high style. Make sure to check out the lenticular mural from both sides.

611 O'Keefe Ave. www.maypoprestaurant.com. © **504/518-6345.** Entrees $15–$18 lunch, $17–$32 dinner. Sun–Thurs 11am–10pm; Sat–Sun 11am–11pm.

Miss River ★★ CONTEMPORARY SOUTHERN The latest from Chef Alon Shaya, he of local and national repute (see **Saba,** p. 141), lands him in the swank new Four Seasons Hotel. The high points are very high; the lows aren't disasters, just unexceptional. Stop first at the fab Chandelier Bar (for something bubbly and to soak up all the glam that a Four Seasons can deliver). Miss River's décor walks the line between shiny glitz and hotel diner, but when it comes to the food, subtle details and flavorings elevate Louisiana classics and comfort foods—dishes commonly found on New Orleans tables are next level here. Sure, the red beans are thrice the price of the nearby diner, but there's a creaminess, a hint of lemongrass and some je ne sais quoi (the recipe is Emily Shaya's, chef's wife). Ingredients convey careful curation and scratch-made attention (there's even an in-house butchery). Fried chicken is presented whole—bronzed, crisped, and juicy beyond belief—then carved nearby for all to gape (and envy). Whole salt-crusted snapper is also a stunner (most everything looks fantastic—Instagrammers are kept busy here), and the dirty rice with sliced duck breast has a bold country-meets-city spirit. All meals become celebrations when they end with the show-stopping baked Alaska. If genial Chef Shaya is greeting diners, as he does often, do engage with him; his telling of the Miss River story would be a highlight of a meal here. *Note:* **Chemin à la Mer,** on the fifth floor of the Four Seasons with stunning views, opened too late to be reviewed.

2 Canal St. www.fourseasons.com/neworleans/dining. © **504/434-5100.** Entrees $32–$70. Daily 10:30am–3pm and 5:30–11pm.

Pêche ★★★ SEAFOOD There's nary a dud on the menu of wood-fired seafood at this über-popular, mega-award winner (Best New Restaurant, Best Chef Ryan Prewitt, blah blah). The raucous room works best for plate-sharing parties, not dates or deep convos. You can skip the shrimp toast and Betty Crockery tuna dip, but not the beer-battered fish sticks (really), hearty craw-fish gratinée, or onion dip with pepper jelly and freshly fried chips. The whole grilled fish (our last one was a buttery fire-crusted redfish with salsa verde) is typically fab. The raw bar is equally fine and fun (tabled patrons can and should eat off that menu). Make full use of the terrific craft beer, cocktail, and European wine menus. For your dessert, the salted caramel cake, of course. No, wait, key lime pie. . . .

800 Magazine St. www.pecherestaurant.com. © **504/522-1744.** Small plates $9–$14, entrees $15–$27, whole grilled fish $45–$69. Sun–Thurs 11am–10pm; Fri–Sat 11am–11pm. Advance reservations essential.

Restaurant August ★★★ CONTEMPORARY SOUTHERN/FRENCH The fine-dining flagship restaurant of the culinary empire John Besh started and has since mostly left (Besh, once a TV food show star, is now a

#MeToo-era fallen star), August remains a marvel of Frenchified Creole and Cajun creativity. There is a rare misfire when a boundary-pushing dish goes one ingredient beyond, or an ordinary dish reaching for extraordinary doesn't get there. But on the whole, your experience will be decorous, cultured, stunningly plated—and memorable. Foie gras here is unfailingly off the charts, done "Three Ways" or in any incarnation. Salads are perfectly composed. Soft luscious gnocchi done with sweet blue crab and slabs of earthy truffles melt on the palate. The signature breaded trout Pontchartrain, in its envelope of paper-thin white bread, with shrimp, crab, and local mushrooms, is Gulf finery. Slowly roasted lamb spiked with andouille produces an orchestra of earthy, rich flavor. A vegetarian tasting menu features buttermilk-laced spring pea soup and smoked eggplant-stuffed squash blossoms. Sweets are urbane yet playful, from a deconstructed banana pudding to a summery pineapple soufflé. Service is utterly professional and unhurried. Tables are well-spaced in the sedate main dining room, where chandeliers glint off tall windows; the warm, wood-paneled wine room with its clever overhead cellar is slightly less formal. If the prices are off-putting (don't expect serving sizes to justify them), the Friday prix-fixe lunch (three courses at $29), makes August a doable experience.

301 Tchoupitoulas St. www.restaurantaugust.com. **©** **504/299-9777.** 3-course lunch $29; dinner entrees $35–$50; tasting menu $98 ($163 with wine). Wed–Sun 5–10pm, Fri 11am-2pm. Reservations recommended.

Moderate

Cochon ★★ CONTEMPORARY CAJUN   Chef/owners Donald Link and Steve Stryjewski pay homage to all things swine at this inspired and authentic Cajun restaurant with a serious moonshine list. It's good, sometimes very good, mega-popular, and one of the few games in town for Cajun food, the rustic country cousin to big-city Creole cooking (see p. 105). The Link/Stryjewski version is amped up several notches, of course. All visits to Cajun country should kick off with some cracklins and a good local beer, like the Parish Canebrake. Follow with boudin balls—crunchy outside, savory and porky inside—with a side of creamy burnished mac 'n' cheese. For a break from hog, briny wood-fired oysters bathed in chili garlic butter, or chicken livers with pepper jelly are astoundingly good (in truth, we like the starters here the most). The fork-tender pork cheeks are disappointing only because of serving size (so get two orders), and the skillet-baked rabbit and dumplings is divine and soul-warming. Oops, same goes for the life-changing mac n' cheese. Ambrosia cake is a potluck-perfect finish—a creamy, fruity, happy ending. Reserve well in advance.

930 Tchoupitoulas St. www.cochonrestaurant.com. **©** **504/588-2123.** Small plates $8–$14, entrees $19–$32. Sun–Thurs 11am–10pm; Fri–Sat 11am–11pm. Reservations strongly recommended.

Domenica ★★ ITALIAN   Bittersweet chocolate walls, soaring ceilings, great art, glossy surfaces, small bar, large crowd. All sets the scene for perfectly bubble-edged Neapolitan pizzas, one of the best salumi in the city, and a kitchen that knows its way around a vegetable. We rarely make it to the *secondi* here because it's such a pleasure to load up on antipasti, *primi*, and a pizza or two. Buttery sautéed chanterelle mushrooms are flavored with marrow and cut through with parsley—decadently rich. A deeply roasted whole cauliflower makes an impressive presentation and a delicious addition to the table. Fresh tagliatelle is sauced with rabbit and porcini mushrooms, hearty and divine (we love that pastas come in two sizes), and we'd never leave home if Mom could make a lamb *stracci* like this one. End with a satiny chocolate hazelnut budino. Domenica's superb daily happy hour, with half-price pizzas from 2 to 5pm, helps explain why it's often cacophonous. The bar pours well-priced boutique Italian wines and homemade limoncellos. Okay, service is inconsistent, ranging from prompt and knowledgeable to perfunctory. Still it's worth it. Also consider the casual uptown outpost, **Pizza Domenica** ★★ (www.pizzadomenica.com; ✆ **504/301-4978**).

123 Baronne St., in the Roosevelt Hotel. www.domenicarestaurant.com. ✆ **504/648-6020.** Pizza $13–$20, pasta $12–$29, entrees $24–$32. Daily 11am–11pm. Reservations recommended.

Drago's ★★ SEAFOOD   The booming Hilton lobby isn't very atmospheric and service can be perfunctory. Fortunately, that's irrelevant, because you're here for one thing and one thing only (okay, two): Drago's buttery, garlicky, Parmesan-y charbroiled oysters—your new paramour, the one you can't get enough of. Other places do them, but none so well and with so much flame. However many you think you want to order, double it. Bargain-priced Maine lobsters are also worth your while, but not much else matters. Sports-minded folks can sit at the bar, order oysters, and watch what's on—there are worse ways to take in a game (though it has no beers on tap—wassup with that?).

2 Poydras St., in the Hilton Riverside. www.dragosrestaurant.com. ✆ **504/584-3911.** Raw oysters $13/dozen, charbroiled $20. Lunch everything under $20; dinner entrees $18–$30, lobster $20–$52. Daily 11am–10pm. Also 3232 N. Arnoult Rd., Metairie, ✆ **504/888-9254.**

Gianna ★★ ITALIAN   Local restaurateur demigod Donald Link's first foray into Italian cuisine is, no surprise, a solid hit. Comfort, atmosphere, and noise levels all land firmly in the winner column (well, the wood chairs could be a titch more cush; try for a booth)—even before the Southern-Italy-meets-Southern-U.S. dishes show up. (Lower the meatball appetizer, tortellini in brodo, and crisped saltimbocca, please.) Flavors are deeply steeped and not overly complex; sauces are light (like the white-on-cream decor), yet each fresh local ingredient is clearly evident. Portions are on the small side, which allows room for ricotta cheesecake and lemon mousse. Our only mis-hit was the intriguing but ultimately uninspiring tummala. Service is on point as expected, given Link's well-oiled machine.

700 Magazine St. www.giannarestaurant.com. ✆ **504/399-0816.** Entrees $22–$29. Mon–Thurs 11am–10pm; Fri–Sat 11am–11pm. Reservations suggested.

Meril ★★ CONTEMPORARY AMERICAN Meril is Emeril Lagasse's breezy, casual, lower-priced concept. The large, popular horseshoe-shaped bar centers on cocktails with local ingredients and fresh herbs; it opens onto a bustling, expansive dining room with floor-to-ceiling windows. The menu is large, but most plates are small, and feature inventive cross-cultural takes, influenced by the docu-series "Eat the World with Emeril Lagasse." Yet it's not too adventurous; meat-and-potato people will find plenty to enjoy. Our successes included chicken mole; a muffuletta flatbread; Korean short ribs wood-grilled Japanese robata-style, served with kimchi cucumbers; and linguine and clams made with guanciale—as well as most of the desserts (Emeril's good at those).

424 Girod St. www.emerilsrestaurants.com/meril. ℂ **504/526-3745.** Small plates $5–$12, entrees $10–$26. Sun–Thurs 11:30am–10pm; Fri–Sat 11:30am–11pm.

Willa Jean ★★★ BAKERY/CASUAL FARE This place goes well beyond pastries, covering all the Southern comfort food and beverage needs exceedingly well, with just enough flair. We know you like specifics, but seriously, anything containing flour is awesome (GFs accommodated, just not as well). So pick whatever bread or pastry item appeals to you—then get a loaf of the cornbread. Yes, you heard right: a loaf. You can thank us later. Biscuits with crab and hollandaise or classic sausage gravy rock your breakfast. For lunch, get fried chicken on a house-made Hawaiian roll with jalapeño slaw, or griddled meat loaf with tomato jam. Or salad heaped with golden beets and feta, or a grilled fig-and-goat-cheese sandwich. Lunch gets crazy-busy; a reservation is not unwise. Dinner entrees are less interesting, or maybe we're just full after eating breakfast and lunch here.

611 O'Keefe Ave. www.willajean.com. ℂ **504/822-9503.** Breakfast/lunch everything under $19; dinner entrees $17–$27. Daily 7am–9pm.

Inexpensive

Auction House Market ★★ CASUAL FARE This chic new food hall is ideal for solos, groups, eclectic appetites, and the indecisive. Ten vendor options ranging from Indian to oysters to avocado toast to empanadas surround a sleek (and seemingly always busy) marble bar. Sushi, sandwiches, and coffee are also available; all are enjoyed by a lively mix of locals, conventioneers, business lunchers, and moms with strollers. Our faves: Happy Jaxx sandwiches and salads, Elysian Seafood for shrimp cocktail and oysters, dosas from Tava, and the Empanolas (handmade empanadas with fillings like gumbo and crawfish étouffée). Definitely use the bathroom here. When you go, you'll know.

801 Magazine St. www.auctionhousemarket.com. ℂ **504/586-8305.** Items $4–$18. Sun–Thurs 7am–10pm; Fri–Sat 7am–11pm.

Bearcat ★★★ CONTEMPORARY CAJUN/CASUAL FARE You know those places where people wait an hour for breakfast? And you think, why? Bearcat is why. It's that good. Also because you can get excellent coffees or

AROUND THE WORLD IN the crescent city

Most visitors anticipate beignets; po'boys; the traditional Creole, Cajun, and French-inflected cuisine for which Louisiana is known; and their modern-ized chef- and ingredient-driven vari-etals. But some of the most exciting local restaurants are serving up other ethnic influences. Consider these when you're ready to go off-roading:

- **Budsi's** This Thai standard-bearer's proof of quality is its leap from pop-up to brick & mortar (p. 116).

- **Dian Xin** Superb traditional dim sum with some localized nods, such as crab and crawfish bao, near the French Market. Well worth the wait you should expect. 1218 Decatur St.; www.facebook.com/dianxinnola; ℭ **504/266-2828.**

- **Fritai** French food is considered the root of NOLA's cuisine, but Haitian may more rightly own the designation. Taste the delicious-ness here. 1535 Basin St. www.fritai.com. ℭ **504/264-7899.**

- **Green Room Kukhnya** Popular "Slavic soul food" like tasty, affordable perogies, kielbasa, bli-nis, and oh that beet burger, in walking distance from the St. Claude clubs (p. 219). 1300 St Bernard Ave.; www.greenroomnola.com; ℭ **504/766-1613.**

- **Lola's** Mmm, paella. See full review p. 119.

- **LUVI** About as far uptown as you can go, this itty-bitty Shang-hai-meets-sushi hybrid turns out ultra-fresh, tastebud-tantalizing dishes to rival the best San Francisco has. There, we said it. Reservations a must. 5236 Tchoupitoulas St.; www.luvi restaurant.com; ℭ **504/605-3340.**

- **Mais Arepas** Consistently deli-cious house-made Columbian specialties. 1200 Carondelet St.; www.facebook.com/maisarepas; ℭ **504/523-6247.** Also check out **Avila,** p. 213.

- **Manolito** Cuban snacks and drinks. See full review on p. 224.

- **Maypop** A "Best of" choice. See full review on p. 126.

- **Pho Tau Bay** The city's exten-sive Vietnamese community has blessed us all with its scrumptious cuisine. Many of the best are in East New Orleans or across the river (see **Dong Phuong,** p. 144), but this one's right in town. 1565 Tulane Ave.; www.photaubay restaurant.com; ℭ **504/368-9846.**

- **Saffron** See review p. 141.

juices to tide you over while you're waiting. And because servings are huge. And because there's something for everyone to love here—starting with the menu concept: a "good" section for relatively healthy dishes and a "bad" sec-tion for indulgences. There's a robust variety of breakfast burritos, topped biscuits (the "daddy" biscuits are personal faves), and other carb-laden options, as all good breakfast spots must serve. But vegans, ketos, paleos, and other dietary preferences are gladly accommodated; a mushroom scramble oozing with boursin will please all. We're so enamored of the breakfasts here that we forget the lunch, but it deserves your attention too, for all the reasons we've enumerated—plus the crab dip and bison burger. The loft-like interior and sprawling patio are jumping most hours, but servers are kind and efficient here and at the smaller uptown location (2521 Jena St.; ℂ **504/309-9011**). What's that you ask? Yes, of course there are cocktails.

845 Carondolet St. www.bearcat845.com. ℂ **504/766-7399.** Everything under $20. Tues–Fri 8am–2pm; Sat–Sun 8am–3pm. No reservations.

Cochon Butcher ★★★ CONTEMPORARY CAJUN/CASUAL FARE This could easily be a three-word review: Just. Eat. Everything. As the name belies, meat is butchered and cured on-site, turning house-smoked meaty goodness into small plates and world-rocking sandwiches. The boudin sausage is one of the best east of Lafayette; the muffuletta may surpass Central Grocery's (p. 111); pork belly with cucumber and mint is wondrous. Get the vinegary brussels sprouts, some potato chips, and dreamy mac n' cheese or rue your decision. If there's caramel doberge cake in the case, get it, and grab a couple bags of handmade chips for later. Casual high-top tables open to the street via garage-style doors, and good local beers are offered at the full bar. Bonus points for the mad *Star Wars* diorama/table.

930 Tchoupitoulas St. www.cochonbutcher.com. ℂ **504/588-7675.** Sandwiches $10–$14, small plates $3–$9. Mon–Thurs 10am–10pm, Fri–Sat 10am–11pm, Sun 10am–4pm.

Mother's ★ CREOLE/SOUL FOOD/CASUAL FARE Legendary Mother's gets the "touristy" rap, but hey, Paris is touristy. And if it's good enough for Beyoncé and Jay-Z (who selfied from here), it's . . . actually that has no bearing on anything. If there are more than four or five parties ahead of you, go elsewhere; if you can waltz right in, the combo platter makes a decent introduction to Creole cuisine. Best bet is any po'boy with Mother's signature baked ham, like the top-selling Ferdi (ham, roast beef debris), or with turkey and cheese, our preference (or with biscuits at breakfast). Laugh if you will at the bread pudding's retro inclusion of canned fruit cocktail, but it's freakishly good. Follow the line rules lest you get some hostess lip: 1) no table-saving; 2) get steam-table items and order po'boys and plates; 3) order and receive drinks; 4) pay; 5) then and only then, find a table—don't send a scout to save one; 6) a server delivers the rest of the food.

401 Poydras St. www.mothersrestaurant.net. ℂ **504/523-9656.** Most menu items under $20. Daily 7am–10pm.

UPTOWN/THE GARDEN DISTRICT/CENTRAL CITY

Expensive

Avo ★★★ ITALIAN Bet someone $5 that you'll witness a marriage proposal tonight. Then book a table on the ultra-romantic, candle-lit patio at Avo. Even if you don't witness The Big Moment, you're a winner when you dine at this uptown beauty, considering chef-owner Nick Lama's impressive and indisputable qualifications: deep Sicilian roots, experience in some of the city's best kitchens, and his family's decades-long immersion in New Orleans'

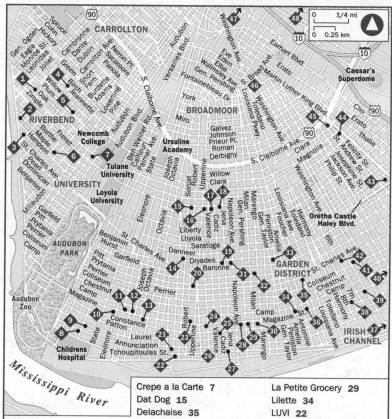

Crepe a la Carte **7**
Dat Dog **15**
Delachaise **35**

Avo **10**
Ancora **18**
Boucherie **4**
Bouligny Tavern **34**
Brigtsen's **2**
Café Reconcile **43**
Cajun Seafood **46**
Camellia Grill **3**
Casamento's **28**
Charlie's Steak **19**
The Chloe **32**
Clancy's **8**
Coffee Science **48**
Commander's Palace **41**
Company Burger **17**
Coquette **39**
Creole Creamery **20**

District Donuts.
   Sliders. Brew **40**
District Donuts
   & Coffee Bar **12**
Domalise's **21**
French Truck Coffee **19, 38**
Gautreau's **14**
Good Bird **15**
Gracious Bakery **20, 42, 47**
Gris Gris **40**
Hansen's Sno-Bliz **26**
Heard Dat Kitchen **44**
High Hat **18**
Imperial Woodpecker **36**
Jacques-Imo's **1**
Joey K's **38**
La Boulangerie **25**

La Petite Grocery **29**
Lilette **34**
LUVI **22**
Mister Mao **27**
Molly's Rise and Shine **40**
Mosquito Supper Club **33**
Pascal's Manale **31**
Patois **9**
Pee Wee's Crab Cakes **45**
Pizza Domenica **23**
PJ's Coffee **6, 13**
Plum Street Snoball **5**
Saba **11**
Saffron **30**
San Lorenzo **40**
Seafood Sally's **1**
Surrey's **24, 40**
Turkey and the Wolf **37**
Vals **17**
Windowsill Pies **16**

food scene. When his talents met this tantalizing locale, lightning—and love—struck. We fell for the perfectly charred, tender octopus, and a just-al-dente pasta with shrimp, artichokes, and a zip of chili. The delicious meatballs and lasagna don't stray far from tradition (both are simultaneously hearty and delicate), and gulf fish piccata is a delightful, light version. We're sorry it's not as inventive as it once was, but everything is Seasoned. Just. So. Skip the cocktail standards and go straight to the winning, almost all-Italian wine list. Service is prompt and perfunctory. If only the desserts were must-do's (you're too full, anyway). We're excited to try the just-launched brunch.

5908 Magazine St. www.restaurantavo.com. © **504/509-6550.** Pastas and entrees $21–$37. Mon–Sat 5–10pm. Reservations recommended.

Brigtsen's ★★★ CONTEMPORARY CAJUN/CREOLE Brigtsen's was one of the early modern Creole revolutionaries, and one of the first to convert a beautiful 19th-century house into an upscale neighborhood restaurant, way back in 1986. This perennial favorite still maintains a warm, romantic intimacy, with the hostess circulating amiably though the sweet little memorabilia- and mural-decorated rooms. The service and cuisine—which shows homey, Cajun-country roots—have been polished to consistent excellence. The "Shell Beach Diet," the famously grand seafood platter, changes seasonally but includes five or six sauced, baked, or otherwise unfried seafood items—an impressive extravagance for sharing or for a one very hungry diner ($36). Chef Brigtsen has a special touch with game and rabbit. His panéed sesame-crusted rabbit in a tangy Creole mustard sauce, as well as his crispy, moist roast duck, are known far and wide; his pecan pie with its perfect, copious crust is also justifiably revered. A modest wine list satisfies but could be expanded. Reserve well in advance during peak periods, and expect a comfortable, relaxed, thoroughly enjoyable adult evening.

723 Dante St. www.brigtsens.com. © **504/861-7610.** Entrees $28–$32. Tues–Sat 5:30–10pm. Reservations highly recommended.

Charlie's ★★★ STEAK There are fancier steak houses in town. All of them, actually. But none with the literal sizzle of Charlie's, which doesn't even have a menu, just a recitation. Start with a heap of onion rings, follow with a massive wedge salad (save some rings to crunch onto the wedge). There are five cuts, seared tuna for those who must, and various sides (we get shrooms and asparagus; if there is such a thing in as overkill in New Orleans, it's the rich crabmeat au gratin. But you do you). Ending with a scoop of Angelo Brocato's ice cream is de rigueur. Steaks arrive plattered, buttered, sizzling (as we said)—and perfectly cooked. Tucked away in an unassuming neighborhood, it's all friendly and efficient, and the ageless dining room, packed with locals, is just as it should be.

4510 Dryades St. www.charliessteakhousenola.com. © **504/895-9323.** Steaks $45–$65. Tues–Sat 5–8:30pm.

Clancy's ★★★ CONTEMPORARY CREOLE Clancy's epitomizes the New Orleans tradition of fine neighborhood dining, where white tablecloths meet good ole boys. Thing is, everyone's a good ole boy here—it's been that way for 70 years. It's got the look: tuxedoes on the waiters, linen on the laps, bead board on the walls. It's got the attitude: It's fun fine dining, aspirational for some, a weekly ritual for others. It's got a menu full of new Creole classics, superbly done: flash-fried oysters topped with brie; creamy, succulent shrimp and grits; a colossal smoked duck leg that stands on its own with the simplest of sides. When softshell crab is in season, it's de rigueur on every menu in town, but Clancy's is smoked—and it's a wonder. We've had great success with veal here, like one with luscious Béarnaise and crabmeat. If we were going all-in, we'd order several of the pricey starters—the mussels with andouille in tomato broth and crawfish vol au vent, to name two. Alas, the ample wine list is short on lower-end options. But once you give in to the kind of splendid evening to be had here, you may choose to give in to all that, too, and commune over conversation and cognac. (If not, consider lunch, when the atmospheric aura still permeates.)

6100 Annunciation St. www.clancysneworleans.com. (C) **504/895-1111.** Entrees $17–$20 lunch, $27–$47 dinner. Mon–Wed 5:30–10:30pm; Thurs–Fri 11:30am–2pm and 5:30–10:30pm, Sat 5:30–10:30pm. Reservations advised

Commander's Palace ★★★ CONTEMPORARY CREOLE The Commander's Palace miracle: It has an uncanny ability to serve up just the amount of formality your mood requires (and a room to match it). An elegant "event" evening? Got it. Rollicking (civilized) good time? Jaded foodie who wants a wow? They're on it. Marriage proposal in the offing? Just tell them when to serve the ring. Party-dressed kids being introduced to fine dining? They'll get the royal treatment, and maybe a rubber duckie garnish. Late, great matriarch Elle Brennan understood that service reigns supreme and that for the ultimate New Orleans experience, stately needn't be stuffy, formal can still be fun, and tradition is often best honored through innovation. Her philosophy still reigns. The family also mentors and fosters the city's culinary scene: A who's who of New Orleans restaurant owners, chefs, and front-of-house managers resembles a Commander's family tree. Yet regardless of how many "best of" lists and awards Commander's racks up, it never rests on its laurels.

The continually changing menu reflects James Beard award–winning Tory McPhail's fervent imagination and commitment to local ingredients, on best display in the seven-course "Chef's Playground." The a la carte menu mixes its classics—spicy-sweet shrimp and tasso henican (the gateway drug of Commander's Palace dishes); consistently perfect pecan-crusted Gulf fish—with seasonal newbies, like a sublime boudin-stuffed quail with a pepper jelly and sugarcane reduction. The gumbo can be a tad salty; opt for the robust turtle soup instead. For enders, the famed bread pudding soufflé is a puff of gladness with whiskey sauce. The wine list is one of the finest in this or any city, with a good selection offered by the glass in half or full pours. Everyone should dine at Commander's, and everyone can. Its unintimidating finery—plus multi-course lunch and happy-hour deals (did we mention 25¢ martinis at lunch?)—starts at around $18 at lunch (less than some po'boys), $28 at dinner. So worth it.

1403 Washington Ave. www.commanderspalace.com. ℗ **504/899-8221.** Entrees $28–$42, tasting menu $95 ($149 w/ wine pairing); 3-course dinner or brunch $38–$46. Mon–Fri 11:30am–1:30pm and 6–10pm; Sat 11am–1pm and 6–10pm; Sun 10am–1:30pm and 6–10pm; opens 6:30pm June–Aug. No shorts or T-shirts; jackets preferred for men at dinner. Reserve well in advance.

Coquette ★★★ BISTRO It feels like Coquette has occupied this tin-ceilinged, chandeliered, bistro-chic space forever. We mean this in the best way—because it's altogether contented in its skin, even if that skin changes daily. The culinary creativity of chefs/owners Michael Stoltzfus and Kristin Essig keeps Coquette comfortable and yet eternally fresh; most everything this potent power-couple produces is absolutely smart, polished, and of the moment. Their dedication to perfect ingredients, and top talent heading the bar and pastry programs, land Coquette firmly in the upper echelon of New Orleans's restaurants and make it one of our perennial favorites. Whatever we suggest will be long gone by the time you dine; what you must do, if possible, is spring for the five-course blind tasting menu (occasional discounts show up; check the website). Crawfish agnolotti with bits of sweet corn and country ham was beautifully bright. Tuna crudo interspersed with compressed cantaloupe and garnished with herb-dusted popcorn had us chuckling with delight. A mélange of asparagus, burrata, and crab with crunchy pumpernickel was just right on a humid afternoon. Finishes are light and often herb-driven and servings aren't enormous—you won't leave here uncomfortably overfull. If any version of cheesecake is on the menu, make that your choice; if you're a chocolate lover, get the pudding, too. Brunch, more of a down-home experience, is also a treat, including the family-style fried chicken feast.

2800 Magazine St. www.coquettenola.com. ℗ **504/265-0421.** Entrees $16–$29 brunch, $28–$34 dinner, tasting menu $80 ($120 w/ wine pairing). Mon–Fri 5:30–10pm; Sat–Sun 10:30am–2pm and 5:30–10pm. Reservations highly recommended.

Gautreau's ★★ CONTEMPORARY SOUTHERN Tucked away in a residential Uptown neighborhood, with no signage to speak of, there's a reclusive spot most every major food magazine and organization has managed to find and lavish with praise and awards. The finery of its food hews close to classic French treatments, but steps forward by virtue of modernity, ingredient perfection (particularly seafood), and artisanal everything. A starter of seared scallops and kabocha squash over arugula is married with a bright pomegranate beurre blanc. A dewy foie gras torchon adds a reduction of stone fruit and huckleberries, with bits of macadamia for crunch. Moist steelhead trout is roasted and uncluttered by a snappy caramelized satsuma juice with pearl onions and hazelnuts. The grown-up wine list matches the low-ceilinged room, with its trompe l'oeil linen walls and warm lighting. Service is flawless.

1728 Soniat St. www.gautreausrestaurant.com. ℗ **504/899-7397.** Entrees $25–$48. Mon–Sat 6–10pm. Reserve in advance.

La Petite Grocery ★★★ BISTRO Among the many bistros along Magazine Street, this way-Uptown standard-bearer is more traditionally French than some in terms of decor and wine selections. Ambience-wise, there's a comfortable welcoming groove here. Food is a distinctive mélange of Creole creativity; local ingredients; keen, classic technique; and the adroit palate of chef/owner/*Top Chef* contestant Justin Devillier. We believe deeply in the steak tartare (which comes and goes from the menu) and require the blue-crab beignets as well as ricotta dumplings with lobster and fresh peas. The chefs are also soup geniuses, making preliminary courses a tough choice. For entrees, smoky shrimp and grits with roasted mushrooms is one of the better treatments we've tried; and beef tenderloin gets a deep, satisfying pan-roasted sear. The kitchen also delivers a perfect cheeseburger with perfect fries. The desserts crush it: Lemon pound cake with local blackberries, topped with a quenelle of basil ice cream, changed our view of that simple dessert forever; a silken cheesecake wafted cardamom, with candied kumquats atop. The bar can get pretty lively—good or not-so-much depending on your goals for the evening (we start there, munching on sides of fried green beans). The usually on-point service might suffer a tad at peak periods.

4238 Magazine St. www.lapetitegrocery.com. © **504/891-3377.** Entrees $18–$35. Tues–Sat 11:30am–2:30pm; Sun 10:30am–2:30pm; Sun–Thurs 5:30–9:30pm; Fri–Sat 5:30–10:30pm.

Lilette ★★★ BISTRO Lilette's pedigreed chef-owner trained in some of New Orleans' finest kitchens and at Michelin-starred restaurants in France, resulting in an artistic, serious approach. The NOLA classic space—high-ceilinged, columned, tiles—is made East Village–ready with tobacco-toned walls. Lunch is thick with businesspeople and ladies who lunch; dinner sees a staid mixed crowd of tourists, neighbors, and young hipsters, all here for the chef's tasteful, clean lines. Start with truffled Parmigiano toast with wild mushrooms, marrow, and veal glace (you may end with it, too; it's divine) or chunky crab claws doused in slightly sweet passion-fruit butter, rich yet restrained (if you stop now, you've done well). A roast chicken breast with brussels sprouts and balsamic-glazed onions is flawless simplicity; gnocchi with intensely unctuous beef cheeks and chanterelles is immorally rich. Desserts are worth the indulgence, notably the curious signature of goat-cheese crème fraîche rounds, paired with vanilla-poached pears sprinkled with pistachios and lavender honey. If you're a wine enthusiast trying to decide between the Uptown bistros, opt for Lilette.

3637 Magazine St. www.liletterestaurant.com. © **504/895-1636.** Entrees $21–$28 lunch, $26–$39 dinner. Tues–Sat 11:30am–2pm; Mon–Thurs 5:30–9:30pm; Fri–Sat 5:30–10:30pm.

Mosquito Supper Club ★★★ CAJUN Mosquito Supper Club has cornered the local market on experiential dining, one which often becomes a highlight of a visit to New Orleans. Four nights a week, 12 diners come together around two rustic picnic tables, as host/chef Melissa Martin serves a multi-course prix-fixe Cajun supper in her charming home. This hearty, homestyle communal meal stars seafood, seasonal vegetables, and the flavors passed through centuries of people in Martin's hometown of Chauvin, Louisiana. Along the way, Martin pays homage to her native land and its waters, her ancestors, the cultures of shrimpers, farmers, and the Cajuns, and conveys her passion for the issues they (and we) face. Woven through are understated lessons around sustainability, climate change, and the viability of a lifestyle. There are no dry lectures, just dialogue and deliciousness—and in the process, knowledge, friends, and memories are gained.

3824 Dryades St. www.mosquitosupperclub.com. No phone. $105–$150 per person; optional cocktails or wine pairing additional. Thurs–Sun 1 seating at 7:30pm (bar open 5:30–9:30pm). Advance reservations and non-refundable pre-payment required.

Patois ★★★ BISTRO/CONTEMPORARY CREOLE This tucked-away, near-perfect bistro is chic and inviting, the locally sourced ingredients pop with freshness, and service is practiced. Its refined, modern Southern Creole menu is shot through with French influences and an occasional dash of something international, like an octopus carpaccio made lively with a pepper-and-chorizo citrus vinaigrette, and a tea-brined smoked duck with rice grits, okra, and a shock of jalapeno tomato compote. We loved a simple lamb ribs appetizer—just right with a dollop of marinated eggplant and Creole tomato jam. The grilled hanger steak, in a rich red-wine bone-marrow reduction, is deeply flavored. Desserts bring a sense of whimsy—the fanciful bread pudding has strawberries and white chocolate sauce; but in the end, the chocolatey, caramelly, peanutty "Snickers" cake got us. All are sweet and worthy.

6078 Laurel St. www.patoisnola.com. ℂ **504/895-9441.** Entrees $15–$29 lunch, $25–$41 dinner. Wed–Thurs 5:30–10pm; Fri 11:30am–2pm and 5:30–10:30pm; Sat 5:30–10:30pm; Sun 10:30am–2pm. Reserve well in advance.

San Lorenzo ★★ ITALIAN We're smitten with the general coolness of the newly renovated Hotel Saint Vincent (p. 86), the latest iteration of this historic orphanage-turned-hostel. San Lorenzo is the upscalest of its three on-site eateries (we're also fond of **Elizabeth Street Café** and drinks by the beautiful-peopled pool), yet it leans more toward comfy and calm than cool. Which is a-okay with us (actually the cushy banquettes might be a bit too serene—you'll sink in a good 3 in.). But cool is in the details, and they're here—those light fixtures! The menu is Milanese, with its best items coming from the sea. All things raw are worth ordering: Hamachi crudo is particularly memorable; delicate flounder piccata also impressed. A bland shrimp risotto was a rare miss, but our desserts—a gorgeous pavlova and lovely olive oil doberge cake—made up for it. Terrif selection of wines by the glass, albeit a bit pricey.

1507 Magazine St. www.stvincentnola.com. ℂ **504/350-2450.** Entrees $14–$45 lunch, $18–$45 dinner. Mon–Fri 11am–3pm and 5–10pm, Sat-Sun 10am–3pm and 5–10pm. Reservations recommended.

Moderate

Boucherie ★★★ CONTEMPORARY SOUTHERN When Boucherie first opened, we wrestled with the selfish tell-or-don't-tell moral dilemma. That didn't last. Word got out, and it's been popular ever since. The food retains its original sense of playfulness, and prices remain solidly affordable for what chef/owner (and *Chopped* alum) Nathaniel Zimet calls "fine dining for the people." The menu is limited, but most everything has Cajun-inflected, meaty goodness, with dashes of global influences. At dinner, a deeply savory brisket is piled with crispy, Parmesan-sprinkled fries (too good to share; get an extra side); at lunchtime you can rock a po'boy loaf, topped with fresh horseradish sauce, or sweet pulled-pork cake piled with tangy, acidic purple slaw or slivers of pickled pear. We wouldn't ignore the blackened shrimp and grit cake, either. Super-sweet Krispy Kreme bread pudding is no longer the hilarious curiosity it once was; choose the Thai chili chocolate pie instead (or don't choose—get both). *Tip:* Around the corner, Boucherie's spinoff **Bourrée** (1510 S. Carrolton Ave.; www.bourreenola.com; ☎ **504/510-4040**) is crushing it as an amped-up wing, barbecue, and daiquiri shack.

1506 S. Carrollton Ave. www.boucherie-nola.com. ☎ **504/862-5514.** Lunch entrees $12–$21; dinner small plates $7–$15, large plates $18–$30. Wed–Fri 11am–3pm and 5–9:30pm; Sat 5–9:30pm; Sun 10:30am–2:30pm and 5–9:30pm.

The Chloe ★ CONTEMPORARY SOUTHERN   Oh Chloe, you enchanting tease. We so want to love you, and perhaps someday we will. For now, let's just be friends. In other words, there's room for growth here (we know your chef and his capabilities), but the charming porch and terraced lawn fronting this newly renovated boutique hotel make such delightful spots to pass a pretty afternoon that we'll keep you in our good graces (and in Frommer's, for now). But we'll only commit to a luncheon or happy hour snacks, so we can enjoy your canopy of oaks, dappling sun, and the clackety clack of the passing St. Charles Avenue streetcar. Even your flighty servers can't dampen that loveliness, and the Chloe salad and flavorful pork belly lettuce cups were dandy enough, while the bartender's crafty concoctions kept us hydrated and duly satisfied.

4125 St. Charles Ave. www.thechloenola.com. ☎ **504/541-5500.** Entrees $13–$34 lunch, $16–$36 dinner. Mon–Fri 11am–3pm and 5–9pm, Sat-Sun 10am–3pm and 5–9pm.

Delachaise ★★ FRENCH/BISTRO   Sitting on its own little island on St. Charles Avenue, this bistro feels so distinctly Parisian that you might crave a Gauloise. It's a worthy hangout for the stellar wine selection (French-leaning and fairly priced; booze and beer options are also plentiful); for the atmosphere (streetside bistro tables and a long narrow tin-ceilinged interior); and for the small but excellent bar-food menu. The best options are the logical ones: pate; frog legs; moules frites; steak frites. Okay FINE, just get the frites. We always end with chocolate souffle and a tawny port. Servers with attitude and A/C set to frigid don't seem to dissuade a youthful crowd that populates the tables for hours on end. Bring a wrap and join them.

3442 St. Charles Ave. www.thedelachaise.com. ☎ **504/895-0858.** Entrees $11–$18 (steak $33). Mon–Thurs 4pm–1am; Fri–Sat noon–2am; Sun noon–1am.

Gris Gris ★★★ CONTEMPORARY SOUTHERN   This ain't yo mama's open kitchen. Gris Gris's entertaining, wrap-around chef's kitchen counter is a great place for fans of cooking shows, communal conversation, or hearty, Southern cooking (you can order based on what appeals as it's prepared and plated before your eyes, but be warned—it looks and tastes universally great). Start with the rare indulgence of chicken gizzards, smothered in caramelized peppers and onions, and a cup of gumbo (one of the better versions around). Whole branzino, seared, encircling a rustic ratatouille, is a visual and taste TKO; the wow-factor pork chop will be enjoyed for at least two meals (while still managing to stay moist). Mom's chicken and dumplings is irresistible on a chilly day. Dessert should be pie (if they're not too busy, ask about the pie man). Upstairs in the bar or casual balcony you'll miss the show but still console yourself with a stellar meal and a street view.

1800 Magazine St. www.grisgrisnola.com. © **504/272-0241.** Entrees $12–$16 lunch, $16–$28 dinner. Mon, Wed-Sat 11am–10pm; Sun 11am–9pm.

Jacques-Imo's ★★ CREOLE/SOUL FOOD   Speaking of food trucks, the gator-painted pickup in front of Jacques-Imo's actually has a table set up in its bed, where some lucky couple can dine (they'll have way more space than in the crowded dining room). This funky, colorful spot with the long line (longer in proportion to who's playing next door at the **Maple Leaf;** see p. 220) is hugely popular for all that jacked-up fun, not to mention giant portions and Creole soul-food stylings. Fortunately, the drinks are well made, and as soon as you're seated you'll be appeased with righteous cornbread muffins. The signature shrimp and alligator-sausage "cheesecake" (more like a quiche) has fans and detractors (we're on board); the diamond-hard crunchy fried chicken and less-complicated Creole specialties fare best. Blackened redfish with a crab-chili hollandaise is a winner, and the lightly batter-fried softshell-crab "Godzilla" worked. The food may ride a bit on the coattails of the rowdy party atmosphere, but it'll feel like a reward worth the wait.

8324 Oak St. www.jacques-imos.com. © **504/861-0886.** Entrees $19–$34. Mon–Thurs 5–10pm; Fri–Sat 5–10:30pm. Reservations required for 5 or more.

Mister Mao ★★ INTERNATIONAL   The décor is a "tell:" you're in for a little mischievousness, some wackiness, a fair amount of spice, and a lot of fun. Owner/wife is a Cambodian-American who heads the kitchen; owner/husband, a white dude who goes by "Wildcat," heads the bar, which could also be tells. Abandon all culinary rules and expectations, ye who enter here, and ye shall be rewarded. Bits of Southeast Asia, Latin America, the Caribbean, and other globe-hopping flavors zing off the teal tiger mural, zebra rugs, and grandmotherly tableware in bewildering, refreshing, and sometimes riotous ways. It's a drinking place for sure, so get in the mood with a yummy, rummy Billion Dollar Betsy, accompanied by sikil pak (addictive habanero and pumpkin seed dip) and the now-signature escargot Wellington, horseradish-laden flavor bombs encircled in puff pastry. A section of the menu lists items at the far end of the Scoville scale—steer clear if heat is not your thing. (Fair warning: Some of those in other sections aren't exactly benign, and Wildcat doesn't have milk on the bar menu. Yet.) Try the enchanting pani puri, crispy lentil popper cups filled with potato masala, marinated blueberries, and mint water. The menu changes often, but octopus and scallop preparations are consistent. Save room for chocolate garlic tart (for real). Servers are kindly, cognizant guides through the menu and equally eclectic wine list. Consider it if you're heading to Tipitina's (p. 220), it's a few steps away.

4501 Tchoupitoulas St. www.mistermaonola.com. © **504/345-2056.** Entrees $18–$30. Mon 5–9pm; Thurs–Sat 5–10pm; Sun 11am–3pm.

Pascal's Manale ★★★ ITALIAN/STEAK/SEAFOOD We adore the old-school neon, and the where-everybody-knows-your-name feel at this century-old neighborhood joint. But more than anything we love the barbecued shrimp—the bowl of colossal, buttery crustaceans that made Manale (mu-*nah*-lee). Make sure you get them (schedule a long workout tomorrow), some turtle soup, and—trust us—classic spaghetti and meatballs. Starting a meal at the oyster bar is compulsory: The bivalves might be frigid, but if Thomas "Uptown T" is shucking, his repartee is hot. Ask him anything, and your party is officially started. When it's crowded it can be boisterous—Pascal's is the kind of place where neighboring tables spontaneously converse, but unlike at a cozy bistro, it's a welcome intrusion (people eat with their hands and wear bibs, fer Pete's sake).

838 Napoleon Ave. www.pascalsmanale.com. © **504/895-4877.** Entrees $22–$28 (steak $44). Mon–Fri 11:30am–9pm; Sat 5–10pm. Reservations advised.

Saba ★★★ ISRAELI/INTERNATIONAL Soon after Alon Shaya left the eponymous, mega-award-winning restaurant he helped originate (we'll spare you the breakup details), chef Shaya roared back by opening Saba. Its menu and amped-up Israeli recipes resemble those at Shaya: The fresh, modern Middle Eastern flavorings are intact, with a bit more localism woven through. That's evident in the blue crab topping velvety hummus, and the rich duck broth in the matzo-ball soup. The Middle Eastern herbs and spices are as subtle as the textures are supple, and the menu encourages a table full of shared plates—tiny, small, medium, and major. Start with some pretty plates of salatim, like *ikra* (lox shmear on steroids) or *lutenitsa,* oven-fired peppers, tomatoes, and eggplant pureed and seasoned to pure perfection. Order as many plates as your table can fit—that way your server will keep bringing the glorious steam-puffed pita bread, piping-fresh from the wood oven. The harissa-roasted whole chicken is moist and perfect, and the astute wine list is stocked with a contingent of beautifully complementary rosés. Close with the divine labneh cheesecake, grit notwithstanding, or carob-fudge cake with black sesame gelato, carob notwithstanding.

5757 Magazine St. eatwithsaba.com. © **504/324-7770.** Small plates $8–$20; family-style entrees $45–$55. Wed–Thurs 11am–10pm; Fri 11am–11pm; Sat 10am–11pm; Sun 10am–10pm.

Saffron ★★★ INDIAN Who comes to New Orleans and eats Indian food? Smart people who appreciate stellar, unpretentious service and sophisticated, delicately seasoned food in a comfortable, elegantly contemporary setting.

IN-THE-KNOW treasure TROVE: FRERET STREET

Like a proper Southern belle, Freret Street, a lesser-known foodie zone, beckons with a "come hither" wink: **Ancora's** excellent wood-fired pizza (4508 Freret St.; www.ancorapizza.com), hipster **Val's** tacos (4632 Freret St.; www.valsnola. com), and our beloved **High Hat** (p. 145) get the block party started. **Good Bird** rotisserie chicken (5041 Freret St.; www.goodbirdnola.com) and **Windowsill Pies** (4714 Freret St.; www.windowsill piesnola.com) are worthy recent adds to the scene. **Company Burger** (4600 Freret St.; thecompanyburger.com) and **Dat Dog** (p. 143) started here, and famed **Cure** (p. 226), arguably the city's foremost craft drinking and small-plate locale, started it all.

Share a few sathi, small bowls served with crisp roti flatbread for dipping or spooning: an excellent daal (lentil stew) or saag paneer. And/or the chargrilled oysters, a NOLA staple done here with curry leaf. Standout entrees include the goat masala, subtle and unctuous, and a spice-crusted gulf fish—another perfect melding of the two cuisines. Cocktails mirror the menu, with crafty hints of tamarind or cardamom; beer and wine are thoughtfully paired. If you think Indian desserts are an immaterial afterthought, the ethereal "Curry is My Jam" ginger cake will change your mind.

4128 Magazine St. www.saffronnola.com. ✆ 504/323-2626. Entrees $18–$30. Tues–Thurs 5–9:30pm; Fri–Sat 5–10:30pm. Reservations recommended.

Seafood Sally's ★★ SEAFOOD Sally's is a straightforward, approachable seafood spot in a delightful converted-house setting that draws neighbors and visitors (Oak St. is outside the typical tourist zones, but a fun stroll). The outside space is especially welcoming, with small and large picnic tables and perhaps a few kids playing between them. If, on the way to your table, you notice something tasty on someone else's plate, you'd feel comfortable stopping to ask them about it, and they'll offer an opinion and a taste. Sharing a platter of the super-fresh seasonal selections, boiled or fried, is good fun; we can also attest to either of the crab claw starters and the Buffalo fried oyster sandwich (fried oysters + bleu cheese = winning combo). If you're uncertain about how to eat all these local seafood standards (whole crabs, head-on shrimp, raw oysters), it's an affordable place to practice and the sociable servers will help you. So might some of the folks at the neighboring tables. *Tip:* good pre-show option if you're headed to the **Maple Leaf** (p. 220).

8400 Oak St. www.seafoodsallys.com. ✆ 504/766-8735. Entrees $14–$30. Mon and Wed–Thurs 4–10pm, Fri–Sat 11am–10pm, Sun 11am–9pm.

Inexpensive

Camellia Grill ★★ DINER/CASUAL FARE Even though it's only been a part of the city's food culture since 1946, the white-columned Camellia Grill seems to have always been here. We go for luncheonette-style counter service with white linens, Southern hospitality, witty banter dished out by white-jacketed servers, and a classic grill-top burger. The omelets manage to be simultaneously hefty and fluffy and come in the standard varieties (if it's been a rough night, we go with chili cheese; that would be American cheese—the square stuff). Late-night hours make it a popular after-club spot, but any time is good for the chocolate pecan pie (heated on the grill and a la mode, please). Good prices, true character.

626 S. Carrollton Ave. ℂ **504/309-2679.** All items under $12. Sun–Thurs 8am–midnight; Fri–Sat 8am–2am.

Casamento's ★★★ SEAFOOD Probably the best "erster" joint in the city, Casamento's takes its oysters so seriously that it simply closes down when they're not in peak season (well, Gulf oysters are always in season nowadays, but everyone needs a vacation). The subway-tiled restaurant has been family owned since 1919. The oysters are scrubbed clean and well selected; the shucker is a hoot (if you dare him, he'll shoot a bivalve into your mouth from across the room). You should absolutely take the plunge and order oyster loaf: a whole loaf of bread fried in butter, filled with oysters (or shrimp), and fried again to seal it. Seriously.

4330 Magazine St. www.casamentosrestaurant.com.ℂ **504/895-9761.** Entrees $9–$24; some items, including oysters, market price. No credit cards. Thurs–Sat 11am–2pm and 5:30–9pm, Sun 5–9pm. Closed mid-May to mid-Sept.

Dat Dog ★ CASUAL FARE This darling of the gourmet hot-dog boom ought to satisfy any dog-related craving, what with 16 types of franks and sausages (including vegan options) and umpteen toppings. Success depends on your personal selections—as dog traditionalists, we prefer brats and imported German wieners over the gator, turducken, or crawfish dogs. Still, we admit the duck version with blackberry sauce was darn good, and the fluffy buns held up well. There are burgers and chicken-breast sammies, too. The bright blue buildings make for an easy, fun hang with a brew and your crew (the gallery overlooking Frenchmen St. has a stellar view of the madding crowds) and an inexpensive dinner (though it's still a $10+/– hot dog).

5030 Freret St. www.datdog.com. ℂ **504/899-6883.** All items under $10. Mon–Sat 11am–10pm; Sun 11am–9pm. Also at 3336 Magazine St. ℂ **504/324-2226**) and 601 Frenchmen St. ℂ **504/309-3362**).

District Donuts. Sliders. Brew ★★ LIGHT FARE/BAKERY The idea sounds like it emerged from a 4am brainstorm after a very long frat party. At the genius frat. The sliders come in cheeseburger, fried chicken, and tofu every day and three other rotating varieties. Pork belly and oysters show up frequently (which is to your benefit). They're invariably carefully topped with house-made dressings, slaws, or a balancing bit of greenery—like a spicy avocado goat-cheese schmear on softshell crab. Donuts follow a similar pattern: You can always get a good ol' glazed, chocolate, or cinnamon sugar, and then the donut heavens open. Fresh-fruit-jelly-filled (pomegranate, muscadine, whatever's at the farmer's market), Nutella-drenched, tart lemon ginger,

road trip EATS

You can snag plenty of good eats in the city's nearby suburbs and parishes. These local favorites are well worth the 10- to 30-minute drive:

- **Blue Crab ★★** For a city that lies between two bodies of water, there's scant waterfront dining. Here's your opportunity. It's seafood, 'natch. Boats tie up. Partying happens. 7900 Lakeshore Dr., Metairie; www.thebluecrabnola.com; ℂ **504/284-2898;** $12–$26; Tues–Sun 11am–9pm.

- **Dong Phuong ★★★** New Orleans has a huge, vibrant Vietnamese population and the restaurant scene reflects it. Head east for the best *banh mi* (on legendary French bread) and baked goods, as a 2018 James Beard Award corroborated. 14207 Chef Menteur Hwy., N.O. East; ℂ **504/254-0214;** $3–$12; Wed–Mon 8am–5pm.

- **Middendorf's ★★★** This classic on-the-water joint fries up the crispiest, freshest catfish imaginable. 30160 Hwy. 51 South, Akers; ℂ **985/386-6666;** $12–$22.50; Wed–Sun 10:30am–9pm.

- **Mosca's ★★★** Generations of New Orleanians make the drive, wait the wait for killer old-school Sicilian classics served family style, and categorically deny allegations that it's a former (or current) mob hangout. 4137 U.S. Hwy. 90 West, Avondale; www.moscasrestaurant.com; ℂ **504/436-8950;** $12–$40; no credit cards; Tues–Sat 5:30–9pm; closed Tues during summer.

- **R&O's ★★** This thoroughly unpretentious old-school neighborhood joint serves po' boys, fried seafood, Italian essentials. 216 Hammond Hwy., Metairie; www.r-opizza.com; ℂ **504/831-1248;** $9–$23; Mon–Tues 11am–3pm; Wed–Thurs 11am–3pm and 5–9pm; Fri–Sat 11am–10pm; Sun 11am–9pm.

maple bacon Sriracha . . . Ri.Di.Culous. Surprisingly, the "Brew" has nothing to do with beer (pardon our misguided frat presumption): It's coffee, pulled from taps, including a super-smooth nitrogen cold-brewed version. Go at off-peak times to avoid lines. The Uptown outpost, **District Donuts & Coffee Bar** (5637 Magazine St.; ℂ **504/313-1316**) offers savories and sweetness tucked into a dainty, buttery half-moon crusty.

2209 Magazine St. www.districtdonuts.com. ℂ **504/570-6945.** Everything under $9. Daily 7am–9pm.

Domilise Po' Boys ★★ LIGHT FARE   Under "Classic Neighborhood Joint," reference materials list a picture of Domilise's (or could). At this century-old, cluttered, lowdown poor-boy shop tucked away Uptown, your hands-down order is the wet-dry, battered-and-fried-to-order shrimp, piled onto puffy poor-boy loaves by friendly fry-counter ladies. Peak lunchtime can move slowly along (take a number), and tables are scant. Don't ever change, Domilise.

5240 Annunciation St. www.domilisespoboys.com. ℂ **504/899-9126.** Po'boys $8.50–$19. Mon–Fri 10am–6:30pm; Sat 10:30am–7pm.

Heard Dat Kitchen ★★ SOUL FOOD The restaurant seats about a dozen people—but the napkins are linen. The neighborhood looks sketchy—but the neighbors are friendly. It makes no matter; the food is worth the trip for those interested in "The Real New Orleans" (you're well out of the tourist zones, into an area where the city's 24% poverty rate is evident). You'll also see some beautiful old homes, a sparkling new community center, and plates presented with the pride of ownership that Jeff Heard imbues in all his soulful, home-cooked dishes. His "Superdome," a dome of mashed potatoes atop a crispy catfish filet, topped with wafer-thin onion rings and surrounded by crab and crawfish creamed corn, is pretty much all you need to eat this week—and so worth it. But get the stuffed bell pepper if it's available.

2520 Felicity St. www.HeardDatKitchen.com. ℂ **504/510-4248.** Entrees $10–$17. Mon–Sat 11am–9pm.

High Hat ★★★ CONTEMPORARY SOUTHERN Located on popular and post-Katrina pioneer Freret Street (see the box on p. 142), this casual neighborhood spot had nothing to go on but an idea and original tile floors. What a go they've made of it. It's become one of our no-fail, go-to spots for unfussy, reasonable lunches and dinners made with obvious care. We come for the always interesting drinks. We come for graceful oyster fennel soup, and upgraded Southern comfort foods, like a mound of fork-tender slow-roasted pork with sublime braised greens and addictive mac n' cheese. But mostly we come for the plateful of fried awesomeness that is the catfish: crispy, light, piled high, and accompanied by tangy slaw and house-made tartar sauce (everything here save the Delta tamales is chef-made on-site, even the condiments). Then we get whatever oven-fresh pie is available, and the insane Grillswith—a grilled donut topped with melting ice cream—because it would be equally insane to skip it.

4500 Freret St. www.highhatcafe.com. ℂ **504/754-1336.** Everything under $20. Daily 11am–9pm.

Joey K's ★ CREOLE/SEAFOOD/DINER This corner hangout gets locals and a few visitors who know that the trout Tchoupitoulas—a rocking pan-fried trout topped with grilled veggies and shrimp—is worth a stop if you're out for a shop. Service is beyond friendly, and the menu is a solid mix of local dishes. Daily blackboard specials such as brisket, lamb shank, and white beans with pork chops are tasty, and somehow we often end up around this stretch of Magazine when hunger strikes.

3001 Magazine St. www.joeyksrestaurant.com. ℂ **504/891-0997.** Everything under $21. Mon–Sat 11am–9pm; Sun 10:30am–3pm.

Surrey's ★★★ CASUAL FARE No embellishment needed, just a straightforward, unfancy breakfast-and-lunch cafe with a straightforward menu and fresh-juice bar, where most everything is homemade and really good. Corned-beef andouille hash is outstanding; deeply house-smoked turkey uplifts a no-fuss turkey-avocado sandwich. OMG award goes to the felonious sugar- and rum-drenched French toast stuffed with bananas Foster. The creamy crab melt isn't far behind. No wonder there's always a line of locals at both locations (no reservations).

1418 Magazine St. (© **504/524-3827**) and 4807 Magazine St. (© **504/895-5757**). www. surreysnola.com. Daily 8am–3pm. Everything under $15. No reservations.

Turkey & the Wolf ★★★ CASUAL FARE   In 2017, *Bon Appetit* magazine named this Irish Channel hideaway best new restaurant in the country. *In the country,* people. *For a sandwich shop.* With counter service and a menu loaded with elevated stoner food. And yet, go . . . taste . . . understand. The goodness stems from comfort, creativity, a dollop of hilarity, a side of wackiness, and talent. Thick-cut fried custom-made bologna, kettle chips, and gooey American cheese are stuffed between fat white bread slabs. Even slow-stewed, heat-spiked collard greens make their way into a sandwich, oozing with cheese and Russian dressing. Deviled eggs are topped with chicken-skin *chicarrones* and house-made hot sauce. Then, for those who have (or make) room, homemade vanilla soft-serve comes with rainbow sprinkles (okay) or tahini and date molasses (whoa). I mean, you gotta laugh. And you gotta eat. *Bonus:* Drinks are equally creative and carefully wrought. *Double-bonus:* Adorbs vintage salt and pepper shakers. Madcap sister spot **Molly's Rise & Shine** (2368 Magazine St.; www.mollysriseandshine.com; © **504/302-1896**) follows the pattern (tasty wacky retro excess) for breakfasts.

739 Jackson Ave. www.turkeyandthewolf.com. © **504/218-7428**. Everything under $13. Mon and Wed–Sat 11am–5pm; Sun 11am–3pm.

COFFEE, BAKERIES & DESSERT

For other sweet treats, see **"Candies, Pralines & Pastries"** in chapter 9, p. 239; also **Bakery Bar** (p. 225); **Bywater Bakery** (p. 116); and **Willa Jean** (p. 130).

Angelo Brocato Ice Cream & Confectionery ★★★ ICE CREAM/DESSERT   Though this sweet, genuine ice cream parlor celebrated its 100th birthday under 5 feet of water, it's long since come back—and ostensibly not a thing has changed. The Brocato family (who have run this since 1905) make rich Italian ice cream and ices, cookies, and pastries amid a wonderful throw-back atmosphere (anchored by a portrait of Angelo himself, and a stunning copper-and-brass espresso machine). Italian flavors like *stracciatella* (chocolate chip) and panna cotta are capital-P Perfect; hard-to-find specialties like spumoni and cassata are spot-on; and the fresh lemon ice is legendary (don't try to decide between that and seasonal fresh fruit ices, blood orange or passion fruit; just get both). After that we get a freshly filled cannoli. Heck yeah, we do. And a slice of the ricotta torta. We tell them it's for a party.

214 N. Carrollton Ave. www.angelobrocatoicecream.com. © **504/486-1465.** Everything under $10. Tues–Thurs 10am–10pm; Fri–Sat 10am–10:30pm; Sun 10am–9pm.

Café du Monde ★★★ COFFEE/DESSERT   Excuse us while we wax rhapsodic. Since 1862, iconic Café du Monde has been selling café au lait and beignets (and nothing but) on the edge of Jackson Square. A New Orleans

bean FREAKS

Single-source, third-wave, cold-pressed, pour-over-only people might be satisfied at one of these spots. *Might*. All except purist Spitfire offer some variation on pastries and light savory fare.

- **Backatown ★★** (Tremé): 301 Basin St. (www.backatownnola.com; ✆ **504/372-4442;** Mon–Fri 7am–7pm, Sat–Sun 8am–5pm).

- **Coffee Science ★★★** (Mid-City): 410 S. Broad St. (www.coffeesciencenola.com; ✆ **504/814-0878;** daily 7am–5pm).

- **French Truck ★★★**: www.frenchtruckcoffee.com. **French Quarter:** 217 Chartres St. (✆ **504/605-2899;** Mon–Fri 7am–6pm, Sat–Sun 8am–6pm). **Lower Garden District:** 1200 Magazine St. (✆ **504/298-1115;** Mon–Fri 7am–6pm, Sat–Sun 8am–6pm). **Uptown:** 4536 Dryades St.

(✆ **504/702-1900;** Mon–Fri 6:30am–6pm, Sat–Sun 7:30am–6pm). **CBD:** 640 Poydras St. (✆ **504/800-8090;** Mon–Fri 7am–6pm, Sat 8am–2pm). Other locations.

- **Mammoth Espresso ★★** (Warehouse District): 821 Baronne St. (www.mammothespresso.com; ✆ **504/475-4344;** Mon–Fri 7am–5pm, Sat–Sun 7am–3pm).

- **Old Road Coffee ★★★** (Tremé): 2024 Bayou Rd. (www.oldroadcoffee.com; ✆ **504/354-8814;** daily 6:30am–6pm).

- **Orange Couch ★★★** (Marigny): 2339 Royal St. (www.theorangecouchcoffee.com; ✆ **504/267-7327;** daily 7am–5pm).

- **Spitfire ★★** (French Quarter): 627 St. Peter St. (✆ **504/384-0655;** daily 8am–8pm).

landmark, it's a must-stop for fried goodness and people-watching, 24 hours a day. A beignet (ben-*yay*) is a square French doughnut–type object, steaming-hot and covered in powdered sugar. You might be tempted to shake off some of the sugar. Don't. Trust us. Spoon more on, even (just beware not to inhale as you ingest); at three to an order for under $4, they're a hell of a deal. Wash them down with chicory café au lait (good with extra powdered sugar) or really good hot chocolate. Feeling guilty? The fresh orange juice is excellent, too, and presumably has vitamins. *Tip #1:* Don't wait for a clean table. Just sit—if it's dirty, the surly servers will eventually clear them. *Tip #2:* The takeout line is around the back. If that line is long, be advised that the line for a table generally moves faster. *Tip #3:* Or just go to the location in the Outlet Collection at Riverwalk (p. 234), or the one in the midst of glorious oak-filled City Park (p. 181). *Tip #4:* Don't wear black.

800 Decatur St. www.cafedumonde.com. ✆ **504/525-4544.** 3 beignets $2.73. Cash only. Daily 24 hr. Also in City Park (3325 Severn Ave. in the Casino Bldg.; Sun–Thurs 7am–9pm, Fri–Sat 7am–10pm) and Outlet Collection (500 Port of New Orleans; ✆ **504/218-7993;** Mon–Sat 10am–7pm, Sun 11am–6pm). All closed Christmas Eve & Day.

Creole Creamery ★★★ ICE CREAM/DESSERT Shakes and malts and scoops, oh my! Thick, luscious, truly fabulous ice cream and sorbets with a rotating list of standard and exotic flavors, from lavender-honey and absinthe

A snoball's CHANCE

Shaved-ice clone? Let us assure you: It's no such thing. These mouthwatering concoctions are made with custom machines that shave the ice so fine that skiers envy the powder. The better proprietors make their own flavored syrups, and the flavors—including exotic ones such as wedding cake (almond, mostly), nectar (think cream soda, only much better), and orchid cream vanilla (bright purple that must be seen to be believed)—are absolutely delectable. Order them with condensed or evaporated milk if you prefer your refreshing drinks on the decadently creamy side, or go further—some shops have started spiking them with booze. Or double the decadence with a **hot rod**—a snoball stuffed with ice cream. At any time on a hot day, lines can be out the door, and like so many other local specialties, loyalties are fierce. You should stop in at any snoball stand you see, but the following are worth seeking out. Hours vary, so call ahead; most open midday until 7 or 8pm, and many close for winter. Go with a sweet tooth and get plenty of napkins.

The snoballs at **Hansen's Sno-Bliz** ★★★ (4801 Tchoupitoulas St.; www.snobliz.com; ℂ **504/891-9788**) are a revered city tradition, still served with a smile by third-generation owner Ashley Hansen, who officially took over after her grandparents died in the months following Katrina (and won the 2014 James Beard "American Classic" award). Those grandparents invented the shaved-ice machine in use here and elsewhere and concocted their own proprietary syrups. Snoballs come in a souvenir cup. Try the bubble-gum-flavored Sno-bliz.

Plum St. Snoballs ★★★ (1300 Burdette St.; www.plumstreetsnoball.com; ℂ **504/866-7996**) has been cooling New Orleanians for more than 70 years, serving favorites in Chinese food containers. Fans of **Pandora's** ★★★ (901 S. Carrollton Ave.; ℂ **504/289-0765**) say its ice is the softest anywhere, and the flavor list is so long it's taking over the neighborhood. You'll have to fight the hordes of school kids in line, even, it often seems, during school hours. **Imperial Woodpecker** ★★ (3511 Magazine St.; www.iwsnoballs.com; ℂ **251/366-7777**) has the edge on exotic and contemporary flavors, like black sesame, cardamom, and cereal cream, while **NOLA Sips** (2633 St. Claude Ave.; www.nolasips.com; ℂ **504/314-1192**) covers the boozy and over-the-top snoball market.

to red velvet cake and tiramisu. Fortunately, they offer a sampler of four or six mini-scoops. Refreshing, maybe even mandatory in summer, and open late enough for a scoop on the way to or from an Uptown club or bar.

4924 Prytania St. (look for the old McKenzie's sign). www.creolecreamery.com. ℂ **504/894-8680.** Most items under $10. No credit cards. Sun–Thurs noon–10pm; Fri–Sat noon–11pm.

Croissant D'Or ★★ COFFEE/BAKERY A quiet and calm place with the same snacks you might find in a cosmopolitan coffeehouse, and you can almost always find an open table inside or in the pretty courtyard. Are the pastries and croissants made of gold? The prices feel like it sometimes, but they are credibly, crustily French. Quiches and light sandwiches as well.

617 Ursulines St. www.croissantdornola.com. ℂ **504/524-4663.** Everything under $8. Wed–Mon 6am–3pm.

Gracious Bakery ★★ COFFEE/BAKERY/CASUAL FARE   Three cute locations serve fresh and yummy pastries, sweets, and terrific sandwiches.

Garden District: 2854 St. Charles Ave. Uptown: 4930 Prytania St. Mid-City: 1000 S. Jefferson Davis Pkwy. www.graciousbakery.com. ℂ **504/301-3709.** Everything under $12. Garden District & Uptown Mon–Fri 7am–6pm; Sat–Sun 7am–4pm. Mid-City Mon–Fri 7am–3pm, Sat–Sun 8am–2pm.

La Boulangerie ★★ BAKERY/CASUAL FARE   Crusty baguettes and oven-warm loaves of many varieties; fresh fruit tarts and Danish; house-smoked salmon on house-baked bagels; sandwiches with cured meats from **Cochon Butcher** (p. 132); and homemade ice cream (on waffle cones baked here) . . . this French bakery is an Uptown neighborhood staple, with good reason. Don't let anyone tell you how good it was under the former owner—just enjoy how good it is now, especially as it adds even more lunch options.

4600 Magazine St. laboulangerienola.com. ℂ **504/269-3777.** Everything under $12. Mon–Sat 6am–6pm; Sun 7am–4pm.

Parish Ice Cream Parlor ★★ ICE CREAM/DESSERT   The luscious small-batch homemade ice creams, sorbets and custards here drew us in with their creamy fruit-and-ganache combos (strawberry with white chocolate ganache; coconut with dark chocolate ganache), but rotating seasonal flavors made us habitual users (please oh please oh please bring back the maple custard with waffle pieces and bacon bits). Is there rehab for Parish Parlor abusers? Be glad your vacation has an end date, lest you end up with a habit like ours.

1912 Magazine St. www.parishparlor.com. ℂ **504/302-2244.** $4–$8. Sun–Thurs noon–9pm; Fri–Sat noon–10pm.

P.J.'s Coffee & Tea Company ★★ COFFEE   This locally based chain has many locations, roasts locally, and offers a great variety of teas, coffees, and espressos. The iced coffee is made with a 12-hour cold-water process. The granita "slushee" is great on hot, muggy Louisiana days.

510 Decatur St.; 2140 Magazine St.; 630 St. Charles Ave.; in the Royal Sonesta and Doubletree hotels; and about 15 other New Orleans locations. www.pjscoffee.com. Everything under $8. Most locations open 6am–9pm (sometimes later Sat and Sun).

EXPLORING NEW ORLEANS

By Lavinia Spalding

7

We've made no secret of our favorite New Orleans activities: walking, eating, people-watching, listening to music, dancing, and eating again. But between those activities, there's much to see, do, and experience. New Orleans is a vibrant, visual, utterly authentic city with a rich history and gobs of culture worthy of your time.

While the French Quarter is certainly a seductive place, going to New Orleans and never leaving the Quarter is like visiting Times Square and believing you've seen New York. Stroll the lush Garden District, marvel at the live oaks in City Park, ride the streetcar on St. Charles Avenue and gape at the gorgeous homes, or go visit some gators on a swamp tour. Take a walk along Bayou St. John, tour the remarkable Tremé neighborhood, or ride a bike through the Bywater. We'll guide you to some of the city's amazing museums, diverse neighborhoods, and prettiest parks, with suggestions for action-lovers and armchair adventurers, history buffs, and party animals.

Exploring New Orleans Safely

During the pandemic, many attractions began to require that visitors show vaccination proof or results of a recent negative test. At the time of publication, mask mandates were in place even for vaccinated individuals, and masks were required on public transportation, in ride-shares, and in healthcare facilities. Depending on surges and variants, the mandate could be reinstated when you visit, so pack a mask in case. Depending on public health orders, some business hours may also be curtailed, and guided tours may be limited. Please keep in mind that a number of attractions closed temporarily when Covid and Ida hit the city hard but should be reopened in time for your visit. It's always best to check social media sites or call, since, to be frank, keeping websites updated isn't on the list of things New Orleans does best.

THE FRENCH QUARTER

Those who have been to Disneyland might be forgiven if they experience some déjà vu upon first seeing the French Quarter. The same might be said for those who have visited Paris. It's more worn than Disneyland, of course, and more compact than Paris, on which it was based. But despite the fact that Walt actually did replicate a French Quarter street in Disneyland's New Orleans Square, there ain't nothing like the real thing, baby—and there's certainly no other square mile in the U.S. that resembles the French Quarter. This one turned 300 years old in 2018 and is one of the most interesting neighborhoods in America. The endless eyefuls of florid architecture, the copious cultural oddities, and the stories that emanate from the very streets make it easy to look beyond the ubiquitous souvenir shops and bars. We make the occasional foray to Bourbon Street in all its tacky, outlandish, odoriferous glory, and we believe there's an argument for experiencing it (at least once). But the operative word is "occasional." (And you also have our blessing to skip it *entirely* and spend your time and money elsewhere.) The key to this city is getting out and fully exploring it. Still: It's New Orleans, so as the Rebirth Brass Band song goes: "Do Whatcha Wanna." (Within reason, of course.)

A French engineer named Adrien de Pauger designed the Quarter in 1718. Almost all of the buildings burned in the fires of 1788 and 1794, though, and were rebuilt while the city was under Spanish ownership, so in truth, the architecture is mostly Spanish, not French. But much French culture remains, and today the Vieux Carré ("Old Square") is a great anomaly in America, where many other cities have torn down or gutted their historic centers. Thanks to a strict local preservation policy, the area looks much as it has since the late 18th century, and it's still the heart of town.

Jackson Square bustles with musicians, artists, fortune-tellers, jugglers, and those mesmerizing "living statue" performance artists who entertain for change (we try to always carry some $1 bills to throw in the hat of those who catch our eye or ear). Pay attention to that seemingly ad hoc jazz band playing right in front of the Cabildo—these talented musicians might be in jeans now but may very well be in tie and tux later, playing high-end clubs. **Royal Street,** our favorite for strolling, is home to stellar street musicians, numerous antiques shops, and galleries. You'll also encounter interesting stores on **Chartres** and **Decatur Streets** and the cross streets between.

The closer you get to **Esplanade Avenue** and toward **Rampart Street,** the more residential the Quarter becomes (in the business sections, the ground floors are commercial and the stories above are often apartments). Peep in through any open gate, where surprises await in the form of graceful brick- and flagstone-lined courtyards filled with foliage and bubbling fountains. At the same time, be mindful that throughout the Quarter, you are walking by people's homes. Please be courteous, quiet, and clean, folks.

The Vieux Carré Commission is ever vigilant about balancing contemporary economic interests in the Quarter with historical preservation. There are

New Orleans Attractions

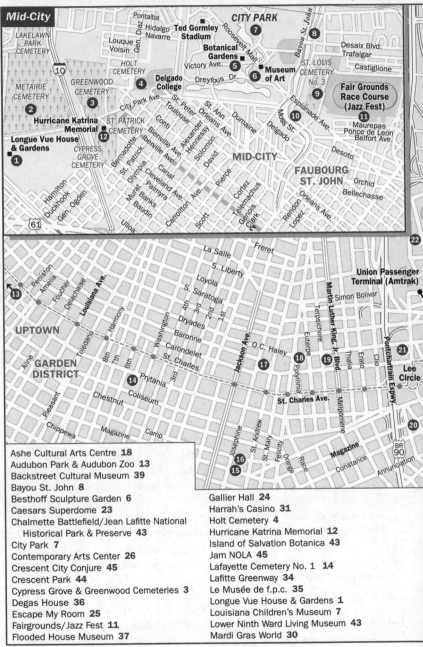

7

The French Quarter

EXPLORING NEW ORLEANS

Mid-City

LAKELAWN PARK CEMETERY

METAIRIE CEMETERY

2 Hurricane Katrina Memorial

ST. PATRICK CEMETERY

12

Longue Vue House & Gardens

1

CYPRESS GROVE CEMETERY

GREENWOOD CEMETERY

HOLT CEMETERY

4 Delgado College

City Park Ave.

Pontalba

Hidalgo

Navarre

Louque

Voisin

Gen. Diaz

5 Botanical Gardens

Victory Ave.

Dreyfous Dr.

Ted Gormley Stadium

CITY PARK

Roosevelt Mall

7

6 Museum of Art

8

Bayou St. John

Desaix Blvd.

Trafalgar

ST. LOUIS CEMETERY No. 3

Castiglione

9

Fair Grounds Race Course (Jazz Fest)

11 Maurepas

Ponce de Leon

Belfort Ave.

Esplanade Ave.

10

Moss St.

Delgado

Desoto

MID-CITY

FAUBOURG ST. JOHN

Orchid

Bellechasse

St. Peter

Orleans Ave.

St. Ann

Dumaine

Toulouse

Conti

Bienville Ave.

Bernadotte

St. Patrick

Ibervia Ave.

Olympia

Murat

Banks

Baudin

Ulloa

Alexander

Hennessy

Solomon

David

Canal

Cleveland Ave.

Palmyra

Carrollton Ave.

Scott

Pierce

Cortez

Telemachus

Genois

Clark

Rendon

Lopez

Orleans Ave.

Hamilton

Duckhook

Gen. Ogden

La Salle

Freret

22

Penison

Amelia

Foucher

Delachaise

Louisiana Ave.

S. Liberty

Loyola

S. Saratoga

4th

3rd

2nd

1st

S. Dryades

Union Passenger Terminal (Amtrak)

13

UPTOWN

GARDEN DISTRICT

Aline

Toledano

Harmony

Washington

Baronne

Carondelet

St. Charles

Prytania

Coliseum

Chestnut

Magazine

Camp

Pleasant

Chippewa

8th

7th

6th

3rd

14

Jackson Ave.

O.C. Haley

17

18

19

Martin Luther King, Jr. Blvd.

Simon Bolivar

Terpsichore

Euterpe

Polymnia

Thalia

Clio

Erato

21

Lee Circle

St. Charles Ave.

Melpomene

Pontchartrain Expwy.

Josephine

St. Andrew

St. Mary

Felicity

Orange

Race

Magazine

Constance

Annunciation

16

15

20

BR 90

Information
Riverfront streetcar route/stops
St. Charles streetcar route/stops
Canal St. streetcar route/stops
Rampart St./ St. Claude Ave. streetcar route/stops
0 1/4 mi
0 0.25 km
Lake Pontchartrain
Mid-City
CITY PARK
Superdome
Main Map
N. Broad St.
N. Dorgenois
N. Rocheblave
N. Tonti
N. Miro
N. Galvez
N. Johnson
N. Prieur
N. Roman
Derbigny
LAFITTE GREENWAY
LaFitte Ave.
Orleans Ave.
St. Ann
Dumaine
St. Phillip
Ursulines Ave.
Bayou Rd.
Esplanade
TREMÉ
N. Claiborne Ave.
St. Bernard Ave.
ST. LOUIS CEMETERY NO. 2
Caesar's Superdome
See "French Quarter Attractions" map
ST. LOUIS CEMETERY NO. 1
LOUIS ARMSTRONG PARK
N. Villere
Congo Square
Basin St.
N. Rampart
Poydras
Common
Loyola Ave.
S. Rampart
O'Keefe St.
Lafayette
Gravier
Perdido
Union
Univ. Pl.
Conti
St. Louis
Toulouse
St. Ann
Dumaine
Dauphine
Burgundy
Barracks
Esplanade
Iberville
Bienville
FRENCH QUARTER
Bourbon
Royal
Ursulines
Gov. Nicholls
Chartres
Decatur
French Market
FAUBOURG MARIGNY
Touro
Frenchmen
Elysian Fields Ave.
Chartres St.
Marigny
Mandeville
Spain
CENTRAL BUSINESS DISTRICT
Carondelet
St. Charles Ave.
Lafayette Square
Poydras
Canal
Camp
Julia
Girod
Magazine St.
Tchoupitoulas
Commerce
S. Peters
Fulton
Conv. Ctr. Blvd.
St. Joseph
Howard Ave.
Calliope
RIVERFRONT
Riverfront streetcar closed for construction until 2022-2023
Mississippi River
Canal St. Ferry (Toll)

McKenna Museum of African-American Art **17**
Metairie Cemetery **2**
Museum of the Southern Jewish Experience **21**
National World War II Museum **20**
New Orleans African American Museum **40**
New Orleans Botanical Gardens & Train Garden **5**
New Orleans Museum of Art **6**
Lower Ninth Ward Living Museum **43**
Ogden Museum of Southern Art **27**
Pitot House **10**
Sazerac House **29**
Smoothie King Arena **22**
Southern Food and Beverage Museum/ Museum of the American Cocktail **19**
St. Alphonsus Church **15**
St. Augustine Church **41**
St. Louis Cemetery No. 1 **33**
St. Louis Cemetery No. 2 **32**
St. Louis Cemetery No. 3 **9**
St. Mary's Assumption **16**
St. Patrick's Church **28**
St. Roch Cemetery and the Campo Santo **43**
Studio BE **43**
Treme's Petit Jazz Museum **38**
Voodoo Spiritual Temple **42**

few chain stores or restaurants, and no traffic lights in the whole interior of the French Quarter (they're relegated to fringe streets); streetlights are the old gaslight style. Large city buses are banned, and during part of each day, Royal and Bourbon streets are pedestrian malls. No vehicles are *ever* allowed around Jackson Square. The Quarter streets are laid out in an almost perfect rectangular grid, so they're easily navigable. They're also well-traveled and thus relatively safe. Again, as you near the fringes and as night falls, you should exercise caution; stay in the busy, well-lit parts, walk briskly, and try not to walk alone.

The French Quarter **walking tour** in chapter 10 will give you the best overview of the historic structures in the area and its history. Many other attractions that aren't in the walking tour are listed in this chapter (and mapped on p. 152), so make sure to cross-reference as you go along.

As mentioned elsewhere, driving in the French Quarter isn't ideal. But if you must, and you're planning a full day of sightseeing in the Quarter, check out our parking tips on p. 289.

Major Attractions

Audubon Aquarium of the Americas ★★★ Penguin evacuees made a star-studded post-Katrina return via a chartered FedEx flight here, waddling home down a (FedEx) purple carpet as news cameras rolled. Then, rescued sea turtles were rehabilitated here after the Gulf oil spill. In Hurricane Ida—the city's most recent big storm—no aquarium lives were lost. In fact, a life was added: A cownose ray gave birth to a pup (named, of course, Ida). These instances point up just how relevant this world-class aquarium is, besides being full of cool fishies. Its focus on the Mississippi and Gulf of Mexico is highly entertaining and painlessly educational for kids and grown-ups. We love the huge interior rainforest, complete with birds and piranhas. A major highlight is feeding the birds at Parakeet Pointe, an outdoor space on the second floor: You can buy a seed stick from the concession stand for $1.50 and prepare to be popular with parakeets! (At press time, this was closed due to Covid-19, but it's truly delightful, so check back!) Also unmissable: a fine exhibit on seahorses, a rare leucistic (white, blue-eyed) gator, and a 13,000-gallon shark and ray touch pool. The outdoor splash fountain is irresistible on a warm day. Right on the edge of the Quarter, the aquarium is a handy refuge from the heat or rain. Big plans are afoot now to move the **Audubon Insectarium and Butterfly Garden,** formerly nearby on Canal Street, into the Aquarium in 2023, with new immersive exhibits dedicated to all things bug and arachnid. Many favorites from the Insectarium's previous location will make the move, and an expansive glass-roofed butterfly pavilion will be an especially beautiful and peaceful departure from the hustle outside.

1 Canal St., at the river. www.auduboninstitute.org. (C) **800/774-7394** or 504/861-2537. $30 adults, $25 seniors and children 2–12. Thurs–Mon 10am–5pm. Closed Mardi Gras, Thanksgiving, and Christmas.

French Quarter Attractions

Audubon Aquarium of the Americas **27**
Beauregard-Keyes House **22**
The Cabildo **11**
Café du Monde **20**
The 1850 House **17**
The French Market **24**
Gallier House Museum **21**
Germaine Wells Mardi Gras Museum **4**
Hermann-Grima House **6**
Historic New Orleans Collection **7**
Jean Lafitte's Old Absinthe House **5**
Madame John's Legacy **15**
Museum of Death **3**
New Orleans Historical
   Pharmacy Museum **10**

New Orleans Historic
   Voodoo Museum **14**
New Orleans Jazz Museum
   at the Old U.S. Mint **25**
Old Ursuline Convent **23**
Our Lady of Guadalupe Chapel –
   International Shrine of St. Jude **2**
Pontalba Buildings **18, 19**
The Presbytère **13**
Preservation Hall **8**
St. Louis Cathedral **12**
St. Louis Cemetery No. 1 **1**
Williams Research Center **9**
Woldenberg Riverfront Park **26**
Voodoo Authentica **16**

The French Market ★★ The site of the French Market was originally used as a bartering market by Indigenous peoples, including the Chitimacha, Choctaw, Ishak, Tunica, and Natchez nations. What's known today as the French Market is said to have been founded by the Oumas people, who sold goods to travelers (including Bienville, "founder" of New Orleans). It grew into an official market in 1812. From around 1840 to 1870, it was part of Gallatin Street, a rough area full of bars, drunken sailors, and criminals. Today it's a mixed bag and not nearly as dynamic as its past, but still a fun, historic amble. The foodstuffs, from produce and seafood to more tourist-oriented items like hot sauces and Cajun spice mixes, are pricier than at local supermarkets—but here they'll pack it for air travel or ship it home. Snacks like gator on a stick will amuse the kids, while the oyster bar and food vendors will satisfy grown-ups (**Meals from the Heart** is a standout). The **farmer's market** is open every day (10am–5pm), and in non-Covid times, there's entertainment (music, cooking demos) on Saturdays and Wednesdays, which livens things up and harkens back to what it was once like here. The famed **flea market** section (daily 10am–5pm) is kind of junky, but sprinkled among the T-shirts, caps, and cheap sunglasses are a few original art vendors (some original art here is tax-free). It's convenient for souvenir shopping and New Orleans–related trinkets, especially inexpensive silver jewelry and all manner of fleur-de-lis. If you've outshopped your luggage, you can pick up a duffle bag or small suitcase. There are all-important clean public bathrooms here. 1235 N. Peters St. (from Jackson Sq. to Barracks St.). www.frenchmarket.org. ⓒ **504/522-2621.** Shop hours vary but generally 10am–5pm.

St. Louis Cathedral ★ St. Louis Cathedral is the oldest continuously active site of a cathedral in the U.S. The stately, iconic building is certainly pretty, but the rather staid interior barely gives a nod to the grand cathedrals of Europe. Still, history and spirituality seep from within, so venture in—if you're lucky, you may catch a choir practice. Volunteer docents, available most weekdays, are full of fun facts about the windows and murals and how the building nearly collapsed once from water-table sinkage. Note the sloping floor: Clever architectural design somehow keeps the building upright even as it continues to sink. Outside, a statue and plaque mark the visit by Pope John Paul II in 1987.

The cathedral formed the center of the original settlement and remains the French Quarter's central landmark. This is the third building to stand on this spot. A hurricane destroyed the first in 1722. On Good Friday 1788, the bells of the second cathedral structure were kept silent for religious reasons (or wind, some say) rather than ringing out the alarm for a fire—which eventually burned down that cathedral and 850 other buildings. It was rebuilt in 1794 and remodeled and enlarged between 1845 and 1851. The structure's bricks were taken from the original town cemetery and covered with stucco to protect the mortar from dampness. That issue arose again during Katrina, which caused a leaky roof to ruin the $1-million organ (it's been rebuilt).

Outside in back, you can see where two magnificent ancient live oaks fell, narrowly missing a statue of Jesus. A forefinger and thumb were amputated, however, and Archbishop-emeritus Hughes, in his first post-Katrina sermon in the cathedral, vowed not to replace them until all of New Orleans was healed. The statue was repaired in 2015. (Current Archbishop Aymond acknowledged that there was still work to be done, but he wanted to celebrate and focus on a symbol of hope as the city moved forward.) The dramatically lit statue makes a resplendent, if somewhat eerie, nighttime silhouette. Well, we think so; others call it "Touchdown Jesus"—do make a point to walk by at night to see why.

615 Pere Antoine Alley. www.stlouiscathedral.org. © **504/525-9585.** Free admission. Self-guided-tour brochure available ($1 donation); formal tours by advance reservation. Daily 9am–4pm; Mass Mon–Fri at 12:05pm, Sun 9 and 11am.

Woldenberg Riverfront Park ★★ This 16-acre linear park along the river serves as promenade and public art gallery, with numerous works by popular local and internationally known artists amid green lawns and hundreds of trees. Seek out the kinetic Holocaust memorial sculpture by noted Israeli sculptor Yaacov Agam and make a slow circle around it to get the full impact of its changing perspectives, which use a rainbow to unexpected symbolic effect. At the upriver end, you're rewarded with a splash fountain for a soggy cool-down (an excellent incentive to get kids to take a scenic walk).

It connects to the nearby **Moonwalk ★★★**, a paved pedestrian thoroughfare along the river near Jackson Square. It's a wonderful walk on a pretty New Orleans day, or in fact for any weather other than pouring rain. Newly renovated steps allow you to get right down to Old Muddy—on foggy nights, you feel as if you are floating above the water. There are many benches from which to view the city's busy port—perhaps while enjoying sugar-dusted beignets to a street musician's song, or watching the moon rise over the river. To your right is the Crescent City Connection bridge; the former World Trade Center of New Orleans skyscraper (now a super-swanky Four Seasons Hotel; see p. 78); and the Toulouse Street wharf, the departure point for excursion steamboats. There are plans to potentially connect the downriver section of the French Quarter's riverfront walkway with **Crescent Park** (p. 182) at the Faubourg Marigny border. For now, make a short jog along N. Peters St. (beside the French Market) to reach the Mandeville Crossing (a pedestrian bridge and elevators) into Crescent Park.

Along the Mississippi River from the Moonwalk to the Aquarium of the Americas at Canal St. © **504/581-4629.** Daily 6am–10pm.

Historic Buildings

Beauregard-Keyes House ★ This "raised cottage," with its Doric columns and handsome twin staircases, was built as a residence for a wealthy New Orleans auctioneer, Joseph LeCarpentier, in 1826. It's named for two other past residents: Confederate General P. G. T. Beauregard, who lived here between 1865 and 1867, and novelist Frances Parkinson Keyes (pronounced *Kize*), who resided here from 1944 until 1970. Her most famous book, *Dinner* *at Antoine's,* was penned here, as was *Madame Castel's Lodger,* concerning General Beauregard's stay in this house. Mrs. Keyes left her home to a foundation. The house, gardens, and her collections of dolls and porcelain veilleuse teapots are open to the public. Hourly tours are available, with renewed emphasis on telling the stories of the enslaved and free people of color who lived in and contributed to the building.

1113 Chartres St., at Ursuline St. www.bkhouse.org. © **504/523-7257.** $10 adults; $9 seniors, students, and AAA members; $4 children 6–12; $7.50 military; free for children 5 and under. Mon–Sat 10am–3pm. Tours on the hour. Closed holidays.

The 1850 House ★★ James Gallier, Sr., and his son designed the historic Pontalba Buildings, which include the 1850 House, for the Baroness Micaela Almonester de Pontalba (see the box on p. 159). She had these rows of town houses on either side of Jackson Square built in 1849 to combat the deterioration of the older part of the city; at the time, they were the largest private buildings in the country. Legend has it that the baroness, miffed that her friend Andrew Jackson wouldn't tip his hat to her, had his statue erected in the square, where to this day he continues to doff his chapeau toward her top-floor apartment. It's probably not true, but we never stand in the way of a good story.

The 1850 House, a branch of the Louisiana State Museum, demonstrates life in 1850, when the buildings opened for residential use. The self-guided tour uses a fact-filled sheet explaining the history of the interior, and a "soundscape" feature lets you "earwitness" sounds and conversations in the house that you might have heard in 1850. Period furnishings vividly illustrate the difference between the upstairs portion of the house, where the upper-middle-class family lived in comfort (and the children, largely confined to a nursery, were raised by enslaved people and indentured servants), and the downstairs, where servants and enslaved toiled in considerable drudgery to make the family comfortable. It's an insightful look at life in the good, and not so good, old days.

Lower Pontalba Bldg., 523 St. Ann St., Jackson Sq. www.louisianastatemuseum.org. © **800/568-6968** or 504/524-9118. $5 adults; $4 students, seniors, military; free for kids 6 and under. Tues–Sun 9:30am–3:30pm (free museum tour if you take the **Friends of the Cabildo** French Quarter walking tour, p. 193, which starts here). Closed Mon and all state holidays.

Jean Lafitte's Old Absinthe House ★ The drink for which this 1806 building was named was once outlawed in this country (unsanitary production and chemical additives, not the wormwood flavoring, caused blindness and madness). Now you can legally sip the infamous libation here and feel at one with the famous types who came before you, listed on a plaque outside: William Thackeray, Oscar Wilde, Sarah Bernhardt, and Walt Whitman—and of course, the unlikely team of Andrew Jackson and the Lafitte brothers, who plotted their desperate—and successful—defense of New Orleans here in the War of 1812. It became a speakeasy during Prohibition; before it was raided by federal officers in 1924, the antique bar and absinthe fountain mysteriously

lady bountiful: **BARONESS DE PONTALBA**

New Orleans owes a great debt to Baroness Micaela Almonester de Pontalba and her family. Without them, Jackson Square might still be a soggy mess. Her father, Don Almonester, used his money and influence to have St. Louis Cathedral, Cabildo, and Presbytère built. The baroness was responsible for the two long brick apartment buildings that flank Jackson Square and for the renovation that turned the center of the Quarter into what it is today.

Born in 1795 into the most influential family in New Orleans, the baroness married her cousin, who subsequently stole her inheritance. When she wanted a separation, at a time when such things were unheard of, her father-in-law shot her several times and then shot himself. She survived, though some of her fingers did not (nor did he). In subsequent portraits, she would hide the wounded hand in her dress. In the end, she got her money back—she used it for those French Quarter improvements—and also ended up caring for her slightly mad husband for the rest of his life. She died in Paris in 1874; her home there is now the American ambassador's residence. The book *Intimate Enemies*, by Christina Vella (Louisiana State University Press, 1997), details this remarkable woman's life.

disappeared (just as mysteriously, they later reappeared in a warehouse down the street, safe from the raiders' axes). The now divey bar is wallpapered with business cards (and day drinkers), so you won't recapture any classy, old-timey atmosphere You'll just have a drink in a genuinely fun, historic hangout. For a more upscale absinthe experience, pop across the courtyard to speakeasy-style **Belle Epoque,** where the restored original cypress bar and marble absinthe fountains live.

240 Bourbon St. www.ruebourbon.com/old-absinthe-house. © **504/523-3181.** Mon–Wed 9am–2am, Thurs and Sun 9am–3am, Fri–Sat 9am–4am. Cash only (but there's an ATM).

Old Ursuline Convent ★★   Forget tales of America being founded by brawny, brave tough guys in buckskin and beards. The real pioneers—at least, in Louisiana—were well-educated Frenchwomen clad in 40 pounds of black wool robes. That's right; you don't know tough until you know the Ursuline nuns, and this city would have been a very different place without them.

The Sisters of Ursula came to the mudhole that was New Orleans in 1727 after a journey that nearly saw them lost at sea or succumbing to pirates or disease. Here, they provided the first decent medical care (saving countless lives) and later founded the first local school and orphanage for girls. They also helped raise girls shipped over from France as marriage material for local men, providing exacting lessons in languages and etiquette, laying the foundation of many local families.

The convent dates from 1752 (the sisters themselves moved uptown in 1824, where they remain to this day), making it the oldest building in the Mississippi River Valley and the only surviving building from the French colonial period in the United States. It also houses Catholic archives dating back to 1718. The **self-guided tour** of the convent shows rooms typical of the era, as well as religious and artistic icons (the top floor, where a ghost supposedly lives, is off-limits, unfortunately). It includes access to St. Mary's Church, original site of the Ursuline convent and a former archbishop's residence. Tours take an hour or less.

1100 Chartres St., at Ursuline St. www.stlouiscathedral.org/convent-museum. © **504/529-3040.** $8 adults; $7 seniors; $6 students and military. Mon–Fri 10am–4pm (last tour 3:15), Sat 9am–3pm (last tour 2:15).

Our Lady of Guadalupe Chapel—International Shrine of St. Jude ★★

This "funeral chapel" was erected in 1826 conveniently near St. Louis Cemetery No. 1, specifically for funeral services, so as not to spread disease through the Quarter. We like it for three reasons: the catacomb-like devotional chapel with plaques thanking the Virgin Mary for favors granted; the gift shop full of religious medals, including a number of obscure saints; and the statue of St. Expedité. The saint got his name, according to legend, when his unidentified crate arrived, stamped EXPEDITE. Now he's the "saint" you pray to when you want things in a hurry (for real). Sunday 7:30 and 9:30 masses are backed by a jazz-tinged band and choir.

411 N. Rampart St. at Conti St. www.judeshrine.com. © **504/525-1551.** Gift shop Mon–Sat 9am–5pm, Sun 7am–6pm. Mass Mon–Sat starting at 7am, Sun from 7:30am.

Museums

In addition to the destinations listed here, you might be interested in the **Germaine Wells Mardi Gras Museum** at 813 Bienville St., on the second floor of **Arnaud's** restaurant (p. 97; www.arnaudsrestaurant.com/about/mardi-gras-museum; © **504/523-5433**). It has a collection of dazzling gowns worn by Wells, who reigned as queen of more than 22 Mardi Gras balls from 1937 to 1968. Admission is free, and the museum is open daily during restaurant hours.

The Cabildo ★★

One of two fine museums flanking St. Louis Cathedral in the heart of the French Quarter, the Cabildo houses the premier collection of New Orleans and Louisiana historical artifacts. It starts with the earliest explorers and covers slavery, post–Civil War reconstruction, and statehood. It is well qualified to do so: The Cabildo is where the Louisiana Purchase transfer was officially signed (this 1795 building was the seat of government at the time; at other times it served as a courthouse and a prison). The detailed history is covered from a multicultural perspective and touches on topics like pre-Civil War music, mourning and burial customs (a big deal during yellow fever epidemics), immigration and assimilation, and the role of the Southern woman. The **Napoleon Room** houses the crown jewel: Napoleon's death mask. The item and its story (it almost ended up in a trash dump) are quite fascinating.

701 Chartres St. www.louisianastatemuseum.org/museum/cabildo. © **800/568-6968** or 504/568-6968. $10 adults; $8 students, seniors, and military; free for children 6 and under. Discounts if visiting multiple Louisiana State Museums. Tues–Sun 9am–4pm (last ticket sale 3:30); closed Mon and state holidays.

Gallier House Museum ★★ James Gallier, Jr. (it's pronounced *Gaul-ee-er*, by the way—he was Irish, not French), and his father were the leading architects in New Orleans in the mid-1800s. They designed the French Opera House, Municipality Hall (now Gallier Hall), and the Pontalba Buildings (see 1850 House, p. 158). This was Junior's personal home, now meticulously restored, with the fancy furnishings appearing much as they would have when the family resided there (some claim Gallier's ghost still does). The home displays some of his innovations—such as early indoor plumbing—and a decided lack thereof in the slave quarters. It's made even more gorgeous for holiday season, with period decor; check the website for other special programs. Discounted combination tickets with the Hermann-Grima House are available.

1132 Royal St., btw. Gov. Nicholls and Ursuline Sts. www.hgghh.org. © **504/274-0748.** $15 adults; $12 seniors, students, and children 8–18; free for children 7 and under. Fri–Sun 9:30am–3:30pm; guided tours hourly starting at 9:30 or by appt; advance booking recommended. Fewer tours in summer; call to confirm.

Hermann-Grima House ★★ This symmetrical Federal-style building (perhaps the first in the Quarter) is very different from its French-style neighbors. The house, which stretches from St. Louis Street to Conti Street, passed through two different families before becoming a boardinghouse for women in the 1920s. It has been meticulously restored and researched, and a tour of the house is one of the city's more historically accurate offerings. Significant efforts are made to tell the stories of the enslaved who lived in the house (including a brand-new tour called "Urban Enslavement in New Orleans"). The knowledgeable docents make this a satisfactory stop at any time, but keep an eye out for the occasional special tours. At Halloween, the house is draped in typical 1800s mourning cloth, as docents explain mourning customs. Cooking demonstrations, using methods of the era, take place in the authentic 1830s kitchen twice a month on weekends from November to April. The house also contains the Quarter's last surviving stable, complete with stalls. A small but excellent gift shop carries women-made, local, artisanal treasures. (We love the bitters.) Discounted combo tickets with the Gallier House are available.

820 St. Louis St. www.hgghh.org. © **504/274-0750.** $15 adults; $12 seniors, students, military, and children 8–18; free for children under 8. Daily 10am–4pm; guided tours on the hour; advance booking recommended but not required.

Historic New Orleans Collection ★★★ Nine of the 10 buildings in this treasured complex have a centuries-old tale to tell; one newly built stunner is just starting to create memories. The HNOC was already chock-full of wonderful artworks, maps, and documents, but with the 2019 completion of a mega-million, tech-forward upgrade, it has vaulted to the pantheon of New Orleans' museums. (And it's free!) The new galleries, at 520 Royal Street, feature excellent interactive displays, a hands-on educational center, and the captivating, quad-projected "French Quarter at Night" film with imagery covering 300 years. Look through the virtual reality viewfinders for scenes that might have happened a few decades or centuries ago in the courtyard you're overlooking (where you can enjoy something savory or sweet from Café Cour). Another building, an elegant 1889 Italianate town house, gives a glimpse into the lives of the 1% circa the 1940s. Don't overlook exhibits at the Williams Research Center (410 Chartres St.), a grandly restored, Beaux Arts–style building that houses historical archives for serious researchers and inquisitive visitors.

520 & 533 Royal St. and 410 Chartres St. www.thnoc.org. ℂ **504/523-4662.** Free admission. Tues–Sat 9:30am–4:30pm; Royal St. locations also open Sun 10:30am–4:30pm. Advance appt. required for Williams Research Center.

Madame John's Legacy ★ This is the second-oldest building (well, parts of it) in the Mississippi Valley, after the Ursuline Convent, and a rare example of Creole architecture that miraculously survived the 1794 fire. Built around 1788 on the foundations of an earlier home that was destroyed in the fire of *that* year, the house has had a number of owners and renters (including the son of Governor Claiborne), none of them named John—or even Madame! It acquired its moniker courtesy of author George Washington Cable, who used the house as a setting for his short story *'Tite Poulette*. The protagonist was a quadroon, Madame John, named after the lover who willed this house to her. Now a Louisiana State Museum, it's undergoing extensive renovations and should reopen in fall 2022.

632 Dumaine St. www.louisianastatemuseum.org. ℂ **800/568-6968** or 504/568-6968. Free admission. Tues–Sun 10am–4:30pm.

Museum of Death ★ If vampire tours are too banal and you need more death in your death, here's all the gore you could ask for. It's graphic, no-holds-barred gruesome, for the thick-skinned only (the lobby rocking chairs are for companions who opt out; those touring the collection are advised to "sit on one of the coffins if you feel faint"). It's an outpost of a similar museum in Hollywood, one man's lurid collection of crime, accident, and autopsy photos (gunshot victims, dismemberments); serial killers' correspondence, diaries, and doodles (John Wayne Gacy's clown drawings; love letters to Jeffrey Dahmer); videos of a cannibal discussing his act; and much more. Perhaps the most thought-provoking item is the rare Thanotron, Dr. Kervorkian's suicide machine. Pick up a serial-killer "tarot card" T-shirt on the way out.

227 Dauphine St. www.museumofdeath.net/nola. ℂ **504/593-3968.** $15. Daily 10am–6pm.

New Orleans Historical Pharmacy Museum ★★★ Leeches. LEEEEECHES. Yeah, they're here. So are many other icky things, and fascinating potions, and instruments-of-torture-looking artifacts (antique surgical devices, in actuality). The first licensed pharmacist in the United States, Louis J. Dufilho, Jr., opened an apothecary shop in this Creole-style town house in 1823. This bizarre and beguiling museum opened in 1950 and displays old apothecary bottles, voodoo potions, opium products of every ilk, suppository molds, and all variant of snake oil—in exquisite wood and glass cases. Also interesting are old makeup and perfume paraphernalia, which were brewed up by pharmacists back in the day. You'll never appreciate a modern doctor's appointment more. If there's a guided tour going on, join it: They're insightful, shocking, and worth it.

514 Chartres St., at St. Louis St. www.pharmacymuseum.org. © **504/565-8027.** $10 adults; $7 students and seniors; free for kids 6 and under. Wed–Sat noon–5pm. Closes early for private events some Sat; check website calendar.

New Orleans Historic Voodoo Museum ★ This small museum is packed with dusty displays of Voodoo objects from around the world and right here in New Orleans, including some that allegedly belonged to the legendary Voodoo queen, Marie Laveau. While serious practitioners might scoff at the tourist orientation of this place, it offers a good introduction to the truth behind the myths of this much-maligned practice. You'll get the most out of your visit if you engage with whoever is manning the front desk, usually someone involved in Voodoo, who can answer inquiries, arrange a reading, or hook you up with a custom gris-gris bag or Voodoo doll.

724 Dumaine St., at Bourbon St. www.voodoomuseum.com. © **504/680-0128.** $10 adults; $8 students, seniors, military, kids 12 and under. Daily 10am–5:30pm.

New Orleans Jazz Museum at the Old U.S. Mint ★★ Dedicated to an original American art form, this museum near Frenchmen Street features stellar art and collectibles. You might see Louis Armstrong's first cornet, Fats Domino's upended (from Katrina) piano, Sidney Bechet's soprano saxophone, or Edward "Kid" Ory's trombone. A "Drumsville" exhibit launched in 2018 includes equipment and instruments from legendary and contemporary New Orleans drummers. The rotating exhibits come from an archive of irreplaceable treasures ranging from costumes, photos, manuscripts, and historic recordings to rare film footage. Best of all, there are **free concerts** (in the lovely third-floor performance space or sometimes, during warm months, on an outside stage— check schedule). The building, the only mint that was both a U.S. *and* a Confederate mint, also has exhibits of interest to numismatists (O-minted coins, struck right here!) and other curious folk. *Fun fact:* Ghost hunters believe William Mumford, who met the noose here in 1862, still hangs around.

400 Esplanade Ave. www.louisianastatemuseum.org and www.nolajazzmuseum.org. © **800/568-6968** and 504/568-6993. $8; free for children 6 and under. Discounts for visiting multiple Louisiana State museums. Tues–Sun 9am–4pm; last ticket sale 3:30pm. Closed Mon and state holidays.

The Presbytère ★★★ The Presbytère, which flanks St. Louis Cathedral to the right, was originally built to house the clergy serving in the cathedral. That never came to pass, and the clergy's loss is our gain. It's now a museum with two excellent permanent exhibits. Upstairs, the Mardi Gras exhibit walks visitors through the holiday's history—which is so much more (and so much more interesting) than cwazy kids doing cwazy kid stuff. It shows ornate Mardi Gras Indian costumes and antique Mardi Gras Queen jewels, and there's even a replica float so you can toss mock beads at mock crowds. (To see the real thing, visit Blaine Kern's **Mardi Gras World; p. 167**.) On the first floor, the multimedia exhibit "Living with Hurricanes: Katrina and Beyond" is an in-depth look at the human drama of hurricanes. First-person audio, video, and interactive displays create an educational but wholly accessible experience, and an emotionally evocative one at that (but with enough optimism, humor, and science to keep it from being too downcast). One man's IN CASE OF EMERGENCY memo hangs on a wall: his jeans, scrawled with his name, blood type, and next of kin. A reproduction of a small attic with a rough hole chopped through its ceiling—and the very axe one woman used to commit a similar act—accompany her voiceover describing the incident. It's powerful stuff.

751 Chartres St., Jackson Sq. www.louisianastatemuseum.org. (ℓ) **800/568-6968** or 504/568-6968. $7 adults; $6 seniors and students; free for kids 6 and under. Discounts if visiting multiple Louisiana State Museums. Tues–Sun 9am–4pm (last ticket sale 3:30).

BEYOND THE FRENCH QUARTER
Uptown & the Garden District

If you can see just one thing outside the French Quarter, make it the **Garden District ★★★**. These two neighborhoods are the first places that come to mind when one hears the words "New Orleans." The Garden District has no significant historic buildings or important museums—it's simply beautiful—enough for authors as diverse as Truman Capote and Anne Rice to become enchanted by its spell. Gorgeous homes stand quietly amid lush foliage, elegant but ever so slightly (or more) decayed. You can see why this is the setting for so many novels; it's hard to imagine that anything real actually happens here.

But it does. Like the Quarter, this is a residential neighborhood, so please be courteous as you wander about. To see the sights, you need only mosey around and admire the exteriors and gardens of beautiful houses. We've mapped out a comprehensive **walking tour** (p. 257) to help guide you to the Garden District's treasures and explain a little of its history. Naturally, it starts with a ride on the St. Charles streetcar. You might also check out the listings starting on p. 234 to find the best shops, galleries, and bookstores on **Magazine Street,** the eclectic shopping strip that bounds the Garden District.

Meanwhile, a little background: Across Canal Street from the Quarter, "American" New Orleans begins. After the Louisiana Purchase of 1803, an essentially French-Creole city came under the auspices of a government determined to develop it as an American city. Tensions between Creole society and the encroaching American newcomers began to increase. Some historians lay this tension at the feet of Creole snobbery; others blame the naive and uncultured Americans. In any case, Creole society succeeded in maintaining a relatively distinct social world, deflecting American settlement upriver of Canal Street (Uptown). The Americans in turn came to outpace the population with sheer numbers of immigrants. Newcomers bought up land in what had been the old Gravier Plantation (now the Uptown area) and began to build a parallel city. Very soon, Americans came to dominate the local business scene, centered along Canal Street. In 1833, the American enclave now known as the Garden District was incorporated as Lafayette City, and—thanks in large part to the New Orleans–Carrollton Railroad, which ran the route of today's St. Charles Avenue streetcar—the Americans kept right on expanding until they reached the tiny "resort town" of Carrollton, a few miles away. It wasn't until 1852 that the various sections came together officially as a united New Orleans.

Bayou St. John, Esplanade & Lake Pontchartrain

Bayou St. John ★★★ is one of the key reasons New Orleans exists. This body of water originally extended from the outskirts of New Orleans to Lake Pontchartrain. Indigenous people, including the Chapitoulas and Choctaw, lived along the bayou, or Bayouk Choupic. In 1699, they showed the waterway to French explorers Pierre Le Moyne Sieur d'Iberville and Jean-Baptiste Le Moyne, Sieur de Bienville. Soon after, Bienville was commissioned to establish a settlement in Louisiana that would both make money and protect French holdings in the New World from British expansion. Bienville chose the spot where New Orleans now sits because he recognized the strategic importance of the Bayou St. John's "back-door" access to Lake Pontchartrain, and ultimately to the Gulf of Mexico. The French renamed it Bayou St. John. Boats could enter the lake from the Gulf, then follow the Bayou to its end. From there, they were within easy portage distance of the mouth of the Mississippi River. The mellow waterway provided some protection from detection and attack, while avoiding the trickier river waters.

The early path from the city to the bayou is today's Bayou Road, an extension of Governor Nicholls Street in the French Quarter. Modern-day Gentilly Boulevard, which crosses the bayou, was another trail used by Indigenous people—it led around the lake and on to settlements as far as Florida.

As New Orleans grew and prospered, the bayou became a suburb as planters moved outward along its shores. In the early 1800s, a canal was dug to connect the waterway with the city, reaching a basin at the edge of Congo Square (which begat today's Basin St.). The Bayou became a popular recreation area, lined with fine restaurants and dance halls (and meeting places for Voodoo practitioners, who held secret ceremonies along its shores). Gradually, New Orleans reached beyond the French Quarter and enveloped the whole area—overtaking farmland, plantation homes, and resorts.

The canal was filled in long ago, and the bayou is a meek re-creation of itself (though reopening nearby floodgates, allowing more natural ebb and flow from Lake Pontchartrain, should bring its ecosystem closer to its thriving original state). It is no longer navigable (even if it were, bridges were built too low to permit the passage of watercraft other than kayaks), but residents still prize their waterfront sites, and kayaks, rowboats, and paddleboards make use of the bayou's smooth surface. This is one of the prettiest areas of New Orleans—full of the old houses tourists love to marvel at without the hustle, bustle, and confusion of more high-profile locations. A stroll along the banks and through the nearby neighborhoods is one of our favorite things to do on a nice afternoon. To gain a much more comprehensive understanding of the city's most beloved waterway, read Cassie Pruyn's excellent *Bayou St. John: A Brief History.*

The simplest way to reach Bayou St. John from the French Quarter is to drive or ride straight up **Esplanade Avenue** about 20 blocks (or grab the bus that says ESPLANADE at any of the bus stops along the avenue). Right before you reach the Bayou, you'll pass **St. Louis Cemetery No. 3** (just past Leda St.). It's the final resting place of many prominent New Orleanians, among them Father Adrien Rouquette, who lived and worked among the Choctaw; Storyville photographer E. J. Bellocq; and Thomy Lafon, the Black philanthropist who bought the old Orleans Ballroom as an orphanage for African-American children and put an end to its infamous "quadroon balls" (p. 21). Walking just past the cemetery, turn left onto Moss Street, which runs along the banks of Bayou St. John. To see an example of an 18th-century West Indies–style plantation house, jog left at Moss Street and stop at the **Pitot House,** 1440 Moss St. (p. 171).

Esplanade leads into **City Park** (p. 181) at Wisner Boulevard. Turn left on Wisner for about 3 miles as it hugs the border of City Park. It'll jog right into Beauregard Avenue; then turn right on Cloverleaf and look for water—and Lakeshore Drive. Turn left. You've reached **Lake Pontchartrain,** which you've probably figured out. Meander along Lakeshore Drive for a couple of miles until you reach a marina (the road will curve and become W. End Blvd.). It's hard to believe this area (known as the **Lakefront**), home to commercial fishing since the late 1800s, was devastated by the 17th Street Canal breach after Hurricane Katrina. The storm piled boats atop each other, smashed buildings into rubble, and destroyed a lighthouse. Now, there's a thriving restaurant hub and shopping along Harrison Avenue, and the nearby **Lakeview** residential neighborhood boasts some of the highest property values around. That canal is just ahead of you, as is the fishing-oriented **Bucktown** neighborhood. But this is probably a good spot to turn back—or hit up Deanie's for old-school seafood just like a local.

Lake Pontchartrain, technically an estuary connected to the Gulf of Mexico, is some 40 miles long and 25 miles wide, and is bisected by the 24-mile **Pontchartrain Causeway,** the world's longest continuous over-water bridge.

Museums & Galleries

CBD/WAREHOUSE DISTRICT/LOWER GARDEN DISTRICT

Contemporary Arts Center ★★ The CAC's two stories of airy galleries (about 10,000 sq. ft.) anchor the city's thriving arts district. (The third and fourth stories are a co-working space.) The center shows influential work by regional, national, and international artists in various mediums, and often presents theater, performance art, dance, or concerts. It's worth a walk-by to

African-American Cultural Heritage

New Orleans' Black history is rich with important milestones, from the birth of jazz to the horrors of the slave trade to crucial civil rights achievements. The ways in which Black people contributed to the creation of the city's culture, cuisine, politics, and literature are endless, and their influence is incalculable. In this majority-Black city, many businesses we list are Black-owned, and almost all museums you visit will cover some aspect of Black heritage.

If you have only a little time to explore, here's a short list to get you started. Begin in the **historic Tremé neighborhood** (America's oldest Black neighborhood), which has a number of significant sights (see p. 173), including **Congo Square** inside Louis Armstrong Park (p. 208); the **Backstreet Cultural Museum** (p. 173), which highlights street culture and Mardi Gras Indian traditions; the nearby **Tomb of the Unknown Slave** (in the yard of **St. Augustine Church;** p. 176); the **New Orleans African-American Museum** (p. 173); and **Treme's Petit Jazz Museum** (p. 163). In the Upper Tremé, **Le Musée de f.p.c.** (p. 173), dedicated to sharing the story of free people of color, is a must. In the **9th Ward,** the **Lower Ninth Ward Living Museum/ TEP Center** (p. 174) is an essential visit, for the oral and photography history of the neighborhood. A trip to the **McKenna Museum of African American Art** (p. 173) in the Lower Garden District is worth your time. Do not miss **Studio BE** (p. 172) or a day trip out to **The Whitney Plantation** (p. 276).

Definitely visit the shops on **Bayou Road** (p. 233), especially **Community Books** (p. 238). The *Essence* Festival is a huge draw (p. 32), of course, and among the city's Black-owned restaurants, **Dooky Chase** (p. 118) is a classic, and **Compère Lapin** (p. 124) is another highlight. The statewide **African American Heritage Trail,** a network of cultural and historic points, is also a good source (information and maps are available at www.astorylikenoother.com).

Know NOLA Tours is wonderful and specializes in African-American heritage tours (www.knownolatours.com; ☎ **504/264-2483); AllBoutDat** (p. 191) is another tour company we highly recommended, and **Hidden History Tours** (www.hiddenhistory.us) gives brilliant walking tours. (See "Organized Tours," p. 190.) **Tours by Judy** (toursbyjudy. com; ☎ **504/416-6666)** offers a number of excellent tours, including one that educates about Free People of Color and one dedicated to the Civil Rights Movement. All are guided by a former history teacher.

check out whatever provocative, large-scale installation is showing in the street-level windows—and often worth checking out in deeper detail.

900 Camp St. cacno.org. ☎ **504/528-3805.** $10 adults; $8 seniors and students; free for K–12 students. Performances may have additional charge. Wed–Mon 11am–5pm.

Mardi Gras World ★★ The Kerns, the first family of float-making, design and build some 75% of the floats used by the Mardi Gras krewes during Carnival Season. You'll see floats from previous years and those in the works for next season. Sketches, sculptures (and sculptors at work), engineers' drawings, and king cake and coffee are all included on the tour—plus you can try on some of the elaborate, sparkling costumes that float riders wear. It's pretty nifty to see the handiwork up close, and if you can't come for

Mardi Gras, at least you can get a taste here—and a better understanding of what goes into it.

1380 Port of New Orleans Place. www.mardigrasworld.com. © **504/361-7821.** $22 adults; $17 students and seniors; $14 children 2–12. Daily 9am–5:30pm. Last tour 4:30pm. Closed Mardi Gras, Easter, Thanksgiving, Christmas. Free shuttle from Canal St.

Museum of the Southern Jewish Experience ★   Shalom, y'all! This new 9,000-square-foot museum offers a thorough history of the Jewish experience across the South. It houses some 4,000 artifacts, including an original Steinmart cash register, antique housewares, letters, photos, an 1800s-era quilt, even a prosthetic leg. Moving stories are shared by holocaust survivors via videos. You can learn some Yiddish, and your own creativity can become part of the collection when you digitally design a corner of a community "crazy quilt"—sure to be a hit with any techy teens or old-school crafters in your entourage.

818 Howard Ave. www.msje.org. © **504/384-2480.** $15 adults; $13 seniors; $10 children; free for kids under 6. Wed–Mon 10am–5pm.

National World War II Museum ★★★   This must-see, world-class facility boasts a collection of artifacts that is beyond abundant. The exhibits include stellar videos and advanced digital techniques, but still manage to emphasize the personal side of war. Descriptions don't do justice to the incredibly moving, interactive experiences.

Founded by the late historian and best-selling author Stephen Ambrose, with support from actor Tom Hanks (Ambrose wrote *Band of Brothers* and consulted on the film *Saving Private Ryan,* both of which starred Hanks), the museum now spans 6 acres and multiple buildings. Visitors are given the dog tag of a soldier whose story unfolds when the tag is scanned at stations along the route. In the **Road to Berlin** and **Road to Tokyo** exhibits, atmospheric floor-to-ceiling decor re-creates battle locations—right down to the temperature and scent. In the U.S. Freedom Pavilion, seven original warplanes hang from a 10-story ceiling. From the ground up, it's an imposing sight; from eye level, it's an almost intimate perspective. Other exhibits of note are the "What Would You Do?" kiosks, which pose thoughtful moral and technical questions; a short, shocking film about the atomic bomb (not for kids)—appropriately silent except for a few excerpts of classical music; a copy of Eisenhower's backup speech apologizing to the nation in the event that D-Day failed; and the amazing story of the B-17 known as **My Gal Sal**—its desolate downing, the daring rescue, and its comeback decades later.

BB Stage Door Canteen lightens the mood with live, 1940s-era USO-style shows. It's good, clean swinging fun for a dinner or brunch show ($40–$65 with modest discounts for kids under 12; $15–$30 show only). (**The American Sector,** the museum's restaurant, is pretty good.) Showing in the **Solomon Victory Theater,** *Beyond All Boundaries* is a short film with "4D" multisensory effects—shaking seats, flashing lights, falling snow—which may be moderately successful at interesting kids in war history ($7). Time is better spent on **Final Mission: USS *Tang,*** which enlists visitors into "silent service" inside a realistic mock submarine as it undergoes its harrowing final sea battle ($7—and worth it). Perhaps most affecting are the intimate stories told through the artifacts and personal items of former soldiers and their loved ones. Take every opportunity to hear these first-person audio stories at the listening stations.

War veterans and civilians who were involved in the war effort often volunteer at the museum. Say thanks and talk with them. We met Jim Weller, who told us how he lied about his age to enlist; he showed us his photo at the Battle of the Bulge and said of the woman and baby next to us: "That's why I won the war—for the babies." That's about the best possible museum experience one can have. Allow for 3 hours, though you could easily spend days here— and if that's your plan, consider staying at the spiffy new museum-owned, 1940s-themed **Higgins Hotel** (www.higginshotelnola.com), named for local boat builder Andrew Jackson Higgins, whose boats helped win the war.

945 Magazine St. www.nationalww2museum.org. © **504/528-1944.** Museum $30 adults; $26 seniors; $18 K–12, college students, and military with ID. Free for WWII veterans and children under 5. Second-day pass $7. Daily 9am–5pm. Closed holidays.

The Ogden Museum of Southern Art ★★★

If NOMA is the crown jewel, this is the crown, the premier collection of Southern art in the United States. The artists' works are impressive, and the graphics are informative and even clever. We particularly like the permanent exhibit of self-taught and outsider art, including some from the local area. Though the building itself is quite dazzling, anchored around a sky-high atrium, one can't help wondering if that soaring space could be put to better use if it were hung with even more fine Southern art (we do appreciate the Ogden-installed sculptures along Poydras St.). If you're visiting on a Thursday, call to see if Ogden After Hours is happening, during which there's music in the atrium. An afternoon of art gazing followed by old Delta blues, the New Orleans Philharmonic, 1930s country, or straight-up jazz makes for a stellar outing. We're also keen on the well-curated gift shop, which has consistently covetable souvenirs with a local spin.

925 Camp St. www.ogdenmuseum.org. © **504/539-9600.** $14 adults; $11 seniors, students, and military; $7 children 5–17; free for kids 4 and under. Mon–Sun 10am– 5pm.

Sazerac House ★★

We're guessing this stunning new distillery exhibit/ tasting room/interactive museum looks nothing like the original Sazerac House, once located 350 feet away, where (so the much-debated story goes) the Sazerac, the first branded cocktail, was invented in the mid-19th century. It's now the city's official cocktail, and the Sazerac Company produces 22 brands, displayed here in a 3-story glass case. That, and much more, will impress even teetolers at this all-ages attraction. The gloriously restored 1860s building, complete with a working rye-producing still, offers self-guided tours covering the history of distilled spirits in New Orleans. There's a small bottling operation, merch, and yes, samples (for 21+, natch). We especially dig the virtual bartenders who "prepare" an adult beverage based on your preferences and text you the recipe.

101 Magazine St. www.sazerachouse.com. ℭ **504/910-0100.** Free admission. Tues–Sun 11am–6pm; last tour begins 4:20pm. Reservations required.

MID-CITY/ESPLANADE/GENTILLY

Degas House ★ Legendary French Impressionist Edgar Degas had a tender spot in his heart for New Orleans. His mother and grandmother were born here, and he spent several months in 1872 and 1873 visiting his brother René and sister-in-law Estelle Musson at this house. A number of paintings resulted, and this is the only residence or studio associated with Degas anywhere in the world that is open to the public. One of the artist's paintings showed the garden of a neighboring house. His brother liked that view, too: He later ran off with the wife of the judge who lived there. Estelle and her children reclaimed her maiden name, Musson. The Musson home, as this is formally known, was erected in 1854. It has since been sliced in two, redone in an Italianate manner, and restored as a B&B and events space, and was recently inducted into the prestigious *Maisons des Illustres* network of homes of noted Frenchmen (only the second such home in the U.S.). It's open to the public for tours, which can be combined with a Creole breakfast.

2306 Esplanade Ave., near N. Broad Ave. www.degashouse.com. ℭ **504/821-5009.** Guided tours $29/person; senior, student, military discounts available. Tour plus breakfast and mimosas $50. Breakfast 9am; tours daily 10:30am and 1:45pm. Reservations required for breakfast, requested for tours.

Flooded House Museum and Levee Exhibit Hall ★ Peer through the windows of this average brick house for an eerie appreciation of the ways in which the 2005 federal flood (p. 12) turned suburban normalcy into upended nightmare. Through sights like a decrepit, waterlogged teddy bear, this mild but effective artist's rendition shows what the homes in this area, abutting the London Avenue canal breach, may have experienced. Next door the extremely informative **Levee Exhibit Hall** display is capped by a simple tribute of two empty rocking chairs.

5000 Warrington Dr. www.levees.org/flooded-house-museum. ℭ **504/722-8172.** Free admission. Go during daylight hours (visitors observe from outside the house; there is no entry).

New Orleans Museum of Art ★★★ The crown jewel of City Park, and of New Orleans art, NOMA houses a 40,000-piece collection of 16th-through 20th-century European paintings, drawings, sculptures, and prints; early American art, Asian art, pre-Columbian and Indigenous ethnographic art, and a vast collection of photography, African works, and decorative glass. Not everything is on display, of course, and this very manageable museum does not take hours to visit. From the front, the original 1911 neoclassical building is an imposing sight among the greenery of City Park. The contemporary rear portion is all angles and curves, steel and glass; and the handsome interior galleries are well lit and organized. It all works to the visitor's advantage. (Well, Lichtenstein's *Five Brushstrokes* sculpture, prominently installed at the front entrance in late 2013, met with comparisons to streaky bacon. But what's art without controversy?) The curation is unfailingly impressive, like 2022's retrospective of pioneering multimedia artist Dawn DeDeaux.

Next door, the already superb **Besthoff Sculpture Garden** ★★★ doubled in size in 2019, bringing this truly world-class attraction to nearly 100 large-scale works set in 11 serene, lushly landscaped acres winding around reflecting lagoons. Works by noted 20th- and 21st-century artists George Segal, Henry Moore, Louise Bourgoise, Frank Gehry, Lin Emery, Hank Willis Thomas, Fred Wilson, Maya Lin, and Frank Stella are here, as well as a version of Robert Indiana's famous pop-art *LOVE* sculpture and the Canal Link Bridge, an unusual walkway that puts visitors at lagoon level (watch your fingers, thar be turtles). It's a cultural highlight, and admission is free. Early risers: Register in advance for $5 yoga classes on Saturday mornings. Or sleep in, grab a **Parkway Bakery** po' boy (p. 122) en route, and picnic amid the artwork. Alternately, **Ralph Brennan's Cafe NOMA** inside the museum has light lunch fare and wine during museum hours; or beignet it up at City Park's branch of **Café du Monde** (p. 146).

1 Collins Diboll Circle, at City Park and Esplanade. www.noma.org. ✆ **504/658-4100.** $15 adults; $10 seniors and active military; $8 students; free for kids 19 and under. Museum Tues–Sun 10am–5pm; sculpture garden daily 10am–5pm. Closed major holidays.

Pitot House ★★ Set along pretty Bayou St. John, the Pitot House is a typical West Indies–style plantation home, restored and furnished with early-19th-century Louisiana and American antiques. Dating from 1799, it originally stood where the nearby modern Catholic school now stands. In 1810 it became the home of James Pitot, the first mayor of incorporated New Orleans (he served from 1804–05). Tours, given by knowledgeable docents or architecture students, are surprisingly interesting and informative.

1440 Moss St., near Esplanade Ave. www.pitothouse.org. ✆ **504/482-0312.** $10 adults; $7 seniors and students; free for kids 6 and under. Wed–Fri 10am–3pm by appt. only (last tour 2:15pm).

CENTRAL CITY

See also the **McKenna Museum of African American Art** (p. 173).

Ashe Cultural Arts Center ★★ This multi-use facility in the historic Central City neighborhood emphasizes the contributions of people of African descent through programs and creative works. With 10,000 square feet of gallery space and 20,000 square feet of performance space, there's always something moving to see and experience here, through fine art and folk art exhibitions, dance performances, concerts, conversations, and film screenings.

1712 Oretha Castle Haley Blvd. www.ashenola.org. ✆ **504/569-9070.** Tues–Sat 10am–6pm.

Southern Food & Beverage Museum & Museum of the American Cocktail ★★

Located in a historic but off-the-tourist-beat part of town, the South's first food-and-beverage museum features clusters of alimental artifacts from each Southern state. It's a jumbled, informative assemblage, showcasing farms, tables, and everything in between, and illustrating how different ethnic groups, geography, and time have contributed to the regional cuisines of the American South. Creole-Cajun cooking classes in the gorgeous demo kitchen run $100 (includes museum admission and private tour). Interesting events and rotating exhibits detail obscure but fascinating topics from absinthe drips to Appalachian soups.

Along one side of the single-room facility, the **Museum of the American Cocktail** (MoTAC) presents 200 years of cocktail history and New Orleans' vital role in the same; exhibits come largely from founder Dale "King Cocktail" Degroff and curator Ted "Dr. Cocktail" Haigh's mind-blowing collection, offering a lively glimpse into the history of everyone's favorite poison (including, of course, absinthe). The booze-obsessed will lose it over the extensive historical artifacts here, including defunct product packaging, glassware, and Prohibition-era photos. (We love the branded bottles of liquor flavorings used to make homemade rotgut palatable.)

1504 Oretha Castle Haley Blvd. www.southernfood.org and www.museumofthe americancocktail.org. ⓒ **504/569-0405.** $11 adults; $5.25 seniors, active military, and students; free for kids under 12 with adult. Thurs–Mon 11am–5pm.

FAUBOURG MARIGNY/BYWATER

JamNola ★

It's a bit pricey, but if you're in the market for wacky, Instagrammable photo ops (bathtub selfie with giant crawfish; 5-ft.-tall bust of Big Freedia), plus immersive exhibits, storytellers guiding you through 12 rooms, and a quick culture primer, this might be your jam. The space is designed by 20+ local artists whose work is largely upcycled, including a wall of vinyl records melted and sculpted into flowers, and floors inlaid with 22,000 Mardi Gras beads.

2832 Royal St. www.jamnola.com. ⓒ **504/233-9152.** $29 adults; $20 seniors, students, and kids 3–12; free for kids 2 and under. Wed–Thurs noon–7pm; Fri noon–9pm; Sat 10am–9pm; Sun 10am–7pm. Tickets must be bought in advance. No cash accepted.

Studio BE ★★★

The power of artist, activist, and educator Brandan "BMike" Odums' astounding work is evident on first glimpse of the exterior murals covering this 35,000-square-foot gallery/museum/warehouse/shop. Inside, the large-format spray-painted and sculptural works, portraying iconic figures important to civil rights, are reflective, instructive, inspiring, and jaw-dropping. It's a must-visit *and* a must-return-often. We love the group art exhibition, "Radical Freedom Dream," a collaboration with local students aged 8–18.

2941 Royal St. studiobenola.com. ⓒ **504/252-0463.** $15 adults; $10 students, seniors, and educators; $5 children 12 free under. Wed–Sat 2–8pm; Sun 2–6pm.

TREMÉ

Backstreet Cultural Museum ★★★ This small cultural gem in the heart of the Faubourg Tremé is dedicated to certain wholly unique New Orleans cultural traditions, mostly of the African-American community. The social aid and pleasure clubs, the second-line parades, brass bands, jazz funerals, and especially Mardi Gras Indians are all well documented and recollected here. We guarantee that the Mardi Gras Indians' ornate beaded costumes are like nothing you've ever seen, and they're best appreciated up close. But the suits are just an entree into the community's intriguing folk traditions. The museum's founder Sylvester Francis, who curated the scrupulous collection, passed away in 2020; his daughter Dominique took over the business. In 2021, Hurricane Ida severely damaged the building, but the beloved collection has found a new home on North Villere Street, right behind the New Orleans African American Museum (see below). Check website or call for hours of operation.

N. Villere St. (exact street number not yet available) www.backstreetmuseum.org. ℭ **504/657-6700.**

Le Musée de f.p.c. ★★★ Louisiana's shameful history of slavery is well-known. In this elegant 1859 Greek Revival house, the lesser-known chronicle of the **free people of color (f.p.c.)** is told through a one-of-a-kind personal collection of artworks and priceless original documents, and a 1-hour tour that's in turns sobering and inspiring. These wealthy, educated, sophisticated, and industrious men and women of French, African, and Caribbean origin populated New Orleans since the early 1700s, and their cultural and commercial formative impact on the city was massive. Exhibited works range from gallant formal portraits of finely attired men and women to copies of the Dred Scott decision and Civil War–era activist newspapers. The **McKenna Museum of African American Art,** a sister museum in Central City, also houses a terrific collection (www.themckennamuseum.com; ℭ **504/323-5074;** by appt. only).

2336 Esplanade Ave. www.lemuseedefpc.com. ℭ **504/323-5074.** $20 adults; $12 K–12 students. Tours by reservation only. Fri 1pm; Sat 11am. Call ahead; museum sometimes closes for private events.

New Orleans African American Museum ★★ The Tremé had to live without this museum for 6 years after it shuttered—a criminal omission considering its location in the oldest African-American neighborhood in the U.S. Finally reopened in 2019, it's currently just a few rooms in a beautifully converted house, displaying collections that tease at what's in store once it returns to its rightful and former glory in the buildings across the street. We love to support it; the artworks and documents shown are a vital telling of the African-American experience in New Orleans and in the U.S. To learn even more, book a half- or full-day "Treme Experience" tour through the museum.

1418 Governor Nicholls St. www.noaam.org. ℭ **504/218-8254.** Self-guided tours $20 adults; $10 students and children under 12. Guided tours $35 adults; $10 students and children. Discounts for Louisiana residents. Thurs–Sun 11am–4pm.

anne rice **IN NEW ORLEANS**

Long before Sookie, Angel, Cassidy, Buffy, any Originals, before anyone cared whether you were Team Edward or Team Jacob, there was Lestat—and the originator of the modern vampire era, the late author Anne Rice. Love her or loathe her, the New Orleans native was one of her hometown's biggest boosters. After *Interview with the Vampire* exploded in the 1980s, hordes of fans descended on her Garden District home, hanging out for days on end, communing with each other and whatever spirits they could conjure. For years Rice famously egged on the whole spectacle, inviting fans into her home, throwing elaborate Halloween bashes, even making appearances in a coffin. Eventually she moved to California, where she died in late 2021, but visitors still come here to honor the doyenne of fang fiction, including obsessed Twihards mining the eerie ore.

Rice's seductive descriptions of her hometown and actual locales are often quite accurate—minus the undead, of course. You can find her books at the **Garden District Book Shop,** 2727 Prytania St. (p. 239). The following landmarks play a role in her books, movies, and inspirations.

FRENCH QUARTER SITES

In Rice's books, the romance of the French Quarter seems to attract vampires, who found easy pickings in its dark corners in the days before electricity. In the *Vampire Chronicles* books, a tomb (empty, of course) with Louis the vampire's name is located in **St. Louis Cemetery No. 1** (p. 186), where Louis occasionally sits and broods. Exteriors for the *Interview with the Vampire* movie were filmed at **700 to 900 Royal St.**—though set decorators had to labor long to erase all traces of the 20th century, covering the streets in mud. What fun for

Tremé's Petit Jazz Museum ★ The smallest museums sometimes deliver the richest experiences, because your chance of connecting with the curators is so much higher—and this one delivers. The only jazz museum located in the birthplace of jazz (the Tremé), it's a must-schedule for both aficionados and beginners. Al Jackson, a lifelong resident, shares his collection of instruments and artifacts, including original recording contracts for Ray Charles and Fats Domino, and a 1954 performing contract signed by Louis Armstrong. But the real treasures in the room are Jackson himself and his vast knowledge of music. 1500 Governor Nicholls St. www.tremespetitjazzmuseum.com. ✆ **504/715-0332.** $15 adults; $8 children 10–13. Weds–Sat tours at 10:30am and 3:30pm or by appt.

NINTH WARD

Lower Ninth Ward Living Museum/TEP Center ★★★ This humble museum has long held a world of insight, telling the full story of this area—not just of the levee failure and its devastation, but of the centuries leading up to it—and why all are so deeply intertwined. It's illuminating, thought-provoking, and even more relevant now that it's relocating to the Lower 9th Ward School, closed for fifteen years since Hurricane Katrina. This is the same school building that "The McDonogh Three" (three 6-year-old girls named Leona Tate, Gail Etienne, and Tessie Prevost) famously and

the present-day residents. Also in the *Interview with the Vampire* movie, caskets are carried from **Madame John's Legacy** (p. 162) as Brad Pitt's voiceover describes Lestat and the little vampire Claudia's night out: "An infant prodigy with a lust for killing that matched his own. Together, they finished off whole families." Yum. **Hotel Monteleone** (p. 65), 214 Royal St., was Aaron Lightner's home in *The Witching Hour.* Rice's characters spent time dining well at **Café du Monde** (p. 146), 800 Decatur St.; **Court of Two Sisters** (p. 100), 613 Royal St.; and **Galatoire's** (p. 103), 209 Bourbon St.

If all this talk of fables and fangs gets you in the mood, head to **Boutique du Vampyre** (709 St. Ann St.; boutique-du-vampyre.myshopify.com; © **504/ 561-8267**) for themed tours, custom fangs, coffin-shaped backpacks . . . you know, the usual. More on vampire tours on p. 198.

GARDEN DISTRICT & LOWER GARDEN DISTRICT SITES

Rice's books also feature many locales in and around the Garden District where she and her family lived and owned properties. **Lafayette Cemetery No. 1** (p. 186) is a frequent setting in Rice's work, especially as a roaming ground for Lestat and Claudia in *Interview with the Vampire* and as the graveyard for the Mayfairs in *The Witching Hour.* The upscale **Pontchartrain Hotel** (p. 87), 2031 St. Charles St., appears in *The Witching Hour.* At **Nolé,** 2001 St. Charles Ave., the vampire Lestat disappeared from this world through an image of himself in the front window (it was then an abandoned car dealership; now it's a special events venue). Rice readers will also recognize **Commander's Palace** (p. 135), 1403 Washington Ave., as a favorite of the Mayfair family.

historically desegregated in 1960. The building has undergone a $14-million renovation, and the center, expected to open in spring 2022, has been reimagined by Tate and her nonprofit Leona Tate Foundation for Change. The new space, the **TEP Center** (for Tate, Etienne, and Provost), is an interpretive center designed to educate the community about New Orleans civil rights history and to help visitors engage in honest conversations about racism.

5909 St. Claude Ave. www.leonatatefoundation.org. © **504/220-3652.** Admission TBD but $10–$15. At press time, tours were by appointment only

Historic New Orleans Churches

Church and religion aren't likely the first things that jump to mind in a city known for debauchery. But New Orleans remains a pious, mostly Catholic city—don't forget Mardi Gras is a pre-Lenten celebration. Religion of one form or another directed much of the city's early history and molded its culture in countless ways. (For a detailed review of **St. Louis Cathedral,** see p. 156, earlier in this chapter.)

St. Alphonsus Art and Cultural Center ★★ The interior of St. Alphonsus is perhaps the most stunning of any church in the city, right up there with some of the lusher Italian splendors. The Irish built St. Alphonsus

REAL GOSPEL, NO brunch

You could do the slick "Gospel Brunch" at the House of Blues. But if you're someone who prefers to experience the real thing in a real place of worship, there are wonderful options. Don't expect fancy robes or masses of choir members, just rooms full of spirit and a seriously joyful noise. Try **St. Peter Claver Catholic Church** (1923 St. Philip St.; ℭ **504/822-8059**), where the voices are beautiful and the congregation welcoming; show some respect when the collection plate comes 'round. Sunday services are at 7:30am and 10am. **Our Lady Star of the Sea Catholic Church** (1835 St. Roch Ave.; ℭ **504/944-0166**) also has a gospel mass on Sundays at 10am, with a fantastic choir. **Franklin Avenue Baptist Church** (8282 I-10 Service Road S; ℭ **504/488-8488**) is a bit of a drive—and it's a *huge* congregation—but they have superb rotating gospel choirs on Sundays at 9am. Alternately, every second Sunday of the month at

6pm, the glorious **Gospel Soul Children** raise their extraordinary voices in praise at **Great Mount Carmel Baptist Church** (3721 N. Claiborne Ave.; ℭ **504/513-0569**). The city's oldest active community choir, the GSPP appears on Jon Batiste's album *We Are*, which was nominated for 11 Grammys. (The choir's church venue may change; check www.facebook.com/nogscinc for updates.)

At the other end of the spectacle spectrum, Bishop (and Internet star) Lester Love incorporates his smooth soul vocals into powerful sermons, adding an R&B backing band and singers at his mini-mega, full-gospel **City of Love Church,** 8601 Palmetto St. in the Gert Town neighborhood (www.thecityoflove. com; ℭ **504/895-5410;** Sun 9:30am). Inspiration is practically preordained. If you're attending the jazzy Sunday mass at **St. Augustine's** (see below), join the throngs walking to brunch afterward at nearby **Lil Dizzy's** (p. 122).

in 1855, in what is now the Lower Garden District, because they wanted to establish their own church, rather than worship at nearby St. Mary's (p. 177) with their German-speaking neighbors. The gallery, columns, and sharply curving staircases lead to spooky, atmospheric balconies with peeling paint and plaster. The church no longer holds Mass—ironically, when St. Mary's was restored, St. Alphonsus closed and the congregation moved there. Hopes for similar restoration here are high, but it's no small undertaking. Katrina caused half a million dollars in damage, and the downriver belltower was blown dramatically across the street. It was completely rebuilt, but in 2021, Hurricane Ida blew a hole in the roof and damaged two stained-glass windows. Meanwhile, it's been used for events (try to catch a concert here) and you can visit the still fabulous-looking interior; free tours (donations gratefully accepted and much in need) are conducted on an informal schedule (Sat 10am–2pm or by advance arrangement; calling ahead recommended).

2025 Constance St., at St. Andrew St. www.stalphonsusno.com. ℭ **504/482-0008** or 504/638-1779.

St. Augustine Church ★★★   One of the great cultural landmarks of New Orleans' Black history, St. Augustine has been a center of community life in the Tremé neighborhood since the mid-1800s. This church was founded by free people of color, who also purchased pews to be used exclusively by enslaved people (to the frustrating dismay of their white masters). This was a first in the history of slavery in the U.S. and resulted in one of the most integrated churches in the country. In the modern era, under the direction of its visionary and charismatic former pastor, Father Jerome LeDoux, St. Augustine integrated traditional African and New Orleans elements into its services. Homer Plessy, Sidney Bechet, and Big Chief Tootie Montana all called this their home church. In late 2005, the archdiocese decided to close St. Augustine because of dwindling membership, but a major public outcry bought a reprieve. It's been going strong since. We're quite enamored of the jazzy 10am **Sunday Mass,** especially when it features a soul-stirring guest performer like James Andrews or John Boutté. The deeply moving **Tomb of the Unknown Slave** (outside on the right side) makes this worth a stop anytime (but call ahead to make sure it's open). Don't forget to leave a donation to help keep St. Aug going. (It was also hit hard by Hurricane Ida and can use the help.) 1210 Governor Nicholls St. staugchurch.org. Ⓒ **504/525-5934.** Mass Sun 10am; Wed 5pm.

St. Mary's Assumption ★

Built in 1860 by German Catholics, this is an even more baroque and grand church than its Irish neighbor across the street, St. Alphonsus (p. 175). These two Lower Garden District churches make an interesting contrast to one another. Along with dozens of life-size saints' statues. St. Mary's houses the national shrine to the hero of the 1867 yellow fever epidemic, Blessed Father Francis Xavier Seelos, who was beatified (one step away from sainthood) in 2000. See his original coffin, a display containing recently discovered locks of his hair, and the centerpiece of the shrine, a reliquary containing his bodily remains. Should Father Seelos become a saint, expect this shrine to be a big deal and place of pilgrimage. Before visiting the shrine, check in at the adjacent welcome center and the interesting **Walk of Life Museum** in the Seelos Shrine Welcome Center at 919 Josephine Street.
2030 Constance St., at Josephine St. www.stalphonsusno.com. Ⓒ **504/522-6748.** Mass Mon–Fri 7:30am, Sat 9am, 10:30am; Sun 9 and 10:30am; vigil Sat 4pm.

St. Patrick's Church ★★

The original St. Patrick's was a tiny wooden building founded to serve the spiritual needs of Irish Catholics—a far cry from this elaborate structure. Begun in 1838, it was built around the old one, which was then dismantled. The distinguished architect James Gallier, Sr. designed much of the interior, including the altar. It opened in 1840, proudly proclaiming itself as the "American" Catholics' answer to St. Louis Cathedral in the French Quarter (where, according to the Americans, God spoke only in French).
724 Camp St., at Girod St. www.oldstpatricks.org. Ⓒ **504/525-4413.** Mass Mon–Fri 7:15am (Latin), 11:30am, noon; Sat 5:30pm; Sun 8am, 9:15am (Latin), 11am, 5:30pm.

St. Roch (Campo Santo) ★★

A local priest prayed to Saint Roch, patron saint of plague victims, to keep his flock safe during the 1867 yellow

floating ACROSS THE RIVER TO ALGIERS POINT

Algiers, established in 1719 and annexed by New Orleans in 1870, is about a quarter-mile across the Mississippi River from the city. The second oldest neighborhood in New Orleans after the French Quarter, it's generally ignored because of its location, but it became a sort of God's country after the hurricane because it did not flood at all; many services, such as mail delivery, were restored quite quickly. It still has the feel of an undisturbed turn-of-the-20th-century suburb, and strolling around here is a delightfully low-key way to spend an hour or two (daytime only). There's a good bit of jazz history in Algiers, the neighborhood that 1920s' musicians called "over da river." There's even a Jazz Walk of Fame at the ferry terminal. Our friends at the **House of the Rising Sun Bed and Breakfast** have a great walking tour on their website (www.risingsunbnb.com). While there, do make a point of visiting **Folk Art Zone** (www.folkartzone.org), a small and wonderful museum of self-taught artists. If Charles Gillam, artist and museum founder, is around, chances are good you'll be treated to a memorable conversation. Algiers is easily accessible via the ferry that runs from the foot of Canal Street. This working ferry, in continuous operation since 1827, is a great way to get out onto the river and see the skyline (and at 30 min., it's perfectly timed for kids' attention spans). See schedule and fares on p. 292.

fever epidemic. When they survived, he made good on his promise to build Saint Roch a chapel. The Gothic result is fine enough, but what is better yet is the small room just off the altar, where successful supplicants to Saint Roch leave *ex voto* gifts in the form of plaster anatomical parts or medical supplies as thanks for their healed affliction. The resulting collection of bizarre artifacts (everything from eyeballs to false limbs) is either deeply moving or a great, creepy spontaneous folk-art installation. While there, do check out the magnificent mural inside **Our Lady Star of the Sea** church, next door. This area of the Bywater district isn't great, so be aware. The chapel, located on the cemetery grounds, has been under restoration but is due to reopen; check ahead.

1725 St. Roch Ave., at N. Derbigny St. nolacatholiccemeteries.org/st-roch-cemetery-1. ℂ **504/482-5065.** Mon–Thurs 8:30am–4:15pm; Fri 8am–4pm except during inclement weather.

A Few More Interesting New Orleans Buildings

The Caesar's Superdome ★ Completed in 1975, the Superdome is a physical and emotional landmark that took on a new worldwide image when it was used as shelter during Katrina. The structure was intended as an evacuation locale of last resort, but quickly turned into hell on earth when tens of thousands of refugees ended up here in a scene of suffering and despair. People were trapped without sufficient food, water, medical care, or, it seemed, hope.

Just months later, the New Orleans Saints reopened the Superdome in 2006 to much hoopla for their first home game (and a halftime show featuring U2) and went on to the playoffs. Three years later they won their first Super Bowl ever (in Miami), to rejoicing far beyond the city boundaries. Atop the team's gleaming success and the Dome's $118-million renovation, the entire building was then "reskinned" in glittery gold tone, a shining beacon of what can arise from the darkest days. Two years later it hosted the 2014 Super Bowl, a huge symbolic comeback. In 2021, the stadium was rebranded as Caesars Superdome and is in the process of a massive multi-year renovation. You can't tour the Superdome (once upon a time, very occasional tours were given), so if you want to see it, your best bet is to attend a game. Not exactly a hardship. Seriously: If you're in town during a home game, GO. Either way, do join the locals in a chant of "WHO DAT?!"

The stats: It's the largest fixed-dome structure in the world (680 ft. in diameter, covering 13 acres), a 27-story windowless building with a seating capacity of 76,000. Inside, there are no view-obstructing posts. The flying-saucer-like building also hosts conventions, balls, and concerts, as does its sister **Smoothie King Center** next door. **Champions Square,** its adjoining outdoor plaza, has become pre- and post-game central and home to many a festival and special event.

1500 block of Poydras St., at LaSalle St. www.mbsuperdome.com. ☏ **504/587-3663.**

Gallier Hall ★ This impressive Greek Revival building in the Central Business District was the inspiration of James Gallier, Sr. Now an events hall, it was erected between 1845 and 1853, served as City Hall for over a century, and has been the site of many key events in the city's history—especially during the Reconstruction and Huey Long eras. Several important figures in Louisiana history lay in state in Gallier Hall, including Jefferson Davis and General Beauregard. Of late, local music legends Ernie K-Doe and Earl King were so honored. Five thousand mourners paid respects to K-Doe, who was laid out in a white costume with a silver crown and scepter. A $10-million exterior renovation was completed in 2017, followed by an interior spiff. Blaine Kern ("Mr. Mardi Gras"), who founded a float-building empire, also lay in state here in 2020. Peek inside if you can, it's a stunner.

545 St. Charles Ave. www.nola.gov/gallier-hall. ☏ **504/658-3627.** Not open to the public.

PARKS, GARDENS & A ZOO

New Orleans' verdant vegetation and expansive tree canopy is one of its many charms, with greenery bursting from small condo courtyards, lavish mansion landscaping, abundantly overflowing terrace pots—and wonderful public parks and gardens. Glorious live oaks are a city hallmark, spreading across streets and over roofs everywhere (an amazing 320 million trees were lost or damaged due to Hurricane Katrina, including many old oaks; thankfully, plenty survived). The city's parks and gardens can be an inviting respite from pounding the sightseeing pavement.

Audubon Park ★★ Across from Loyola and Tulane universities, Audubon Park and the adjacent Audubon Zoo (see below) sprawl over 340 acres, extending all the way from St. Charles Avenue to the Mississippi River. This tract once belonged to city founder Jean-Baptiste Le Moyne and later was part of the Etienne de Boré plantation, where sugar was first granulated in 1794. Although John James Audubon, the country's best-known ornithologist, lived only briefly in New Orleans (at what is now the **Audubon Cottages** hotel; p. 65), the city has honored him by naming the park, zoo, and even a golf course after him.

The huge trees with black bark are live oaks; some are centuries old. More than 200 live oaks were planted to replace the many that didn't survive Hurricane Katrina. The park is a very pretty, wide-open place to stroll or enjoy a shaded picnic among statuary, fountains, and gazebos. There's a nice 1¾-mile paved walking, running, skating, and biking path that loops around the lagoon (and Bird Island rookery) and golf course (which a lovely cafe overlooks). Along the track are 18 exercise stations. You'll also find tennis courts, baseball diamonds, horseback-riding facilities, and three playgrounds (the one on Walnut St., donated by former Saints quarterback Drew Brees, is great and accessible and has ziplines). Audubon Zoo is toward the back of the park across Magazine Street. Behind the zoo, a popular green space on the riverbank, called Riverview but nicknamed **the Fly,** has pleasant views of Frisbee players and the Mississippi.

6500 Magazine St. audubonnatureinstitute.org/audubon-park. © **504/861-2537.** Daily 5am–10pm.

Audubon Zoo ★★★ This is a place of justifiable civic pride that delights even non–zoo fans—small enough to be manageable, but big enough to cover all important zoo bases, including elephant, orangutan, giraffe, and lion exhibits, with bonuses, like Malayan sun bears and gorgeous free-ranging peacocks. Some 15,000 animals (including rare and endangered species) live in natural habitats of subtropical plants, waterfalls, lagoons, and a Louisiana swamp replica complete with rare white gators. For restless kiddos, there's also a playground, a carousel, and some great hot-day diversions, including a wading pond for the little ones, and the **Cool Zoo** splash park with its **Gator Run** lazy river for inner-tube floating. So bring swimsuits and towels if the weather warrants (open seasonally; check website). There are misters and shady oaks for humans of all ages, but hot is hot: For maximum animal action, avoid midday, when the animals are sleeping off the heat. (Bonus track: Crank the Meters' "They All Ask'd for You" before or after you visit. How many zoos have their own hit song?) We like taking the St. Charles Avenue streetcar to Audubon Park, where a free shuttle from the park to the zoo departs every 20 to 30 minutes.

6500 Magazine St. www.auduboninstitute.org. © **504/861-2537.** $25 adults; $20 seniors and children 2–12. Cool Zoo $10. Wed–Fri 10am–4pm; Sat–Sun 10am–5pm. Closed Mardi Gras Day, Thanksgiving, and Christmas.

Chalmette Battlefield/Jean Lafitte National Historical Park & Preserve ★★ These are the grounds where the bloody **Battle of New Orleans** was won on January 8, 1815. Ironically, it should never have been fought: A treaty signed 2 weeks before in Ghent, Belgium, had ended the War of 1812. But word had not yet reached Congress, the commander of the British forces, or Andrew Jackson, who stood with American forces to defend New Orleans and the mouth of the Mississippi River. The battle also succeeded in finally uniting Americans and Creoles. Markers on the battlefield allow you to follow the course of the fighting (or you can just watch the film in the visitor center). Inside the park is a national cemetery, established in 1864. It holds only two American veterans from the Battle of New Orleans, but also some 14,000 Union soldiers who fell in the Civil War. For a terrific view of the Mississippi River, climb the levee in back of the Beauregard House. It's about 6 miles from the French Quarter.

8606 W. St. Bernard Hwy. www.nps.gov/jela. *©* **504/281-0510.** Free admission. Daily 9am–4pm. Visitor center closed Mardi Gras and federal holidays (open Veterans and Memorial Days).

City Park ★★★ Once part of the Louis Allard plantation and named one of America's "Coolest Parks," City Park's 1,300 beautifully landscaped acres provide a charming spot for jogging, birding, or just gazing at the moss-dripping live oaks (the largest collection in the world!). It's also a treasure trove of culture and activity, with botanical gardens, a conservatory, picnic areas, lagoons for boating and fishing, **swan boats** (p. 202), and bike paths and **rentals** (p. 291). Then there are tennis courts; two golf courses; two New Orleans–themed **miniature golf** courses (p. 202), a bandstand with summertime concerts, two stadiums, playing fields, playgrounds, and a miniature train you can ride in. That's just a start. **Carousel Gardens** is a kids' amusement area with rides; **Children's Storyland,** inside Carousel Gardens, has fairytale figures for kids to scamper on and over and an exquisite antique carousel (see "Especially for Kids," p. 200). In 60-acre **Couturie Forest,** you can wander, hike, and reach New Orleans' highest point of elevation, **Laborde Mountain,** which is 43 whole feet. (Birders, bring your binoculars: It's the best spot in town!) During Halloween, City Park hosts the massive **Voodoo Music & Arts Experience** (aka Voodoo Fest), and at Christmastime, the mighty oaks are strung with (literally) a million light displays—quite a magical sight.

You'll also find the **New Orleans Museum of Art** (p. 170) at Collins Diboll Circle, on Lelong Avenue, in a building that is itself a work of art. Flanking it to the left is the wonderful **Besthoff Sculpture Garden** (p. 171); to the right is the **Louisiana Children's Museum** (p. 202). Tucked away inside the **Botanical Gardens** is one of the oddest and most charming attractions in this odd and charming city, the **Train Garden.** Imagine a massive train set located in Dr. Seuss's basement, if Dr. Seuss were obsessed with both New Orleans and organic materials. Along 1,300 feet of track are exacting,

½₂-scale replicas of 1890s streetcars and ornately detailed representations of actual New Orleans neighborhoods and landmarks—all made from plant matter! The Botanical and Train Gardens are open for viewing year-round on Wednesdays from 10am to 8pm, and Thursday through Sunday 10am to 4pm; trains operate Saturdays and Sundays only (weather permitting).

1 Palm Dr. www.neworleanscitypark.com. ℂ **504/482-4888.** Park free. Botanical Gardens $10 adults; $5 kids 3–12; free for kids 2 and under (includes Train Garden). For hours and rates of other attractions, see separate listings. Park daily sunrise–sunset. Admissions and hours may vary seasonally, so check website or call.

Crescent Park ★★

This newish, river-hugging 1.5-mile green space paralleling the Marigny and Bywater neighborhoods is ideal for a picnic, run, or walk, or just to get a different, thoroughly modern perspective on New Orleans. That starts as you cross the enormous, rust-colored steel arc, the Piety Street Bridge (aka the Rusty Rainbow), to reach the park. Or access it via the less dramatic, wheelchair-accessible Mandeville Crossing closer to the French Quarter. From the park's freshly planted and paved paths, the Quarter is a mysterious, distant vision; from its expansive waterfront stage set amid decayed wharves, the area's industrial legacy nips at the heels. Watch for concerts and other events at this substantial welcoming space. For free workout classes, see p. 294.

Enter from bridges near 2300 N. Peters St. at Elysian Fields (accessible); 3360 Chartres St. near Piety St. (stairs only); 3900 Chartres St. near Bartholomew St. (accessible). crescentparknola.org. ℂ **504/636-6400.** Free admission. Daily 6am–7:30pm (may close earlier in winter).

Lafitte Greenway ★★

This 2.6-mile walking trail and bikeway is a former railway and post-Katrina success story that now connects neighbors and neighborhoods: It starts just above the French Quarter and traverses the Tremé, Bayou St. John, and Mid-City. There's a FitLot, a playground, basketball courts, and baseball and soccer fields. If you're renting a bike (p. 291), the greenway will facilitate your explorations with nary a pothole in sight. (*Bonus:* It passes several adjacent eat- and drinkeries.) It's well lit, but use caution after dark. Check the website for free workouts, occasional events, and info about the very important history of this area and the Greenway's storm-water management techniques.

Trailhead begins at Basin and St. Louis Sts. just outside the French Quarter (near St. Louis Cemetery #1); look for signage. Other access points intersect its route. www. lafittegreenway.org. ℂ **504/462-0645.** Open 24 hr.

Longue Vue House & Gardens ★★

Longue Vue mansion is a little pocket of the unexpected. Just 20 minutes from the city center, near the more interesting end of suburban Metairie, is a unique expression of Greek Revival architecture set on an 8-acre estate, constructed from 1939 to 1942 and listed on the National Register of Historic Places. It's like stumbling across a British country-house estate—and since it was never a plantation, it may satisfy

Tara-esque cravings, if you can't get out to River Road (p. 269) or are plantation-averse.

The mansion was designed to foster a close rapport between indoors and outdoors, with vistas of formal terraces and pastoral woods. The charming gardens were partly inspired by the Generalife, the former summerhouse of the sultans in Granada, Spain; look also for fountains and a colonnaded loggia. Unlike at some attractions for garden enthusiasts, kids can actually have fun here in the delightful **Discovery Garden,** with clever and amusing exhibits where they can play (and maybe even learn). All in all, it's a nice place to ramble on a pretty day. Also on occasional offer are twilight or lunchtime garden concerts, volunteering opportunities, yoga, and Tai Chi.

7 Bamboo Rd., near Metairie. www.longuevue.com. © **504/488-5488.** Mon–Sat 9:30am–5pm. Admission to gardens (self-guided) $10; guided house tour $20; guided tour of house and gardens $25. Tours on the hour until 4pm. Closed most major holidays.

NEW ORLEANS CEMETERIES

Along with Spanish moss and lacy cast-iron balconies, the cities of the dead are indelibly associated with New Orleans. Known the world over for their elaborate and beautiful aboveground tombs, their inscrutable ghostly presence enthralls visitors. There are more than 45 cemeteries in New Orleans—33 are considered historic, and 5 are officially listed in the National Register of Historic Places. Iconic tourist attractions as much as Jackson Square or Bourbon Street, the cemeteries have a fascinating backstory—one that has become twisted over time by mythology. But the truth is so fascinating that it needs little embellishment.

Sometimes called "Cities of the Dead" for their resemblance to urban centers, the cemeteries have, of course, been a part of New Orleans nearly since its founding. For the earliest settlers, dying wasn't that big of a deal; everyone was doing it, and the dead were buried in common graves or along the riverbanks (except the hoitiest of the toity, who were buried at St. Louis Cathedral). But when the river rose or a major rain caused flooding, that didn't work out too well. Old Uncle Etienne had an unpleasant habit of bobbing back to the surface, doubtless no longer looking his best. This practice gave rise to some good stories (though experts debate their veracity) of coffins floating downriver, bodies weighted down with rocks, and holes drilled in caskets to let the water through and keep them from popping up from the ground like deathly balloons.

Add to that cholera and yellow fever epidemics, which helped increase the number of bodies and also the possibility of infection. Given that the cemetery of the time was *inside* the Vieux Carré, it's all pretty disgusting to think about.

Around the late 1780s, death was getting to be a bigger deal. Not only was death more *prevalent,* what with fires and epidemics and such, *honoring* death and the dead was also becoming more ceremonial. When new cemeteries became necessary, they were plotted on the outskirts of town where illness and odor were less likely to be troublesome. The first, St. Peter, was begun in 1725 by the Catholic Diocese, and rests where a Superdome parking lot now sits. Bodies were buried in the soil there. When St. Peter was full, the famed St. Louis No. 1 came about, in 1789, on what is now Rampart Street. The first major city of the dead, with fancy tombs and a parklike setting, it provided a more fitting tribute to departed loved ones. When it filled up, others soon followed, improving on the haphazard layout of St. Louis No. 1 to form designated "streets" in a grid pattern.

Following Old-World Style

It's true that the high-water table and muddy soil here influenced the popularity of the aboveground "condo crypt" look—the dead are placed in vaults that resemble miniature buildings. But such tombs are actually customary in France and Spain (and elsewhere); it was just another tradition that the colonists brought with them to New Orleans. Some say St. Louis No. 1 was inspired by the famous Père Lachaise cemetery in Paris. Perhaps it's just because they are both such impressive, prestigious sights.

The aboveground vaults are also often adorned with stunning works of sculptural art, decorations that represent the family name, occupation, or religion (which was invariably Catholic; the first Jewish cemetery was not founded until 1828). Some tombs were not owned by families, but by a group, like the firefighters, police, or a benevolent society. These were decorated accordingly: Witness the enormous elk visible from the corner of Canal Street and City Park Avenue. Group tombs were helpful for families who could not afford a family tomb. The cemeteries may also have fancy ironwork in the gates and fences—and on the whole are well worth a visit.

Hi Honey, I'm Home

So . . . all that tomb for one dead guy? Not so much. The tombs indeed host multiple bodies. The methodology is actually fairly clever. Inside the tomb are long chambers, one above the other, separated by shelves. When a casket goes in, it rests on the top shelf, and the vault is resealed with simple brick and mortar. Heat and humidity act like a slow form of cremation. After a year and a day (by custom and rule—to accommodate the traditional year-long mourning period), another family member may be buried here. Whatever's left of the first one is moved to the bottom level, and the casket bits are removed. In some tombs, that shelf has a gap toward the back, and the remnants just get pushed back, where they fall through the gap to the vault below. Everyone eventually lies jumbled together to continue their quest for a dusty family reunion. And so room is made for a new casket, and the exterior is closed up once again. The result is sometimes dozens of names, going back generations, on a single spot. It's an efficient, space-saving system that gives new meaning to the phrase "all in the family." If a family loses two people within the year, one of them rests in a temporary holding vault until that year-and-a-day period has passed.

Seriously? We. Can't. Even.

If you've read through this section, or if you're a human being, hopefully you have some respect for the historic nature of these cemeteries and their cultural significance. If nothing else, we hope you recognize that these are sacred burial places. Thus, we can't even believe we need to implore you not to mark these tombs in any way or remove anything from these cemeteries. Due to their age, it's best not to even touch the tombs. If you've heard that leaving offerings or scrawling "XXX" on the graves brings good luck or calls up the ancestors, that's bogus. In actuality, it's just defacing someone's hallowed resting place (and it's illegal). Make your memories and take your photos of these beautiful, sanctified spaces. But otherwise, please, please leave them and their inhabitants in peace.

Upkeep Issues

By law, families must maintain their tombs. Traditionally, All Saints' Day (Nov 1) is when families gather to honor their dead, and in the days leading up to it, you will still see people busily tidying up and washing down the sun-bleached, whitewashed brick buildings. Some are treated with lime, leaving a yellow or green tint. Flowers, candles, photos, and memorabilia are left on and around the tombs of loved ones. To this day, if you go to a cemetery on November 1—which we recommend—you may see a tender graveside party atmosphere. The Krewe de Mayahuel (www.facebook.com/krewedemaya huel) also puts on a Day of the Dead cemetery procession, to honor loved ones who have passed.

But many graves have fallen into disrepair, when family members are no longer willing, able, or around to do the maintenance. There are laws that allow the city to take over and transfer a neglected tomb, but these are largely unenforced (and there's the creepy factor). Other laws and customs around these centuries-old tombs are murky, and responsibility for the expensive upkeep gets shifted or shunted off. So sadly, many cemeteries today face moderate to severe dishevelment. For years, crypts lay open, exposing their pitiful contents—if they weren't robbed of them—bricks, shattered marble tablets, even bones, lay strewn around. Several of the worst eyesores have been cleaned up; others still remain in deplorable shape. Concerns were high for the fate of the iconic cemeteries during the Katrina disaster days, but in large part, "the system worked." The tombs survived unscathed, except for some high-water marks much like those borne by any other flooded structure.

Restoration and cleanup efforts have been spearheaded by the nonprofit **Save Our Cemeteries** (www.saveourcemeteries.org; © **504/525-3377**). Consider throwing a few, um, bones their way, or even volunteering. The website accepts online donations. Save Our Cemeteries also offers tours and occasional lectures.

For more information, we highly recommend Robert Florence's *New Orleans Cemeteries: Life in the Cities of the Dead.* It's full of photos, facts, and human-interest stories for those with a deeper interest in this fascinating aspect of New Orleans culture and is available at bookstores throughout the city.

7 Cemeteries You Should (or Must) See with a Tour

Many of the tour companies listed on p. 190 provide cemetery tours. If you haven't pre-planned, guides may be available for hire at the entrances to St. Louis No. 1 and Lafayette No. 1, *when those cemeteries are open.* These two (and St. Louis Cemetery #2) have been closed a while, with unclear opening dates. Check www.nolacatholiccemeteries.org (or peek through locked gates).

Lafayette Cemetery No. 1 ★★★ Right across the street from Commander's Palace restaurant, this is the lush uptown cemetery. Once in horrible condition, it's been mostly restored. (It's also been closed for *years,* unfortunately.) Anne Rice's Mayfair witches have their family tomb here. See p. 175.

1400 block of Washington Ave.

St. Louis Cemetery No. 1 ★★★ Actually you can *only* see this one with a tour. It's the oldest extant cemetery (1789) and the most iconic. It's part of the **African American Heritage Trail.** Here lie Marie Laveau (p. 190), Bernard Marigny, and (eventually) Nicolas Cage, in the pyramid he had inscribed *"Omnia Ab Uno"* (Everything From One). It's also recognizable for the acid-dropping scene from *Easy Rider* shot here. This was closed at press time, too.

Basin St. btw. Conti and St. Louis Sts.

St. Louis Cemetery No. 2 ★ Established in 1823, it's the city's next-oldest cemetery. Although the neighborhood is much improved, its old reputation as a rough one has kept most tours away so it's less trafficked (and more run down). **Save Our Cemeteries** (p. 185) and **Historic New Orleans Tours** (p. 192) offer tours (but it was also closed at press time, with tours suspended). The Emperor of the Universe, R&B legend Ernie K-Doe, was laid to rest here in 2001; his widow, Empress Antoinette, joined him in 2009. Claude Tremé, founder of the historic neighborhood that bears his name (see p. 173), also rests here.

N. Claiborne Ave. btw. Iberville and St. Louis Sts.

Cemeteries You Can See on Your Own

This Mid-City cluster of cemeteries on or near City Park Avenue is an easy streetcar ride up Canal Street from the Quarter. Just take the streetcar called—can you guess?—"Cemeteries." Most of these cemeteries (such as St. Louis No. 3 and Metairie) have offices that can provide maps or direct you to a grave location. All have sort-of-regular hours—anytime from 9am to 4pm is a safe bet. Cemeteries are often secluded spaces, and once were known for thieves preying on tourists. That's no longer common, but going in pairs or groups and being alert is always a good idea.

Cypress Grove and Greenwood Cemeteries ★★ Located across the street from each other, both were founded in the mid-1800s by the Firemen's Charitable and Benevolent Association. Each has some highly original tombs; keep your eyes open for those made entirely of iron.

120 City Park Ave., at Canal Blvd. www.greenwoodnola.com. ⓒ **504/482-8983.** By car, take Canal Blvd. north to City Park Ave.; turn right. The entrance to Greenwood is on the left (lake) side of Canal; Cypress Grove is across the street (right or river side of Canal). Daily 8:30am–4:30pm.

Holt Cemetery ★★★ This one is not so easy to find, but it's worth seeking out. Dating to the mid-1800s, this former burial ground for indigents is the rare New Orleans cemetery with nearly all in-ground graves. They are maintained by the families—or not maintained at all, in many cases—which results in its particular folk-art appeal, with hand-drawn markers and family memorabilia scattered about. It's incredibly picturesque and poignant in its own way. Jazz pioneer Charles "Buddy" Bolden is buried here, in an unmarked grave.

635 City Park Ave. (turn down tiny Rosedale Ave., across City Park Ave. from the Burger King and next to Delgado College). Mon–Fri 8am–2:30pm; Sat 8am–noon.

Hurricane Katrina Memorial ★ On the former site of Charity Hospital's paupers' field, this affecting circle of tombs holds the bodies of 85 unclaimed victims of the 2005 levee failures and the names of others who perished. It's a dignified place that's easily missed (look for a discreet black iron gate), the better for contemplative solitude, perhaps. Surrounded by a storm-shaped series of pathways, the memorial does its duty in giving one substantial pause.

5056 Canal St. Take the Canal St. streetcar to City Park Ave. Mon–Fri 8am–2pm.

Metairie (Lake Lawn) Cemetery ★★ Don't be fooled by the slightly more modern look—some of the most amazing tombs in New Orleans are here. Don't miss the pyramid-and-sphinx Brunswig mausoleum, the "ruined castle" Egan family tomb, and the former resting place of Storyville madam Josie Arlington. Her mortified family had the madam's body moved when her crypt became a tourist attraction (her move may have also resulted from the complaints of blue-blood families, themselves mortified at Josie's proximity). But the tomb remains exactly the same, including the statue of a young woman knocking on the door. Legend has it that the young woman is Josie herself being turned away from her father's house, or a virgin being denied entrance to Josie's brothel—she claimed never to despoil anyone. The reality is that it's just a copy of a statue Josie liked. Other famous residents include Confederate General P. G. T. Beauregard, jazz greats Louis Prima and Al Hirt, *Vampire Chronicles* author Anne Rice, and Ruth Fertel of Ruth's Chris

Steakhouse (in a marble edifice that oddly resembles one of her famous pieces of beef). You'll have to drive or taxi here, but you can also drive the lanes through the cemetery, a good option for a rainy day.

5100 Pontchartrain Blvd. ℭ **504/486-6331.** Daily 8:30am–5pm. By car, take Canal St. to City Park Ave.; turn left until it becomes Metairie Ave., turn right onto Pontchartrain Blvd. (signs for I-10), then make a quick left under highway; stay on Pontchartrain and into entrance.

St. Louis Cemetery No. 3 ★★★ Conveniently located next to the Fair Grounds racetrack (home of Jazz Fest), St. Louis No. 3 was built on top of a former graveyard for lepers. Storyville photographer E. J. Bellocq lies here. It's a scenic cemetery and neighborhood near Bayou St. John, accessible via Esplanade Avenue.

3421 Esplanade Ave. ℭ **504/482-5065.** Mon–Sat 8am–4:30pm; Sun and holidays 8am–4pm.

VOODOO

Voodoo's mystical presence is one of the most common New Orleans motifs—though it is mostly reduced to a tourist gimmick. With kitschy dolls for sale and exaggerated mythology surrounding Voodoo queen Marie Laveau, a very real, culturally important religion with a serious past gets lost amid all that camp.

Voodoo's roots can be traced in part back to the religion of West Africa's **Yoruba** people, which incorporates the worship of several different spiritual forces that include a supreme being, a pantheon of deities, and the spirits of ancestors. When Africans were kidnapped, enslaved, and brought to Brazil, Haiti, and, ultimately, Louisiana, they brought their religion with them.

Later, other African religions met and melded, and when enslaved people were forced to convert to Catholicism, they found it easy to merge and practice both religions and rituals. Rites involved dancing and singing to intricate drum rhythms. Some participants might even fall into a trancelike state, during which a *lwa* (or *loa*), a spirit and/or lower-level deity intermediary between humans and gods, would take possession of them.

Voodoo was banned in Louisiana until the Louisiana Purchase in 1803. The next year, enslaved Haitians overthrew their government, and new immigrants came to New Orleans, bringing along a fresh infusion of Voodoo (or more accurately, Vodou, the Haitian spelling you'll often see in New Orleans).

Napoleonic law (which still holds sway in Louisiana) and the Code Noir (p. 16) gave the enslaved Sundays off, and in 1817, a city ordinance restricted gatherings of enslaved people to one place: **Congo Square** on Rampart Street, part of what is now Louis Armstrong Park. African worship there, including dancing and drumming rituals, gave enslaved people a way to have their own community and a certain amount of freedom. These gatherings naturally attracted white onlookers, as did the rituals held (often by free people of African descent) along **Bayou St. John.** The local papers of the 1800s are full of lurid accounts of Voodoo "orgies" and of spirits possessing both white and Black people. In Congo Square, Voodoo blended with the dominant religion, Catholicism, and gatherings became more like performance pieces than religious rituals. Legend has it that nearby madams would come down to the Sunday gatherings and hire some of the performers to entertain at their houses.

During the 1800s, the famous Voodoo priestesses came to some prominence. Mostly free women of color, they were devout religious practitioners and very good businesswomen with a steady clientele of whites who secretly came to them for help in love or money matters. During the 1900s, Voodoo largely went back underground, but by the end of the century, it was viewed as entertainment and commercialized for tourism.

It is estimated that today as much as 15% of the population of New Orleans practices Voodoo, though the public perception—casting spells or sticking pins in Voodoo dolls—is largely Hollywood nonsense.

Most of the stores and places in New Orleans that advertise Voodoo are set up strictly for tourism. This is not to say that some facts can't be found there or that you shouldn't buy a mass-produced souvenir. For an introduction to Voodoo, check out the **New Orleans Historic Voodoo Museum** (p. 163) or **Voodoo Authentica** (p. 246). For true Voodoo, however, seek out real Voodoo temples or practitioners. You can find them at the temples listed below or by calling **Ava Kay Jones** (yorubapriestess.tripod.com; © **504/484-6499**), who creates custom gris-gris bags (packets of meaning-infused herbs, stones, and other such bits), potions, candles, and dolls by appointment only. If you happen into one of these temples and find no one about, come back or wait quietly; they may be conducting a reading in a side room. And be sure to check out Robert Tallant's book *Voodoo in New Orleans* (Pelican Pocket, 1983).

Voodoo Temples & Spiritual Practitioners

The city has several authentic Voodoo temples and *botanicas* selling everything you might need for potions, spells, and ritual implements for altars. The public is welcome, and employees are happy to educate the honestly inquisitive.

The venerable **Island of Salvation Botanica** in the New Orleans Healing Center, 2372 St. Claude Ave. #100 (islandofsalvationbotanica.com; © **504/948-9961**), is run by Vodou priestess **Sallie Ann Glassman.** The *botanica* is open Monday to Saturday 10am to 5pm and Sunday 11am to 5pm, but call first to make sure they are not closed for readings (or to schedule a reading). Start with a visit here, or a stroll down **Rosalie Alley** to see beautiful voodoo imagery (in the Bywater, off Rampart between Piety and Desire Sts.).

Priestess Miriam, who has practiced for decades at the **Voodoo Spiritual Temple,** 1428 N. Rampart St. (www.voodoospiritualtemple.org; © **504/943-9795**), is the real McCoy, a serene spirit and practitioner in the traditions of the West African ancestors. No pins in dolls here, folks, but healings, prayers, blessings, spiritual consultations, and training are available. The temple is just off Esplanade Avenue, easily accessed from the French Quarter or via the

VISITING marie laveau

The most famous New Orleans Voodoo queen, Marie Laveau was a real woman, although her life has been so mythologized that it is nearly impossible to separate fact from fiction. But who really wants to?

She was born a free woman of color in 1794. A hairdresser by trade, Marie became known for her psychic abilities and powerful gris-gris. Then again, her day job allowed her into the best houses, where she heard all the good gossip and could apply it to her other clientele. In one famous story, a young woman about to be forced into a marriage with a much older, wealthy man approached Marie. She wanted to marry her young lover instead. Marie counseled patience. The marriage went forward, and the happy groom died from a heart attack while dancing with his bride at the reception. After a respectable time, the now-wealthy widow was free to marry her lover.

Marie wholeheartedly believed in Voodoo—and business. Her home at what is now 1020 St. Ann Street was purportedly a gift from a grateful client. A devout Catholic, Marie attended daily Mass and was well known for her charity work. Her death in 1881 was even noted by the *Times-Picayune*.

Her look-alike daughter, Marie II, took over her work, leading some to believe (mistakenly) that Marie I lived a very long time, looking quite well indeed—which only added to her legend. But Marie II allegedly worked more for the darker side than her mother. Her eventual reward, the story goes, was death by poison (delivered by whom is unknown). Visitors have long brought Marie tokens (candles, beads, change) and asked her for favors—she's buried in **St. Louis Cemetery No. 1.** But because misguided or outright disrespectful people marred her tomb with X's (a nasty, illegal fail that, despite what you may hear, does nothing except dishonor her and damage her resting place), the cemetery is now closed to tourists.

Rampart streetcar. Interested, respectful tourists are welcome. Call for an appointment. The vibe feels right at **Crescent City Conjure** (www.crescentcityconjure.us; ✆ **504/421-3189**), a pretty little Marigny shop with supplies and expertise for root, herb, and oil work, along with various other items for practicing hoodoo and witchcraft. Authenticity and education are the watchwords; owner Sen Elias is welcoming of experienced practitioners and patient with the genuinely curious. Readings start at $35 for 15 minutes. For related shops, see p. 246.

ORGANIZED TOURS

The free, self-guided walking tours we've developed for you (see chapter 10) are pretty great, if we do say so ourselves. But there are also great advantages to taking organized tours. Though they're touristy by definition, someone else does the planning, and it's an easy way to get to outlying areas. A good tour guide can entertain, enlighten, and even inspire. We lean toward some of the smaller companies, in hopes that they may have fewer people than the allowable 28 per group. We like to hang close to the guide in case we have questions; they'll often continue to share knowledge while on the way to the next point of interest—and we find that these kinds of serendipitous personal interactions are easier to come by when fewer people are being herded along. It's reassuring that New Orleans tour guides must be licensed, which involves actual study and testing. So not just anyone can load you on a bus and take you for a (literal or figurative) ride.

Tours almost always run rain-or-shine (no refunds), but in some instances you're allowed to move your reservation to another day. Walking tours and large bus tours have a designated meeting point; smaller van tours usually provide pickup at your hotel. Before booking, check for deals on tickets—they pop up regularly on **Groupon** (www.groupon.com) and **Yelp** (www.yelp.com).

Be aware: It's fairly common practice for hotel concierges and storefront tour offices to **earn commission on the tours they sell or recommend** (ditto restaurants). Some may have honest opinions about the merits of one over another, and those may be perfectly good options, but often they're selling you what they get paid to sell. If you're looking for a tour, do the research yourself and cut out the middleman; no matter how you learned about it, pay the fee directly to the company, not to your concierge or a street-corner booth.

And about those "free tours" you may run across: Keep in mind that they're not really free (and they're always packed to the gills). They usually come with a heavy-hitting request for tips, and by the time you tip the guide, you're not far from the cost of tours from established providers. We don't love the business model, and then when we found large chunks of our published walking tours lifted wholesale and republished on their website—without copyright permission or attribution—well, draw your own conclusions about the authenticity of their tours. While you're on the lookout: Hawking tours on the street, including in front of cemeteries, is illegal (although not well enforced). If your guide does that, it's just not a good sign from the get-go about what you're in for.

Tour Companies

We're supportive of legitimate businesses that legitimately support the city we love so much. The following companies offer multiple tours (and may offer discounts if you commit to more than one). Most have walking tours of the **French Quarter,** the **Garden District,** and the **cemeteries,** as well as city van tours and tours to the **plantations** and **swamps** (they provide transportation and tickets to an associated swamp or airboat tour). Other specialty tours are noted, but if you have a particular interest you don't see, contact these companies—customized tours can often be arranged.

All Bout Dat Tours ★★★ This woman-owned, Black-owned tour company is known—and loved—for telling the whole truth, nothing but the truth. On Saturday mornings, singer and storyteller Mikhala leads a moving, powerful Black Heritage tour of Treme, Armstrong Park, and Congo Square. On a 2.5-hour Black Heritage and Jazz tour, you'll be driven around to visit historical sites and meet local shop owners, artists, and elders.

www.allboutdat.com. ℂ **504/457-9439.** Black Heritage Walking Tour $35; Black Heritage and Jazz Tour $60. Check website for other tours and full schedule.

Beyond the Bayou ★★★ We're all thumbs up for this locally owned company. For starters, it's *legitimately* eco-conscious, and one of very few travel companies that's 100% carbon neutral. Groups are small; guides are friendly, fun, factual, and flexible. Tour options are still evolving but include a delightful (and delicious) private 3-hour "cocktail concierge" French Quarter walking circuit (adult bevvies included), an all-day Cajun Country excursion (swamp tour, unique music experiences, and two meals included), and a sustainable swamp tour in the Atchafalaya Basin (breakfast and lunch plus a visit to the Whitney Plantation).

www.beyondthebayoutours.com. ℂ **504/708-5161.** Tours start at $149.

Cajun Encounters ★ This is a large company, but it's also locally owned—a point of pride and also a bit of a hallmark, as they like to hire local guides. It's been around for 25+ years, and tours are on a 33-seat bus. The City & Cemetery bus tour takes you through the French Quarter, St. Louis No. 3 Cemetery, Warehouse and Central Business districts, City Park, and Garden District, with cemetery walk-around opportunities. The company also offers swamp and plantation tours (see chapter 11).

941 Decatur St. www.cajunencounters.com. ℂ **866/928-6877** or 504/834-1770. City + Cemetery Tour $54 adults; $38 children. Swamp tour (with hotel pickup) $59 adults; $38 children. Check website for other tours, schedules, and discount offers.

Gray Line ★ This well-known, well-established (since 1926) nationwide company runs coach and walking tours of the city, swamps, and plantations—in pretty much every combination (including tour/cruise combos with sister companies **Steamboat NATCHEZ** and **City of New Orleans riverboat;** p. 196). River cruises offer fab views and nostalgic fun. As the big kahuna of tour companies, it offers large groups, full-size buses, and a slicker, more scripted presentation—but also a glitch-free operation, from the call center to the deep bench of backup guides to the heavy tour schedule, so one call can set you up.

Toulouse St. at the Mississippi River. www.graylineneworleans.com. ℂ **800/233-2628.** Walking tours start at $29 adults; $15 children. Bus tours start at $49 adults; $20 children. Check website for other tours, prices, and full schedule.

Historic New Orleans Tours ★★★ This is one of our favorite midsize tour companies, mostly because the guides are terrific. Quite often they have advanced degrees in history or other related disciplines, and they're free to bring their own perspectives and interests to the tour, thereby keeping things fresh vs. a noticeably routine script. The company emphasizes authenticity over sensationalism and is particular expert in cemeteries. Guides lead walking tours of the French Quarter, Garden District, and cemetery; plus a fun adults-only "Scandalous Cocktail" tour, which strings together local bars and drinks with tales of historic brothels, organized crime, and even the JFK assassination. The colorful bartenders, when not too busy, also tell their own tales (do pace your drinking, though!). Other special-interest tours (available by advance arrangement, some private) focus on music, literature, film, and the Tremé. If you can get on a tour led by Milton or Rob, all the better. www.tourneworleans.com. ⓒ **504/947-2120.** Most tours $25 adults; $18 students, seniors, and military; $7 children 6–12; free for kids 5 and under. Tours available in French, Spanish, and German.

Hop On, Hop Off City Sightseeing Tours ★ We'll just say it: The Big Red Bus is garish in any city, and downright ugly against this city's historic streets and backdrops (couldn't the local franchise at least have designed them to resemble our local streetcars?). Despite their visual offense, we'll admit these double-deckers offer a good way to get oriented and see the city at your own pace. www.citysightseeingneworleans. ⓒ **800/362-1811.** $39 for unlimited hop on, hop off sightseeing for 1 day ($10 children 3–12). Buses run continuously 9:30am–5:30pm.

Walking Tours

The nonprofit volunteer group **Friends of the Cabildo** ★★ (523 St. Ann St.; www.friendsofthecabildo.org; ⓒ **504/523-3939** or 504/524-9118) offers an excellent 2-hour introductory walking tour of the Quarter, starting from the 1850 House on Jackson Square (see p. 158) daily at 10:30am and 1:30pm. Tour guides are licensed, and often Quarter residents, so they know whereof they speak. Tours cost $25 adults; $20 seniors, students, and military; ages 12 and under free. Purchase tickets online or on-site and arrive 15 minutes early.

One of the more established **walking tours of the Tremé** ★★★, focusing on African-American history and the incredible cultural and musical legacy of this historic neighborhood, is offered by **French Quarter Phantoms** (www. frenchquarterphantoms.com; ⓒ **504/666-8300**). It leaves from 718 N. Rampart St. Saturday through Monday at 10:30am. Reservations are required; it's $22 when booked online. **Know NOLA Tours** ★★★ (www.knownolatours. com; ⓒ **504/264-2483**) also offers a phenomenal African heritage walking tour of the Tremé. Owner/guide Malik is from this culture, and his personal connection to the history and cultural traditions you'll learn about (such as the Mardi Gras Indians and Social Aid & Pleasure Clubs) are an enormous added value to his depth of knowledge. Advance reservations required; times vary. It's $25 for adults and $15 for kids 12 and under.

Two Chicks Walking Tours ★★ (www.twochickswalkingtours.com; ⓒ **504/975-4386**) adds a dollop of sass to its informative, entertaining tours. In the adults-only Bordellos and Ladies of the Night tour, for example, perky guide Christine, adorned in a rainbow tutu, knows her stuff and weaves plenty of standard history through this soft-focus lens, bringing it new interest. Each tour stop has some relation to the oldest profession, from the Ursuline Convent to Storyville. It's a bit bawdy but not at all frivolous (even with the soundtrack of hooker-related tunes played between stops—think "Roxanne" and "House of the Rising Sun"). Our group had men and women of all ages and a mature teen with her parents, and all were equally engaged. The guide went well off-script answering questions, which personalized the tour even if causing it to run a bit over the 2 hours. Most of their tours cost around $30; reservations are required.

For something more high-end and personal, try **Soul of New Orleans Tours** (www.neworleansprivatetours.net; © **504/905-4999**). The delightful, intrepid Cassandra arranges a custom walking or van tour for your small group, however straightforward or unusual. Prices start at $225 for up to six people.

Swamp Tours

Depending on weather, area, and operator, a **swamp tour** can be serene and reverent, eerie and mysterious, or a thrill and a hoot. There's no dearth of tour options, but because of how delicate the eco-system is, we favor those that take measures to preserve the natural environment. The truth is, you'll be hard pressed to find guides who don't throw marshmallows to gators and raccoons, a surefire means of attracting the critters, but one we find pretty cringeworthy (especially since feeding wild animals trains them to view humans as a food source, which can be, um . . . hazardous). We've made efforts to include tours that are ethical and eco-conscious, along with a few of the more mainstream, old-school, locally owned operations. On the following tours, you're likely to see waterfowl such as egrets, owls, herons, bald eagles, and ospreys. Less frequently, you may spot a feral hog, otter, beaver, frog, turtle, raccoon, deer, or nutria. As for alligators, in warm months they're generally plentiful; in cooler months, they sleep, so you probably won't see them. (One note: Regardless of season, keep your hands inside the boat—to a gator, they can look like dinner.) Even during winter hibernation, a morning spent floating on the bayou is pleasant, and learning about how this unique ecosystem contributes to the local culture and economy is quite interesting. Plus, the swamps are simply beautiful.

Most tour operators listed earlier in this chapter under "Tour Companies" (p. 191) provide swamp tours, but they really just coordinate your transportation, narrate the drive, and deliver you to one of the following knowledgeable swamp-tour folks. You can also drive to one of these tours or contact them directly to arrange your transportation from the city.

Dr. Wagner's Honey Island Swamp Tours ★, 41490 Crawford Landing Rd. in Slidell, about 30 miles outside of New Orleans (www.honeyisland swamp.com; © **985/641-1769** or 504/242-5877), takes you into the interior of Honey Island Swamp to view wildlife with native professional naturalist guides, all of whom grew up plying these waters. The guides provide a solid educational experience to go with the pure swamp excitement. They do throw food, so you'll likely see all manner of close-up critters, from gators to raccoons to feral hogs. Small flat-bottom boats—both covered and uncovered—ease through the swamp for about 2 hours. Prices are $25 adults, $15 children 12 and under if you drive to the launch site yourself; or $54 adults and $32 children with hotel pickup in New Orleans.

It's a little farther out and you'll need to provide your own transportation, but we'd be remiss if we didn't add **Annie Miller's Son's Swamp and Marsh Tours** ★, 3718 Southdown Mandalay Rd., Houma (www.annie-miller.com;

EXPLORING THE mighty mississippi

New Orleans has always had a complicated and crucial inter-relationship with water. To understand it better, we recommend **The Great Delta Tour** ★★ (www.thegreatdeltatours.com; ✆ **888/316-1338**), which explores the Mississippi Delta's cultural, economic, and environmental impact on the area. Founder/guide/Master Naturalist Barbara weaves it all together while her van covers a lot of literal and informative ground on this whole-day or half-day eco-tour: from the wetlands to the rivers to canals; from preservation to restoration; and from the shrimpers and fishermen whose families have plied these waters for generations (you'll meet some of them) to the petrochemical industry's effects on them. You'll visit areas that were under 15+ feet of water after the 2005 levee breaches, and areas that will likely be underwater in the very near future. You'll visit the Isleño and Vietnamese communities (lunching at acclaimed Dong Phuong bakery), who've thrived in the Mississippi Delta region for centuries and decades, respectively—with large and largely overlooked impact. This isn't exactly a laugh-a-minute tour, and littler young'uns may get fidgety. But it's a rare opportunity to delve into important topics, and you'll leave wanting to further explore these fascinating regions and issues. Whole-day tours cost $85 adults, $80 seniors and military, $65 under 12; half-day tours are $48 adults, $35 under 12. Departure locations vary (hotel pickups available).

✆ **985/868-4758**). The utterly authentic Jimmy Miller, son of the legendary Alligator Annie, is carrying on in her down-home tradition. Swamp water runs through his veins, and he knows every inch of this bayou. Reservations required; call for schedules. Prices are $30 adults, $15 children 4–12, free for 3 and under; tours run 2 to 2½ hours.

Airboat Adventures ★ (www.airboatadventures.com; ✆ **888/467-9267** or 504/689-2005) is a slick operation with an expansive gift shop (which also houses a rare white gator) and a fleet of boats. Rather than disappearing into swampy seclusion (as you might at some other swamp tour outfits), you're likely to see and hear those other boats as you—and they—speed through on screeching boats (noise-blocking headphones provided), with fearless local captains who get shockingly up close and personal, enough to hand-feed, belly-rub, and even *kiss* the toothy reptiles. Controversial? Yes. Invasive? Probably. Popular? Wildly. Prices are $99 per person for a 6- to 8-passenger boat, or $75 for a 15- to 27-passenger boat; fee includes transportation from New Orleans hotels (about 40 min.); deduct $20 if you arrive on your own. Phone reservations required.

Kayak Tours

Honey Island Swamp Kayak Tours ★★★ (www.honeyislandkayaktours.com; ✆ **504/517-3066**) is owned by friendly, easy-going, eco-conscious Jessica, who knows this swamp like it's her back yard—because it *is her back yard*. Jessica grew up here and takes paddlers into one of the nation's most undisturbed swamps to see ancient cypress trees (one dates from 1803). We love that she walks her eco-talk: She's organized annual river cleanups since

FULL steam AHEAD

C'mon, you know you want to. It's a paddle wheeler on the Mississippi, fer the love of Mark Twain. A river cruise is cheesy, refreshing fun, and gives everyone an excuse to bust out their best "Proud Mary."

The steamboat **NATCHEZ** (www.steamboatnatchez.com; ℂ **800/233-2628** or 504/569-1401), a marvelous three-deck steam-powered sternwheeler, re-creates the 19th-century version that held the record for fastest steamship till the *Robert E. Lee* famously whipped it in 1870—although the

current boat has never lost a race! Now it takes leisurely jazz cruises from 7 to 9pm nightly with the Grammy-nominated Dukes of Dixieland providing the tunes; there's narration for a little history, a steam-engine room for gearheads, and an option to add dinner. There are also daytime cruises at 11:30am or 2:30pm daily, with a lunch option available. Tickets range from $38 to $87 for adults, $15.50 to $40 for kids 6 to 12. *NATCHEZ* is docked at Toulouse Street behind Jax Brewery. Its spiffy newer and newly renovated sister steamboat, the *City of New*

2012 and even grinds into sand the glass bottles she finds. She educates about ecology and wetlands loss and never baits or feeds wildlife. Beginners, kids over 6, and pets are welcome, and guests can swim in certain areas. Also, the launch site is a bar, so if you're hungry or thirsty after the workout, you're set. Tours are 2.5 hours; $59 for adults, $35 for kids 6-12. You'll need your own transportation to get to the launch site.

Kayak-iti-Yat ★★★ (www.kayakitiyat.com; ℂ **985/778-5034** or 512/964-9499) explains city lore from the unique perspective of a kayak along Bayou St. John. When the weather's right, it's a sublime way to explore some historic neighborhoods. Tours range from 2 to 4 hours, with increasing intensity of upper-body workouts (the better to justify last night's indulgent dinner). It's not difficult even for the inexperienced. Tours run daily; times vary, and advance reservations are required. Two-hour tours are $49; 4-hour tours are $84. Two-person minimum. Call for reservations, times, and meeting-place directions. All equipment is provided, but there's no bathroom stop, so plan ahead.

If you're adventuresome and can commit the better part of a day, **Lost Lands Tours ★★** (www.lostlandstours.org; ℂ **504/858-7575**) takes kayakers to the Maurepas Wildlife Management Area, 45 minutes outside of New Orleans, on a 3- to 4-hour paddle through the elegant, mysterious swamps, returning to the city around 3pm. The focus is on the environmental issues surrounding these vital, rapidly disappearing wetlands. It's beautiful and illuminating. Transportation is available between the meeting place and boat launch (four people max); tours are $95 each if four people sign up (otherwise, per-person rates are $120 each for three or $150 each for two people), weather permitting.

Cemetery, Mystical & Mysterious Tours

Interest in the ghostly, supernatural side of New Orleans has always been part of its appeal. It has also resulted in some rather humorous infighting as rival tour

Orleans, which launched in 2019, offers a brunch cruise for a similar range of prices.

The smaller **Creole Queen** (www. creolequeen.com; © **800/445-4109** or 504/529-4567), has a 7:30pm jazz cruise ($52 adults, $26 kids 6–12, free for 5 and under; with buffet dinner $84, $40, and $15 respectively) and a 2½-hour Historical River Cruise, which stops downriver at Chalmette Battlefield, site of the Battle of New Orleans ($36 adults, $15 kids 6–12, free for 5 and under; additional charge for buffet lunch). It's docked at the end of Poydras Street, next to the

Outlets at Riverwalk. The Queen premiered a swanky new sister ship in 2019, the 2,500-passenger, jazz-themed **Riverboat Louis Armstrong;** it doesn't actually cruise the river but offers occasional concerts and events aboard.

All ships have outside decks and inside lounges with A/C or heat as needed, and cocktail bars, of course. Times vary seasonally, so call ahead. Arrive at least a half-hour early to board. **Tip 1:** Check the online coupon sites for discounts. **Tip 2:** There's better food on land. Just sayin'.

operators steal each other's guides, shtick, and customers. We enjoy a good nighttime ghost tour of the Quarter as much as anyone, but we also have to admit that what's available is really hit-or-miss in presentation (it depends on who conducts your particular tour) and more miss than hit with regard to facts. Go for the entertainment value, not for the education, and you won't be disappointed. All the tours stop outside locations where horrifying things supposedly (or actually) happened, or inexplicable sights have been observed. Allegedly. Just be aware that this isn't a haunted-house tour (you don't enter any buildings other than a bar for a mid-tour break), and no ghouls jump out from dark corners. If you do see any spectral action, it'll most likely be due to that bar stop.

We can send you with a clear conscience on the **Cemetery and Voodoo Tour** offered by **Historic New Orleans Tours ★★★** (p. 192), which is consistently fact-based and not sensation-based, though still entertaining. (Some guides are even descendants of people discussed on tours.) At press time, guides were holding court from the gates of both St. Louis Cemeteries 1 and 2. The tour also takes you to Congo Square and the site of Marie Laveau's home. It leaves daily at 10am and 1pm from the courtyard at Backatown Coffee, 301 Basin St. Rates are $25 adults; $18 students, seniors, and active military; $7 children 6 to 12; free 5 and under. They also offer a nighttime **Haunted French Quarter Tour,** 'cause thrills and chills deserve darkness. The tour departs nightly at 7:30pm from 823 Decatur St. (Reserve online.)

A nonprofit organization dedicated to cemetery maintenance, education, tomb restoration, and authentic tours, **Save Our Cemeteries ★★★** (www. saveourcemeteries.org; © **504/525-3377**) offers tours of the Lake Lawn Metairie cemetery (Sun at 10am) and St. Louis Cemetery #3 (Sat at 10am). Tours cost $25, kids under 6 free. Advance reservations required.

New Orleans Secret Tours ★ offers, among other experiences (food, cocktails, LGBTQ), a Voodoo tour led by guides committed to teaching the truths of Voodoo. Tours focus on the actual religion—in history and today—in relationship to slavery and to the City of New Orleans, in myth and reality. The tour visits significant Voodoo locations in and around the French Quarter, including an authentic altar. It's $32; departure dates and times vary. Leaves from the Lost Sock Laundry & Art Gallery at 840 N. Rampart St. Book at www.nosecrettours.com or call ℂ **504/517-5397.**

As for those vampire tours . . . sorry to burst your bubble, friends, but vampires are not real. Personally, we prefer our history with a bit of, well, history—but if tales of bloodsuckery and high drama are what you seek, the current reigning kings are at **French Quarter Phantoms** (www.frenchquarter phantoms.com; ℂ **504/666-8300**). Costumes, fake blood, Dickensian delivery—the whole megillah (but not all the guides do it). Tours cost $20 ($17 when booked online); free for kids 7 and under. They leave from the Voodoo Lounge, 718 N. Rampart St., nightly at 6pm and 8pm. A baby step down on the drama ladder, the 1½-hour New Orleans Vampire tour given by **Haunted History Tours** ★ (www.hauntedhistorytours.com; ℂ **504/861-2727**) departs nightly at 8:30pm from outside St. Louis Cathedral and costs $25 adults, $22 students and seniors, $18 ages 3 to 12, free for 2 and under. Haunted History also offers nighttime French Quarter ghost tours. Advance bookings only via the website.

Tip: These tours usually go out with large groups. Try to stay near the front, so you can see and hear your guide—even the ones with the most booming voices have to regulate their delivery out of respect for French Quarter residents.

Food & Beverage Tours & Classes

Ain't no cuisine in the world like New Orleans cuisine. True dat. Consider taking this fact one tasty step further with a food and beverage tour or class.

Cooking class instructors, just like tour guides, can make or break the experience. **Destination Kitchen Food Tours** ★★ (www.destination-kitchen. com; ℂ **855/353-6634**) delivers a sprightly and cosmopolitan approach to epicurious Big Easy, showcasing culinary and cocktail offerings of the French Quarter and Garden District (or lesser-known areas like Oak and Freret Sts.), with or without a cooking experience. Commentary is offered in English, French, or Spanish, the three languages that New Orleans has spoken for centuries. Food and beverage tours range from $70 to $100. Some include transportation. History and music tours also available.

Doctor Gumbo ★★★ (www.doctorgumbo.com; ℂ **504/473-4823**) offers three tours, including a 4-hour food and cocktail "gastronomic odyssey" to seven establishments, where you're pretty much guaranteed a fun, flavorful, and enormously filling experience. Reservations required. Tours from $70 to $130.

Drink and Learn ★★★ (www.drinkandlearn.com; ℂ **504/578-8280**) is Elizabeth Pearce's aptly named company. The noted cocktail impresario and author of *Drink Dat New Orleans* punctuates her walking tour with stops at cocktail-orientated sites, where participants partake of pre-poured smart beverages. Pearce's lively delivery, depth of knowledge, and visual aids transport guests through centuries of New Orleans' storied cocktail history. Day and night Cocktail Tours meet at Vacherie Restaurant (p. 70), 827 Toulouse St., and cost $55 per person (21 and over only). Book in advance; the small groups fill up fast.

NOLA Brewing Brewery Tour ★★ (3001 Tchoupitoulas St.; www.nolabrewing.com; ✆ **504/896-9996**) isn't a walking tour, but an actual tour through the largest local craft brewery in New Orleans. The 35-minute, brewmaster-led look behind the scenes is wildly popular (read: crowded) not only for the free samples, but also because it's informative. Kickass New York–style **Nola Pizza Co.** is on-site and goes down well with the taproom's brews. For more on local breweries, see p. 229. The taproom is open Sunday to Thursdays 11am to 9pm and Friday and Saturday 11am to 10pm. Call ahead; you may need to book in advance.

One expert mixologist. Up to 10 mixology neophytes. Four drinks. One hour. Or thereabouts. Perched on stools around the nightclub's small upstairs bar, things move snappily along during **The Maison's Mixology Class** ★★ (508 Frenchmen St.; www.maisonfrenchmen.com/mixology; ✆ **504/371-5543**), with an instructor doling out cocktail history and how-tos, prepping the next round, and fielding questions—all with aplomb (while occasionally shouting over the band playing downstairs). You get to mix, stir, and schmooze. It's not meant as a drunk-fest, but simple logistics dictate that there will be buzzing. You'll leave with recipes, a few new friends, some new skills, and the aforementioned buzz. Class is in session Friday and Saturday at 5pm (book in advance through the website) and costs $50. Participants must be 21 or over.

Also see the **Confederacy of Cruisers Culinary Bike Tour** (below).

Bicycle & Other Wheeled Tours

A bike tour is a terrific way to explore some lesser-seen parts of this flat city up close and in depth. Our suggested tours go at an outright leisurely pace, so you needn't be a serious rider, but bike familiarity and a healthy dose of pluck will help you handle potholes and traffic (including stretches along some busy avenues). Do opt-in to the optional helmet; bring sunscreen, a hat, rain poncho, and water (though most tours provide a small starter bottle) as conditions dictate. While a restroom stop is included, you'd be wise to take care of that before departure, too. For regular old bike rentals, see p. 291.

Confederacy of Cruisers (www.confederacyofcruisers.com; ✆ **504/400-5468**) offers a history and culture bike tour with an itinerary that hits parts of the Marigny, Bywater, 7th Ward, and Tremé on comfortable, well-maintained single-gear cruisers with baskets. The eight-person-maximum, guide-led group pulls over about every 10 minutes at such diverse stops as the New Orleans Center for Creative Arts (NOCCA), St. Roch Cemetery, and the *Plessy v. Ferguson* landmark, where guides offer up well-informed cultural and architectural insights. The 3-hour tours are $49 and depart twice daily. Its **culinary bike tour** takes different itineraries, but all go to killer, off-the-beaten-track eateries favored by locals. The "tastes" are copious, and the guides' laidback deliveries bely a serious depth of food knowledge (and history and architecture), which they impart between bites. It's $79 all-inclusive, and worth it. It runs daily at 10:15am. A **cocktail tour** is $10 more, but we're just not sure riding these streets after four or five drinks is such a great idea. Reservations by email are a must. Most tours depart from 634 Elysian Fields Avenue.

Flambeaux Tours (www.flambeauxtours.com; ✆ **504/321-1505**) has thrice-daily bike tours of the French Quarter, Marigny, and Tremé; the Garden District and Uptown; and Mid-City; they can customize your itinerary. They also have weekend nighttime social rides on bikes tricked out with wheel lights—you'll get the looks (10 riders minimum, $350). Bikes are comfy and well-maintained (also available for rental), and if you can get on one of Eric's tours, he's a native New Orleanian and particularly good with the cultural quips ($50; book ahead online).

Or, try **Get Up N Ride** (www.facebook.com/getupnridenola), with hip locals on loosely organized social rides around towns most Tuesday nights. You need your own bike (see p. 291 for rentals) with a light and a lock. Check their Facebook page for meeting location and other details.

Corny it may seem, but a **horse-drawn carriage tour** of the Quarter or beyond has eternal romantic allure. The "horses" are actually mules (they handle the city heat and humidity better), often bedecked with ribbons, flowers, and even hats. Drivers seem to be in a fierce competition to win the "most entertaining" award. They share history and anecdotes (some of dubious authenticity) and can customize itineraries on request. Carriages wait on Decatur Street in front of Jackson Square from 8am to midnight (except in heavy rain). We like Black-owned, family-owned **Mid-City Carriages** (www.mid-citycarriages.com; ✆ **504/581-4415**) and family-owned **Royal Carriages** (www.neworleanscarriages.com; ✆ **504/943-8820**), in business for 80 years, making it the oldest sightseeing carriage company in the U.S. Join a tour on a waiting carriage (you may be sharing with other tourists) for $25 per person per ½ hour. There are French Quarter or ghost-themed 1-hour group tours for $50 per person. Private carriages run about $125 for 30 minutes or $200-$250 for 1 hour, for up to four people. Call for custom tours and hotel pickups.

ESPECIALLY FOR KIDS

If you plan to give the kids a lifelong guilt complex for confining you to your hotel room when you *know* all that clubbing and fooding is going on outside, then perhaps New Orleans is better done *sans enfants*. But the truth is, despite its reputation as a playground for grown-ups, the Big Easy is a terrific family destination, with oodles of only-in-New-Orleans activities to entertain them (and you). **Mardi Gras** (p. 49) and **Jazz Fest** (p. 59) are both doable and enjoyable with kids, as are many of the organized tours (p. 190). *Tip:* Those above spooking age love to tour the cemeteries (no touching!) and haunted places, but long walking tours of historic homes and landmarks may be best left to the grown-ups.

The **French Quarter** in and of itself is cool for kids 6 and over. You can while away a pleasant morning on a Quarter walkabout, seeing the architecture and peeking into shops, checking out the street performers, with a rest stop for powder-sugary beignets at **Café du Monde** (p. 146). If you have kids of museum-going age, the Mardi Gras exhibit at the **Presbytère** (p. 163) or the Hurricane exhibit at the **Cabildo** (p. 160) will hold their attention for a while. You can probably talk them into a riverfront walk along scenic Woldenberg Park in warm weather, ending at a great splash fountain in front of Audubon Aquarium.

Even self-conscious tweens fall for a **carriage ride** around the Quarter (see "Bicycle & Other Wheeled Tours," p. 199), and it works for all ages when it's hot and nap time is closing in—it might even rock the little ones to sleep. The **Canal Street Ferry** (p. 178) crosses the Mississippi River and ends just preboredom (and makes a great intro to reading *Huckleberry Finn* together). Add a clackety-clacking **streetcar ride** (p. 291), and you've hit the trifecta of fascinating transportation options.

If it's just a matter of needing to run, jump, swing, and blow off some energy, head for **Cabrini Playground** (www.cabriniplayground.com) in the residential northeast corner of the French Quarter at Barracks and Dauphine streets.

A number of the city's top attractions are obviously family-friendly, including the wonderful **Audubon Aquarium of the Americas** (p. 154). The St. Charles Streetcar will deliver you to **Audubon Park** (p. 180), home to three great playgrounds. Our top pick is the **Walnut Street Playground** (built by Drew Brees, the Saints' recently retired quarterback, who can sometimes be seen there with his own kids). It's inclusive, offering features—including two ziplines—to kids of all abilities. And right there at the park, the highly regarded **Audubon Zoo** (p. 180), complete with a seasonal splash park for the pool-deprived, is both lovely and a great diversion.

For more animal action, a **swamp tour** (p. 194) is a sure-fire winner. While you're not guaranteed to see gators, it's a pretty good bet (in warm months), and even so, hey, you're on a boat in a swamp. Many also offer speedier **airboats** for young adrenaline junkies.

Older kids may get a kick out of **Escape My Room** ★ (633 Constance St., www.escapemyroom.com; ✆ **504/475-7580**), a New Orleans version of the popular escape room craze. Participants are "locked" in one of four heavily decorated rooms (our fave is the tough Inventor's Attic) themed around an actual local family. They must answer clues to solve a mystery and thereby "escape." It works best when clue hunters' backgrounds and ages are diverse ($34–$53 per person, advance reservations required). It's not for young kids, and those 12 and older must be accompanied by adults. Bring your reading glasses!

Kidding Around in City Park

And then there is the wonder that is **City Park.** We've already mentioned some of the all-ages features (see p. 181), and with the stunning **Louisiana Children's Museum** now located there, you could just make it your base (details below). In December, a million holiday lights turn the City Park landscape into fairy-tale scenery for the **Celebration in the Oaks** (p. 33). Here are a few more of the park's offerings for kids and parents to love:

Big Lake Boating and Biking ★★ Big Lake in City Park is a pretty spot for a boat ride, and the kids can scour the shoreline for turtles. Canoes, kayaks, and glam **swan boats** (LED-lit at night) can be rented from **Wheel Fun,** which also rents **bicycles, tandems,** and **surreys** for use inside City Park. All that pedaling action can be a workout, which means you can justify a visit to nearby **Angelo Brocato's** ice cream parlor afterward (p. 146). Life jackets (provided) required. Check website and www.groupon.com for discounts.

Wheel Fun Rentals, Big Lake Trail. www.wheelfunrentals.com. © **504/252-5655.** Swan boat $11/hr. adults, $6/kids (holds 4–5); kayak $16–$23/hr.; surrey $27–$37/hr.; bike $8–$20/hr. (in-park use only). Check website for various rental hours.

Carousel Gardens and Children's Storyland ★★ The under-8 set will be delighted with this recently updated playground (rated one of the 10 best in the country by *Child* magazine), its charming décor inspired by well-known children's stories and rhymes. It offers plenty of characters to slide down and climb on and generally get juvenile ya-yas out. Kids and adults will enjoy the carousel, Ferris wheels, bumper cars, miniature train, Tilt-a-Whirl, ladybug-shaped roller coaster, and other rides at the **Carousel Gardens** amusement park, also in City Park. Delighting local families since 1906, the gorgeous carousel (or "da flying horses," as real locals call it) is one of only 100 all-wood merry-go-rounds in the country, and the only one in the state. The carousel was recently being reconstructed and was due to reopen in spring 2022.

Victory Ave. www.neworleanscitypark.com/in-the-park/carousel-gardens. © **504/483-9402.** Storyland admission $6; Storyland & Carousel Gardens unlimited rides $25. Free for kids under 36" tall. Storyland Wed–Fri 10am–4:30pm, Sat–Sun 10am–6pm. Carousel Gardens mid-Mar to mid-Nov Sat–Sun 11am–6pm, longer hours June–July.

City Putt Miniature Golf ★ We love the design of these two 18-hole miniature golf courses: On one course, each hole is designed around a New Orleans neighborhood, with iconic statues and signage and stuff; the other course keys off of statewide themes (learning is fun!).

Victory Dr., across from Storyland and Botanical Garden. www.neworleanscitypark. com/in-the-park/city-putt. © **504/483-9385.** $10 adults; $8 children 4–12; free for kids 3 and under. Wed–Fri 3–10pm; Sat–Sun noon–10pm; last rental 1 hr. before closing. Hours may vary during Celebration in the Oaks.

Louisiana Children's Museum ★★★ This stunning, brand-new museum is really a playground in disguise. Set amidst 8 gorgeous acres of nature, it furtively "teaches" sustainability and stewardship of our world and its waters in wonderful, hands-on ways. Geared toward kids 8 and under and their parents and caregivers (but fine for older kids, too), it's a dazzling gem that makes a visit to already-jam-packed City Park de rigueur for families. A few outdoor and lobby exhibits are free; beyond that, five interactive themed galleries focus on "play and learning in equal parts." "Follow That Food" goes from fields and waters to ports, markets, and tables; "Make Your Mark" immerses young'uns in the fun of New Orleans' music, art, and architecture. Other highlights include a kid-powered barge pedaled across a lake to an island made of

GET THE KIDS jazzed

In such a musical town, there aren't as many music options for the younger set as we'd like. Blame it on the booze—most music venues serve alcohol and are legally prohibited from allowing anyone younger than 21 to enter. The street performers along **Royal Street** and in **Jackson Square** work well, but fear not, we've got a few other interesting ideas.

o **Frenchmen Street Clubs** Yes—you can make the Frenchmen Street scene with kids in tow. The **Maison** (p. 216) and **Three Muses** (p. 218) allow kids for the early shows, which usually start around 4 or 5pm (parents must be in attendance). Grab a table, order snacks, and let the little ones shake their miniature groove thangs. They may be asked to leave when the tables break down and the drinking crowd moves in, around 9 or 10pm.

o **Mid-City Lanes Rock 'n' Bowl** Hey, you got cool music in our bowling! Wait, you got bowling in our nightclub! It's two in one, and both work. It's hard to go wrong with this one, although the music usually doesn't get started till 8-ish, so bedtime might need to be pushed back. Kids with parents are welcome. See p. 220.

o **Music Box Village** Kids (like adults) may or may not "get" the performances here—the eclectic music made in this "sonic village" isn't exactly mainstream. But curious minds of all ages will find the musical-instrument structures fascinating. During the hands-on public hours, visitors can explore them and create their own eclectic tunes. See p. 231.

o **Preservation Hall** The historic, inimitable traditional jazz venue is open to all ages. The earliest show starts at 5pm nightly; get there early so the young ones can sit far enough in front to see (if they're really young, sit by the door in case a boredom-induced quick exit is required). See p. 213.

o **New Orleans Jazz Museum at the Old U.S. Mint** This museum has some form of free music nearly every day, and all ages are welcome. See p. 163.

recycled plastic; a "make-your-own-music" garden; and "All About Bubbles," whose perspective is from inside a bubble. While the adults are learning about learning (and gathering ample take-home ideas), kids have plenty of roam, crawl, explore, and play space, including the darling "kindows" (kid-size pop-out window cubbies). The on-site Acorn Café satisfies all bellies.

15 Henry Thomas Drive. www.lcm.org. 𝒞 **504/523-1357.** $14 adults and kids 1 and up; seniors, active military $12. Wed–Sat 9:30am–4:30pm; Sun 11:30am–4:30pm. Admission by timed-entry tickets, available online.

Kid-Oriented Tours

French Quartour Kids Tour ★★ The company's founder—a former schoolteacher and an excellent kid-wrangler—conducts the tours in costume and manages to maintain the enthusiasm level for a full 1½ hours. Six tours cover all age groups, with treasure hunts, spooky tours, and music tours. Her spiels keep it relatable, bringing attention to what life was like for kids in the olden days. History is definitely conveyed as sites are explored, but the lessons use props (which she totes around in a colorful wheeled cart), storytelling, play-acting, and enough gory details to hold most kids' focus. Emphasis on "most." Ask about seasonally themed tours.

www.frenchquartourkids.com. ℂ **504/975-5355.** $20 per person (includes kids and adults; 1 adult chaperone required). Tour times vary, btw 9:30am–5pm daily. Reservations required.

Lucky Bean Tours ★★ This company's 2-hour small-group French Quarter Kids & Family Tour (designed for ages 5–12) is a popular, personalized primer. Kid whisperers explain everything from Mardi Gras to jazz funerals to pirates and voodoo, as well as how NOLA families of old shopped, played, and lived. And what child (or tween or teen or adult) doesn't love snacks, shwag, and crafts? Guides come prepared with food, beads, second-line handkerchiefs, and materials to make toys local kids have crafted for generations.

www.luckybeantours.com. ℂ **504/975-5355.** $30 per person, free for kids 4 and under. Tours leave Jackson Sq. at 10am. Advance reservations required.

SPECTATOR SPORTS

Big Easy Rollergirls ★ Okay, it's a total goof, but a hoot of a goof. By definition, roller derby is going to be a bit wild (though the athleticism can't be denied). Mix in New Orleans, and the resulting outcome is pure wackiness. The Big Easy babes play it up for all it's worth, and the crowd action is equally rowdy. More of a hipster scene but with a smattering of families, it's all in fun, and worth the modest ticket price just to check out the cheerleaders, halftime entertainment, outfits, and food trucks. Season runs March–August.

University of New Orleans' Lakefront Arena, 6801 Franklin Ave. www.facebook.com/bigeasyrollergirls. Tickets $15 at door, $10 in advance online; kids $5, free for ages 6 and under.

New Orleans Pelicans ★★ What to say about the NBA Pelicans? They're up, they're down, they're up again. During a glorious stretch when Chris Paul and Anthony Davis led the team to playoffs and higher heights, tickets were pricey and hard to acquire; nowadays, they're affordable (as in, $5 plus tax) and easily procured. This will likely change as Zion Williamson—the number one draft pick in 2019—returns to the court after his 2021 foot surgery. The Pelicans put on a great b-ball show, and it's worth the price of admission to see the celebrity mascots *USA Today* deemed the two creepiest mascots in sports: Pierre the Pelican, who was revamped after scaring too many kids, and King Cake Baby, whom tourists find terrifying and locals find hilariously, perfectly, weirdly New Orleans.

Smoothie King Center, 1501 Girod St. www.nba.com/pelicans. ℂ **504/525-4667.** Tickets start at $4 and go way up.

New Orleans Saints ★★★ Who dat won the Super Bowl? The Saints' incredible Super Bowl XLIV victory in 2010 was the culmination of the city's

BET YOU CAN FIND places to gamble

The history of the **Fair Grounds Race Course** (1751 Gentilly Blvd.; www.fair groundsracecourse.com; ✆ **504/944-5515**) is *deep*. Founded in 1872, it's the third oldest in the country; General Custer ran his horses here, and it was, until recently, the longest homestretch in North America. The horse-racing season kicks off on Thanksgiving, a tradition for many local families who don their finest attire and silliest hats for the occasion. Horses run through March; simulcasts and OTB continue on and a large slots casino is open year-round (Mon–Sat 9am–midnight, Sun 10am–midnight). Bordering the French Quarter, **Harrah's Casino,** 229 Poydras St.,

(www.caesars.com/harrahs-new-orleansorleans; ✆ **504/533-6000**), is quite like a Vegas casino: 115,000 sq. ft., 1,700 slot machines, more than 100 tables, sports betting, a steakhouse restaurant, and the Masquerade Lounge. *Tip:* The voluminous buffet can satisfy the most serious munchies for not-so-serious cash. A classic riverboat-style casino, **Treasure Chest Casino** (www. treasurechest.com; ✆ **504/443-8000**) is docked on Lake Pontchartrain not far from New Orleans airport. **Slot machines** can be found in every imaginable locale in the city, from bars to laundromats, separated (by law) from the main room by a door or curtain.

43-year collective dream (to say nothing of the end of 43 years of frustration), in which the beloved 'Aints finally won the big one, becoming a metaphor for the city's post-Katrina comeback and a source of frenzied pride. A scandal here and there hasn't come close to dampening the enthusiasm for this team (2019's missed call actually increased it). Whether you're a football fan or not, try to get yourself inside the Superdome (p. 178) for a Saints game—there's really nothing like it. Your best bet is the **NFL Ticket Exchange** (www.ticket exchangebyticketmaster.com). Otherwise, the pregame party at **Champions Square** outside the Superdome is an excellent place to start your game day. Another option: Watching the game in a local bar is a cheap cultural experience—not only will you get to know the city, you'll often find free food.

Caesars Superdome, 1500 block of Poydras St. Saints home office: 5800 Airline Dr., Metairie. www.neworleanssaints.com. ✆ **504/733-0255**. Ticket info: ✆ **504/731-1700**. Tickets around $45–astronomical, depending on the game.

NOLA Gold Rugby ★★ When major league rugby came to the U.S. in 2018, NOLA Gold was one of the inaugural teams. The Gold plays in a 10,000-seat stadium in Metairie where even cheap-seat views are surprisingly good. Games are rowdy, bone-bashing, and boozy, but also family-oriented and affordable—and at 80 minutes, they whip by. We appreciate the commentator who explains the game in real time so we're not entirely lost. Arrive early for the epic parking-lot tailgating; 30 minutes pre-kickoff, a brass band leads fans in a second line parade up the ramp into the stadium and onto the field where the team's practicing, so you can high-five your favorite players as they warm up. The brass band stays for the whole game, because . . . New Orleans. It's a blast.

The Gold Mine at the Shrine on Airline, 6000 Airline Dr., Metairie. www.nolagoldrugby. com. ✆ **504/733-0255**. Tickets $18 and up; season pass $135.

NEW ORLEANS NIGHTLIFE

By Diana K. Schwam

8

New Orleans works her wily exotic charms most effectively after dark, when the cocktail slingers and jazz singers ply their magic. It is impossible to imagine this city without its non-stop melodious soundtrack. After all, this is the town that sends you to your grave with music and then dances back from the cemetery. It's the city that lets the good times roll and lets you take them to go (you can stroll the streets with a drink in hand, as long as it's in a plastic "go-cup"—or "geaux," to use the faux French). Here, some of the world's greatest musicians—no exaggeration—can be seen and heard with relative ease in remarkably intimate surroundings. And when the clubs get too full, no matter: The crowd spills into the street, where the talking, drinking, and dancing continue.

In this chapter, we'll help you wend your way through all the theater, club, and bar awesomeness. (Here, that's "Daylife" as well as "Nightlife.") But keep in mind that tomorrow beckons, with more of the city's enchantments to explore. First, a few things to know:

o **Club-hopping is easy.** The city is compact, so most clubs are within easy walking or taxi distance from your hotel or dinner locale. On Bourbon and Frenchmen Streets they're closely clustered so you can hop from one to another.

o **Showtimes vary.** Posted start and end times range from strict to strictly a suggestion (and sometimes indicate door times, not show times). Call if your schedule depends on it. Shows often start later than promised—except when they start on time.

o **Show proof.** Of age verification (everywhere), and vaccine status (some places, as we write, require proof of Covid-19 vaccination and face masks). A few allow kids to early shows when accompanied by a parent (see p. 203). Mostly, though, it's 21+, and expect to be carded. Even you, grandpa. It's da law.

- **No cover doesn't mean free.** It means buy beverages (boozy or not) and tip the band generously. And/or buy their vinyl, CDs, merch, whatever.
- **Drinking is optional.** Despite its preeminent reputation, non-drinkers can and do enjoy New Orleans. Fun is fun. You be you.
- **Early shows rock.** Shows starting from 2ish to 7pm are often no or low cover, mellower music, and a great way to avoid the crowds and the crazy. Some allow kids.
- **Cover charges vary widely.** During big events and for big acts, they can be much higher than cited here. Crowd sizes also vary accordingly.
- **Music is everywhere.** A blurry line separates "clubs" from bars, restaurants, hotel lounges, streets, parks, front porches, and stoops. All can showcase excellent music, so don't overlook them.
- **Smoking is nowhere.** All clubs, bars, and restaurants are nonsmoking. Take it to the streets, if you must (or courtyards, where allowed).
- **What's going on.** Check **Offbeat.com** and sign up for "Weekly Beat" e-mails or go to **WWOZ.org/livewire** (you can also tune in to 90.7; club lineups are announced at the top of every odd hour). Both have good apps, worthy of downloading for the duration of your visit (and after).

THE RHYTHMS OF NEW ORLEANS

New Orleans R&B legend Ernie K-Doe was once quoted as saying, "I'm not sure, but I think all music came from New Orleans." What might be a more accurate account—and relatively hyperbole-free—is that all music came *to* New Orleans. Any style you can name, from African field hollers to industrial techno-rock to classical, finds its way to the Crescent City. Paul McCartney, Led Zeppelin, Trent Reznor, and Beyoncé have recorded here. Pianist James Booker, an eye-patched eccentric even by New Orleans standards, could make a Bach chorale strut like a second-line umbrella twirler. Then all those styles are blended, shaken, and stirred into a new, distinctive, and frothy concoction that could come *from* nowhere else.

That sublime hybrid is what you'll likely find: jazz descended from Buddy Bolden, Louis Armstrong, and their Storyville compatriots. Head-bobbing R&B transmitted via Fats Domino and Professor Longhair. Hip hop incorporating rhythmic Mardi Gras Indian chants. Brass bands of the second-lines, infused with funk exuberance. Soak it in.

The Jazz Life of New Orleans

—With thanks to jazz historian George Hocutt

Music was of great importance to the Louisiana settlers and their Creole offspring, and early on the city had a fascination with marching bands (records of parades go back to 1787). Bands became de rigueur at occasions from baptisms to funerals ad infinitum—as they still are today.

CAN'T-MISS NEW ORLEANS MUSICAL
experiences

- **Kermit Ruffins,** anywhere he and his rowdy trumpet show up (try Blue Nile, Bullets, or his clubs, Kermit's 9th Ward Juke Joint or the iconic Mother-in-Law Lounge).
- The **Soul Rebels** brass band's roof-raising Thursday sets at Les Bon Temps Roulé (4801 Magazine St.; lbtrnola.com).
- The soul-wrenching, party-starting early set of the sublime **John Boutté** at d.b.a.
- Multi-instrumentalist (and mad musical mastermind) **Aurora Nealand** with her Royal Roses or in other forms. Try to keep your toes from tapping. Just. Try.
- The mellow tones and vivid lyrics of folk-leaning **Paul Sanchez** or troubadour **Andrew Duhon.**
- Piano wizards **Tom McDermott, Josh Paxton,** or **Jon Cleary,** solo or not.
- **Swank hotel lounging.** Besides the Four Seasons' **Chandelier**

Bar (p. 226), Maison de la Luz's **Bar Marilou** (p. 226), the Mazarin's **Patrick's Bar Vin** (p. 225), the Monteleone's **Carousel Bar** (p. 222), the Pontchartrain's rooftop **Hot Tin** (p. 223), the Prince Conti's **Bombay Club** (p. 222), the Roosevelt's **Sazerac Bar** (p. 228), or the Windsor Court's **Polo Club** (p. 228), try the **Davenport Lounge** at the Ritz-Carlton (p. 68) or the Virgin Hotel's rooftop **Dreamboat Lounge** (p. 80).
- Catching someone huge like Pearl Jam or Patti Smith at iconic **Tipitina's** (give the 'Fess Head statue an extra rub for your good fortune).
- Brilliant singer-songwriter-guitarist and Death Valley dry wit **Alex McMurray** solo or in any of his many guises, like the Tin Men trio or, if you hit the jackpot, doing sea shanties with the Valparaiso Men's Chorus.

In the early 19th century, enslaved people were allowed to congregate in the area known as **Congo Square** (now part of Armstrong Park) for dancing and drumming to the rhythms of their African and Caribbean homelands. Eventually these enslaved people and free people of color became accomplished instrumentalists. When blues, work songs, hollers, and spirituals were melded with their native-based rhythms and syncopations, the precursor to jazz was forming. The music was taking on a distinctly New Orleanian aura.

By the late 1890s, cornetist **Charles "Buddy" Bolden,** the "First Man of Jazz" (a film about him was released in 2019), and drummer **"Papa" Jack Laine** were taking the sounds to the next level, and to white audiences—helped along by Black vaudeville crossing the color line. (In a part of the Central Business District once called **Backatown,** their original haunts still stand—barely—awaiting pending renovation. We hope. Check out the **Eagle Saloon** at 401-403 S. Rampart St. and the neighboring **Iroquois Theatre,** where an adolescent Louis Armstrong first played, at 413-415 S. Rampart St.)

Meanwhile, the Storyville brothel zone was flourishing on nearby Basin Street (p. 21). The entertainment lineup at the better houses included a piano

- **Rebirth Brass Band** at the Maple Leaf on a Tuesday. Or anywhere, any day.
- Bowling and dancing at **Rock 'n' Bowl**, especially on Thursday zydeco night.
- Trombonist **"Big Sam" Williams.** He grooves, he moves, and you will, too.
- Excellent modern jazz in the city's premier room, **Snug Harbor.**
- Seeing the Grammy-winning **Nightcrawlers, Stooges, Hot 8, TBC,** or **Rebirth** and finally getting what this brass band thing is all about—and never wanting it to stop.
- The dulcet clarinet of **Dr. Michael White,** which snakecharms even diehard jazz cynics, or **Don Vappie** on banjo, the swingingest strumming around.
- **DJ Soul Sister,** whose rainbow flow jams the floor monthly at the **Hi-Ho Lounge** (p. 219).

- **The Wild Magnolias.** Just. See. Them. Or **Cha Wa.** Or any Mardi Gras Indians band.
- **Meschiya Lake** breaking hearts (and saving **Chickie Wah Wah** from an early demise).
- **Flow Tribe** or **People Museum.** You can say you knew them when.
- The inimitable **Walter Wolfman Washington,** for the blues _and_ the suits.
- The brassy blues belting and skintight rhythms of **Lulu and the Broadsides** at the Starlight or anywhere.
- A show at **Preservation Hall,** where the soul of traditional jazz oozes from the instruments as much as from the ancient-looking walls.
- Breakout national stars **Trombone Shorty, The Revivalists, Tank & the Bangas, Galactic,** or **Big Freedia** if they happen to be back in town on their home turf.

player in the parlor—the immortal **Jelly Roll Morton** among them. By the 1920s, as sleazy Storyville was folding, its players took the new sounds on the road: **Kid Ory** to California; **King Oliver** and his protégé **Louis Armstrong** to Chicago; **Papa Jack and his Original Dixieland Jazz Band** to New York. Their shows drew hordes and their records sold wildly. After World War II, **Sidney Bechet** and horn set up shop in France, and jazz consumed the continent. The jazz genie was officially out of the bottle and the craze was on.

New Orleans is still producing jazz greats and pushing the form forward. Start with **Ellis Marsalis,** father to jazz-playing sons **Branford, Jason, Delfeayo,** and Pulitzer Prize–winning trumpeter **Wynton. Jon Batiste, Christian Scott aTunde Adjuah, Terence Blanchard,** and brothers **Troy "Trombone Shorty" Andrews** and **James "Satchmo of the Ghetto" Andrews** (among others) blow their horns to ever-adventurous distances. Obviously, the city still abounds with creativity.

Meanwhile, the nouveau traditional jazz movement is mad hot. On any given night in any given club, players from their 20s to their 70s share the bandstand, covering Jelly Roll or Django—or playing originals straight outta their eras. The **Jazz Vipers, Smokin' Time Jazz Band, Ibervillianaires, Tuba Skinny, Little Big Horns,** and **Hot Club of New Orleans** start the long list. Cellist **Helen Gillet,** bassist **James Singleton,** percussion madman **Mike Dillon,** and multi-instrumentalist **Aurora Nealand** are among those advancing into newer reaches of the form; **Charlie and the Tropicales** harken back to mid-century calypso hipness.

Brass Bands

Today, there's way more to New Orleans brass bands than the post-funeral "second line" parade of "When the Saints Go Marching In." Now, brass is imbued with funk, R&B, reggae, and hip hop, and appearances on the HBO TV show *Tremé* have engendered a new crop of fans. Classics like the **Tremé Brass Band** and **Olympia Brass Band** still hold court (in their current incarnations), but the revival goes back to the late 1980s, when **Dirty Dozen Brass Band** and **Rebirth Brass Band** started mixing things up. Today this horn-heavy, booty-moving, New-Orleans-born-and-bred style packs the clubs and the streets. Try to catch the sounds of Louis Armstrong-inspired and reigning king **Kermit Ruffins and his Barbecue Swingers; Hot 8; New Birth;** or the **Stooges.** Or newer arrivals like the blazing **TBC Brass Band,** raging **Brass-a-Holics,** or the pumping street-corner gods, **Soul Brass.** Did we mention the ladies-only **Pinettes?** Yeah, see them.

Cajun & Zydeco

Cajun and zydeco don't come from New Orleans at all, despite the soundtrack you hear blaring out of Bourbon Street T-shirt shops. Both genres originated in the bayous of southwest Louisiana, a good 3 hours away. Their foundations lie in the arrival of two different French-speaking peoples in the swamp country: white Acadians (French migrants who were booted out of Nova Scotia by the English in 1755) and Black Creoles (who came from the Caribbean slave trade). Both oppressed groups took to the folksy button accordion, newly introduced from Germany and France, which added a richness and power to their fiddle and guitar music. Later, drums, amplifiers, and steel guitars filled out the sound.

The styles began to separate after WWII, with the Cajuns gravitating toward country-and-western swing and Creole musicians being heavily influenced by urban blues. **D. L. Menard** (the Cajun Hank Williams) and **Clifton Chenier** (the King of Zydeco) pioneered exciting new strains in their respective directions. During the early 1960s folk-music boom, such figures as the **Balfa Brothers** and fiddler **Dennis McGee** performed at folk festivals. A turning point came when a Cajun group received a standing ovation at the 1964 Newport Festival, energizing the form and Cajun pride, and spawning a new generation of Cajun musicians.

The proud new generation was led by accordion guru **Marc Savoy** and his multi-instrumentalist/author wife **Ann,** and fiddler **Michael Doucet** and his band **Beausoleil**—with **Steve Riley** and **Zachary Richard** in quick-step. The next generation of ambassadors, like the Grammy-winning **Pine Leaf Boys, Feaufollet,** and intoxicating hybridists **Sweet Crude, Michot's Melody Makers,** and **Lost Bayou Ramblers,** are mixing in new styles while venerating old-timey music. (The **Ramblers** regularly cover the **Pogues,** scrambling Irish punk with Cajun French in a madcap, Mensa-level mash-up. It works crazy well.)

As for zydeco, the late **Boozoo Chavis, John Delafose,** and **Rockin' Sidney** joined king Clifton Chenier and added their own embellishments. More recently, **Nathan Williams** and the late, great, stately **Beau Jocque** did the same. The form is thriving today thanks to some of their musical progeny, including Chenier's son **C. J.,** Delafose's son **Geno,** various Dopsie kin (**Dwayne** and **Rockin' Dopsie, Jr.**) and **Ardoins** (**Sean** and **Chris**); plus **Keith Frank,** hybridist **'Lil Nathan,** Grammy winner **Terrance Simien,** and powerhouse **Amanda Shaw.** Many of this latest crop of players, including **Corey Ledet** and **Jeffrey Broussard,** are blending in hip hop and other influences du jour. Also see "Cajun Country," p. 277.

Rhythm & Blues (& Hip Hop & Bounce, Oh My)

The Delta isn't far, and the blues' gospel and African-Caribbean bloodlines took deep root in the Crescent City. In the 1950s, **Fats Domino** and his great producer-collaborator **Dave Bartholomew** fused those elements into the seminal hits "Blueberry Hill" and "Walkin' to New Orleans." Simultaneously, **Professor Longhair** and **"Champion" Jack Dupree** were developing trailblazing piano sounds, contrasting mournful woe with party-time spirit. More piano genii followed, from **James Booker** to **Dr. John,** while Grammy winner **Jon Batiste, Jon Cleary, Josh Paxton, Tom McDermott, Joe Krown, David Torkanowsky,** and many more carry on the city's unparalleled piano tradition. Crooners **Johnny Adams** and "Soul Queen" **Irma Thomas** kept it smooth (she still does—don't miss her if you get the chance).

The long-time keepers of the flame, the **Neville Brothers,** retired (R.I.P. saxophonist Charles, who passed in 2018), but their funky offshoot the **Meters** are going strong in various guises. The genre has broadly evolved into funk, jam, and hip hop—with **Lil Wayne** and **Juvenile** and the beleaguered Cash Money label driving that end, not to mention the only-in-New-Orleans, proto-twerking bounce genre led by gender-tweaking post-rapper **Big Freedia.** And we gotta include funksters **Galactic** and **Dumpstaphunk,** resurgent **Choppa,** recently blown-up **Tank and the Bangas,** and breakout superstar **Troy "Trombone Shorty" Andrews.**

The bluesy end of the spectrum is well represented by late greats like **Snooks Eaglin** and **Earl King.** "Deacon" John Moore has been on the scene since the 1950s, as a guitarist, banjo player, singer, and bandleader par excellence, and still rips it up (and oh, the stories he tells). Current keepers of the acclaim include axe men **Tab Benoit, Anders Osborne, Walter "Wolfman" Washington, Little Freddie King,** and **Sonny Landreth,** and harpist nonpareil **Johnny Sansone,** to name a few.

CLUB LISTINGS

Unless otherwise noted in the listings below, clubs are open 7 days a week.

The French Quarter

BB King's ★ We tend to eschew chains. With so many wonderfully individualistic choices, why go cookie-cutter? But there's comfort in familiarity, and if Frenchmen Street's crowds and scruffiness seem overwhelming or off-putting, BB King's won't. The multilevel room is spacious and accessible; the people-pleasin' burgers, barbecue, beers, and blues are reliable. Service isn't perfect, but live music almost all day is a hard-to-find plus. 1104 Decatur St. www.bbkings. com/new-orleans. ℭ **504/934-5464.** No cover except for occasional concerts.

The Famous Door ★★ Open since 1934, it's the oldest music club on Bourbon Street, and many luminaries have played here (including a 13-year-old Harry Connick, Jr.). Great historic value, cheap drinks, no cover (usually), loud but super-solid cover bands. Drunken dancing might happen. 339 Bourbon St. ℭ **504/598-4334.** No cover.

Fritzel's European Jazz Pub ★★ From the open street front, this 1831 building looks sketchy, overlookable even. The pushy door folk will aggressively attempt to hustle you to a seat at the cramped picnic tables and rush you to order a drink. Let them: Some of the best traditional jazz is played on the teensy stage here, and the quasi-hofbrau atmosphere breeds community. Music starts mid-day; good kids and cats can come. 733 Bourbon St. www.fritzels jazz.net. ℭ **504/586-4800.** 1-drink minimum per set.

House of Blues ★ You can find this chain club elsewhere and you can find authentic (vs. ersatz) folk-art-laden roadhouses within a few miles (hello, Tipitina's). It's lost its domineering booking muscle and in-crowd draw, but occasionally a name booking comes through and burlesque nights are fun. These days we're more apt to go for the smaller, lesser-used rooms: The upstairs **Parish** feels inviting and feels real; the lovely **courtyard** actually *is* real. 225 Decatur St. www.houseofblues.com/neworleans. ℭ **504/310-4999.** Cover varies.

The Jazz Playhouse ★★ This Bourbon Street retreat in the Sonesta Hotel is a go-to spot for established and on-the-rise local jazz and funk artists (Big Sam, Shannon Powell, Luther Kent, and Brass-a-Holics are sure things). Trixie Minx, queen of the NOLA burlesque scene, holds court Fridays. The well-prepared drinks aren't inexpensive (and service can be a bit snooty) in the swank, draperied mid-size room. Seating (sometimes club-style at small tables, sometimes theater-style) can get crammed at popular shows. But we're still in the "Yes" column for solid talent, good sound, and FQ convenience. 300 Bourbon St. in Royal Sonesta Hotel. www.sonesta.com/jazzplayhouse. ℭ **504/553-2299.** Cover $25 and up.

Maison Bourbon ★★ Despite its location and the DEDICATED TO THE PRESERVATION OF JAZZ sign (an attempt to confuse tourists into thinking this is Preservation Hall?), Maison Bourbon isn't a tourist trap. The music is authentic, often superb Dixieland and traditional jazz, and the brick-lined room is a respite from the mayhem outside. 641 Bourbon St. www.maisonbourbon. com. ℭ **504/522-8818.** 1-drink minimum per set.

Palm Court Jazz Cafe ★★ This stylish dinner club is a reliable, mature, comfortable venue for top-notch classic and traditional jazz Wednesday through Sunday. Table seating (make reservations), with a small back bar for non-diners. 1204 Decatur St. www.palmcourtjazzcafe.com. ℭ **504/525-0200.** Wed–Sun 7–11pm. Cover $5 and up; entrees $17–$32.

Preservation Hall ★★★ The decaying, ancient-looking building lends just the right air of consecration to this, an essential spot for traditional jazz fans and, well, everyone (Robert Plant and U2's Edge have sat in here). With little air, so-so sight lines, no bathrooms (you are warned), and constant crowds, the awesomeness is in the hallowed, intimate atmosphere and the superb musicianship. And awesome it is, truly. There are three to four shows nightly, starting at 5pm; each lasts about an hour. The bench seats are filled in order of arrival, so go early or prepare to stand or sit on the floor (or book limited first-row seats well in advance). No drinks, no bathrooms. 726 St. Peter St. www.preservationhall.com. ℭ **504/522-2841.** Cover $25 (standing); $40 (bench); $50 (first row). Reserve in advance.

Starlight Lounge ★★★ This blessed refuge, mere feet from Bourbon Street, drips with dusky atmosphere. Respectful audiences and some of the city's best jazz, blues, and cross-genre musicians squeeze in, allowing just a sliver of floor for dancers. A gleaming chandelier and glass-arch-topped pocket doors enhance the sexy vibe of the two intimate rooms, the former parlor of a 1779 Creole Cottage. Across a petite courtyard, **Avila Grill** serves scrumptious *arepas, loma saltado,* and other Venezuelan bar foods (nonclub-goers welcome). 817 St. Louis St. www.starlightloungenola.com. ℭ **504/827-1655.** Cover free–$20. Daily 3pm–late.

Toulouse Theatre ★★ We're awfully excited to see this long-time venue renewed and run under the auspices of Preservation Hall's Ben Jaffe, a beloved local culture keeper. His team has made a few for-the-better changes to the classic boudoir décor and is booking an eclectic line-up of locals and visiting bands spanning funk to world music to jazz to hip hop to country to DJs (we're livin' on a prayer that the popular '80s Night dance party returns). 615 Toulouse St. toulousetheatre.com. ℭ **504/571-9771.** Cover $15-$40.

Frenchmen Street & the Marigny

Bamboula's ★★ Choose Bamboula's if the Frenchmen scene is a bit too scruffy for your taste or your feet are failing you. The food and drinks won't knock your socks off, but said socks will at least be seated (unless they're up dancing). The vibe is reproduced vintage; the unquestionably good music starts early and ends late. 514 Frenchmen St. www.bamboulasnola.com. ℭ **504/944-8461.** Usually noon–2am. Cover free–$20.

New Orleans Nightlife

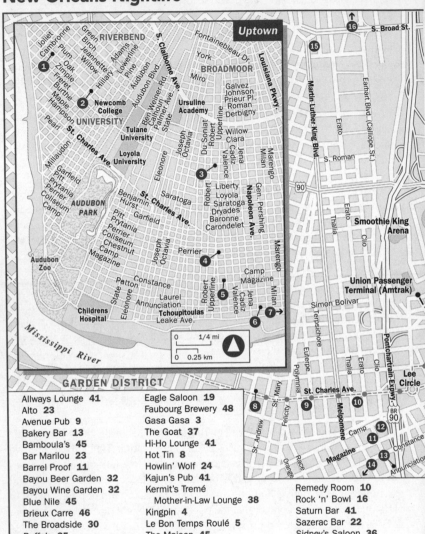

Information

- ●●●● Riverfront streetcar route/stops
- ——●— St. Charles streetcar route/stops
- ——■— Canal St. streetcar route/stops
- ——●— Rampart St./ St. Claude Ave. streetcar route/stops

N. Broad St.

N. Dorgenois
N. Rocheblave
N. Tonti
N. Miro
N. Galvez
N. Johnson
N. Prieur
N. Roman
Derbigny

LAFITTE GREENWAY

Orleans Ave.
St. Ann
Dumaine
St. Phillip
Ursulines Ave.

N. Dorgenois
N. Rocheblave
N. Tonti
N. Miro
N. Galvez

TREMÉ DISTRICT

Bayou Rd.

N. Clalborne Ave.

Caesar's Superdome

Poydras

ST. LOUIS CEMETERY NO. 2

ST. LOUIS CEMETERY NO. 1

N. Villere

LOUIS ARMSTRONG PARK

Esplanade

St. Bernard Ave.

St. Claude Ave.

See "French Quarter Nightlife" map

Basin St.

N. Rampart

Univ. Pl.

Conti
St. Louis
Toulouse

St. Ann
Dumaine

Burgundy

Barracks

FAUBOURG MARIGNY

Loyola Ave.

S. Rampart

O'Keefe St.
Gravier
Union
Perdido

Common
Canal

Dauphine

Bourbon

Ursulines
Gov. Nichols

Esplanade

Touro
Frenchmen

Elysian Fields Ave.

CENTRAL BUSINESS DISTRICT

Lafayette
Carondelet

FRENCH QUARTER

Royal

Marigny

Iberville
Bienville

Chartres

Mandeville

Spain

St. Charles Ave.

Poydras

Lafayette Square

Decatur

French Market

Chartres St.

BYWATER

Camp

Julia
Girod

Magazine St.

St. Joseph

Tchoupitoulas
Commerce
S. Peters
Fulton

River

Convention Center

Howard Ave.

Calliope

Conv. Ctr.

RIVERFRONT

Canal St. Ferry (Toll)

Mississippi

Morgan
Delaronde

Seguin

ALGIERS

0 ——— 1/4 mi
0 ——— 0.25 km

Riverfront streetcar closed for construction until 2022-2023

Gay Nightlife
Country Club **47**
Mag's 940 **42**

Performing Arts, Theaters, Cruises
Café Istanbul **41**
Civic Theater **18**
The Fillmore **27**
Mahalia Jackson Theater
  for the Performing Arts **33**
Marigny Opera House **47**
Mudlark Theater **41**
Music Box Village **41**
Orpheum **21**
Southern Repertory Theater **34**

Blue Nile ★★ This chill, mid-size club has a killer sound system and pretty much zero attitude (or seating, or decor, save some murals), making it a fun hang for the local, reggae, funk and jam bands they book (DJs rule the upstairs room). Trumpeter Kermit Ruffins and funksters the Cesar Brothers have been mainstays. The club recently renovated; so call ahead to make sure it has re-opened. 532 Frenchmen St. www.bluenilelive.com. ✆ **504/766-6193.** Cover free–$15.

Buffa's ★★ "Hey, let's throw some diner-style tables and chairs in our nondescript back room, book some top local jazz-leaning musicians, and create a friendly, laid-back scene." Okay, we're in. The burgers are juicy, the beer cold, and kids are welcome. Post-pandemic policy requires purchase of a whole table ($60, seats six) per party. Still not awful if it's just two of you—the quality of their bookings usually merits $30 each, especially if it's Tom & Aurora. 1001 Esplanade Ave. www.buffasbar.com. ✆ **504/949-0038.** Rarely a cover.

d.b.a. ★★★ A favorite bar/nightclub for its quality bookings and sound, laid-back vibe, and superb beer and spirits selections (scaled back in pandemic times, we hope it revives). Shows (usually) start on time and feature a wide variety of excellent Louisiana talent like magnificent crooner John Boutté, the tight blues of Walter Washington, and breakout bluesy rockers Honey Island Swamp Band, as well as the occasional on-the-cusp national band. Mostly standing-room only, and the low stage doesn't help those in the back (maybe that's why they're so dang chatty). *Tips:* Hit the early shows—always good, often free. Hit the sublime John Boutte's Sunday residency (not free, but well worth the cover). 618 Frenchmen St. www.dbaneworleans.com. ✆ **504/942-3731.** Cover free–$20, occasionally higher.

The Maison ★★ This brick-walled Frenchmen mainstay has civilized, spacious table seating, food service, and old-timey jazz early in the evening; after 10pm the tables get kicked out and it gets funkier, danceable, and down. The second-level wraparound balcony is a good hang when the main floor gets too packed (sometimes it's VIP; the third floor is a dance club on weekends). Drinks and food are serviceable, but brunch and swing dance lessons are awfully fun, and the Smoking Time Jazz Band on Saturdays is a sure bet. Also check out the mixology classes, p. 199. Under 18 okay early in evening. 508 Frenchmen St. www.maisonfrenchman.com. ✆ **504/371-5543.** Cover free–$15.

Snug Harbor ★★★ This sit-down concert-style club, the first music venue on Frenchmen Street, is the city's premier showcase for contemporary jazz. Two levels provide mostly good viewing (beware the pillars upstairs—try to sit along the rail) for the attentive audience. They only book top-tier acts—there's no bad show—but Dr. Michael White, Herlin Riley, Delfeayo Marsalis, and Stanton Moore's regular gigs are sure bets. The adjoining restaurant has great burgers and more, making for a one-stop date night. Monitors screen the concerts in the low-ceilinged bar—for the budget-minded, the next-best thing to live. Advance ticketing is wise. 626 Frenchmen St. www.snug jazz.com. ✆ **504/949-0696.** Cover $15–$40.

French Quarter Nightlife

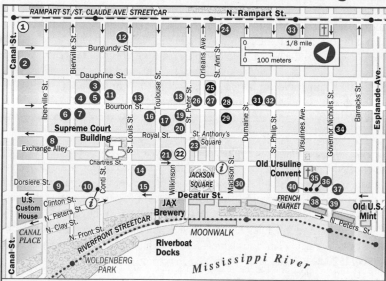

Clubs & Bars ●

The Abbey **36**
Aunt Tiki's **37**
B.B. King's **38**
Bar Tonique **24**
Bombay Club **3**
Cane & Table **35**
Carousel Bar at the Monteleone Hotel **8**
Cat's Meow **26**
Crescent City Brewhouse **15**
Davenport Lounge at the Ritz Carlton **2**
The Dungeon **16**
Effervescence **33**
Erin Rose **11**
Famous Door **5**
French 75 Bar at Arnaud's **4**
Fritzel's European Jazz Pub **27**

House of Blues **9**
The Jazz Playhouse **7**
Jewel of the South **12**
Kerry Irish Pub **10**
Lafitte's Blacksmith Shop **32**
Maison Bourbon **18**
Manolito **30**
Molly's at the Market **40**
Napoleon House **14**
Palm Court Jazz Cafe **39**
Pat O'Brien's **19**
Patrick's Bar Vin **6**
Peychaud's **17**
Pirate's Alley Café and Absinthe House **23**
Preservation Hall **20**
Starlight Lounge **13**
Toulouse Theatre **21**

Gay Nightlife ●

Bourbon Pub—Parade Disco **28**
Café Lafitte in Exile **31**
Golden Lantern **34**
Good Friends Bar & Queens Head Pub **25**
Oz **29**

Theaters, Performing Arts, Cruises ○

Le Petit Théâtre du Vieux Carré **22**
Saenger Theatre **1**

ⓘ Information

 Rampart St./St. Claude Ave. streetcar route/stops

The Spotted Cat Music Club ★★★ Our aesthetic leans toward cramped rooms, little amplification, and scrappy bands with a fresh take on big-band, old timey, gypsy, hot—well, any type of swinging—jazz. So we adore the oft-crowded Cat. The scarce seats are hardly comfy, but when it's swinging the 100% reliably fine music is the real deal, as evidenced by the frenetic-footed jitterbuggers squeezed in front of the minute stage. We love the uncrowded early hours (music starts at 2pm) and scrappy local artwork. Sidewalk seating added post-pandemic works for a drink and a footrest (the music doesn't reach). Cash only, and please tip the band! 623 Frenchmen St. www.spottedcatmusicclub.com. No phone. Cover free–$10, higher for special events. 1 drink per set.

Three Muses ★★★ Sophisticated modern lounge meets classic 1920s saloon, and we likey. It serves up beautifully balanced, new-timey cocktails and mouthwatering small Asian-influenced plates, set to old-timey tunes (it's one of the few Frenchmen St. venues with decent food). The scant tables and stools go fast; reserve in advance or expect a line when the street is hopping. If they're here, don't miss Debbie Davies, Antoine Diel, or Monty Banks. Kids okay early. Tip the band! 536 Frenchmen St. www.3musesnola.com. ℭ **504/252-4801.** Thurs–Sun 4–10pm. $3 music charge.

Elsewhere Around the City

The Broadside ★★ The Broad Theatre was already our favorite place to catch a flick. When communal movie viewing went out the door during the pandemic, so did the Broad. Enter the Broadside, an outdoor music venue alongside the theater, that got many neighbors through Covid-19 when indoor clubs were closed. Dress for the weather and join the locals at this laid-back scene for music or classic films on the outdoor screen (come early to get a chair, or bring your own chair or blanket). There's usually a food truck. 600 Broad St. broadsidenola.com. Tickets $5–$20.

Bullet's Sports Bar ★★ Situated on a residential street named for the civil rights attorney credited with fighting local Jim Crow laws, this unassuming 7th Ward bar comes alive with a bullet on Fridays when the all-female Pinettes brass band plays (and if trumpeter Shamarr Allen plays or, okay, a lot of others). The crowd is friendly, bartenders efficient (order a set-up, it's practically required and part of the fun), and the experience pure booty-shaking

---

Bender Mender

If the aftermath of clubbing leaves you with a morning-after case of the liquid flu, consider the **Remedy Room.** An actual M.D. hooks you up to an actual I.V. packed with fluids, vitamins, and various other restoratives, to get you upright and sharp for that 1pm swamp tour or conference call. Next time, remember: one glass of water with each cocktail (1224 St. Charles Ave.; www.theremedyroom.com; ℭ **504/301-1670;** $149 and up).

Club Listings

NEW ORLEANS NIGHTLIFE

THE ST. CLAUDE & ST. BERNARD scenes

The scruffy local alternative types have gentrified carved out a pulsing metal-punk-and-bluegrass-infused scene (well, all the genres) along stretches of St. Claude and St. Bernard Avenues in the Marigny. If this is what you're into (or if you think Frenchmen St. has jumped the shark), check out the sundry bookings at colorful **Carnaval** (2227 St. Claude Ave.; www.carnavallounge.com; ℂ **504/265-8855**). At the spacious, comfortable **Hi-Ho Lounge** (2239 St. Claude Ave.; www.hiholounge.net; ℂ **504/945-4446**), we dig Monday night's BYOBanjo bluegrass jam, the eclectic local bookings, and poutine from Fry & Pie. The loose, welcoming karaoke at 24-hour **Kajun's Pub** (2256 St. Claude Ave.; www.kajunpub.com; ℂ **504/947-3735**) and the drag-centric **AllWays Lounge** (2240 St. Claude Ave.; www.theallwayslounge.com;

ℂ **504/218-5778**) round out the tatty, happening street scene. These clubs are just a few blocks from the Marigny and Frenchmen Street.

Up the road a bit, **Saturn Bar** in Bywater retains its art-project-meets-*Lost-In-Space* dive vibe with rotating indie, funk, karaoke, trivia, whatever (3067 St. Claude Ave.; ℂ **504/949-7532**). **The Goat** covers the metal/goth/punk/alternative angle (1301 St. Bernard Ave.; www.facebook.com/thegoatneworleans; ℂ **504/252-4747**). **Sidney's Saloon** is less hard-core but completes this block's scruffy trifecta (1200 St. Bernard Ave.; sidneyssaloon.com; ℂ **504/224-2672**). Do take a cab, and don't wander into the transitional bordering areas. Hungry? See p. 116 for nearby food options.

NOLA. There might be a barbecue truck outside for eats. It's about a 2-mile cab ride from Bourbon Street. Don't wander. 2441 A.P. Tureaud Ave. ℂ **504/948-4003**.

Chickie Wah-Wah ★★★ We're ever so fond of this Mid-City club, and especially glad that actual musicians, including regular Meschiya Lake, stepped in to save it from demise after the owner's sudden passing in 2021. Top local roots, rock, blues, and singer-songwriter acts draw reverent crowds to the clean, midsize, shotgun-style room decorated with cool old tin signs. Food usually pops up in the kitchen or outside. It's off the Canal Street streetcar at N. White Street, just past Broad. Try to catch Paul Sanchez, Tom McDermott, Jon Cleary, Susan Cowsill (yup, that one). 2828 Canal St. www.chickiewahwah.com. ℂ **504/304-4714**. Cover $10–$25.

Culture Park ★★ Essentially it's a huge, grown-up backyard party–if you tricked out your sprawling yard with a bar, DJ deck, big screen, dance floor, a bunch of picnic tables, some yard games, a few deck-style seating areas, swings, and, yup, a jacuzzi (no one was in it when we were there, but I'm sure it happens). This former service station is now a venue for a great daytime or gameday hang; crowds can swell at night when the hip hop and R&B cranks. Food trucks provide snacks; drinks are reasonable; and the vibe is casual, with plenty of locals but scant indoor or covered space (or parking, or seating for that matter—skip the stilettos). 3000 Franklin Ave. instagram.com/cultureparknola. ℂ **504/520-0130**. Cover free–$20.

Gasa Gasa ★ Filling the eclectic, indie-rock niche in a single room, Gasa draws a Tulane-to-20-something crowd. Occasional readings, art exhibits, the hopping Freret Street scene, and the mind-blowing exterior mural by Berlin-based street artist MTO augment the allure. 4920 Freret St. www.gasagasa.com. ℂ **504/304-7110.** Cover free–$20.

The Howlin' Wolf ★★ The big (10,000-sq.-ft.) not-at-all-bad Wolf brings to the Warehouse District leading local and occasional mid-level national acts focusing on rock, funk, and jam (Leftover Salmon, of Montreal; local faves like Anders Osborne, and Dumpstaphunk). Good sound, good sight lines, good times—especially Sundays, when the Hot 8 brass band plays the smaller "Den." *Fun fact:* The bar is from Al Capone's Chicago hotel. 907 S. Peters St. www.thehowlinwolf.com. ℂ **504/529-5844.** Cover $5–$50.

Kermit's Tremé Mother-in-Law Lounge ★ All aboard! If you've come to New Orleans to pay homage to its musical past, this brightly muraled, historic spot formerly owned by dearly beloved Ernie K-Doe (who sang "Mother-in-Law") is a requisite touchstone. Décor once featured his illustrious manikin, but no longer, sadly. Lately it mostly draws 7th Ward locals and blasts overamplified beats. But if Kermit or brass bands are blowing (Sun, lately) it's well worth a visit. Bonus if he's also barbecuing or Tootsie's manning the fryer. 1500 S. Claiborne Ave. www.facebook.com/ruffinsbbq. ℂ **504/975-3955.** Cover varies. Most shows 6pm–midnight.

Maple Leaf Bar ★★★ This classic New Orleans club is a locals bar by day, a poetry hub on Sundays (3pm readings, a 30-year tradition), and a medium-size, tin-ceilinged, twinkle-light-strung club at night. Personal space can become a wistful memory when the crowds pack in (usually by 11), and the drunk frat crowd can be maddening; seek temporary refuge on the back patio, at the back bar's junky pool table, or on the sidewalk where the overflow party goes. But it's got that magical, transformative vibe you can't manufacture, and when Rebirth rips it up on Tuesdays it's pretty much a NOLA must-do (if you're only around on Mon, see The Trio). 8316 Oak St. www.mapleleafbar.com. ℂ **504/866-9359.** Cover $10–$20.

Rock 'n' Bowl ★★★ Bowling. Bands. Beer. If you can't have fun here, we give up. There's swing most Wednesdays, zydeco on Thursdays, and local blues, rockabilly, rock, and who cares what else on other nights. It's an utter hoot and an unbeatable experience that draws all ages and types (well, check your politics at the door) to the lanes and spacious, well-air-conditioned dance floor. The custom-embroidered bowling shirts make splendid souvenirs, and the vintage hanging ball return is from the still-missed pre-Katrina location. *Note:* Private parties sometimes take over, so call ahead. 3016 S. Carrollton Ave. www.rocknbowl.com. ℂ **504/861-1700.** Bowling $25/hr. per lane, $1 shoe rental; show admission $5–$25. Mon–Fri 4pm–late; Sat 11:30am–late; Sun check calendar.

Tipitina's ★★★ Dedicated to the late piano master Professor Longhair (that's him in bronze just inside the entrance; rub his head for luck), Tip's is,

NEW ORLEANS NIGHTLIFE Club Listings

cajun & zydeco JOINTS

There are few of these here in the big city; then again Cajun and zydeco music didn't originate in New Orleans. Dance halls are plentiful in Lafayette and environs—see p. 279. You might catch the world-renowned Beausoleil, raucous Pine Leaf Boys, or edgy Lost Bayou Ramblers at **d.b.a.** (p. 216) or **Tipitina's** (p. 220) while they're in town. Tip's hosts a Fais do-do (usually the first Sun at 5, but check) with live Cajun music and dancing;

on Thursday nights at **Rock 'n' Bowl** (p. 220), Zydeco rules and dancers vie for "hottest." The surest bet is **Mulate's** (201 Julia St.; www.mulates.com; ✆ **504/522-1492**), a tourist-friendly, conventioneer-laden dinner-dancehall with so-so food, live music, and patient instructors Wednesday through Sunday. It's folksy all-ages fun, and if I can two-step, anyone can. Call to make sure it's not closed for a private event.

if not *the* New Orleans club, a major musical touchstone and a reliable place for top local and out-of-town roots, brass, jam, and rock bands from Wilco to Willie Nelson. If you can catch locals like Troy "Trombone Shorty" Andrews, Galactic (who bought the place in 2019), or the Funky Meters here, do not waver for a sec. It's nothing fancy: four walls, buncha bars, wraparound balcony (often reserved for VIPs), and a stage (which, if you're under 6 ft., isn't easy to see from the back on crowded nights). This uptown (location, not atmosphere) institution has good (loud) sound and air-con, and there's usually some food truck action. Get advance tix for festival bookings and other big-name acts, and plan on cabbing. They're supposed to open an adjunct piano bar soon. We're looking forward. 18+ okay. 501 Napoleon Ave. www.tipitinas. com. ✆ **504/895-8477.** Cover $10–$40.

THE BAR SCENE

You won't have any trouble finding a place to drink in New Orleans. Heck, thanks to liberal laws and "go-cups," you won't have to spend a minute *without* a drink in hand. But there's more to this town than bars (much), and more to bars than Bourbon Street (ditto), so as with all things, let moderation preside. There, that's our sermon. Our suggestions include some of the most convivial, quaint, or downright eccentric spots; also keep in mind that many hotels and restaurants have excellent bars; see chapters 5 and 6.

The French Quarter & the Faubourg Marigny

Bar Tonique ★★ If we lived in this Quarter's-edge neighborhood, this might be our bar. The crew and clientele (including many service-industry folk) are supremely hip, but they're doing everything so right that they've earned a bit of smug. We don't care, because mostly we're there to glow in the candlelight bouncing off the original brick walls, or cozy up with our honey in the smoochy booths near the working fireplace, and sip on a prodigious punches, a superbly poured cocktail, or a $6 happy-hour special (the best

Pat O'Brien's & the Mighty Hurricane

Pat O'Brien's, 718 St. Peter St. (www. patobriens.com; ℂ **504/525-4823**), is world-famous for the hefty, vivid red drink with the big-wind name. The bar's owners created the Hurricane's rum-heavy formula during a 1940s whiskey shortage. It's served in hurricane-lamp-style glasses (including, if it survives the coronavirus, a 3-gal. magnum size, taller than many small children and shared through long straws, while standing up, at least for the first few sips). Naturally, this attracts drinkers in droves. The entrance line can get long, and the once-peaceful courtyard can get raucous. In all honesty, the $11.50 drink is kinda sickly sweet, but it's a rite of passage and the glass is a great souvenir (they'll pack it up for you). All this means Pat O's is still a reliable, rowdy, friendly introduction to New Orleans. The dark dueling-pianos lounge is awfully fun (music starts 6pm, 2pm weekends)—send up a napkin, a 10-spot, and a prayer with your request and get ready to sing along. Locals populate the main bar up front, but when weather permits, the often-boisterous tropical patio with the flaming fountain is the place to be.

Sazerac deal in town). You know they're serious about the drinks, because there is nothing—nothing—to eat. So order in. 820 N. Rampart St. www.bar tonique.com. ℂ **504/324-6045.**

The Bombay Club ★★ This grown-up, wood-paneled bar/restaurant/British library is an oasis of civility just off Bourbon Street We absolutely order something with gin from the long martini list, along with the boudin croquettes (the food is quite good; so is the happy hour). We're supremely fond of the fetching curtained back booths, and most eves someone talented is tickling the upright keys. 830 Conti St., in the Prince Conti Hotel. www.bombay clubneworleans.com. ℂ **504/577-2237.**

Cane & Table ★★★ C&T's "sophisticated faded" decor is marked by perfectly distressed plaster and brick walls, sparkly chandeliers, a gleaming white-marble bar top, and a slim, sexy patio. But rum (that's the cane) is the star, mixed with house-made ingredients and squeezed-to-order juice by some of New Orleans' most revered craft cocktail revivalists. They call it proto-tiki; we call it high-culture colonialism. The complex flavors may not be for everyone, so start with the fruity Hurricane & Table. Excellent small and large plates follow the Latin/Caribbean tide: Share the tostones, but bogart the crispy spiced ribs. Love. There's no sign; it's next to Coop's. 1113 Decatur St. www.caneandtablenola.com. ℂ **504/581-1112.**

Carousel Bar at the Monteleone Hotel ★★ No, you're not drunk (or maybe you are). The bar *is* spinning (one drink per rotation is the purported ratio—don't worry, its slo-o-o-w). There's plenty of soignée sofa seating and fine piano-based entertainment, but the classic experience requires a coveted seat at one of the 25 barstools ringing the Carousel, sipping a Vieux Carré cocktail, invented here some 70 years ago. Be prepared to wait for your (literal) turn. 214 Royal St. www.hotelmonteleone.com/carouselbar. ℂ **504/523-3341.**

Cat's Meow ★   The drinks and drink specials flow aplenty—the better to loosen the larynx at this Bourbon Street karaoke mecca. Whether or not you take the mic, the scene is entertaining, and the crowds get thick. Then they get drunk. The action starts at 4pm daily and goes late. 701 Bourbon St. www.cats karaoke.com. © **504/523-2951.**

Crescent City Brewhouse ★★   When it was opened by a world-renowned master brewer in 1991, CCB was the first new brewery in New Orleans in more than 70 years. Its German-style beers still hold up, and come with a full menu, an excellent balcony view, and live jazz. 527 Decatur St. www. crescentcitybrewhouse.com. © **888/819-9330** or 504/522-0571.

Effervescence ★★   What's not to love? This white-on-white-on-crystal bub-pub on a low-key stretch of Rampart Street is ideal for a languid evening or a sparkling Sunday morning. It's low-commitment fancy: dressy or jeans, a flute or a magnum, a date or a chick night. The expansive list of all things bubbly ranges from a $6 half-glass of prosecco to fun flights to a Roederer magnum. Oysters and small plates (emphasis on the small) provide spot-on accompaniments. 1036 N. Rampart St. www.nolabubbles.com. © **504/509-7644.**

Erin Rose ★★★   Triple threat: friendly, unassuming Irish Pub, cocktail bar, and **Killer PoBoys** in the back room. That's the name *and* the bold-but-accurate description of the enterprise. Try the rum-marinated pork-belly po' boy with citrus lime slaw. Killer, indeed (so good they opened another location, **Big Killer PoBoys,** at 219 Dauphine St.). Erin's signature frozen Irish coffee eradicates humidity: highly recommended as a mid-afternoon pick-me-up. 811 Conti St. www.erinrosebar.com. © **504/522-3573.**

French 75 Bar at Arnaud's ★★★   A beautiful, intimate bar space in one of the Quarter's most venerable restaurants (p. 97), French 75 has won a James Beard Award for Outstanding Bar Program. It feels like drinking in New Orleans should: classic and classy. Bartenders are adept at vintage mixes (including a perfect Ramos Gin Fizz and the namesake French 75 champagne cocktail) and original concoctions. Order a side of Arnaud's dreamy soufflé potatoes to munch on. Perfection. 813 Bienville St. www.arnaudsrestaurant.com/bars/french-75. © **504/523-5433.**

Hot Tin ★★★   Leading the pack among the explosion of rooftop bars (also see **Alto** at the Ace Hotel [p. 78] and **Monkey Board** at the Troubadour [p. 83]), the gorgeous Ponchartrain Hotel's Hot Tin is designed to resemble a 1940s writer's studio (but with fancy cocktails). The vintage vibe is cool, but the main draw is THE VIEW. One of the best in the city, day or night. Be sure to seek out the less astounding back terrace for an alternate perspective. 2301 St. Charles Ave. (take lobby elevator on right). www.hottinbar.com. © **504/323-1500.**

Jewel of the South ★★★   At this upper-Quarter gem, the "Jewel" reference is not just a nod to a classic Southern cocktail. Truly, everything here is jewel-like, from the exquisitely prepared cocktails (no surprise—the

GAME on

proprietors are two revered stalwarts of New Orleans' modern cocktail era) to the demure dining room and come-hither courtyard. While they're intentional, passionate, and proud about their products, they're not precious. Those interested in mixology are willingly indulged; those with an appetite can enjoy finely plated modern tapas and caviar; those who come for fun or flirtation will find their needs fulfilled. 1026 St. Louis St. www.jewelnola.com. ✆ **504/265-8816.**

Kerry Irish Pub ★   This pub has darts, pool, a proper pint of Guinness, and, occasionally, Beth Patterson, who mashes traditional Celtic folk, honeyed originals, metal-to-acoustic conversions, and hilariously filthy knockoffs. Sometimes a Bob Dylan tribute, too. The Kerry specializes in very-late-night drinking. Nightcap, anyone? 331 Decatur St. www.facebook.com/Kerry-Irish-Pub-163926209622. ✆ **504/527-5954.**

Lafitte's Blacksmith Shop ★★   Even if it wasn't a legendary pirate's lair and the oldest bar (and maybe building) in the Quarter, Lafitte's would merit a visit. It's ancient and ultra-atmospheric, so despite the crowd chatter and blaring jukebox (when much-preferred piano man Mike Hood isn't around), sipping an ale in this crumbling, cavern-like, candlelit interior is nearly akin to time traveling. Avoid the vaunted Voodoo daiquiri, a.k.a. Purple Drank, and stick with beer and ambience instead. 941 Bourbon St. www.lafittesblacksmithshop.com. ✆ **504/593-9761.**

Manolito ★★   This teensy divot just off Decatur Street, helmed by some of the city's shiniest bar luminaries, will likely be populated by cocktail nerds geeking out on the Cuban-inspired craft cocktails. Nerd or not, join them. These are serious, good, seriously good drinks. And get the tortilla Española. 508 Dumaine St. Ave. www.manolitonola.com. ✆ **504/603-2740.**

Molly's at the Market ★   The hangout for bohos and literary locals, who chew over the state of their world and their city in this casual, comfortable, East Village–feeling bar. A kind of platonic-ideal locals' bar, it's perpetually popular. **Junction** (p. 116) sometimes pops-up here, ably tending to the peckish with burgers and wings out of the back patio kitchen. 1107 Decatur St. www.mollysatthemarket.net. ✆ **504/525-5169.**

Napoleon House ★★★ Set in a landmark 1815 building, the cave-dark barroom and romantically faded courtyard seem almost too perfectly aged. No plastic surgery here: The building, a National Historic Landmark, was owned by the same family for 101 years until a 2015 sale; the new owners would have been exiled had they changed a thing. Even locals come for the toasty muffuletta, subtle classical music, and signature Pimm's Cup–a cucumber-infused glass of summer any time of year. Trying to figure out where to propose? This might work. 500 Chartres St. www.napoleonhouse.com. ✆ **504/524-9752.**

Patrick's Bar Vin ★★ Half a block and a million miles from Bourbon Street, Patrick Van Voorebeek, self- and aptly described bon vivant and one of the city's premier sommeliers, serves conviviality and an excellent selection of wines (and other spirits) by the glass. The bar feels like your great uncle's decorous but restful library; the sweet courtyard screams for something bubbly. 730 Bienville St., in the Hotel Mazarin. www.patricksbarvin.com. ✆ **504/200-3180.**

Peychaud's ★★★ Joined here are two of the most important people in the city's storied cocktail history . . . separated by about 3 centuries. Antoine Peychaud, namesake, apothecary, and former resident of this lovely locale (ca. 1830ish), devised Peychaud's Bitters, an essential ingredient of the sublime Sazerac, the city's official cocktail (the nation's first, say some). Around 2009, Neal Bodenheimer opened Cure (p. 226), the city's first serious craft cocktail bar, largely credited with reviving the city's fine drinks culture. We'd follow Neal anywhere—his imprint virtually guarantees a good drink—but following him to this classic bar and delightful courtyard is a thorough pleasure. 727 Toulouse St. www.maisondeville.com. ✆ **504/324-4888.**

Pirate's Alley Café ★ In a tucked-away location behind St. Louis Cathedral, on the corner of two actual alleys, this hideaway doubles down with a pirate theme, lending cheesy fun. Purists will balk at the absinthe service here, but it's entertaining—flaming sugar cube and all. The food's handy but nothing more. 622 Pirate's Alley. www.piratesalleycafe.com. ✆ **504/524-9332.**

Elsewhere Around the City

Avenue Pub ★★ This is beer-geek heaven, what with 40+ options on tap and many more in bottles—any hour of the day (well, let's hope those pre-Covid hours return). Proper glassware and occasional cask ales show they're serious about their suds, but even the PBR crowd enjoys the upstairs balcony overlooking St. Charles Boulevard (and the currywurst and fries). 1732 St. Charles Ave. www.theavenuepub.com. ✆ **504/586-9243.** Tues–Wed 4pm–midnight; Thurs 10am–midnight; Fri–Sat 10am–1am.

Bakery Bar ★★ There are two important reasons to recommend this comfy, oddly located spot tucked in the shadows of the Pontchartrain Expressway: 1) It is a bar. 2) It is a bakery, featuring the elusive, exceptional Debbie

Does Doberge cakes: moist, multi-layered mouthgasms worth the taxi fare. There's other food, too, and board games. But ultimately, it's a bar. With cake. Don't wake me. 1179 Annunciation St. www.bakery.bar. © **504/513-8664.** Tues–Fri 11am–midnight, Sat–Sun 10am–midnight.

Bar Marilou ★★★   In a remarkable transformation from stodgy to stunning, this former law library is arguably the city's most stylish bar. Opened in 2019 as part of the Warehouse District's luxe Maison de la Luz hotel (entryway along the building's left side), it's a feast for the senses. Deep gold tones, kicky animal prints, fringe, and those old bookshelves—now persimmon-red and secreting a private speakeasy for hotel guests—anchor the dramatic high style. The menus and vogue vibe, shaped by a group behind some of Paris's top spots, lean swank and French. Artistic apertifs are a specialty; bar bites include anchovies and a liver terrine as well as fluffy *gougeres* and seared scallops. 546 Carondolet St. www.barmarilou.com. © **504/814-7711.**

Barrel Proof ★★   As the name implies, whiskey is the leading man at this shadowy, wood and tin-walled room in the Lower Garden District. And beer, for the beer-and-a-shot specials. If you know and love your brown liquor, the substantive selection of 300+ options (primarily American, Japanese, and Scottish), will blow your hair back. If you don't, ask nicely and the bartenders will share their expertise. Customized flights work well for both scenarios. They've invariably got something tasty coming out of their pop-up kitchen. 1201 Magazine St. www.barrelproofnola.com. No phone.

Bayou Beer Garden and Bayou Wine Garden ★★   For visitors looking for the "real" New Orleans, here's a taste. Two, actually. Bayou Beer Garden is a neighborhood bar with a big covered backyard deck, big screens, and a big beer list. The sister wine bar, connected by a walkway, has a slightly upper-scaler atmosphere and food. Where the Beer Garden serves wings and jalapeño poppers, the Wine Garden goes for charcuterie and crab Rangoon dip (then again, **Piece of Meat** [p. 120] is next door). Either is a hang with the locals, for a game or after a visit to nearby City Park. Beer: 326 N. Jefferson Davis Pkwy. bayoubeergarden.com. © **504/302-9357.** Wine: 315 N. Rendon St. bayouwine garden.com. © **504/826-2925.**

Chandelier Bar ★★   The fact that you enter the soignée new Four Seasons Hotel directly into the Chandelier Bar is a calculated choice: You are ensconced from the get-go in shimmery indulgence, of the sort that only 15,000 crystals overhead can create. There's more than the high-drama atmo, though: If you opt to stray from the logical menu choices (champagne and caviar), the drinks program is headed by one of the city's best, and food choices come from Miss River, the hotel's terrif celeb-chef-led restaurant. 2 Canal St. www.fourseasons.com/neworleans. © **504/434-5100.**

Cure ★★★   This mixologist mecca helped instigate the resurgence of craft cocktails in New Orleans as well as now-booming Freret Street. It's an oasis of sleek, boasting great small plates and some of the most knowledgeable bar chefs in town, who blend exceptional ingredients with personable chat.

dive RIGHT IN

If you'd rather drink with Tom Waits than Tom Cruise, you'll appreciate New Orleans' fine dive bars—and by fine, we mean down-and-dirty, neighborhood holes-in-the-wall with regulars straight out of a Jim Jarmusch casting call. Uptown, **Snake & Jake's Christmas Club Lounge** (7612 Oak St.; www.snakeandjakes.com; Ⓒ **504/861-2802**) is illuminated only by dwindling Christmas lights, which doesn't make it easier to find this crowded, sweat-soaked, off-the-beaten-path shack. There's a new oddly normal backyard space, and it's BYOD (dog), so you know it's friendly. Also Uptown, at the Elvis-themed **Kingpin** (1307 Lyons St.; Ⓒ **504/891-2373**), 20-somethings in CBGB tees come for shuffleboard and cheap drink specials. In the depths of the French Quarter's Decatur Street, **Aunt Tiki's** (1207 Decatur St.; Ⓒ **504/680-8454**) is laden with stickers, Halloween dreck, and affable, slouching degenerates. As if that's not draw enough, drinks are strong and cheap. Down the street, **The Abbey** (1123 Decatur St.; Ⓒ **504/523-7177**) has a few motley stained-glass windows, but everything else is the antithesis of church. While a David Lynchian clientele prays at the bar 24/7, any jukebox offering both Merle Haggard *and* the Cramps is worthy of worship. Elsewhere in the Quarter, **The Dungeon** (738 Toulouse St.) covers the dark end of the dive spectrum: with blackness, skulls, metal, and more blackness.

Avoid the late crowds and go at happy hour. 4905 Freret St. www.curenola.com. Ⓒ **504/302-2357.**

Double Dealer ★★   To enter this literal underground club is to instantly desire some fringed attire (ladies), a very thin 'stache (gents), and a cigarette holder (all, including nonsmokers). The weekends-only, reservations-required speakeasy tucked below the elegant Orpheum Theatre plays off the theatrical "special event" vibe. Deco-meets-decay décor features old theater costumes and velvet curtains to partition off the spaces for partying or privacy. Ooh, la, and la. (Be advised: no food options). 129 Roosevelt Way. doubledealernola.com. Ⓒ **504/300-0212.**

Le Bon Temps Roulé ★   Another way-uptown, rundown shack with a cramped bar and decent beer list. So? So schedule your visit for a Thursday, when the Soul Rebels brass band blows this here roof off. Or Fridays during oyster season, when the bivalves are free. The archetypal local characters are quite welcoming the other five nights of the week, too. 4801 Magazine St. www.lbtrnola.com. Ⓒ **504/895-8117.**

NOLA Brewing Taproom ★★★   See p. 199.

Pluck Wine Bar ★★   We're blessed with several attitude-free wine bars in New Orleans, including this friendly newbie, whose food menu helps elevate it above the other options. Its modern-not-sleek decor mirrors the approachable vibe—the other reason we choose Pluck (no bottles over $100; no menu items over $20). Ask and ye shall receive if you're wine-curious, or just chill with a few friends and a few glasses in the comfy booths. 722 Girod St. www.pluckwines.com. Ⓒ **504/233-9780.**

Polo Club Lounge ★★★ Upstairs in the Windsor Court Hotel (p. 80), the Sazerac-and-cigar crowd lounges on velvet sofas and leather armchairs to a cool piano combo (often with songstress Robin Barnes), as big-money deals and serious romances discreetly work themselves out in this dignified room. 300 Gravier St. www.windsorcourthotel.com/polo-club-lounge. ℂ **504/523-6000.**

Sazerac Bar at the Roosevelt ★★★ If the New Orleans bar scene were a monarchy, the historic Sazerac Bar in the glamorous Roosevelt Hotel might be queen. Its sinuous wood walls and Deco-era murals have borne witness to movie stars, political scandals, and we don't want to know what (check the bullet hole in the paneling to the left of the bar). You're here for all that panache as much as the namesake cocktail (now $18). Bar service could be friendlier, but never mind, the ambience is stellar. 123 Baronne St. www.the rooseveltneworleans.com. ℂ **504/648-1200.**

GAY NIGHTLIFE

Most of these bars catering to New Orleans' thriving LBGTQ+ community are along the French Quarter's illustrious 4-block "fruit loop." Expect late hours, friendly folk, and *insane* crowds during Southern Decadence (p. 32), Mardi Gras, Halloween, Easter (yes)—basically at the drop of any quasi-celebratory hat. Also see gaynola.com.

Bars & Clubs

In addition to those reviewed below, you might try the long-running **Golden Lantern,** 1239 Royal St. (ℂ **504/529-2860**), the über-diverse Cheers of NOLA. It typically has one of everything—one drag queen, one leather boy, one guy in a suit, one beer-drinking dog at the bar. Everybody is friendly and it's open 24/7 (or will be again soon, we hope). For drag and more friendliness, there's the neighborly neighboring **Mag's 940** at 940 Elysian Fields Ave. (ℂ **504/948-1888**).

If your proclivities lean in any other direction, you probably know how to find what you're looking for. It's out there.

The Bourbon Pub—Parade Disco ★★ Of the two hyper-popular bars, the downstairs pub is a bit calmer. Upstairs, Parade Disco's high-tech dance setup comes alive on weekend nights, especially pre- and post- the Sunday 8pm glam drag show. 801 Bourbon St. www.bourbonpub.com. ℂ **504/529-2107.**

Café Lafitte in Exile ★★ One of the oldest gay bars in the U.S., this was established in 1933 and claims Tennessee Williams as a patron. Downstairs is more of a cruise bar (not so much for teeny-boppers or twinks), upstairs has a friendly, pub-like atmosphere. Fun happens on both levels including the famed Sunday night Trash Disco (we don't really get the storied "Love Is in the Air" napkin toss, but we still love it). 901 Bourbon St. www. lafittes.com. ℂ **504/522-8397.**

getting crafty: MAKING THE BREWERY SCENE

We'll never be Portland, but if they've got Voodoo donuts, we've got actual Voodoo. Here are a few brew spots worth the Uber.

o **Courtyard Brewery:** Beer-wise, this funky converted warehouse in the Lower Garden District offers the best of the local IPA lot. 1020 Erato St.; www.court yardbrewing.com.

o **Parleaux Beer Lab:** Deep in Bywater, the fruit trees and herbs in the simple backyard beer garden may turn up in their creative brews. Stouts are standouts, as is proximity to the **Joint** barbecue (p. 115). 634 Lesseps St.; www. parleauxbeerlab.com; ℂ **504/702-8433.**

o **Urban South:** The social scene is the main attraction at this huge warehouse-style spot. 1645 Tchoupitoulas St.; www. urbansouthbrewery.com; ℂ **504/267-4852.**

o **Brieux Carre:** They're having fun with beer here, an experimental hop oasis steps from the Frenchmen Street madness. 2115 Decatur St.; www.brieuxcarre.com; ℂ **504/304-4242.**

o **Zony Mash:** Locals flock here for the fun scene, cool space (a converted old movie theater in Mid City), music venue, sours, and seltzers. 3940 Thalia St. www.zony mashbeer.com; ℂ **504/766-8868.**

o **Faubourg Brewery:** The brewery formerly known as Dixie now has better brews; great entertainment programming; and a huge almost-new facility about 15 minutes from the city. Great for large groups & families. 3501 Jourdan Rd,; faubourgbrewery.com; ℂ **504/867-4000.**

o **Crescent City Brewhouse** (p. 223) and **NOLA Brewing** (p. 199): The ones who started it still do it well.

Country Club ★★ We still miss the days when this bar, pool, restaurant, and club was an anything-goes, clothing-optional, mostly gay retreat. But we'll admit that the new dressed-up, mostly not-gay version is quite delightful (and cleaner, with a legit menu and chef). The converted Creole cottage tucked away in the residential Bywater offers a staycation for locals and visitors of all persuasions, with a pretty veranda, airy dining room, pool, and Jacuzzi. *Fair warning:* The hilarious weekend drag brunch (10am and 1pm Sat and Sun) books up months in advance. 634 Louisa St. www.thecountryclub neworleans.com. ℂ **504/945-0742.** Day pass for pool $20; more for events.

Good Friends Bar & Queens Head Pub ★★★ This truly is a friendly spot, drawing mixed genders, types, and ages, my favorite of those listed for its unpretentious vibe. I like that the decor and music aren't generically techno'ed out—it at least tries to maintain some NOLA feel—and that the straight-welcoming local denizens will gladly chat you up. The upstairs Queens Head Pub is quite entertaining with its Saturday 4pm singalong. On a hot day, the frozen concoction called the Separator goes down easy. 740 Dauphine St. www.goodfriendsbar.com. ℂ **504/566-7191.**

Grrl Spot ★★ Infrequent but super-popular pop-up events for grrls of all types. Location and entertainment varies, so check website to see what's in the queue. facebook.com/grrlspot.

Oz ★★ This world-renowned, bass-heavy dance club might be overrated, but it still has an incredible light show, go-go boys atop the bar (usually), and drag on Wednesdays and Saturdays. It's a see-and-be-seen spot for a mostly young crowd including plenty of straights. The dance-floor view from the upstairs balcony is worth it alone. 800 Bourbon St. www.oznew21.com. ℂ **504/593-9491.** Cover varies.

8 PERFORMING ARTS, THEATERS & CONCERT HALLS

Culture vultures may also want to see what's on tap at local colleges, including **Tulane University** (www2.tulane.edu/calendar); and several eclectic, occasional performance spaces: **Marigny Opera House** (725 St. Ferdinand St.; www.marignyoperahouse.org; ℂ **504/948-9998**), **Mudlark Public Theatre** (1200 Port St.; www.facebook.com/mudlarkpublictheatre), and **Café Istanbul** (2372 St. Claude Ave.; www.cafeistanbulnola.com; ℂ **504/975-0286**). Also check www.theneworleansboxoffice.com for theater events.

Civic Theatre ★★ Before 2013, there was nothing here but an exquisite Deco chandelier and a flock of pigeons. Little was spared in restoring the original 1906 architecture and plasterwork of this triple-tiered mid-size theater. The lineup has stretched from John Prine to Slayer to Belle and Sebastian and Trey Anastasio. 510 O'Keefe St. www.civicnola.com. ℂ **504/272-0865.** Ticket prices vary.

The Fillmore ★★ Scale the daunting entry stairway on the Canal Street side of Harrah's (there IS an elevator, if you want to ask) and you'll find that the industrial black interior and huge crystal chandeliers in the 2,200-capacity main room ably honor the sister club in San Francisco (with NOLA nods like a brass instrument fixture and Louis Armstrong mural). Sound is outstanding (rock shows get LOUD, but clear), and sight lines are almost unobstructed (save for a few on the sides of the tiered premium seats; otherwise, those VIP seats are worth the extra pop). Food and drink prices are reasonable, and food is surprisingly good. 6 Canal St. www.thefillmorenola.com. ℂ **504/881-1555.** Tickets $25–$120.

Le Petit Théâtre du Vieux Carré ★★ One of the oldest community theaters in the U.S., Le Petit has occupied this building since 1923, save for a scary 2011 shutdown. Fortunately, the opening of restaurant **Tableau** (p. 106) in the shared building enabled the 350-seat theater to reopen, and patrons to enjoy a dinner-and-a-play night out. Local productions of classic dramas, musicals, and comedies vary from very good to stellar. 616 St. Peter St. www.lepetittheatre.com. ℂ **504/522-2081.** Tickets $10–$55.

Mahalia Jackson Theater for the Performing Arts ★ This handsome midcentury theater in Armstrong Park (bordering the French Quarter) is spacious but not big, so every seat is decent. Over the years it has hosted the local Philharmonic, opera, and ballet companies; it also offers touring theater productions, dance troupes, rock concerts, and other live acts. 1419 Basin St. www.mahaliajacksontheater.com. ℂ **504/287-0350.** Ticket prices vary.

Music Box Village ★★★ We haven't been *every*where, but we're pretty sure there's nothing like the Music Box Village *any*where else. It's an enchanted collection of artisan-fabricated structures, each at once an edifice, an artwork, and a musical instrument—the love child of Burning Man and the London Philharmonic, born and being raised in Bywater. A performance in, on, and around these magical musical houses is a mesmerizing experience that should not be missed. Dress for outdoor conditions; seating is rustic, so come early to snag a bench or a hay bale, or bring a folding chair or blanket. If there are no performances while you're in town, try to check it out during public hours or for whatever oddball event may be happening here. 4557 N. Rampart St. www.musicboxvillage.com. Performances $20–$85; suggested donation for visits $5–$15.

The NOLA Project ★★ This excellent ensemble presents boldly conceived and staged productions in a variety of settings (think "Legend of Sleepy Hollow" at the CAC; p. 166). Locations vary. www.nolaproject.com. ℂ **504/302-9117.** Ticket prices vary, but usually $20–$25.

Orpheum ★★★ It took $15 million, 10 years, and lots of elbow grease to restore this drop-dead-stunning, 1,500-seat Beaux Arts theater to its original 1908 glory after it languished in post-Katrina ruin. It now hosts the Louisiana Philharmonic and New Orleans Ballet Theater, plus all manner of performers from Kraftwerk to David Sedaris to Charlie Puth. Also see Double Dealer, p. 227. 129 Roosevelt Way. www.orpheumnola.com. ℂ **504/274-4870.** Ticket prices vary.

Saenger Theatre ★★★ Following an extensive, gajillion-dollar, post-Katrina renovation, and a near flattening when the adjacent Hard Rock Hotel collapsed, this 1927 stunner from the glory movie-house days is now technologically state-of-the-art. The Saenger hosts concerts, comedy shows, Broadway shows, and more. 1111 Canal St. www.saengernola.com. ℂ **504/287-0351.** Ticket prices vary.

Southern Repertory Theatre ★★ Focusing (mostly) on Southern playwrights and themes, these consistently high-quality productions take place in a pretty fabulous, newly renovated 1915 church. Comedy and cabaret also fill out the calendar. 2541 Bayou Rd. www.southernrep.com. ℂ **504/522-6545.** Ticket prices vary, usually $5–$45.

NEW ORLEANS SHOPPING

By Lavinia Spalding

9

Shopping in New Orleans is a highly evolved leisure activity, with a shop for every strategy and a fix for every shopaholic—and for every budget. Think of the endless souvenir shops on Bourbon Street and swanky antiques stores on Royal Street as the bookends for all the shopping New Orleans has to offer. There are sweet deals to be had, lavish riches to be spent, artworks to be admired. But as all shoppers know, the fun is in the hunt. And New Orleans has some smashing hunting grounds.

Just one word of warning: In the listings below, we outline stores' hours of business, but ever since the pandemic hit, those hours have been in major flux, especially in summer, when many shops reduce hours. Call before you go!

MAJOR HUNTING GROUNDS

ART MARKETS On the second Saturday of every month, the **Arts Market New Orleans** takes place at **City Park's** Goldring/Woldenberg Great Lawn (8 Victory Ave.), and on the last Saturday of the month, in **Marsalis Harmony Park** (formerly Palmer Park; S. Carrollton and S. Claiborne Aves., last stop on the St. Charles streetcar line; www.artsneworleans.org; © **504/523-1465**). From 10am to 4pm you'll find paintings, pottery, glass, mosaics, jewelry, handmade frames, soaps, clothing, and much more from high-quality juried artists (plus music and food). At the Marigny's open-air **Art Garden** (artgardennola.com) on Friday, Saturday, and Sunday nights, the browsing is free; goods are original, local, and affordable. (It's mostly art and jewelry, with the occasional awesome vintage box camera upcycled as a lamp.) We also love snooping through the booths at **Secondline Arts & Antiques** (1209 Decatur St.; secondlinenola.com) and browsing the locally made works at **Zèle** (2481 Magazine St.; zelenola.com) and **Garden District Marketplace** across the street (2855 Magazine St.; www.

SHOPPING ON THE bayou

It's not the busiest shopping stretch (by far), but Bayou Road might be the friendliest—and one of the most historic. In fact, without it, New Orleans probably wouldn't exist. This is the city's oldest road, first used by indigenous people who later introduced it as a trade route to French settlers. The handful of sweet businesses, several of which are Black-owned, includes **Community Book Center** (p. 238), a social hub specializing in African-centered books; **King and Queen Emporium Int'l,** where you can stock up on pomegranate soap, African shea butter, and Orisha incense; and **CupCake Fairies,** where you should treat yourself to the bourbon-chocolate cupcake you surely deserve. Some *lagniappes* (bonuses): **Whiskey and Sticks** for drinks and cigars, **Old Road Coffee** for a great cup of joe, **Coco Hut** for Jamaican cuisine, and **McHardy's** fried chicken around the corner.

instagram.com/gdm_nola). And we always mark our calendars for the **Freret St. Market** (freretmarket.org) on the first Saturday of every month (except in summer). Great finds, eats, music, beer, produce—and even a kids' area!

CANAL PLACE At the foot of Canal Street (333 Canal St.) near the Mississippi River, this sophisticated shopping mall holds more than 30 shops, many of them elegant retailers like Louis Vuitton, Tory Burch, Michael Kors, G-Star Raw, Saks Fifth Avenue, and Tiffany & Co. There's also a two-story Anthropologie, the **Louisiana Crafts Guild** gallery of locally made goods, and SALON, a new rotating art gallery. Canal Place (www.canalplacestyle.com) is open Monday to Saturday 11am to 7pm, Sunday noon to 6pm.

THE FRENCH MARKET These historic shops begin in the colonnade along Decatur Street across from Jackson Square. Offerings include candy, housewares, fashion, crafts, and toys. The open-air section—originally an indigenous peoples' intertribal trading grounds, it's the oldest continuously operated open-air market in the country—begins at Ursulines Avenue and N. Peters Street. There's a stage for live music and cooking demos, and food booths including an oyster bar, a terrific fresh juice bar, and tasty-healthy **Meals from the Heart Cafe.** The farmers market and foodstuff stalls—including local seafood, meats, and spices—will pack your purchases for travel or shipping. The flea market section has low-end souvenirs (good buys, if not good quality) and a smattering of actual art and handmade goods. (Some of the best art finds are in nearby **Dutch Alley Artist's Co-op.**) It's always a fun stroll. Open daily 10am to 5pm (www.frenchmarket.org). See also p. 156.

JAX BREWERY Just across from Jackson Square at 600-620 Decatur St., the old brewery building is now a jumble of shops and cafes (and good bathrooms, and great views). It's an easy stop for clothing and souvenirs, particularly the crawfish-logo'd polo shirts and other preppie wear at **Perlis.** Open daily 10am to 7pm (www.thejaxbrewery.com; ✆ **504/566-7601**).

JULIA STREET Some of the city's best contemporary art galleries (many listed under "Art Galleries," p. 235) line Julia Street from Camp Street to the river (and fork off into surrounding side streets). The quality of talent exhibited here—among both creators and curators—is quite astounding.

MAGAZINE STREET This premier shopping drag is 6 miles (you read that right: *6 miles*) of antiques, boutiques, galleries, salons, and all manner of restaurants in 19th-century brick storefronts and quaint Creole cottages, from Canal Street to Audubon Park. Prime sections are roughly the 1900 to 2200 blocks; 2800 to 3100 blocks; 3400 to 4600 blocks (with the odd block or so of nothing); and 5400 to 5700 blocks. A car or JazzyPass (p. 292) will help you browse the lengthy, lively avenue (www.magazinestreet.com).

THE OUTLET COLLECTION AT RIVERWALK Whoa. **Coach, Kate Spade, Nordstrom Rack, Le Creuset,** and 75 other outlet stores fill this sprawling three-story mall. Bargains are a bonus when you can walk from the French Quarter, shop with a daiquiri in hand, and enjoy the best mall food-court view in existence at tables overlooking the Mississippi. It's behind the Hilton at 500 Port of New Orleans Place, just steps from the ferry and cruise terminals. Open Monday to Saturday 10am to 7pm, Sunday 10am to 6pm (www.riverwalknewMuorleans.com; © **504/522-1555**).

RIVERBEND, MAPLE & OAK STREETS To reach these cute Carrollton-area shops, ride the St. Charles Avenue streetcar to stop no. 212 (S. Carrollton and Maple Sts.) and walk down Maple Street, where shops like **Sarah Ott** (cool local designs) and the delectable **Maple Street Patisserie** inhabit renovated Creole cottages and old buildings. Return to Carrollton, walk 4 blocks away from the river to Oak Street, and turn left. Along this happening shopping strip, you'll find the excellent **Blue Cypress Books,** high-end knives at **Coutelier,** snazzy decor at **Eclectic Home,** guitars and vintage duds at **Glue,** and folky and funky **Malarky** art gallery. For refreshments, try iconic **Camellia Grill** (p. 142), Jamaican fare at **14 Parishes,** vegan **Breads on Oak,** spicy crab and quaffable cocktails at **Seafood Sally's,** or something frosty from **Ale on Oak.** (And if you're there in the evening, catch a show at the **Maple Leaf Bar,** of course.)

SHOPPING A TO Z

Antiques

Collectible Antiques ★★ One of our favorites of the dusty, jumbled, and eclectic antiques/junk stores on the Esplanade end of Decatur, its stock runs from Art Deco to 1960s collectibles. 1232 Decatur St. collectible-antiques. hub.biz. © **504/766-2343.** Daily noon–6pm.

James H. Cohen & Sons ★★ A serious place for serious collectors. The fifth generation of antique-dealing Cohens specialize in antique weapons, coins, and currency from points near and far, dating back to 400 B.C. A locally minted antique coin, a gold doubloon, or a coin from actual sunken treasure

makes a fine souvenir. 437 Royal St. www.cohenantiques.com. © **504/522-3305.**
Mon–Sat 9:30am–5pm.

Keil's Antiques ★★ Established in 1899 and currently run by the family's fourth generation, Keil's has a considerable collection of 18th- and 19th-century French and English furniture, chandeliers, jewelry, and decorative items spanning three crowded floors. Ask a staff member about the doorman who worked his spot here for 78 years and you may coax out some other stories as well. 325 Royal St. www.keilsantiques.com. © **504/522-4552.** Mon–Sat 9am–5pm.

Magazine Antique Mall ★ Diggers will dig the superb browsing and many good deals found among the 50-ish variegated stalls in this 7,000-square-foot space. 3017 Magazine St. www.magazinestreet.com/merchant/magazine-antique-mall. © **504/896-9994.** Daily noon–5pm.

M.S. Rau ★★★ The sheer scale of the inventory makes century-old Rau a destination for serious buyers. Every opulent item that could possibly be crafted from fine metals, gems, crystal, wood, paint, china, and marble, plus articles made by every name known to the antique world, is here for the ogling, filling room after jaw-dropping room across three historic buildings. It recently doubled its size to 40,000 square feet and is now even more museum-like than before. We particularly love the selection of walking canes, fifteenth-century iron floor safes, and orchestrion (self-playing) instruments. Most every item has a story to tell, and the knowledgeable sales reps pleasantly indulge your curiosity. 622 Royal St. www.rauantiques.com. © **888/557-2406.** Mon–Sat 9am–5:15pm.

Art Galleries

Galleries share the **Royal** and **Magazine Street** landscapes with the aforementioned antiques shops, while in the Warehouse District, the 300 to 700 blocks of **Julia Street** (and surrounding streets) house some 20 contemporary fine-arts galleries, anchored by the **Contemporary Arts Center** and **Ogden Museum of Southern Art** (p. 169). Go from 6 to 9pm on the first Saturday of each month for the Arts District Gallery Openings. In addition to the Julia Street galleries listed below, be sure to also check out **LeMieux, Octavia,** and fantastic newcomer **Spillman Blackwell.** For the more intrepid, explore the burgeoning lowbrow and outsider art movement around **St. Claude Avenue** (no current collective website, but hit UNO St. Claude, Good Children, and The Front Galleries at 2429, 4037, and 4100 St. Claude Ave., respectively). And whatever else you do, don't miss **Studio BE ★★★**, at 2941 Royal Street, home to the astounding works of artist, activist, and educator Brandan "BMike" Odums. For more on Studio BE, see p. 172.

Angela King Gallery ★★★ Opened in 2007 in a show of much-needed post-Katrina solidarity, this is still one of the best contemporary art galleries in the city. King shows works by artists such as Peter Max, Andrew Baird, Richard Currier, Raymond Douillet, Patterson & Barnes, and Michelle

Gagliano. 241 Royal St. www.angelakinggallery.com. © **504/524-8211.** Wed–Sat 11am–5pm or by appt.

Antieau Gallery ★★★ We adore artist Chris Roberts-Antieau's whimsical side (sewn works that riff on current events and social mores) and her dark side (macabre snow globes and a dollhouse re-creation of the *In Cold Blood* crime scene). 719 Royal St. www.antieaugallery.com. © **504/304-0849.** Daily 10am–6pm.

Arthur Roger Gallery ★★★ Arthur Roger pioneered the Warehouse District and fine-arts scene when he opened in New Orleans over 40 years ago, tying the local community to the New York art world. Still blazing trails, the expansive gallery represents Francis X. Pavy, Ida Kohlmeyer, Dawn DeDeaux, Dale Chihuly, Demond Melancon, and the stunning figurative photographs of the late George Dureau. 432-434 Julia St. www.arthurrogergallery.com. © **504/522-1999.** Tues–Sat 10am–5pm.

Ashley Longshore ★★ Not for the faint of heart or wallet, Ashley's clever, controversial art riffs on pop culture and wealth-worship in bright hues and high gloss. She slams (or glorifies?) materialism and winks at celebrity on pillows and paintings, but they're flower-strewn and alit with butterflies, so hey, it's all good. We were smitten with a fanciful pair of Crest-white armchairs with lipstick-red metallic auto upholstery, emblazoned with "No F**ks Given." Then, some 14-year-old girl bought them for $6,000/pair. 4Realz. 4537 Magazine St. www.ashleylongshore.com. © **504/333-6951.** Mon–Fri 9am–5pm; Sat 11am–4pm.

Carol Robinson Gallery ★★ The grande dame of the local contemporary Southern arts scene, Robinson shows accessible but surprisingly affordable works, including Sandra Burshell's arresting pastels, Jere Allen's mysterious milky-white figures, James King's haunting oils, and Christina Goodman's exquisite minute tableaus. 840 Napoleon Ave. carolrobinsongallery.net. © **504/895-6130.** Tues, Fri 1–5pm; Sat 11am–3:45pm.

Christopher Porche-West ★★ Porche-West's portrait photographs are themselves works of art, but then he sculpts and frames them within magnificent assemblages of architectural remnants, mechanical parts, natural materials, and found oddities, creating highly collectible, singular statement pieces in his **Bank of Soul** studio. Check them out, or sit for one yourself. 3201 Burgundy St. www.porche-west.com. © **504/947-3880.** Open by appt.

Dr. Bob Art ★★★ In his one-of-a-kind Bywater studio, Dr. Bob turns out his colorful, iconic "be nice or leave" folk art signs, rimmed in bottle caps and other found materials. Available in a variety of sizes, materials, and sentiments. 3027 Chartres St. drbobart.net. © **504/701-7297.** Daily 10am–5pm.

Frank Relle Gallery ★★★ Sometimes spooky, sometimes serene, Relle's nightscapes of the local swamps and architecture are undeniably stunning. 910 Royal St. www.frankrelle.com. © **504/265-8564.** Daily 10am–6pm.

A Gallery for Fine Photography ★★★ This incredibly well-stocked photography gallery emphasizes the historic and contemporary culture of New Orleans and the South. Images include Ernest J. Bellocq's legendary Storyville photos, Herman Leonard's jazz images, the haunting work of Sebastião Salgado, and something from just about every period, style, or noted photographer (including books, if photos aren't in your budget). 241 Chartres St. www.agallery.com. ℂ **504/568-1313.** Thurs and Mon 10:30am–5pm; Fri–Sun 10:30am–5:30pm.

Jonathan Ferrara Gallery ★★★ Since 1998, Ferrara has been showing emerging cross-media artists in thought-provoking exhibitions that lean playful and ironic. Skylar Fein's pop-pundit pieces are both hilarious and horrifying in their truth; Paul Villinski's winged sculptures are magical. 400a Julia St. www.jonathanferraragallery.com. ℂ **504/522-5471.** Tues–Sat 10am–5pm or by appt.

Martine Chaisson Gallery ★★ The stark, sweeping space screams for high-impact, highly saturated imagery, and Martine delivers. Hunt Slonem's neo-expressionist bunnies, birds, and butterflies are a bright delight; Katrine Hildebrandt's mesmerizing geometrics are oddly serene. 727 Camp St. www.martinechaissongallery.com. ℂ **504/302-7942.** Currently by appt only.

Michalopoulos ★★★ James Michalopoulos's thickly painted, topsy-turvy renderings of shotgun houses and creole cottages can be found on the walls of many a *real* local house, and his portraits of jazz musicians are nothing short of gorgeous (proof: He's done six Jazz Fest posters, more than any other artist in the festival's history). Original works are definitely an investment, but prints are available, too, and affordable. 617 Bienville St. www.michalopoulos.com. ℂ **504/558-0505.** Mon–Sat 10am–6pm, Sun noon–4pm.

Modernist Cuisine Gallery ★ Those familiar with his *Modernist Cuisine* cookbooks may recognize Nathan Myhrvold's vibrant food photos. Great as they look on the page, the large-format, resin-coated prints are even yummier up close. 305 Royal St. modernistcuisinegallery.com. ℂ **504/571-5157.** Sun–Wed 10am–6pm, Thurs–Sat 10am–8pm.

New Orleans School of GlassWorks & Printmaking Studio ★★★ This institution, with 35,000 square feet of studio space, houses an 850-pound tank of molten glass, a letterpress, and a printing press. At this sister school to the Louvre Museum of Decorative Arts, glasswork artists, bookbinders, and master printmakers display their work, demonstrate glassblowing, and teach classes, including the popular "Wine & Design" gatherings. 727 Magazine St. neworleansglassworks.com. ℂ **504/529-7279.** Mon–Sat 10am–5:30pm.

Tax-Free Art
Many original works of visual art in New Orleans are exempt from sales tax, thanks to a statewide program promoting cultural activity in designated districts. Be sure to ask about sales tax where you buy.

Photo Works ★★ Photographer Louis Sahuc's life's work was photo-documenting iconic New Orleans imagery, such as Jackson Square swathed in fog, diners at Galatoire's, or fragments of ironwork. They're emotion-laden keepsakes. 521 St. Ann St. www.louissahuc.com. ℭ **504/593-9090.** Thurs–Mon 11am–6pm.

Rodrigue Studio New Orleans ★ The late Cajun artist George Rodrigue's ubiquitous Blue Dog is the Zelig of New Orleans art: The cobalt kitsch canine appears in every imaginable pose and setting and invades your consciousness. Adorable? Obnoxious? You be the judge. The gallery also displays some of Rodrigue's more classical works. 730 Royal St. www.georgerodrigue.com. ℭ **504/581-4244.** Mon–Sat 11am–5pm; Sun noon-5pm.

Terrance Osborne ★★★ If you want your walls to telegraph your devotion to New Orleans, this may be the gallery—and artist—for you. Rich, dynamic paintings (including original Jazz Fest posters) of streetscapes, musicians, cultural icons, parades, and more from $50 prints to $50,000 originals. 3029 Magazine St. www.terranceosborne.com. ℭ **504/232-7530.** Thurs–Mon 11am–5pm.

Books

Arcadian Books ★★ Bibliophiles will bask in these wondrous, dusty stacks, especially lovers of the classics (in English and Latin); the history inquisitive (local and far beyond); and seekers of French, German, or Russian literature in the original. The personable proprietor, Russell Desmond, is ridiculously knowledgeable and knows every item in this gloriously decrepit grotto. 714 Orleans Ave. ℭ **504/523-4138.** Mon–Sat 9am–5pm.

Baldwin & Company ★★★ This mindfully designed bookshop/café named for James Baldwin is an oasis of good books, cozy couches, thoughtful art, and sublime iced lattés, in one of the city's rare Art Deco buildings. It emphasizes community, creativity, and Black literature, and hosts occasional poetry slams and concerts. 1030 Elysian Fields Ave. www.baldwinandcobooks.com. ℭ **504/354-1741.** Mon–Sun 7am–3pm.

Beckham's Bookshop ★★ Some 60,000 volumes collected by the store's owners (and one cat) jam the bottom two floors at beloved Beckham's—a pillar of the Quarter's thriving indie bookshop scene since 1967. It has used books for all interests (browse the glass cases for rare gems) and a fine small selection of new, locally focused titles. The third floor is all vintage vinyl. 228 Decatur St. www.facebook.com/BeckhamsBookshop. ℭ **504/522-9875.** Daily 10am–4pm.

Community Center Bookstore ★★★ The city's oldest Black-owned bookstore has been a social and cultural hub since 1983; we've stopped by for a quick browse and wound up staying hours, engrossed in conversation with the proprietors. African-centered literature reigns, from new fiction and memoir to classics, poetry, history, cookbooks, plus a sweet selection of kids' books. Also trinkets and textiles (and a cat). 2523 Bayou Rd. www.readcbc.com. ℭ **504/948-7323.** Tues–Sat 10am–6pm.

Crescent City Books ★★ This small, friendly shop of mostly used books offers serious literature for the seriously literate, with an emphasis on history, local interest, literary criticism, philosophy, and art. It's also a hub of info about literary events and has a small selection of maps and art prints. 240 Chartres St. www.crescentcitybooks.com. Ⓒ **504/524-4997.** Daily 11am–7pm.

Faulkner House Books ★★★ Yes, Nobel prize–winner William Faulkner lived here while writing his early works, but that's only one ingredient in this winning recipe for a perfect small bookshop. Shelf after high shelf is occupied by desirable titles, from first editions to Southern authors and current bestsellers. Just one room and a hallway, Faulkner House feels like somebody's private home (it is)—but the gracious advice and judicious selection make manifest the art of bookselling. No cats; occasional dogs. 624 Pirate's Alley. faulknerhousebooks.com. Ⓒ **504/524-2940.** Daily 10am–5pm.

Garden District Book Shop ★★★ Set in an old (1884) roller-skating rink, this lovely, medium-size shop is stocked with just about every New Orleans– or Louisiana-themed book you can think of, no matter the focus: interiors, exteriors, food, Creoles, fiction, poetry, you name it—including many signed copies. Best-sellers, too. 2727 Prytania St. www.gardendistrictbookshop.com. Ⓒ **504/895-2266.** Mon–Fri 7am–6pm, Sat–Sun 8am–5pm.

Octavia Books ★★★ For those who adore independent bookstores, this uptown beauty with its sweet, tiny patio (complete with waterfall) is well worth a visit. There's much to savor here, in the extensive, well-selected stock, and in the frequent signings and readings. 513 Octavia St. at Laurel St. www.octaviabooks.com. Ⓒ **504/899-7323.** Mon–Sat 10am–6pm; Sun 10am–5pm.

Candies, Pralines & Pastries

Bittersweet Confections ★ Ideal for fortification after (or before) a tough gallery- or museum-hopping stint, this bakery/café is known for its chocolates, but the cupcakes also are hard to resist. Wish it were open later for a little something after a Warehouse District dinner. 725 Magazine St. www.bittersweetconfections.com. Ⓒ **504/523-2626.** Tues–Sat 7:30am–2pm.

Laura's Candies ★ Charming Laura's is said to be the city's oldest candy store, established in 1913. The pralines are fabulous, but the rich, delectable golf-ball-size truffles are a personal favorite indulgence. 331 Chartres St. www.laurascandies.com. Ⓒ **504/525-3880.** Daily 10am–6pm.

Loretta's Authentic Pralines ★★★ You may not see a ghost in New Orleans, but these pralines (and praline beignets) will haunt you. The shop carries on the spirit of the late "praline queen" Loretta Harrison, the city's first African American woman to run her own successful praline company. www.lorettaspralines.com. French Market: 1100 N. Peters St. Stall #9, Ⓒ **504/323-8350;** Thurs–Mon 9am–5pm. 2101 N. Rampart St. Ste 9., Ⓒ **504/944-7068.** Wed–Fri 9am–5pm, Sat 9am–3:30pm. lorettaspralines.com.

Southern Candymakers ★★★ Our top choice for pralines, it offers the usual suspects and some nontraditionals (coconut and sweet potato!), all extra creamylicious and made fresh right in front of you—if the display doesn't reel you in, the aroma will. We swoon for the pecan-laden *tortues;* the boxed chocolate crawfish and gator pops make fine gifts. 334 Decatur St. www. southerncandymakers.com. ℰ **504/523-5544.** Daily 10am–6pm. Also in the French Market at 1010 Decatur St., ℰ **504/525-6170.**

Costumes & Masks

Costumery is big business and big fun in New Orleans, and not just for Mardi Gras; most households boast a well-stocked year-round costume closet. In addition to these shops, try thrift stores, where outfits can sometimes be found at a fraction of their original cost. (Troll Dauphine St. in the Bywater.)

Carl Mack Presents ★★ Mack, doyen of Mardi Gras entertainment, rents or creates ornate costumes for Fat Tuesday or any day. This is high-production-value stuff—no naughty nurses here. 1010 Conti St. www.carlmack. com. ℰ **504/949-4009.** By appt.

Fifi Mahony's ★★ Wig wackiness, why not? Have the hair you've always wanted (even if just for the day). Worth visiting to see their outrageous custom pieces. Salon and makeup services, too. 934 Royal St. facebook.com/pg/fifimahonys. ℰ **504/525-4343.** Sun–Wed noon–6pm; Thurs–Sat 11am–7pm.

Uptown Costume & Dancewear ★★ This is headquarters for Mardi Gras, Halloween, and whenever the costuming bug happens to bite. (In New Orleans, it bites often!) It's hard to imagine anyone leaving this big, well-stocked shop empty-handed. 4326 Magazine St. facebook.com/uptowncostumeand dancewear. ℰ **504/895-7969.** Tues–Thurs 11am–6pm; Fri noon–7pm; Sat 10am–6pm.

Fashion, Vintage Clothing, Hats & Accessories

Art and Eyes ★★★ Eyeglass wearers who demand something above average: For a souvenir you'll use daily, consider something from this extensive assortment of fabulous frames. Artisan-made, unusual materials, vintage, designer, imported . . . too much gorgeousness to pick just one. 3708 Magazine St. www.artandeyesneworleansla.com. ℰ **504/891-4494.** Mon 11am–5pm, Tues–Fri 11am–7pm; Sat 10am–6pm; Sun noon–5pm (closed Sun in Aug).

Century Girl ★★★ High-end curated vintage gems. Just choose your decade, be it a shimmering beaded '20s gown; a wasp-waisted mid-century cocktail confection a la Midge Maisel; a '70s Gucci butterfly-patterned silk kerchief; or an Oscar de la Renta gown so slinky it might escape the store (straight into your closet). 2023 Magazine St. www.centurygirlvintage.com. ℰ **504/875-3105.** Mon 11am–5pm, Tues–Fri 11am–7pm, Sat 10am–6pm; Sun noon–5pm.

Dollz & Dames ★★ If the Frenchmen Street jitterbugging scene has released your inner pin-up gal, this is your store. The vintage-y frocks make for darling datewear, but we'd don them any time. Tops cost $60 to $130, and dresses are under $200. Cute accessories, custom T-strap dance shoes, and helpful help. 216 Decatur St. www.dollzanddames.com. ℰ **504/522-5472.** Daily noon–6pm.

Fleur de Paris ★★★   The 1920s and 1930s elegance displayed here is positively swoonworthy. Hand-blocked, stylishly trimmed hats are expensive, but works of art; you'll also find luscious stockings and scarves, an ever-changing collection of vintage gowns, and custom design services. 523 Royal St. www.fleurdeparis.shop. ℂ **504/525-1899.** Mon, Wed–Sat 10am–6pm, Sun noon–6pm.

Funky Monkey ★★★   For 25 years, this place has brought the retro. You'll be the life of any party in glittery boots and a 70s-style mini, or a bulky sweater, or a stunning ball gown, or a beaded mosaic vintage vest. Or just scoop up one of the many awesome graphic tees. 3127 Magazine St. www.funky monkeynola.com. ℂ **504/899-5587.** Mon–Wed 1am–6pm, Thurs–Sat 11am–7pm, Sun noon–6pm.

Luca Falcone ★★   Bespoke suits of Italian fabric and shoes of Spanish leather, all cut to custom perfection by master tailors. If clothes make the man, many a gentleman has been made here (and if you can afford these suits, you can afford to come back for the fitting . . . and you'll have a good excuse to do so). 2049 Magazine St. www.lfsuits.com. ℂ **504/309-5929.** Mon–Sat 10am–6pm or by appt.

Meyer the Hatter ★★★   Family-owned for more than 125 years, this haberdashery has one of the South's largest selections of fine hats and caps, with distinguished international labels such as Bailey, Stetson, Kangol, Dobbs, and Biltmore for men (the women's collection is smaller). Let these hat whisperers fuss over you and pick out the proper feather for your new chapeau—they know just how to top every head. 120 St. Charles Ave. www. meyerthehatter.com. ℂ **504/525-1048.** Mon–Sat 10am–5:45pm.

Miss Claudia's Vintage Clothing & Costumes ★★   Gold sequined short-shorts and pink rhinestoned dresses, bright turquoise wigs to put over our tresses, bedazzled leggings and sparkling blings—these are a few of our favorite things. (Also floral maxis, leather, Hawaiian shirts, men's vintage . . .) This tiny shop is a good time waiting to happen. 4204 Magazine St. www.face book.com/missclaudiasvintage. ℂ **504/897-6310.** Mon, Wed–Fri 11am–6pm, Sat 10am–6pm, Sun noon–5pm.

No Rules Fashion ★   Glam, costume-y, and adventurous stuff for pirates, fetishists, and everyday nonconformists. Think velvet corsets, spangly bust-iers, sequined jumpsuits, two-piece suits in skull or flamingo patterns, or go-with-anything Edwardian and military-inspired jackets. Reasonably priced, no-regrets funwear. 927 Royal St. www.norulesfashion.com. ℂ **504/875-4437.** Mon–Thurs 11am–5pm, Fri–Sat 11am–6pm, Sun noon–5pm.

odAOMO ★★   Owner/designer Dr. Sophia Aomo Omoro designs dresses, bags, and accessories that are hand-crafted in Kenya by her own small team. The looks are breezy, fashion-forward, and eminently wearable; the real standouts are the statement neckpieces, belts, and bags of leather, beading, and metals. Fair wages and eco-friendly materials are central to the odAOMO philosophy. 839 Chartres St. www.odaomo.com. ℂ **504/460-5730.** Thurs–Sun 10am–5pm.

Rubenstein's ★★★ Many a proper young New Orleans man learned the art of attire here. For almost a century this hallowed haberdasher has outfitted gents in custom suits, fine menswear, and perfect prepwear. Their pros will dress you to the nines, with quick-turnaround tailoring to get you Galatoire's-ready. 102 St. Charles Ave. www.rubensteinsneworleans.com. ℭ **504/581-6666.** Mon–Sat 10am–5pm.

ShoeBeDo ★★ As much a gallery as a shoe store, it's worth a visit just to gawk. The window display's full of glam, outrageous, I-can't-pull-that-off footwear, but oh, you can. (There are cute flats and sandals, too.) 324 Chartres St. www.shoebedousa.com. ℭ **504/523-7463.** Sun–Thurs 10am–6pm, Fri–Sat 10am–7pm.

SoSuSu ★★★ Upscale, contemporary day-, foot-, and night-out wear that will spark joy. Susu selects labels you'll hear about next year, with a practiced eye for elegance, fine lines, and a minimalist pop of quirk. 3427 Magazine St. www.sosusuboutique.com. ℭ **504/309-5026.** Mon–Sat 10am–5pm.

Trashy Diva ★★★ There's actually nothing trashy about the '40s and '50s vintage-inspired clothes here. Flirty, curve-flattering numbers in silks and velvets appeal to both Bettys and Goths, as do the shoes and va-va-voom corsets and lingerie. Check sales racks for bargains, and ask to be pointed to the nearby lingerie shop. 537 Royal St. trashydiva.com. ℭ **504/522-4233.** Sun–Mon and Thurs noon–6pm, Fri–Sat noon–7pm. Also at 2048 Magazine St. ℭ **504/299-8777.** Tues–Fri noon–6pm, Sat 11am–6pm, Sun 1–5pm.

West London Boutique ★★★ This gorgeous destination for local and visiting fashionistas offers apparel by emerging female designers from around the world. Think elegant fun: dramatic embroidery and romantic lace, bright flowers and mixed prints, satin and ruffles, softness and sparkle. 3952 Magazine St. www.westlondonboutique.com. ℭ **504/558-4649.** Mon–Sat 11am–5pm; Sun noon–5pm.

Food, Wine & Liquor

Every souvenir shop in town stocks spices, hot sauce, coffee, and beignet mix. The French Market vendors do, too, along with meat and seafood, and they're set up to ship it home or pack it for travel. If you get a hankering from home, try **www.cajungrocer.com**.

Grand Krewe Fine Wine & Spirits ★★ Whatever libations you seek, this warm and friendly local shop will sort you out, with fairly priced international wines, boutique bubbles, and small-batch spirits. Plus, free "Thirsty Thursday" tastings and the two cutest shop pugs in the known universe. 2305 Decatur St. www.grandekrewe.com. ℭ **504/309-8309.** Mon–Sat noon–8pm, Sun noon–5pm.

Keife & Co. ★★ If you just can't get out the door, Keife & Co. will deliver a basket with gourmet meats, cheeses, and wine to your Central Business District hotel room. If you *can* get out, grab a bottle on your way to the restaurant or to take home. Great selection; even better service. 801 Howard Ave. www.keifeandco.com. ℭ **504/523-7272.** Mon–Sat 10am–7pm.

WINE TASTINGS a la carte

Sip, shop, sip, shop. Rinse and repeat! With the Wine Institute of New Orleans' enomatic system, you can top up a debit card and set to dispensing 1-, 2-, or 3-ounce pours of some 120 wines at these three great wine stores. The Institute's own wine bar and shop **W.I.N.O** (610 Tchoupitoulas St.; www.winoschool. org; ℂ **504/324-8000**) is a good starting point in the Warehouse District. **Faubourg Wines** (2805 St. Claude Ave.; www.faubourgwines.com; ℂ **504/342-2217**) always has a nice selection of $5 to $8 pours and a fab take-home selection. Uptown, **Second Vine Wine** (4212 Magazine St.; www.facebook.com/secondvinewine; ℂ **504/353-9125**) is a friendly, low-key place to sip decently priced wines from around the globe. Or taste your day away at the state's first micro-winery, **Ole' Orleans** (1232 O. C. Haley Blvd.; www.oleorleans.com; ℂ **504/568-9463**), where all wines are Louisiana-made and NOLA-named, like the Gumbeaux merlot and a white blend called Wards. Reserve online.

Vieux Carré Wine and Spirits ★★ Whether you're a serious wine buyer, or looking for a souvenir bottle of Herbsaint, absinthe, or Sazerac rye—or just want a BYOB for tonight's dinner—this densely packed 35-year-old French Quarter shop will fit the bill. 422 Chartres St. www.instagram.com/vcwineandspirits. ℂ **504/568-9463.** Mon–Thurs 10am–6pm, Fri–Sat 10am–7pm.

Gifts, Home Decor & Bath

Bevolo ★★★ Even if you don't intend to take home a handmade copper gaslight lantern as a vacation memento, check out Bevolo because 1) the lanterns are a gorgeous local tradition; 2) master craftsmen fabricate them right in front of you at the on-site workshop (weekdays only); and 3) you might change your mind about your souvenir choice. Or select something more modern from the adjoining Interior Collection. 316 Royal St. www.bevolo.com. ℂ **504/522-9485.** Mon–Sat 9am–5:30pm.

The Collective Shop ★★ This new boutique is a favorite for handcrafted local gifts at great prices. We're especially into the Louisiana-themed pop-art paper products with illustrations of Zapps Potato Chips, Sazeracs, crawfish boils, sno-ball syrups, oysters, and Slap Ya Mama hot sauce. 3512 Magazine St. www.statementgoods.com. Thurs–Sat 11am–6pm, Sun–Mon 11am–4pm.

Derby Pottery ★★ One of Mark Derby's hand-pressed tiles, glazed in gleaming single hues, makes for a lovely keepsake (particularly the New Orleans street-name tile reproductions); 100 make for a dazzling backsplash or fireplace surround. Ceramic mugs and water-meter clocks make excellent handmade souvenirs. 2029 Magazine St. www.derbypottery.com. ℂ **504/586-9003.** Mon–Sat 10:30am–5pm.

The Good Shop ★★★ Good is how you'll feel supporting this collective where the wares are locally, ethically, and eco-consciously crafted by makers who give back to the community. We adore the mission. We also adore the jasmine candles, Smoke perfume, and "brass fed" onesies. 1114 Josephine St. www.thegoodshopnola.com © **504/784-0900.** Weds–Sat 11am–6pm, Sun 11am–5pm.

Hazelnut ★ The housewares and gifts here are generally cute, with one dazzling standout: the line of toile items with a customized pattern of iconic New Orleans scenes—the St. Charles streetcar, a live oak tree, St. Louis Cathedral, and such. We want it all: bedding, tote bag, tray, picture frame, even the face mask. Sigh. If you're lucky, co-owner actor Bryan Batt (*Mad Men*) will be in the shop. 5525 Magazine St. www.hazelnutneworleans.com. © **504/891-2424.** Mon–Sat 10am–6pm; Sun noon–5pm.

Hové ★★★ The oldest perfumery in the city, Hové features a fabulous selection of all-natural scents for men and women. Original creations ("Kiss in the Dark") and Southern smells such as vetivert and tea olive, available in many forms (bath products, travel candles), make lovely presents—even for yourself. Book buffs will appreciate the copy of *Jitterbug Perfume* signed by author Tom Robbins, confirming the shop in his bestseller was roughly based on Hové. 434 Chartres St. www.hoveparfumeur.com. © **504/525-7827.** Wed–Sat 10am–5pm.

NOLA Boards ★★★ Need a gift or souvenir that's a few (big) steps up from a magnet? We're nuts about all things wooden from this sweet local shop—especially the handcrafted roux paddles, cheese boards, rolling pins, fleur de lis oven pulls, and Louisiana-shaped cutting boards. 4228 Magazine St. www.nolaboards.com. © **504/256-0030.** Sun 11am–5pm, Mon–Sat 11am–6pm.

Simon of New Orleans/Antiques on Jackson ★★ Folk artist Simon, whose brightly painted signs hang in homes and businesses throughout New Orleans, will paint-to-order your own personal sign and ship it to you. The studio also has a particularly good of primitive furniture, antiques, and hodgepodgery. 1028 Jackson Ave. www.facebook.com/simonofneworleans. © **504/524-8201.** Mon–Sat 10am–5pm.

Sunday Shop ★★ Entering this boutique is like stepping into a glossy magazine—everything just looks, feels, and smells soothing and refined. Luxe linens, lavender soaps, ostrich feather dusters, the odd vintage objet d'art, oh my. Shopping here is an extravagance, but a divine one. 2025 Magazine St. www.sundayshop.com. © **504/342-2087.** Mon, Wed–Sat 11am–5pm; Sun 11am–4pm, Tues by appt.

Jewelry

Marion Cage ★★★ Cage's ultrafine, exquisitely wrought work is popular with collectors in Paris and New York, where she worked before opening this gallery in her native New Orleans. Crafted in matte rose and yellow gold, rhodium, leather, and hardwoods, items start around $85; a delicate sterling talon runs $245. 3807 Magazine St. www.marioncage.com. © **504/891-8848.** Mon–Sat 10am–5pm or by appt.

Mignon Faget, Ltd. ★★ Faget, a New Orleans native, lends her signature style to New Orleans–specific designs in gold, silver, and bronze d'oré (and housewares)—all superb souvenirs or gifts. 3801 Magazine St. www.mignonfaget.com. © **504/891-2005.** Mon–Sat 10am–6pm, Sun noon–6pm.

Saint Claude Social Club ★★★ This gorgeous boutique stocks *all* the pretty things—flouncy vintage frocks, dreamy feather headpieces—but it's the jewelry, sourced mainly from independent female designers around the world, that keeps us running back to the bright yellow door a block off Magazine Street. We obsess over the store's namesake Saint Claude designs, such as Wonder Woman cuffs, locally inspired alligator rings, gingko earrings, and crawfish-claw necklaces. 1933 Sophie Wright Pl. www.saintclaudesocialclub.com. ℂ **504/218-8987.** Mon–Sat 11am–6pm, Sun 11am-5pm.

Music

Domino Sound Record Shack ★★ A one-room beats shop off the beaten track. Stellar ska, rock steady, and R&B collections; world music from countries you've never heard of; local weirdness; and pretty much everything Sun Ra ever put out. All vinyl except for about 37 cassettes. Bonus points for proximity to McHardy's Chicken (p. 117). 2557 Bayou Rd. www.dominosound records.com. ℂ **504/309-0871.** Wed–Mon noon–6pm ('til 7:30 Fri).

Euclid Records ★★ If you love the smell of vinyl in the morning, or any time, Euclid will fire your pheromones. This younger-than-it-feels Bywater shop (sistah of the iconic St. Louis shop) stocks two floors of platters from every era and hosts occasional in-store performances. 3301 Chartres St. www. euclidrecordsneworleans.com. ℂ **504/947-4348.** Daily 11am–5pm, Sat 11am–7pm.

Louisiana Music Factory ★★★ *The* place to get yourself stocked up on New Orleans music, with helpful staff and a large selection of regional music—Cajun, zydeco, R&B, jazz, blues, gospel—plus books, posters, record players, original art, musicians' supplies, and T-shirts. It's especially hopping during Jazz Fest, when it hosts live performances. 421 Frenchmen St. www. louisianamusicfactory.com. ℂ **504/586-1094.** Thurs–Tues 11–6pm.

Peaches Records ★ Peaches' first store (ca. 1975) was a stop-off for R&B royalty (Stevie Wonder!) and helped launch local hip-hop artists like Juvenile and Lil Wayne. Still family-owned and a hip-hop hub, the spacious store stocks a broad swath of locally focused CDs, vinyl, books, DVDs, super-kitschy gewgaws, and one of the better logo'd T-shirts in town. 4318 Magazine St. www.peachesrecordsandtapes.com. ℂ **504/282-3322.** Daily 10am–5pm.

The Occult

Bottom of the Cup Tearoom ★ Open since 1929, it bills itself as the "oldest tearoom in the United States," so a reading with Otis, its premier psychic, is a pretty classic experience. The tearoom psychics can read palms, tarot cards, and tea leaves. Great selection of teas for purchase and various psychicy goods. 327 Chartres St. www.bottomofthecup.com. ℂ **800/729-7148** or 504/524-1997. Daily 10am–6pm.

Boutique du Vampyre ★ Of course, New Orleans has a brick-and-mortar vampire shop—are you really surprised? (It's one of only a few in the U.S.) Proprietress Marita Jaeger showcases local artisans, custom-made

DIVING DEEPER INTO voodoo

What better souvenir to bring back from New Orleans than some genuine Voodoo paraphernalia? Touristy it may be, but **Marie Laveau's House of Voodoo** ★ (739 Bourbon St.; www.voodooneworleans.com; ℂ 504/581-3751) has loads of Voodoo dolls and gris-gris bags that make great souvenirs for the right friends. With two big rooms of Voodoo paraphernalia, **Voodoo Authentica** ★★ (612 Dumaine St.; www.voodooshop.com; ℂ 504/522-2111) feels like a regular retail establishment, just one selling locally made Voodoo dolls, potions, spell candles,

and daubs that range from cheap to costly; there are simple souvenirs as well as serious works of art—plus readings. Or venture to the Lower Garden District to **Haus of Hoodoo** ★★ (1716 St. Charles St.; hausofhoodoo.com; ℂ 504/302-2042), run by Vodou Priestess Jessyka Winston; it offers ritual baths, spiritual waters, oils, candles, herbs, bundles, divinations, books . . . and the opportunity to be liberated from any voodoo-related misconceptions you might be harboring. Also see p. 188 for Voodoo temples and practitioners (they usually have shops, too).

fangs, coffin-shaped backpacks . . . and for the faint of heart, temporary bite tattoos. 709½ St. Ann St. feelthebite.com. ℂ **504/561-8267.** Daily 10am–9pm.

T-Shirts & More

If crass and mass market suits your style, by all means buy up the Bourbon Street goods. But for garments with local flavor, cleverness, and a decent design aesthetic, there are many better options. Shirts (and hats, hoodies, and so forth) in these shops will probably run $5 to $10 more than your average show-me-your-whatever tops, but they're softer. And smarter.

DNO (Defend New Orleans) ★★   Small shops with stylish locally inspired goods, comfy shirts and hoodies, caps, home decor, plus some lesser-known NOLA-related books. 1101 First St. www.dno.la. ℂ **504/941-7010.** Mon–Fri noon–6pm; Sat–Sun 11am–4pm. Also at 600 Carondelet St. ℂ **504/324-7463.** Sat–Mon 11am–4pm.

Dirty Coast ★★   With two locations, Dirty Coast sells utterly witty, eye-catching, original T-shirt designs like the "Crawfish Pi," with the Greek symbol composed of a tasty pile of mudbugs, and "504Ever." 5631 Magazine St. ℂ **504/324-3745.** Also 713 Royal St. ℂ **504/324-6730.** www.dirtycoast.com. Sun–Thurs 11am–5pm, Fri–Sat 11am–6pm.

Fleurty Girl ★★★   It's hard to leave here without one (or more) of its pithy NOLA-centric T-shirts. Dig the cocktail-related tees, like KEEP CALM AND CARRY A GO-CUP and the Mardi Gras–inspired EVERYWHERE ELSE IT'S JUST TUESDAY. Also excellent jewelry, housewares, and accessories. 617 Chartres St. ℂ **504/304-5529.** Mon–Thurs 10am–6pm; Fri–Sat 10am–7pm; Sun 9am–6pm. Also 3137 Magazine St. ℂ **504/301-2557.** Daily 10am–6pm. www.fleurtygirl.net.

WALKING TOURS OF NEW ORLEANS

By Diana K. Schwam

We've said it before, and we'll keep saying it: This town was made for walking. Even at the height of the humid summer months, when everyone's main motivation is to laze in the shade and sip cool drinks, you can still flit between air-conditioned restaurant and air-conditioned museum.

With every step in undeniably unique New Orleans, there is something extraordinary to marvel at and commit to memory, in your mind's eye or on your phone: a gorgeous building more interesting than the last, a "colorful" character, a tuba-lugging musician in formal wear. Granted, the sidewalks and streets are a bit crumbly, but it's laden with eye candy and void of elevation, save the bar stools.

Stroll along the city streets, or the banks of Bayou St. John, turning when it strikes your fancy. You might have a street to yourself—or share it with a fleeting ghost. Imagine it 100 years ago, without the cars and overhead wires: It wouldn't have looked much different than it does now.

One recent development that only adds to a delightful walk is the launch of **Yardi Gras,** the outbreak of elaborately decorated homes and yards (aka **"house floats"**) that popped up citywide when the parade floats were sidelined by the pandemic in 2020 and 2021. We're hoping this silver lining becomes a lasting tradition. If you're in town during **Carnival season,** do venture into the neighborhoods. Halloween, Christmas, St. Patrick's Day, Valentine's Day, and most holidays also portend a good chance of seeing ornate, ostentatious or outrageous home décor—we New Orleaneans need little excuse to dress up ourselves or our homes.

The French Quarter, Garden District, and Bayou St. John—each has its own distinct appearance, fascinating history, and a bit of mystery, and all are easily manageable on foot. So put on some good walking shoes, breathe in that Southern breeze, and mosey. Go slow. Take it (big) easy. Admire the lacy ironwork. Peek through

French Quarter gateways, where simple facades hide exquisite courtyards with elaborate fountains and thick foliage. Gawk at the mighty oaks, some dripping with swaying Spanish moss.

These self-guided walking tours provide a solid introduction to what is simply one of the most beautiful cities anywhere, and answer some "That looks interesting—what the heck *is* it?" queries. For professional guided tours, see p. 190.

WALKING TOUR 1: **THE FRENCH QUARTER**

START:	**The intersection of Royal and Bienville streets.**
FINISH:	**Jackson Square.**
TIME:	**Allow approximately 2 hours, not including time spent in shops or historic homes.**
BEST TIME:	**Any day between 8am and 10am (the quiet hours).**
WORST TIME:	**At night. Some attractions won't be open, and you won't be able to get a good look at the architecture.**

If you only spend a few hours in New Orleans, do it in the exquisitely picturesque French Quarter. In these 80 city blocks, the colonial empires of France and Spain intersected with the emerging American nation. It's called the Vieux Carré or "old square," but somehow it's timeless—venerable yet vibrantly alive. Today's residents and merchants are stewards of a rich tradition of individuality and creativity. This tour will introduce you to its style, history, and landmarks.

Start at the corner of Royal and Bienville streets, heading into the Quarter (away from Canal St.). That streetcar named Desire rattled along Royal Street until 1948 (then came the bus named Desire. Really). Imagine how noisy these narrow streets were when the streetcars ran here. Your first stop is:

1 337–343 Royal St., Rillieux-Waldhorn House

Now housing art galleries, shops, and apartments (upstairs), this elegant structure was built between 1795 and 1800 for Vincent Rillieux, the great-grandfather of the French Impressionist artist Edgar Degas. The wrought-iron balconies are an example of excellent Spanish colonial workmanship.

2 334 Royal St., Bank of Louisiana (Police Station)

Across the street, this former bank was erected in 1826, with its columned Greek Revival portico added in the early 1860s. It suffered fires in 1840, 1861, and 1931, and has served as the Louisiana State Capitol, an auction exchange, a criminal court, a juvenile court, and an American Legion social hall. Now a creamy yellow, it houses the Vieux Carré police station.

Walking Tour 1: The French Quarter

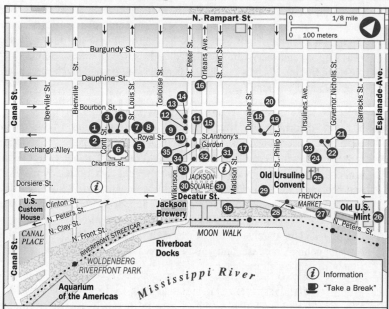

3 403 Royal St., Latrobe's

Benjamin H. B. Latrobe died of yellow fever shortly after completing designs for the Louisiana State Bank, which opened here in 1821. One of the nation's most eminent architects, he contributed to the design of the U.S. Capitol and the White House. Note the monogram LSB on the Creole-style railing. It's now an elegant banquet hall named for the architect. Peek inside if you can.

4 417 Royal St., Brennan's Restaurant

The famed, bright-pink Brennan's opened in this historic building in 1955 and was crowned restaurant royalty almost immediately. Shuttered in 2013 following a sad financial, legal, and family squabble, the restaurant changed hands (but stayed in the family) and was gloriously restored and reopened in 2014. One of 200 buildings destroyed in the 1794 fire and rebuilt (also by Vincent Rillieux) in 1855, it has been home to the Banque de la Louisiane, the world-famous chess champion Paul Charles Morphy, and the parents of Edgar Degas. If it's open, take a gander at the elegant center staircase and pretty courtyard, with the turtle-stocked fountain. And by all means, eat!

5 437 Royal St., Peychaud's Drug Store

When Masons held lodge meetings here in the early 1800s, proprietor and druggist Antoine A. Peychaud served after-meeting drinks of bitters and cognac to lodge members in small egg cups, called *coquetier*—later Americanized to "cocktails." And so it began (the cocktail and the much-debated legend).

6 400 Royal St., Louisiana Supreme Court

Built in 1909, this was and still is a courthouse, covering the length of the block. The ostentatious baroque edifice laden with Georgia marble seems out of scale here. Sadly, many original Spanish-era structures were demolished to pave its way. Granted, those original buildings were indeed run down; the new construction was positioned as slum-clearing. But all this was well before the Vieux Carré Commission formed in the early 1930s to protect the historic French Quarter buildings. Ironically, rulings in this very courthouse upheld the preservation regulations fueled by the Vieux Carré Commission.

7 519–521 Royal St., Antoine's Wine Cellar

See the little barred window between these buildings? Watch how many people walk right by this hidden marvel. Peer inside to spy the 165-foot-long, wow-factor wine cellar belonging to **Antoine's Restaurant** (p. 97), around the corner. The 25,000-bottle capacity leaves oenophiles envious.

8 533 Royal St., Merieult House

Built for the merchant Jean François Merieult in 1792, this house was the only building in the area left standing after the 1794 fire. Legend has it that Napoleon offered Madame Merieult great riches in exchange for her hair, to create a wig to present to a Turkish sultan (she refused). Nowadays, it's home to the excellent **Historic New Orleans Collection** (p. 161).

Cross Toulouse Street to:

9 613 Royal St., the Court of Two Sisters

This structure was built in 1832 for a local bank president on the site of the 18th-century home of a French governor. The two sisters were Emma and Bertha Camors, whose father owned the building; from 1886 to 1906, they ran a curio store here. Consider a charming courtyard cocktail.

10 640 Royal St., Le Monnier Mansion

No one thought this 1811 building would survive a fourth-floor addition in 1876, creating the city's first "skyscraper." Sieur George, fictional hero of George W. Cable's scandalous *Old Creole Days,* "lived" here. In the mid-1960s, the building housed Loujon Press, legendary in literary circles for its early embrace of avant-garde writers and Beat poets including Burroughs and Bukowski.

Cross St. Peter Street to:

11 700 Royal St., LaBranche House

The lacy cast-iron grillwork, with its delicate oak-leaf and acorn design, makes this one of the most photographed buildings in the Quarter. This is one of 11 three-story brick row houses built from 1835 to 1840 for the widow of wealthy sugar planter Jean Baptiste LaBranche.

Turn left at St. Peter Street and continue to:

12 714 St. Peter St., Lacoul House (Old Coffee Pot)

Built in 1829 by prominent physician Dr. Yves LeMonnier, this was a boardinghouse run by Antoine Alciatore in the 1860s. His cooking became so popular that he eventually gave up catering to open the famous Antoine's restaurant (p. 97), 2 blocks away and still operated by his descendants. The Old Coffee Pot restaurant operated in this space from 1894 until 2019. Walk through and check out the gorgeous arched ceilings.

13 718 St. Peter St., Pat O'Brien's

Now the de facto home to the famed Hurricane cocktail (p. 222), this building was completed in 1790. Later, Louis Tabary put on plays here, including, purportedly, the first grand opera in America. The popular courtyard is well worth a look, and maybe even a refreshment.

14 726 St. Peter St., Preservation Hall

The exquisitely decrepit early 1800s building is now best known for its tenant since the 1960s—Preservation Hall. Scores of people descend here nightly for traditional New Orleans jazz (p. 213). A daytime stop affords a glimpse, through the ornate iron gate, of a lush tropical courtyard in back. Author Erle Stanley Gardner, of *Perry Mason* fame, lived upstairs.

Continue up St. Peter Street until you reach Bourbon Street, and turn right: Walk 1 block to Orleans Street and **stop at the corner.** The beige, three-story hotel with the wraparound balcony is the:

15 Bourbon Orleans Hotel

Site of the notorious quadroon balls, where wealthy white men were introduced to potential mistresses: free women (and girls) of color who were one-fourth Black (quadroon) or one-eighth (octoroon). During these balls, the young women's mothers would carefully negotiate *placage* arrangements with the men, which often included financial, educational, housing, and child support for the mistresses. Imagine the discussions on those balconies.... The building later became a convent for the Sisters of the Holy Family, the second-oldest order of Black nuns in the country. Their founder (whose mother was a quadroon mistress!), Henriette DeLille, has been presented to the Vatican for consideration for sainthood.

Look up and down Bourbon Street and try to imagine what it was like in the 1950s and '60s during that particular heyday of jazz and burlesque. A couple blocks to the right, clarinetist Pete Fountain held court over the wild, swinging scene at his French Quarter Inn; a few blocks to your left at the Sho Bar, Blaze Starr stripped her way into the limelight and the hearts of tens of thousands of men.

Turn left on Orleans, heading lakeside (past the Bourbon Orleans Hotel), and follow Orleans a block to Dauphine (pronounced Daw-*feen*) Street. On the corner is:

16 716 Dauphine St., Le Pretre Mansion

In 1839, Jean Baptiste Le Pretre bought this 1836 Greek Revival house and added the romantic cast-iron galleries. The house is the subject of an oft-told horror story: In the 19th century, a conspicuously wealthy Turk, supposedly the exiled brother of a sultan, rented the house. He brought an entourage of servants and beautiful young girls—all thought to have been stolen from the sultan—and threw lavish parties. One night, screams came from inside; the next morning, neighbors found the tenant and the young beauties lying dead in a pool of blood. The mystery remains unsolved. Local ghost experts say you can sometimes hear exotic music and piercing shrieks. This story is strangely similar to "The Brother of the Sultan," a 1922 fictional tale by Helen Pitkin Schertz. Draw your own conclusions.

Turn right on Dauphine Street and go 2 blocks to Dumaine Street. Hydrate at the **Good Friends Bar** (p. 229) along the way if necessary. Turn right on Dumaine and walk 2 blocks, crossing Royal Street, to:

The French Quarter

WALKING TOURS OF NEW ORLEANS

17 632 Dumaine St., Madame John's Legacy

This structure was once thought to be the oldest building on the Mississippi River, built in 1726, 8 years after the founding of New Orleans. Recent research, however, suggests that only a few parts of the original building survived a 1788 fire. Its first owner was a ship captain who died in the 1729 Natchez Massacre; upon his death, the house passed to the captain of a Lafitte-era smuggling ship—and 21 subsequent owners. The structure is a rare example of the once-prevalent French "raised cottage," with an aboveground basement of brick-between-posts construction (locally made bricks were too soft to be the primary building material). Its name comes from George W. Cable's fictional character who was bequeathed the house in the short story "Tite Poulette." It's now part of the Louisiana State Museum complex but has been shuttered for renovations for some time.

Turn around and double back to Royal Street. Turn right.

18 915 Royal St., Cornstalk Hotel

Legend persists that the fence surrounding this sweet Victorian was ordered by the home's owner to ease his wife's homesickness for her native Iowa. Oddly, the same story is told about a house in the Garden District with a similar fence (p. 258). It was forged in Philadelphia, and only one more exists (at the Banning Museum in California, but from New Orleans). In any case, it's awfully pretty, isn't it? Enough so that Bill and Hillary Clinton and Elvis himself have walked the supposedly haunted halls here.

19 919 Royal St., Andrew Jackson Hotel (Old Federal Courthouse)

Just after General Andrew Jackson slammed the British in the 1815 Battle of New Orleans, Louis Louaillier, a member of the legislature, criticized the popular general. Jackson responded by jailing Louis, as well as a judge who tried to order Louis' release. When the war ended and the prisoners were freed, the judge hauled Jackson back into a courthouse on this site, citing him for contempt and fining him $1,000. Twenty-nine years later, Congress ordered Jackson to be repaid with interest. The courthouse survived until 1890, when this hotel was built.

Continue down Royal Street for half a block (good gallery browsing here). Turn left on St. Philip. Go 1 block to:

20 941 Bourbon St., Lafitte's Blacksmith Shop

This National Historic Landmark claims to be the oldest continually operating bar in the country (see p. 224). Legend is that it was the headquarters of Jean Lafitte and his pirates, who posed as blacksmiths and used it to fence goods they'd plundered on the high seas. It still reflects the architectural influence of late-1700s French colonists. It may also be the oldest building in the Mississippi Valley, but that has not been documented. An unfortunate exterior renovation that tried to replicate the original brick and plaster makes it look fake (it's actually not), but the candlelit interior is still an excellent place to imagine 19th-century Quarter life and swill some grog.

Turn right onto Bourbon Street and follow it 2 blocks to Governor Nicholls Street. Turn right and go 1 block to the corner of Royal Street:

21 1140 Royal St., Lalaurie House

Two-time widow Madame Delphine Macarty de Lopez Blanque wed Dr. Louis Lalaurie and moved into this residence in 1832, where the couple seduced the city with extravagant parties. When a fire broke out, neighbors crashed through a locked door to find seven starving slaves chained in painful positions. The sight, combined with Delphine's stories of past slaves having "committed suicide" and rumors of hideous live-subject medical experiments conducted within, enraged her neighbors. Madame Lalaurie and her family escaped a mob's wrath and fled to Paris. After her death, her body was secretly returned to New Orleans for burial. Tales of hauntings persist, especially that of a slave child who fell from the roof trying to escape Delphine's cruelties. The building was a Union headquarters during the Civil War, a gambling house, and home to actor Nicolas Cage. Haunted himself by financial difficulties, Cage was forced to return the house to the bank. It now houses luxury condos.

22 1132 Royal St., Gallier House Museum

James Gallier, Jr., built this house as his residence in 1857. He and his father were two of the city's leading architects (p. 161). Anne Rice based Lestat and Louis's home in *Interview with the Vampire* on this house.

Continue on Royal Street to Ursulines Avenue and turn left, toward the river.

23 617 Ursulines Ave., Croissant D'Or ☕

For a little rest or sustenance, stop in the popular **Croissant D'Or,** 617 Ursulines Ave. (www.croissantdornola.com; ✆ **504/524-4663;** p. 148). The pastries here are very good, as is the ambience—inside or out.

At the next corner, turn left onto Chartres Street. You'll be in front of:

24 1113 Chartres St., Beauregard-Keyes House

This raised cottage was built as a residence in 1826 by Joseph Le Carpentier, though it has other important claims to fame (detailed on p. 157). Notice the Doric columns and handsome "boy/girl" twin staircases.

Across the street is the imposing:

25 1100 Chartres St., Old Ursuline Convent

Built in 1752, this is officially the oldest building in the Mississippi River Valley. It was home to the hearty French nuns of Ursula, who helped raise young girls into marriageable prospects for the lonely men settling this new territory (more on p. 159). Many locals claim to be direct descendants of those proper young girls—so many, in fact, that the math doesn't

10

The French Quarter | WALKING TOURS OF NEW ORLEANS

add up. But it beats the alternate original settler ancestry of criminals and other heathens.

Continue along Chartres until you get to Esplanade Avenue and turn right. This is one of the city's most picturesque historic thoroughfares, with grand 1800s town houses gracing the tree-lined avenue. Just past Decatur Street, you'll see:

26 400 Esplanade Ave., New Orleans Jazz Museum at the Old U.S. Mint

This was the site of Fort St. Charles, built to protect New Orleans in 1792. Andrew Jackson reviewed the "troops" here—pirates, ragtag volunteers, and a nucleus of actual trained soldiers—whom he later led in the Battle of New Orleans. It's now a Louisiana State Museum housing the New Orleans Jazz Museum, and a coin and minting collection (p. 163).

Follow Esplanade toward the river and turn right at the corner of North Peters Street. Follow North Peters until it intersects with Barracks Street. This is the back end of:

27 The Historic French Market

This European-style market (p. 156) has been here for well over 200 years, and today it has a farmers market, food booths, arty-crafty goods, and flea-market stalls with souvenirs. Do stop to shop or nosh.

When you leave the French Market, exit on the side away from the river onto Decatur Street. Follow Decatur to St. Philip St. and look for four tall flags flying in the middle of the pavement, surrounding the:

28 Jeanne d'Arc Statue

Locally dubbed "Joni on the Pony," this gilded replica of mighty Joan of Arc riding into battle was a 1958 gift from France, recognizing sisterhood between the two countries. It took a circuitous and controversial route to this location, and now serves as rallying point for the magnificent Krewe de Jeanne d'Arc parade each January 6 (Joni's bday and Twelfth Night).

Across the street, you'll pass 923 and 919 Decatur Street, where the Café de Refugies and Hôtel de la Marine stood, gathering places in the 1700s and early 1800s for pirates, smugglers, European refugees, and outlaws. Now, it's muffuletta time:

29 923 Decatur St., Central Grocery ▇

If it's lunchtime, pop into **Central Grocery** (© **504/523-1620;** p. 111) and pick up a famed muffuletta sandwich. Eat inside at the little tables, or take it with you and dine alfresco in Jackson Square, near your next stop.

Decatur Street will take you to Jackson Square. Turn right onto St. Ann Street; the twin four-story, red brick buildings here and on the St. Peter Street side of the square are:

30 The Pontalba Buildings

These highly coveted buildings sport some of the most impressive cast-iron balcony railings in the French Quarter. They also represent early French Quarter urban revitalization—and early girl power. In the mid-1800s, Baroness Micaela Almonester de Pontalba inherited rows of buildings along both sides of the Place d'Armes from her father, the wealthy Spanish nobleman-turned-magnate Don Almonester (who rebuilt St. Louis Cathedral [p. 156], among other developments). In an effort to counteract the emerging American sector across Canal Street, Baroness Pontalba had the structures razed, and under her supervision the Pontalba Buildings were begun in 1849 (you can see her mark today in the entwined initials A.P. in the ironwork). These high-end apartments were built in the traditional Creole-European style, with commercial space at street level, housing above, and courtyards in the rear. The Baroness also had Jackson Square built, including the cast-iron fence and the equestrian statue of Andrew Jackson. Her scandalous personal story (see p. 159) is equally fascinating.

Follow St. Ann to Chartres Street, turn left, and continue around Jackson Square; you will see:

31 751 Chartres St., the Presbytère

This, the Cabildo, and the St. Louis Cathedral—all designed by Gilberto Guillemard—were the first major public buildings in the Louisiana Territory. The Presbytère was originally designed as the cathedral's rectory. Baroness Pontalba's father financed the building's beginnings, but he died in 1798, leaving only the first floor done. It was finally completed in 1813. Never used as a rectory, it became a city courthouse and now houses the excellent **Louisiana State Museum** (p. 163).

Next you'll come to:

32 St. Louis Cathedral

Although it is the oldest Catholic cathedral in the U.S., this is actually the third building erected on this spot—the first was destroyed by a hurricane in 1722, the second by fire in 1788. The cathedral was rebuilt in 1794; the central tower was later designed by Henry S. Boneval Latrobe, again remodeled and enlarged between 1845 and 1851 under the direction of Baroness Pontalba. The bell and stately clock (note the nonstandard Roman numeral 4) were imported from France (much more on p. 156).

The building on the cathedral's right is:

33 701 Chartres St., the Cabildo

In the 1750s, this was the site of a French police station and guardhouse. Part of that building was incorporated into the Spanish government state-house (known as the "Very Illustrious Cabildo"). It was still under reconstruction in 1803 when the transfer papers for the Louisiana Purchase were signed in a room on the second floor. Since then, it has served as New Orleans' City Hall, the Louisiana State Supreme Court, and, since 1911, a Louisiana State Museum (p. 160).

Think those old Civil War cannons out front look pitifully obsolete? Think again. In 1921, in a near-deadly prank, one was loaded and fired.

The French Quarter

WALKING TOURS OF NEW ORLEANS

That missile traveled across the wide expanse of the Mississippi and landed 6 blocks inland in a house in Algiers, narrowly missing its occupants.

Walk up the narrow alley between the Cabildo and St. Louis Cathedral. You'll come to Pirate's Alley:

34 624 Pirate's Alley, Faulkner House Books

In 1925, William Faulkner lived here. He contributed to the *Times-Picayune* and worked on his first novels, *Mosquitoes* and *Soldiers' Pay*, making this lovely store a requisite stop for literature lovers and book buyers of any persuasion (p. 239).

To the left of the bookstore, a small alley leads to St. Peter Street, which is behind and parallel to Pirate's Alley.

35 632 St. Peter St., Tennessee Williams House

Have a sudden urge to scream "Stella!!!" at that second-story wrought-iron balcony? No wonder. This is where Tennessee Williams wrote *A Streetcar Named Desire*, one of the greatest pieces of American theater. He remarked that he could hear "that rattle-trap streetcar named Desire running along Royal and the one named Cemeteries running along Canal Street and it seemed the perfect metaphor for the human condition."

Backtrack toward Jackson Square. Walk toward the river on St. Peter Street to Decatur Street. Make a left on Decatur and pass the carriages and artists in front of Jackson Square. Cross Decatur at St. Ann to get to:

36 800 Decatur St., Café du Monde 🍽

You've finished! At **Café du Monde** (✆ **504/525-4544;** p. 146), get beignets and café au lait (of course). Do climb the adjacent stairs to the landing–a micro-park renamed in the wake of the 2020 social justice uprising for Louisiana lieutenant governor Oscar Dunn (when he took office in 1868, he was the U.S.'s first elected Black lieutenant governor). Enjoy the expansive views of Jackson Square and the Mississippi River, take a selfie, relax on a bench and rest your feet, and watch the river roll.

WALKING TOUR 2: THE GARDEN DISTRICT

START:	**Prytania Street and Washington Avenue.**
FINISH:	**Lafayette Cemetery.**
TIME:	**45 minutes to 2 hours.**
BEST TIME:	**Daylight.**
WORST TIME:	**Night, when you won't be able to get a good look at the architecture.**

Walking around the architecturally astounding Garden District, you may get the impression that you've entered an entirely separate city—or time period— from the French Quarter. The Garden District was indeed once a separate city (Lafayette) and established later, after the 1803 Louisiana Purchase. But what most profoundly distinguishes the two is that they were developed by two different groups: The French Quarter was settled by Creoles during the French and Spanish colonial periods, and the Garden District was created by Americans.

Thousands of Americans moved here after the Louisiana Purchase, drawn by a booming local economy fueled by lucrative Mississippi River commerce, abundant slave trade, and national banks. Friction soon arose between these new residents and the Creoles, sparked by language barriers, religious division, commercial competition, and mutual snobbery. With inferior business experience, education, and organizational skills, the Creoles worried that *les Americains* would drive them out of business, and Americans were barred from the already overcrowded French Quarter. The snubbed Americans moved upriver and created their own residential district of astounding, in-your-face opulence: the Garden District. It is, therefore, a culture clash reflected through architecture, with Americans creating an identity by introducing bold, new styles.

Note: With few exceptions, houses on this tour are private homes and not open to the public. Several are owned by celebrities (names are omitted for privacy). Please be respectful of the residents.

To reach the Garden District, take the St. Charles streetcar to Washington Avenue (stop no. 16) and walk 1 block toward the river to:

1 2727 Prytania St., Garden District Book Shop

A stellar collection of national and regional titles, with many signed editions, makes this bookshop (p. 239) an appropriate kickoff for a Garden District tour. The historic property was built in 1884 as the Crescent City Skating Rink, and subsequently acted as a livery stable, mortuary, grocery, and gas station. Today "the Rink" also offers a coffee shop, restrooms, and air-conditioning (appreciated if you're doing this tour in summer).

Across Prytania Street, head to the corner of Fourth St. to find:

2 1448 Fourth St., Colonel Short's Villa

This house was built by architect Henry Howard for Kentucky Colonel Robert Short. The story goes that Short's wife missed the cornfields in her native Iowa, so he bought her the cornstalk fence (for a laugh, see Cornstalk Hotel; p. 253). But a revised explanation has the wife requesting it because it was the most expensive, showy fence in the building catalog. Second Civil War occupational governor Nathaniel Banks was quartered in this 9,800-square-foot beauty, which is currently owned by Scott Rodger, manager/producer of Sir Paul McCartney and Andrea Bocelli. The interior design is inSANE (photos on nola.com, 8/3/21).

Walking Tour 2: The Garden District

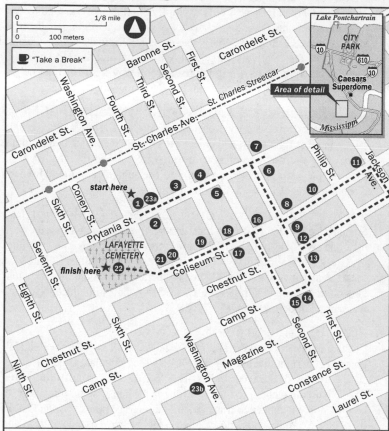

1 The Garden District Book Shop
2 Colonel Short's Villa
3 Briggs-Staub House
4 Our Mother of Perpetual Help
5 Women's Opera Guild Home
6 Toby's Corner
7 Bradish Johnson House
    & Louise S. McGehee School
8 Pritchard-Pigott House
9 Morris-Israel House
10 The Seven Sisters
11 Buckner ("Coven") House
12 Carroll-Crawford House

13 Brevard-Mahat-Rice House
14 Payne-Strachan House
15 Stained Glass House
16 Joseph Merrick Jones House
17 Musson-Bell House
18 Robinson House
19 Koch-Mays House
20 Benjamin Button House
21 Commander's Palace
21 Lafayette Cemetery
22a Still Perkin' 🍵
22b Coquette 🍵

Continuing down Prytania, you'll find:

3 2605 Prytania St., Briggs-Staub House

This is the Garden District's only example of Gothic Revival architecture (unpopular among Protestant Americans because it reminded them of their Roman Catholic Creole antagonists). Original owner Charles Briggs built the relatively large adjacent servant quarters for his Irish slaves, who were also starting to create the nearby Irish Channel neighborhood (across Magazine St. from the Garden District).

4 2523 Prytania St., Our Mother of Perpetual Help

The original owner, Henry Lonsdale, made his fortune selling burlap sacks, and was the first to add chicory to coffee. Once an active Catholic chapel, this site was one of several in the area owned by novelist Anne Rice and the setting for her novel *Violin*. The author's childhood home is down the street at 2301 St. Charles Avenue.

5 2504 Prytania St., Women's Opera Guild Home

Some of the Garden District's most memorable homes incorporate more than one style. Designed by William Freret in 1858, this one combines his Greek Revival design with Queen Anne–style additions. It's now an events center owned by the Women's Opera Guild. Tours are occasionally offered through Gray Line (p. 273) or the guild. facebook.com/womensguildnooa; © **504/453-7051.**

6 2340 Prytania St., Toby's Corner

The Garden District's oldest known home was built in 1838 for Philadelphia wheelwright Thomas Toby in the then-popular Greek Revival style—by way of the West Indies. The "non-Creole" style still followed Creole building techniques, such as raising the house up on brick piers to combat flooding and encourage air circulation. The house changed hands in 1858 to a family whose descendants still live here, six generations and many renovations and expansions later.

7 2343 Prytania St., Bradish Johnson House & Louise S. McGehee School

Paris-trained architect James Freret (cousin of William; see stop #5 above) designed this French Second Empire–style mansion for sugar factor Bradish Johnson in 1872 at a cost of $100,000 ($2 million plus today). Contrast the house's awesome detail with the stark, classical simplicity of Toby's Corner across the street—illustrating the effect that one generation of outrageous fortune had on Garden District architecture. Since 1929 it has been the private Louise S. McGehee School for girls.

Back track to First Street and turn left (away from St. Charles); it's a short block to:

8 1407 First St., Pritchard-Pigott House

This grand Greek Revival double-galleried town house shows how, as fortunes grew, so did Garden District home sizes.

10

The Garden District

WALKING TOURS OF NEW ORLEANS

Note the marble carriage block in front of the house across the street. Past residents used these like a step stool when mounting their horses and carriages.

9 1331 First St., Morris-Israel House

As time passed, the trend toward the formal Greek Revival style took a playful turn. By the 1860s, Italianate was popular, as seen in this (reputedly haunted) double-galleried town house, designed by architect Samuel Jamison. designed this house and note the identical ornate cast-iron galleries.

From the Morris-Israel House, turn right onto Coliseum Street. Along this block you'll see:

10 2329–2305 Coliseum St., the Seven Sisters

This row of "shotgun" houses gets its nickname from a (false) story that a 19th-century Garden District resident built these homes as wedding gifts for his seven daughters. Actually, there are eight "Seven Sisters," and they were built on speculation (the eighth looks somewhat different). "Shotgun"-style homes are so named because, theoretically, if one fired a gun through the front door, the bullet would pass unhindered through a series of rooms and out the back. (Or maybe because a West African word for this native African house form sounds like "shotgun.") Common in hot climates, the shotgun style effectively circulates air. The relatively small homes are popular in New Orleans, but rare along the imposing Garden District streets.

Follow Coliseum 1more block to Jackson St., to:

11 1410 Jackson St., Buckner ("Coven") House

The setting for Miss Robicheaux's Witch Academy from *American Horror Story: Coven,* this stunning 1865 mansion built for a cotton baron has three ballrooms and 48 columns. You can rent them all (and the rest of the house) for a silly sum.

Now turn right on Jackson for 1 block; go right again on Chestnut St. for 2 blocks. At the corner of First and Chestnut, you'll see:

12 1315 First St., Carroll-Crawford House

On the right-hand corner, the Carroll-Crawford House is another of Samuel Jamison's Italianate beauties. An even bigger cousin to the Morris-Israel House down the street, it was built in 1869 for Virginia cotton factor Joseph Carroll.

13 1239 First St., Brevard-Mahat-Rice House

On the left-hand corner, this 1857 Greek Revival town house was later augmented with an Italianate bay, in a fine example of "transitional" architecture. The fence's rosettes begat the house's name, "Rosegate," and its woven diamond pattern is said to be the precursor to the chain-link fence. This was novelist Anne Rice's home and a setting in her *Witching Hour* novels.

14 1134 First St., Payne-Strachan House

As the stone marker out front notes, Jefferson Davis, president of the Confederate States of America, died in this classic Greek Revival antebellum home, that of his friend Judge Charles Fenner. The sky-blue ceiling of the gallery is believed to keep winged insects from nesting there and to ward off evil spirits. (Now that you're aware of this local tradition, you'll notice it everywhere.)

Turn right on Camp. At the corner of Camp and Second St. is:

15 1137 Second St., Stained Glass House

This house exemplifies the Victorian architecture popularized in uptown New Orleans toward the end of the 19th century. Many who built such homes were from the Northeast and left New Orleans in the summer; otherwise, it would be odd to see this claustrophobic, "cool climate"–style house. Note the exquisite stained glass and rounded railing on the gallery.

Turn right onto Second Street and go 2 blocks to the corner of Coliseum:

16 2425 Coliseum St., Joseph Merrick Jones House

When previous owner Trent Reznor of the band Nine Inch Nails moved in, new anti-noise ordinances were introduced at city council. His next-door neighbor was Councilwoman Peggy Wilson. Coincidence?

Turn left onto Coliseum Street and go 1 block to Third Street. Turn left to get to:

17 1331 Third St., Musson-Bell House

This is the 1853 home of Michel Musson, one of the few French Creoles then living in the Garden District and the uncle of artist Edgar Degas (who lived with Musson on Esplanade Ave. during a visit to New Orleans). On the Coliseum Street side of the house is the foundation of a cistern. Most of these once-common water tanks (Mark Twain commented that it looked as if everybody in the neighborhood had a private brewery) were destroyed at the turn of the 20th century when mosquitoes, which breed in standing water, were found to be carriers of yellow fever. Yellow fever epidemics infamously killed 41,000 New Orleanians between 1817 and 1905.

Turn around and cross Coliseum to see:

18 1415 Third St., Robinson House

This striking Italianate villa was built between 1859 and 1865 by architect Henry Howard for tobacco grower Walter Robinson. Walk past the house to appreciate its scale—the outbuildings, visible from the front, are actually connected to the side of the main house. The entire roof is a large vat that once collected water. Add gravity and water pressure: Thus begat the Garden District's earliest indoor plumbing. The lavish 10,500-square-foot interior features a ballroom, a dining table seating 26 guests, and a grand, curving staircase with 28 stairs, each covered in their own design.

10

WALKING TOURS OF NEW ORLEANS | The Garden District

Hard to believe that, in sorrier, post-Depression times, it was sold for just $500...especially considering that the seven-bedroom home was on the market a few years back for $12 million but sold for a trifling $4 million.

Continue down Coliseum Street to the corner of Fourth St:

19 2627 Coliseum St., Koch-Mays House

This picturesque chalet-style dollhouse (well, for a large family of dolls) was built in 1876 by noted architect William Freret for James Eustis, a U.S. senator and ambassador to France (perhaps justifying the full-size ballroom). It and four other spec homes he built on the block were referred to as Freret's Folly. No detail was left unfrilled, from the ironwork to the gables and finials.

20 2707 Coliseum St., Benjamin Button House

Half a block further down Coliseum, this 8,000-square-footer is best known as the title character's home in the film *The Curious Case of Benjamin Button*. Ergo Brad Pitt slept here, fictionally (he bought his own French Quarter home soon after filming). The house was owned by the same family from 1870 until its 2009 sale. Thus when the *Button* location scouts came calling, they dealt with the family's 90-year-old matriarch, who had raised seven kids under this roof. Or *roofs,* since it's actually two houses combined: The original 1832 house has been significantly renovated over the years.

At the corner of Coliseum and Washington Ave.:

21 1403 Washington Ave., Commander's Palace

Established in 1883 by Emile Commander, this turreted Victorian (a bordello in the 1920s) is now the pride of the Brennan family, the most respected restaurateurs in New Orleans. Commander's Palace has long reigned as one of the city's—nay, the country's—top restaurants (p. 135).

22 1400 Washington Ave., Lafayette Cemetery

Established in 1833, this "city of the dead" is one of New Orleans' oldest cemeteries. While it's currently closed for renovations, a peek through the gates provides a glimpse of the classic above ground tombs. Typically they house numerous corpses from an extended family—one here lists 37 entrants; others are designated for members of specific fire departments or fraternal organizations.

Walk to St. Charles Avenue to pick up the streetcar (there is a stop right there) or flag down a cab to return to the French Quarter.

23 Wind Down at Still Perkin' or Coquette ☕

Now go back to your first stop, the Rink, where you can enjoy a cup of coffee and some light refreshments at Still Perkin'. Or head south on Washington to Magazine Street, where an early dinner at Coquette (p. 136) or any of the many eateries along this street will satisfy most appetites.

10

WALKING TOURS OF NEW ORLEANS

The Garden District

START:	Esplanade Avenue and Johnson Street.
FINISH:	City Park.
TIME:	It's a healthy trek, about 3 hours and 3 miles, not including museum, cemetery, and lunch stops. If that's too much, you could do stops 1–9 (1 mile) or 12–21 (2 miles) separately. Or bike or drive!
BEST TIME:	Monday through Saturday, early or late morning.
WORST TIME:	Sunday, when attractions are closed, or after dark. If you decide to stay in City Park or in the upper Esplanade area until early evening, plan to return on the bus, streetcar, or by taxi or rideshare.

If you're heading to City Park, the New Orleans Museum of Art, or the Jazz & Heritage Festival, consider some sightseeing in this overlooked region. I particularly enjoy the quiet, meandering stretch along Bayou St. John and walk here many mornings. Historically, Esplanade Ridge was Creole society's answer to St. Charles Avenue—another lush boulevard of stately homes and seemingly ancient trees stretching overhead. The lots are not quite as expansive as along St. Charles, so the grand front lawns are not in evidence. Originally home to the descendants of the earliest settlers, the avenue had its finest days toward the end of the 19th century, and some of the neighborhoods along its path have seen better days. Still, it's closer to the soul of the city than St. Charles Avenue (read: Regular people live here, whereas St. Charles always was and is for the well-heeled). For more interesting facts, look for the bronze historic markers in the median along Esplanade Ave.

You can catch a bus on Esplanade Ave. at Rampart Street, headed toward City Park and your chosen starting point. Otherwise, stroll (about 15 min.) up Esplanade Avenue to:

1 2023 Esplanade Ave., Charpentier House

Originally a plantation home, this elegant Greek Revival house was built in 1861 for businessman and railroadman A. B. Charpentier. It's now Ashton's Bed & Breakfast (p. 76), which maintains a Charpentier room.

2 2033–2035 Esplanade Ave., Widow Castanedo's House

Juan Rodriguez purchased this land in the 1780s, and his granddaughter, Widow Castanedo, lived here until her death in 1861 (when it was a smaller, Spanish colonial–style plantation home). Before Esplanade Avenue extended this far from the river, the house was located in what is now the middle of the street. The widow tried and failed to block the extension of the street. The late-Italianate house was moved to its present site and enlarged sometime around the 1890s. It's been split down the middle and is inhabited today by two sisters.

Walking Tour 3: The Esplanade Ridge

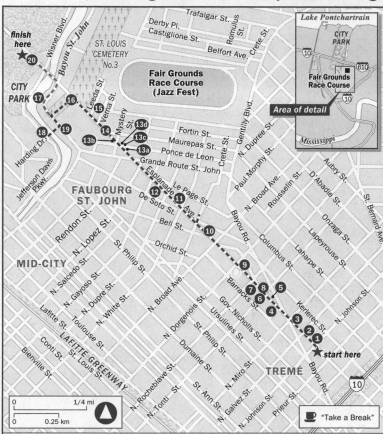

1 Charpentier House (Ashton's)
2 Widow Castanedo's House
3 2139 Esplanade Ave.
4 2212, 2216 & 2222 Esplanade Ave.
5 Goddess of History—
   Genius of Peace Statue
6 Degas House
7 Reuther House
8 2337 & 2341 Esplanade Ave.
9 2453 Esplanade Ave.
10 2623 Esplanade Ave.

11 2809–2911 Esplanade Ave.
12 2936 Esplanade Ave.
13a Café Degas 🍵
13b Canseco's 🍵
13c Fair Grinds 🍵
13d 1000 Figs 🍵
14 3330 Esplanade Ave.
15 Luling Mansion
16 St. Louis Cemetery No. 3
17 Bayou St. John
18 Magnolia Bridge
19 Pitot House
20 City Park

3 2139 Esplanade Ave.

A great example of the typical Esplanade Ridge style. Note the Ionic columns on the upper level.

After you cross North Miro Street, Esplanade Avenue crosses the diagonal Bayou Road, which was the route to the French-Canadian settlements at St. John's Bayou in the late 17th century. Bear left at the fork to stay on Esplanade Avenue and look for:

4 2212, 2216 & 2222 Esplanade Ave.

Originally built as spec town homes in 1883, these three Candy Crush–colored Italianate houses now comprise Le Belle Esplanade B&B inn. Although they look like triplets, each has its own architectural identity, and the intricate millwork and detailing surely stood out long before the eye-catching paint job was applied.

5 Goddess of History—Genius of Peace Statue

The triangular plot across the street was given to the city in 1886 by Charles Gayarre. George H. Dunbar donated the terra-cotta statue, a victory monument. It was destroyed in 1938 and replaced with this cement and marble model.

6 2306 Esplanade Ave., Degas House

French Impressionist artist Edgar Degas stayed and painted here, home to his brother and sister-in-law. The scandalous family story is on p. 170.

7 2326 Esplanade Ave., Reuther House

Check out the collection of metal and cinderblock sculptures in this front yard. The current resident is an artist, co-founder of the Contemporary Arts Center, and a major figure in the city's arts community.

In passing, take a look across the street at nos. 2325, 2327, 2329, and 2331—all interesting examples of Creole cottages. Then, continue to:

8 2337 & 2341 Esplanade Ave.

These houses were identical structures when they were built in 1862 for John Budd Slawson, owner of a horse-drawn-streetcar company that operated along Bayou Road. Back then, both were single-story shotgun-style houses. Notice the unusual ironwork beneath the front roof overhang.

Cross North Rocheblave Street to:

9 2453 Esplanade Ave.

This house was one of a matching pair at the corner of Dorgenois Street; the other was demolished. Though its architecture has been greatly altered, it's one of the few remaining mansard-roofed homes on Esplanade Ridge.

If you're just doing the lower portion of this tour, turn left on North Dorgenois Street, head 1 block to Bayou Road, and you'll find a trove of locals' favorite casual eateries including **Pagoda** and **Leo's Breads**. **McHardy's Chicken** (p. 117) is also close by. If you're continuing along the upper portion of this tour, cross North Broad Street to:

10 2623 Esplanade Ave.

Thank booze for this beauty. The Corinthian columns denote the classical revival style of this home, built in 1896 by absinthe and bitters magnate Louis A. Jung. The Jungs donated to the city the adjoining triangle of land at Esplanade Avenue, Crete Street, and DeSoto Street. on the condition that it remain public property. The pretty pocket park features a fountain (well, planter) and is graced by an unusual Art Nouveau fence.

11 2809 Esplanade Ave., Cresson House

This decorative, Queen Anne–style center-hall Victorian is just one of many pretty houses on Esplanade Ridge.

12 2936 Esplanade Ave.

This Gothic villa–style house is now an ISKCON (Hare Krishna) center (free vegetarian dinners on Sunday eves!). At the corner of Lopez St., look down the block for a glimpse of the historic **Fair Grounds Race Course** (p. 205).

13 a–d Take a Break at Café Degas, Canseco's, Fair Grinds, or 1000 Figs 🍵

The shops and restaurants at the intersection of Mystery Street and Esplanade Avenue offer fine lunchtime options. If the weather is nice, the semi-outdoor setting is exceedingly pleasant at **Café Degas** (p. 118). For snacks or picnic food (you're near Bayou St. John and City Park), try **Canseco's**, 3135 Esplanade Ave. (✆ **504/322-2594**), or turn down Ponce DeLeon Street, where **1000 Figs** offers very good Mediterranean fare (3141 Ponce de Leon St.; ✆ **504/301-0848**), and local fave **Fair Grinds** coffeehouse pours a good cup of joe (3133 Ponce de Leon St.; ✆ **504/913-9072**).

Continue to:

14 3330 Esplanade Ave.

This galleried frame home was built in the Creole-cottage style. Note the orientation of this stretch (and many of the houses along Esplanade Ave.). The lots are on a diagonal, so houses face Esplanade at a slight angle—a remnant either from the original plantation plots or from fortifications built at strategic angles to protect the city from attack.

Continue along Esplanade until Leda Court; turn right for a ½-block detour to:

15 1436 Leda Ct., Luling Mansion

Florence Luling, a German sugar and cotton baron, purchased 80 acres and commissioned famed architect James Gallier, Jr. to design this elaborate, three-story Italianate mansion. Built in 1865 with a full moat and ornate formal gardens that stretched all the way to Esplanade Avenue, it later it served as the Louisiana Jockey Club (it abuts the Fair Grounds Race Track). Time, weather and unfortunate modern adjustments have taken a toll, but its original magnificence is still apparent. It's apartments now, and a film site.

10

WALKING TOURS OF NEW ORLEANS | Esplanade Ridge & Bayou St. John

I've got to give it to my friends at WWOZ radio and the Ponderosa Stomp Foundation, who developed **www.acloserwalknola.com/tours**. This interactive site dishes up deep, rich history on historic musical locations and touchstones around the city. It's kinda like geocaching for music history nerds.

Return to Esplanade Avenue and turn right. On your right is:

16 St. Louis Cemetery No. 3

The public Bayou Cemetery, established in 1835, was purchased and expanded by the St. Louis diocese in 1854. It contains the burial monuments of many of the diocese's priests and religious orders. It might also be called "Restaurateurs' Rest": The tombs for the Galatoire, Tujague, and Prudhomme families are here. You can comfortably explore this cemetery without a group. As always, be respectful and alert. Open 8am-4pm daily.

Continue walking on Esplanade Ave. toward City Park. At the bridge, cross over to **City Park,** or turn left on Moss Street to walk along:

17 Bayou St. John

You probably wouldn't be standing here if it weren't for this peaceful, historic waterway, since it's responsible for the city's founding. It's explained on (p. 165).

Continue along Moss St.

18 Magnolia Bridge (aka Cabrini Bridge)

Originally built in the 1800s over Esplanade Avenue as a swing bridge to allow boat traffic, it was moved here in 1909. Streetcar rails were added in the late 1800s, and the Works Project Administration rehabbed it in 1936 (along with other bridges across the Bayou and in City Park). It was converted to pedestrian-only use in 1989, and got its bright blue paint job in 2018, to many neighbors' consternation (for years, the steel had a dark patina; historians claim blue is the original color).

Back-track on Moss St. to find:

19 1440 Moss St., Pitot House

This Creole country house overlooking the historic Bayou was home to the city's first mayor. It's open to the public, with docents offering a window onto life when Bayou St. John was the city's main trade route. See p. 171.

Return to Esplanade Avenue, cross the bridge, and walk into:

20 Esplanade & City Park Aves., City Park

Across the traffic circle, white pillars mark the entrance to your final destination: expansive City Park (p. 181), with its glorious live oaks, museums, gardens, lakes, and much, much more.

SIDE TRIPS FROM NEW ORLEANS

By Lavinia Spalding

I f you have time (say, 3 days), a sojourn into the countryside outlying New Orleans makes for an interesting cultural and visual contrast to the city. This chapter starts off by following River Road along the banks of the Mississippi, visiting the plantation homes and museums that line it, heading upriver from New Orleans. The second part takes you 150 miles west of New Orleans to the heart of the prairie Cajun Country.

The River Road trip can be done as a day trip, or you could keep rambling north to the St. Francisville area and stay overnight. The Cajun Country trip requires a 1- or 2-night stay, more if you can. A third option is a day trip to a bayou Cajun town. GPS will be your friend for either jaunt.

PLANTATIONS & MUSEUMS ALONG THE GREAT RIVER ROAD

The River Road plantation homes, with their elaborate architecture, opulent décor, and meticulously tended gardens, have long been among Louisiana's top tourist destinations, idealized in books and movies. But the decision of which homes to visit—or whether to visit at all—remains complex. There's simply no getting around the fact that New Orleans was once the center of the U. S. slave trade. It would be unconscionable to downplay the truth: This joyful, exquisite city we love has a brutal, ugly past. And River Road is where much of that brutality occurred.

So the question is: Should we tour the plantation homes built by the enslaved? In doing so, might we find answers to important questions about the legacy of people of African descent in America—and the roots of systemic racism? Or, by visiting the homes, are we enabling a side of the tourism industry that sugarcoats or ignores slavery? Some argue it's essential to visit so that we never forget the evils of slavery; others say that by touring the homes, we perpetuate the cycle of people profiting from dehumanizing the enslaved.

Here's our humble take: Until recently, most plantation tours were devoid of any authentic discussion concerning the hundreds of thousands of human beings who were captured and carried to Louisiana and forced to build, furnish, clean, maintain, and do every other kind of back-breaking work in and around the homes. But ever-so-slowly, tours are bringing to light these essential stories, and they're important to hear. We've listed a handful of plantation homes near New Orleans where the stories of enslaved people are being brought forward.

Most notable is **The Whitney** (p. 276). In 2014, this former plantation home became one of the nation's first museums dedicated to memorializing the enslaved, and a visit is profoundly edifying and moving. So if you're conflicted about touring plantations, we recommend the Whitney. And if you're *not* conflicted about touring plantations, we recommend the Whitney.

As for other, more mainstream tours, some persist in focusing solely on "the big house" (the enslaver's extravagant home) and make little or no mention of those who actually built the home. We aren't fans of tours that skirt the topic of slavery. But near New Orleans, there are two—**Oak Alley** (p. 275) and **Laura** (p. 275)—where serious efforts have been made to include this history. If a tour glosses over it, feel free to ask for it directly. You still may not get an accurate portrayal of the lives and contributions of the enslaved, but requesting the info is at least one small step toward combating racial injustice.

THE EARLY PLANTERS & THE ENSLAVED The early planters of Louisiana were rugged frontier people, most of whom had small plots of land by the river. In 1719, the first two ships carrying 451 captive Africans (rice farmers, mostly) arrived, and over the next 12 years, some 6,000 people were brought to Louisiana and sold into slavery. As the planters spread out along the Mississippi from New Orleans, they relied on the labor of these enslaved Africans, as well as European indentured servants and enslaved Indigenous people, to work their land and to clear vast swamplands, creating waterways for transporting indigo, tobacco, and other crops.

In 1795, enslaved workers successfully granulated cane-sugar crystals, after which sugar replaced indigo as the dominant crop. At this time, there were 19,926 enslaved Africans in Louisiana. Most of them worked on plantations.

By the 1800s, Louisiana planters had introduced large-scale farming and brought more acreage under cultivation. King cotton, rice, and sugarcane were popularized, bringing huge monetary returns, although natural dangers, a hurricane, or a swift change in the course of the capricious Mississippi could wipe out entire plantations and fortunes. In 1808, the importation of enslaved people was banned, ending the transatlantic slave trade. But the domestic slave trade boomed, with Louisiana at its center. By 1812, there were 35,000 enslaved people in Louisiana.

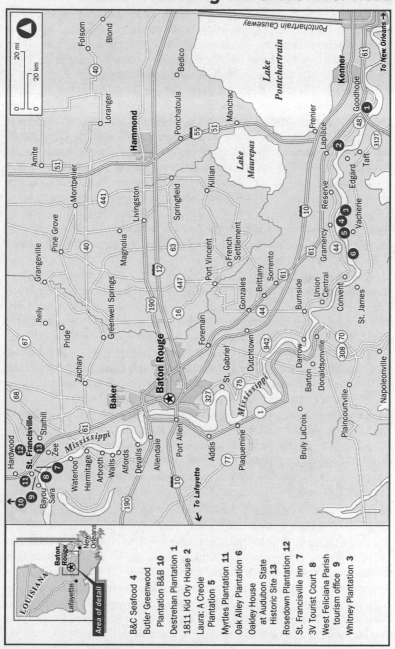

B&C Seafood 4

Butler Greenwood
Plantation B&B 10

Destrehan Plantation 1

1811 Kid Ory House 2

Laura: A Creole
Plantation 5

Myrtles Plantation 11

Oak Alley Plantation 6

Oakley House
at Audubon State
Historic Site 13

Rosedown Plantation 12

St. Francisville Inn 7

3V Tourist Court 8

West Feliciana Parish
tourism office 9

Whitney Plantation 3

BUILDING PLANTATION HOUSES Generally located near the riverfront, the plantation home was the focal point of a self-sustaining community. Most were modest, but some had wide, oak-lined avenues leading from their entrance to a wharf. The kitchen was separated from the house because of fire danger. Close by was the overseer's office. Some plantations had pigeon houses or dovecotes—and all had the inevitable cramped slave quarters lining the lane to the crops or across the fields and out of sight.

The first houses were simple "raised cottages," with long, sloping roofs, cement-covered brick walls on the ground floor, and wood-and-brick (brick between posts) construction in the living quarters on the second floor. Influenced by West Indian styles, these colonial structures suited the sultry climate and swampy building sites and made use of native materials. In the 1820s, however, Greek Revival and Georgian influences began to be added, creating a style dubbed Louisiana Classic. As prosperity flourished, homes became more grandiose, many embracing the styles of extravagant Victorian architecture, northern Italian villas, or Gothic lines. Planters and their families brought back ornate furnishings and skilled artisans from their European travels. Glittering crystal chandeliers and *faux marbre* (false marble) mantels appeared. Social lives, families, and egos also grew.

But such enormous wealth still stemmed from an economy based on human servitude. Enslaved people did the grueling work of producing all of the crops. They also raised farm animals, cooked and sewed, cared for their enslavers' children, and served as carpenters, masons, and smiths. They typically worked 10 to 16 hours a day, 6 days a week, from sunrise to beyond sunset. In 1860, just before the Civil War, Louisiana was producing about one-sixth of all cotton grown in the U.S., and almost all of the sugar. By this time, there were 332,000 enslaved people in the state. Nine out of 10 worked on plantations and farms.

The injustice and cruelty of slavery became the seeds of its own demise. After the Civil War, large-scale farming became impossible without that labor base. During Reconstruction, lands were confiscated and turned over to people who proved unable to run them; many were subdivided. Increasing international competition eroded the cotton and sugar markets. The culture represented by the plantation houses you'll see emerged and died in a span of less than 100 years.

PLANTATION HOUSES TODAY Where scores of stately homes once dotted the riverfront, few remain. Several that survived the Civil War fell victim to fires, floods, or industrial development. Others, too costly to be maintained, were left to the ravages of dampness and decay. But a few have been preserved and upgraded with electricity and plumbing. Most are private residences; some are B&Bs; a handful are open to visitors, the admission fees supplementing upkeep. Tours are hit-or-miss; much depends on your guide. After you visit a few, you'll begin to hear many of the same facts about plantation life, sometimes as infill for missing or boring history. For far too long, the era has been romanticized. The fact is that these plantations would not exist were it not for unthinkably savage, yet real, human cruelty.

Planning Your Trip

All the plantation homes shown on the map on p. 271 are within easy driving distance of New Orleans. If you're returning late, the small highways can be a little intimidating after dark. Don't expect broad river views along the Great River Road (the roadway's name on *both* sides of the Mississippi); it's obscured by tall levees. You'll see sugarcane fields and plenty of evidence of Louisiana's petrochemical industry. But spontaneous detours through little, centuries-old towns might result in finding a choice resale shop or good road food.

The **Whitney, Laura,** and **Oak Alley** are minutes apart, and each offers a different perspective on plantation life and the tourism industry. All three honor stories of the enslaved. The Whitney is unmissable, as it is focuses entirely on the enslaved perspective. Laura is classic understated Creole and has a low-key but superb presentation. Tara-esque Oak Alley represents the showy Americans and is slicker and glitzier (one could even do an Oak Alley drive-by; the huge, ancient trees are impressive). All are approximately an hour from New Orleans.

Organized Tours

Seeing plantation houses via a bus tour is a comfortable, planning-free option, and you get some bonus narration along the route. Almost every New Orleans tour company operates a tour to one or two plantations; most offer pickup at hotels or a central French Quarter locale. Costs include transportation and admission, and the offerings are always subject to change.

The reliable 5- to 7-hour tours (including travel time) given by mainstay **Gray Line** (www.graylineneworleans.com; © **800/233-2628** or 504/569-1401) typically offer a choice of two of three plantations: Laura, Oak Alley, or Whitney. (In late 2021, due to Covid and Hurricane Ida, tours only went to Oak Alley; check to see what current offerings are.) Daily tours depart Gray Line's Toulouse Street station (near Jax Brewery in the French Quarter). Times vary, so call ahead (Oak Alley tour $69 adults, $35 children 6–12). A combo Destrehan Plantation and swamp tour at 9am on most days is $109 adults, $60 kids 6 to 12.

Legendary Tours (www.legendarytoursnola.com; © **504/471-1499**) visits Oak Alley, Laura, or the Whitney for $68 including round-trip transportation (one plantation). For smaller groups, **Tours by Isabelle** (www.toursby isabelle.com; © **877/665-8687** or 504/398-0365) takes groups of 6 to 13 people in a comfortable van on a half-day or 9-hour expedition to multiple planta-tions. Check website for details.

Plantations & Museums Between New Orleans & Baton Rouge

The houses and museums below are listed in the order in which they appear on the map, running north along the Mississippi from New Orleans. Tours range from 1½ to 2½ hours; most people do one or two in a day (and may drive past others). Depending on your choices, you may have to cross the

Mississippi River by bridge a few times. The winding river makes distances deceiving; give yourself more time than you think you'll need. Several well-known plantation homes are in this area. If you're more interested in learning the deep history of the river parishes (that is, stories of the enslaved), take the 10-mile **1811 Slave Revolt Trail,** which begins at the **1811 Kid Ory House** (see below) and ends at the **Destrehan Plantation** (see below). It commemorates the brutal uprising that some call America's first freedom march.

Destrehan Plantation ★★ Its proximity (30 min. from New Orleans), in-character docents wearing period clothing, and role in *Interview with the Vampire* and *12 Years a Slave* have made Destrehan Manor a popular plantation to visit. It's the oldest intact plantation home in the lower Mississippi Valley open to the public. Built in 1787 by a free person of color for a wealthy Frenchman, it was modified from its "dated" French colonial style to Greek Revival in the 1830s. Its warmly colored, graceful lines are aesthetically pleasing, and some original furnishings remain. One room has been left un-renovated, to show the humble rawness beneath the usual public grandeur. Important history related to the enslaved occurred at Destrehan, and an education center offers exhibits dedicated to these events, including the 1811 uprising. A house display also honors Marguerite, an enslaved cook and laundress, and a new tour (about $5 extra, Sat and Mon at 10:15am) gives voice to marginalized groups, including Indigenous and enslaved. *Note:* Destrehan is a good choice for those with mobility issues, because unlike most plantation homes, it has ramps and an elevator.

13034 River Rd., La. 48, Destrehan. www.destrehanplantation.org ⓒ **877/453-2095** or 985/764-9315. $23 adults, $20 military, $18 seniors, $12 children 7–17, free for kids 6 and under. Daily 9am–4pm. Closed Jan 1, Mardi Gras, Easter, Thanksgiving, and Dec 24–25.

1811 Kid Ory Historic House ★★ This museum is a bit off River Road, on I-61, but it's a worthy detour. Its founder, John McCusker, a former staff photographer for the *Times-Picayune,* is a passionate authority on early jazz and the role New Orleans musicians played in shaping this uniquely American art form. McCusker was there when the levees broke in 2005 and shared the 2006 Pulitzer Prize for Public Service Journalism for coverage of Hurricane Katrina and its aftermath. He used to give jazz history tours but recently switched gears and founded this museum on the grounds of a former plantation. The museum is dedicated to two important stories connected to the property: the 1811 rebellion (the largest uprising of enslaved people in the nation's history), which began inside the house, and the life of Edward "Kid" Ory, jazz pioneer,

---

River Road Pit Stop

Restaurants are in short supply along the River Road. The cafe at Oak Alley is the best of the mostly so-so eateries at the plantations. Instead, stop at down-home **B&C Seafood,** just east of Laura Plantation, where you can join the locals digging into steaming trays of boiled seafood and Cajun standards (2155 Hwy. 18, Vacherie; ⓒ **225/265-8356**; all items $7–$25; Mon–Sat 9am–5pm).

born in the slave quarters in 1886. You'll see Ory's century-old trombone, other historic instruments, and a collection of maps, antiques, and interactive displays. The museum is also the starting point of the 10-mile 1811 Slave Revolt Trail. 1128 LA 628, Laplace. www.1811kidoryhistorichouse.com. ℭ **985/359-7300.** $15 adults, $7.50 kids under 10. Tues–Sun 10am–3pm.

Laura: A Creole Plantation ★★★ Laura is simple on the outside but absorbing within. It has no hoop-skirted guides, offering instead a thorough view of daily life on an 18th- and 19th-century sugar plantation, a cultural history of Louisiana's Creole population, and an in-depth examination of one Creole family. Much is known about this house and its residents thanks to extensive records (more than 5,000 documents researched in France), including the detailed memoirs of its namesake, proto-feminist head-of-household Laura Locoul. In 1994, Laura was Louisiana's first plantation to delve into stories of the enslaved. In 2004, many original artifacts were saved by employees in a fire, after which the main house and a slave cabin were accurately restored to the 1805 period. And in 2017, a small onsite museum opened, dedicated to sharing stories of the enslaved and history of the slave trade and resistance. Two more standout facts: The beloved Br'er Rabbit stories were first collected here by a folklorist in the 1870s, and Fats Domino's parents were born on this plantation.

2247 Hwy. 18, Vacherie. www.lauraplantation.com. ℭ **888/799-7690** or 225/265-7690. $25 adults, $23 military, $15 teens 13–17, $10 children 6–12, free for children 5 and under. ($2 discount online for adult tickets.) Tours daily 10am–4pm every 40 min; last tour 3:20pm. Tours in French available some days; check website. Special-interest tours available with advance notice for groups of 20 or more. Closed Jan 1, Mardi Gras, Easter, Thanksgiving, and Christmas.

Oak Alley Plantation ★★★ If your image of plantation homes comes strictly from Tara in *Gone With the Wind,* you can see something reasonably close to that Hollywood creation here. A massive white house, its porch lined with giant columns, approached by a quarter-mile drive lined with stately oak trees (the 1839 house has 28 fluted Doric columns to match the 28 trees). Consequently, this is Louisiana's most famous plantation house. It's also the slickest operation, with golf carts traversing the blacktopped property. Oak Alley lay disintegrating until 1914; new owners and restorers were responsible for its National Historic Landmark designation. In 2012 a row of re-created slave quarters was added. The well-researched displays do a good job of illuminating the lives of the enslaved and the means by which this plantation survived. A memorial wall and database honor enslaved residents. Big-house tours now also tell the unvarnished truth, highlighting the stark dichotomy between the lives of the owners and those of their forced laborers. A sit-down restaurant and casual cafe are on-site, as well as bed-and-breakfast rooms.

3645 La. 18, Vacherie. www.oakalleyplantation.com. ℭ **800/442-5539** or 225/265-2151. Admission with "Big House" exhibit: $27 adults, $9 children 6–17, free for children 5 and under. Discounts for seniors, AAA members, and active military. Admission without "Big House" exhibit $2 less. Grounds open daily 9am–5pm, tours every 30 min 9am–4:30pm. Restaurant open 8:30am–5pm. Closed Jan 1, Thanksgiving, and Christmas.

St. Francisville doesn't look like much on approach, but history buffs, nature lovers, and ghost hunters will be charmed. This is not Cajun Country—this area has American plantations only and no French history, but if you're interested in plantations from an architectural, historical, or cultural perspective, you can do well by planting yourself here for an overnighter. (And if you're interested in ghosts, we'll point you straight to the **Myrtles Plantation**—www.myrtlesplantation.com— billed as "one of American's most haunted homes.") The town is 30 miles northwest of Baton Rouge and 2 hours by car from New Orleans. Contact the West Feliciana Parish **tourism office** at 11757 Ferdinand St. (www.explorewest feliciana.com; ℂ **800/789-4221** or 225/635-6769; Mon–Sun 9am–5pm). The tourism office is located in the Historical Society Museum—stop by here first to get the lay of the land.

Recommended places to stay include the **St. Francisville Inn,** at 5720 Commerce St. (stfrancisvilleinn.com; ℂ **225/635-6502;** $185–$335), a recently renovated boutique hotel with antiques-laden rooms, fab restaurant **The Saint,** a craft cocktail bar, and pool, all of which welcome guests and locals. There's also **Butler Greenwood Plantation B&B,** at 8345 U.S. 61 (www. butlergreenwood.com; ℂ **225/635-6312;** double $150–$250), with modest guest cottages, some with Jacuzzis or fireplaces, on oak-laden grounds; and the budget-friendly, hippie-friendly downtown **3V Tourist Court,** at 5687 Commerce St. (www.themagnoliacafe. net/3v-tourist-courts; ℂ **225/721-7003;** $85–$145), a collection of cute, quirky historic efficiency cabins (hello, fans of tiny houses) built in 1938. (Bonus: Local favorite **Magnolia Café** is onsite.)

Whitney Plantation ★★★   Again, if you see only one plantation, make it the Whitney. Slavery may get meager mention at other plantations. Here, at the first museum of its kind in the U.S., history comes from the perspective of the enslaved. Visitors receive a name tag with the biography of an enslaved individual, immediately personalizing the experience, and begin the 90-minute guided walking tour with a short film shown in a church. They share the pews with life-size sculptures by artist Woodrow Nash of enslaved children, which are beautiful, spiritual, and heartrending. The tour moves to expansive gardens of somber monuments etched with personal testimonials and 107,000 names; a separate "Field of Angels" remembers enslaved children (40 perished on this very land). These contemplative spaces lay the emotional foundation as the tour moves to sparse cabin homes; the historic kitchen; endless fields; murky creeks that gave cover during escape attempts, and the blacksmith cabin where men toiled over the instruments of their own confinement.

Among the most affecting is the three-cell jail, a crude, iron cage positioned with cruel irony such that, now twice confined, the prisoner's barred view is of the gleaming "big house" (where appropriately scant tour time is spent). Elsewhere, 60 ceramic heads on spikes pay noble, resonant tribute to enslaved

Area attractions include:

o **Oakley House at Audubon State Historic Site ★** John James Audubon received room and board in exchange for giving art lessons to the young resident of this 1801 plantation home. After class, he painted 32 of his "Birds of America" series (those lessons helped finance the books' publication). A tour of the just-restored, 17-room colonial is worthwhile, and leave time to walk among the gardens and nature trails, part of a 100-acre wildlife sanctuary. There are original slave quarters and occasional special programs highlighting the influence of African Americans on the development of early America. 11788 Hwy. 965, St. Francisville; www.lastateparks.com/historic-sites/audubon-state-historic-site; ℭ **225/635-3739;** $10 adults, $8 seniors, $5 students 6 to 17, free for kids 3 and under; daily 9am to 5pm.

o **Rosedown Plantation ★★** Rosedown is by far the most impressive and historic of the more far-flung plantations, starting with its wide avenue of ancient oaks and dramatic gardens. Tours educate about 19th-century culture, family customs, and the lives and contributions of enslaved workers. 12501 Hwy. 10, at La. 10 and U.S. 61, St. Francisville; www.lastateparks.com/historic-sites/rosedown-plantation-state-historic-site; ℭ **888/376-1867** or 225/635-3332; house tour and historic gardens $12 adults, $10 seniors, $6 students 6 to 17, free for kids 5 and under; daily 9am to 5pm; tours begin at 10am; last tour at 4pm.

persons decapitated during the uprising in 1811. Not everything is original (much was razed), but it's all deeply authentic, haunting, and vital.

5099 Hwy. 18, Wallace. www.whitneyplantation.com. ℭ **225/265-3300.** $25 adults; $23 seniors, students, active military; $11 kids 6–18; free for children 6 and under. Wed–Mon 9:30am–4:30pm. Tours hourly; book in advance; no self-guided option. Most of tour is outdoors, rain or shine. Paths wheelchair-accessible (some parts rough); 2nd floor of house not wheelchair-accessible. Closed Jan 1, Mardi Gras Day, July 4, Thanksgiving, Dec 25.

CAJUN COUNTRY

This area, also called Acadiana (though you won't find that on the maps) has a history and culture unique in the US. It consists of a rough triangle of Louisiana made up of 22 parishes (counties), from St. Landry at the top of the triangle to the Gulf of Mexico at its base. Lafayette is the unofficial capital of Acadiana.

Meet the Cajuns

The Cajuns' history is a sad one, but it produced a people and a culture well worth knowing. In the early 1600s, colonists from France began settling the southeastern coast of Canada in a region of Nova Scotia they named Acadia.

tuning in **TO CAJUN COUNTRY**

Our standard soundtrack for the drive from New Orleans to Cajun Country begins with the excellent **WWOZ 90.7 FM** (to which we're assiduously tuned while in the city). After an hour on the road, static takes over, signaling the unwrapping of whatever new music we've recently purchased from **Louisiana Music Factory** (p. 245). In about half a CD's time, we can usually pull in **KBON 101.1 FM** for some rollickin' Cajun and zydeco tunes. At that point we know we've arrived, as much in geography as mood.

They developed a peaceful agricultural society based on the values of a strong Catholic faith, deep love of family, and respect for their relatively small landholdings.

This pastoral existence was isolated from Europe for nearly 150 years, until Acadia became the property of the British. The king's representatives tried to force the Acadians to pledge allegiance to the British Crown, renounce Catholicism, and embrace the king's Protestantism, but for decades they steadfastly refused. Finally, the British governor of the region sent in troops. Villages were burned and families separated as ships were loaded to deport them. A 10-year diaspora began, scattering them to France, England, America's East Coast, and the West Indies. Hundreds of lives were lost to the terrible conditions onboard.

In 1765, Bernard Andry brought 231 men, women, and children to reestablish a permanent home in Louisiana, a natural destination thanks to its strong French background. These industrious settlers worked the swampy, wildlife-teeming lands, building levees, draining fields, and planting many of the farms you still see here.

Cajun Language

Much of this essay was provided by author, historian, and four-time Grammy nominee Ann Allen Savoy, who, along with her husband Marc (an acclaimed accordion maker), are members of the Savoy-Doucet Cajun Band and several other groups. The Savoys are celebrated keepers of the culture, not least for having spawned a musical dynasty. All four of their talented children are carrying the cultural torch through their own music and art.

The French influence in Louisiana is one of the things that sets the state apart from the rest of the United States. Although French is spoken by many older Cajuns (ages 60 and up), most middle-aged Louisianans don't speak the language. This is partially because knowledge of the French language, from the 1930s on, became associated with a lack of business success or education. Cajun music was considered hokey, and Cajun culture on the whole was denigrated and stigmatized.

Today, Cajun culture has experienced a resurgence of popularity and respect. Young people are emphatically adopting their ancestors' language, music, recipes, and other traditions, and proudly speak with the sharp, bright Cajun accent.

Cajun French is peppered with beautiful old words dating from Louis XIV, unused in France and historically intriguing. It is not a dialect of French; however, many words have been localized (a mosquito can be called a *marougouin* in one area, a *moustique* in another, a *cousin* elsewhere), and "Franglish" is common (*"On va revenir right back"*—We'll be right back).

Additionally, the fascinating Creole language is still spoken by many Black Louisianans. A compilation of French and African dialects, it is quite different from standard French, though Cajuns and Black Creoles can speak and understand both languages.

Cajun Music

It's hard to decide which is more important to a Cajun: food or music. In the early days when instruments were scarce, Cajuns held dances to a cappella voices. With roots probably found in medieval France, the strains came in the form of a brisk two-step or a waltz. Traditional groups still play mostly acoustic instruments—a fiddle, an accordion, a triangle, maybe a guitar, and the traditional high, loud vocal wail.

The best place to hear real Cajun music is on someone's back porch, the time-honored spot for eating some gumbo and listening to several generations of players jamming. If you can't wrangle an invitation, the local dance halls on any weekend will do just fine. It's quite the social scene, and there are usually willing dance coaches for newbies (don't be shy—everyone will be watching the really good dancers; you should, too). The following 3-day Cajun weekend takes you on a well-rounded musical introduction to this region. For Cajun music clubs in New Orleans, see p. 221.

Planning Your Trip

You'll see and do a lot during this 3-day weekend, which includes options to customize the trip based on your own interests. A bit of adventurous meandering on your own will most definitely reward you with more finds.

It's awfully fun to visit Acadiana during **Cajun Mardi Gras** (p. 59), **Festival International de Louisiane** (p. 31), **Festivals Acadiens et Creoles** (p. 33), or the **Breaux Bridge Crawfish Festival**—but any weekend will do. There's plenty of music throughout the year and often a small festival somewhere in the area. If you find one, you simply have to go: They're almost guaranteed to be a memorable social, cultural, and musical experience. (We'll never forget our first Yambilee.)

For tons of good, detailed information, contact the **Lafayette Convention and Visitors Commission** (www.lafayettetravel.com; © **800/346-1958** in the U.S., 800/543-5340 in Canada, or 337/232-3737), and check **Downtown Lafayette** for goings-on (www.downtownlafayette.org; © **337/291-5566**).

Boudin: Get Linked In

Boudin (boo-*dan*) is a Cajun sausage link made of pork, pork liver, rice, onions, and spices and stuffed inside a casing. If it's done right, it's spicy and sublime. In these parts, you can get this inexpensive (about $4 per pound) snack at just about any grocery store or gas station. Disputes rage about whose reigns supreme (**www.boudinlink.com** has digitized the argument). It's best eaten while leaning against a car, chased with a Barq's root beer. Conducting a comparison test is great fun, but the singular choice in these parts is the **Best Stop** (615 Hwy. 93 N., Scott, exit 97 off the I-10; www. beststopinscott.com; ✆ **337/233-5805**). It's always busy, so the links and crunchy pig-fat cracklins (aka *chicharones*) are always fresh. Did we mention that they ship? Send us some *now*, please. Best Stop is open Monday to Saturday 6am to 8pm and Sunday 6am to 6pm.

Organized Tours

A terrific and oh-so-easy way to explore Cajun Country is with **Gondwana Ecotours** (www.gondwanaecotours.com; ✆ **504/708-5161**), which offers completely customizable, all-inclusive 2- to 5-day itineraries including transportation, meals, and lodging. On our 3-day tour, we spent hours chatting with a zydeco legend in his studio; we met a Cajun chef-musician who taught us to cook an unforgettable dinner then played music for us under the stars; we glided through Cypress and Tupelo trees on a private, eco-friendly swamp tour (and spotted a bald eagle, a red-shouldered hawk, and eight alligators). We bunked in a roomy country-style cottage on the edge of a placid pond, equipped with canoes and life jackets. For all you get—attentive guide, comfy transport, cozy digs, more-than-you-could-ever-eat food at cool local joints, unique experiences, and plenty of sightseeing stops—the price, from $699 for 2 days) is money well spent.

If it's strictly the food you're after (can't blame ya), you can drive to Lafayette, where **Cajun Food Tours** (www.cajunfoodtours.com; ✆ **337/230-6169**) will save you from additional driving by shuttling you to six Cajun food stops in a comfy 14-seater bus. They're not all the little down-home holes-in-the-walls you might stumble onto yourself, but it's convenient, fairly priced, and you'll get plenty of variety. Tours cost $59 adults; kids 12 and under $35; reservations required). Plan in advance because they may not be offered every day. Each year, **Festival Tours International** (p. 63) offers a stellar music-focused tour of the area during the 3 days between Jazz Fest weekends. Also see "Organized Tours," p. 190.

A CAJUN 3-DAY WEEKEND

The suggested itinerary for a 3-day side trip from New Orleans to Cajun Country is designed to introduce you to this marvelous, singular culture. The drive from New Orleans is about 2½ to 3 hours, mostly via I-10 (140 miles from New Orleans). If you opt to drive back via U.S. 90, it's about 170 miles.

You'll be based in Lafayette and going to the smaller towns of Eunice, Mamou, and St. Martinville for a thorough immersion in real Cajun culture. We've provided main highway directions; some form of GPS is recommended to help get you to the in-town destinations.

Friday, Day 1: Lafayette ★★★

Leave New Orleans early in the day and head for the River Road (Hwy. 18) plantations to tour a plantation (p. 269). Or head directly to Lafayette. *Tip:* Try to avoid going through Baton Rouge at afternoon rush hour.

Lafayette is a midsize city of 120,000, with a university (University of Louisiana Lafayette) and plenty of hotel options. But we recommend you opt for an atmospheric B&B instead. Check in at the 130-year-old (but recently renovated) **T'Frere's Bed & Breakfast** (1905 Verot School Rd., Lafayette; www.tfrereshouse.com; 𝄞 **800/984-9347** or 337/984-9347; double $135) or **Mouton Plantation Bed & Breakfast** (338 N. Sterling St., Lafayette; www.moutonplantation.com; 𝄞 **337/233-7816**; double $125; suites $175). For a more freewheeling, downtown experience, **Blue Moon Saloon & Guesthouse** offers en suite rooms or cottage accommodations in the main house, with shared kitchen and public areas adjacent to the storied outdoor live music venue (215 E. Convent St., Lafayette; bluemoonpresents.com; 𝄞 **337/234-2422**; double from $105, bungalow $275). Three-night minimum stay during certain festivals.

Plan to arrive in time for lunch, and if it's a weekday, go directly to **Creole Lunch House** (713 12th St., Lafayette, in a residential area; www.facebook.com/creolesstuffedbread; 𝄞 **337/232-9929;** Mon–Fri 11am–2pm). Get a couple of stuffed breads and whatever's been smothered that day (chicken thighs, pork chop, shoe, it's all gonna be ridiculously good home cooking). We'll toss out three other casual, worthy eatin' options to bookmark during your Lafayette stay: **Johnson's Boucaniere** (1111 St. John St.; www.johnsonsboucaniere.com; 𝄞 **337/269-8878;** Tues–Fri 10am–3pm, Sat 8am–3pm, Sun 10am–2pm), especially the sublime pulled pork; **Olde Tyme Grocery** for po' boys (218 W. St. Mary Blvd.; www.oldetymegrocery.com; 𝄞 **337/235-8165;** Mon–Fri 8am–10pm, Sat 9am–7pm); and the relative newcomer **Pop's Poboys** (740 Jefferson St.; www.popspoboys.com; 𝄞 **337/534-0621;** Mon–Wed 10:30am–2pm, Thurs–Sat 10:30am–9pm), whose menu includes great salads (a rare find in these parts) and creative twists on po'boys, like "the Kathy Bates"—fried green tomatoes with spicy chili-garlic shrimp salad and Crystal hot sauce. Oh yeah.

Relax or stroll the shops and galleries in downtown. Take in the exhibits at the **Acadiana Center for the Arts** (101 W. Vermilion St., Lafayette; acadianacenterforthearts.org; 𝄞 **337/233-7060;** daily 9am–5pm). Or visit the **Church of St. John the Evangelist** (914 St. John St., Lafayette; www.saintjohncathedral.org; 𝄞 **337/232-1322**), a splendid Dutch Romanesque edifice done in red and white brick, with fine stained glass dating to 1916. Then hop in the car and drive 10 minutes to **Martin Accordions** (2143 Willow St., Scott; www.martinaccordions.com; *C* **337/232-4001**), a friendly family-owned business for 30-plus years, to lay eyes on their dazzling handmade instruments. Tours and demonstrations are available by appointment, or sometimes by request. (We popped over unannounced when they were hard at work and wound up staying an hour, learning about how accordions are made and hearing incredible music.)

For dinner, reserve a table at brand-new hotspot **Vestal** (555 Jefferson St., Lafayette; www.vestalrestaurant.com; *C* **337/534-0682**). The elegant Southern-meets-French menu focuses on food sourced from local vendors and artisans, cooked over "live fire" on hot, hardwood coals. (In other words, there's a 14-ft. fire in the middle of this restaurant.) All steaks are served with bone marrow herb butter, so steak is a good bet; other standouts are koji-cured duck breast topped with bourbon foie gras (the duck is locally and humanely raised) and the blue crab spaghetti. If you have room, flip back the time-travel clock and squeeze in a sundae from **Borden's** (1103 Jefferson St., Lafayette; www.bordensicecream shoppe.com; *C* **337/235-9291**), the last retail Borden's shop in the world, and hardly changed since it scooped its first cone of creamy goodness back in 1940. Otherwise, head back and hit your relaxing veranda and cushy bed—Saturday is a full day.

Saturday, Day 2: Eunice & Mamou ★★

Grab a quick B from your B&B before heading out to supplement it. If you haven't already stopped for boudin, now's a good time, because a) pork sausage for breakfast = yes, always; b) you might want to stop here again tomorrow; and c) you'll instantly become more welcome at your next stop. Choose the **Best Stop** (see the box on p. 280), but if you require a little egg or biscuit action with your sausage, head across Highway 10 to **Don's** (730 I-10 S. Frontage Rd., Scott; www.donsspecialty meats.com; *C* **337/234-2528**). A half-link per person is a minimal sampling of boudin; get a few more links to take to the **Savoy Music Center,** 3 miles east of downtown Eunice (about a 35-min. drive; 4413 U.S. Hwy. 190 E.; www.savoymusiccenter.com; *C* **337/457-9563;** Tues–Fri 9am–5pm, closed for lunch noon–1:30pm; Sat jam 9am–noon). On weekdays this working music store sells instruments, equipment, and Marc Savoy's exquisite, world-renowned handcrafted accordions (check out the folk-art aphorisms scrawled on his workshop cabinets, if you can). At the Saturday-morning jam sessions, this nondescript faded-green building becomes the spiritual center of Cajun music. Local and visiting musicians young and old gather to savor this unpretentious, unparalleled music and culture. It's probably the closest thing to that back-porch experience you'll find.

Stay and savor this utter authenticity, or cut out to head for the alternate universe known as **Fred's Lounge** in Mamou, about 20 minutes north (west on U.S. 190, then right on LA 13; 420 6th St.; *C* **337/468-5411;** Sat 8am–1:30pm; music starts at 9am). This is the other end of the Cajun

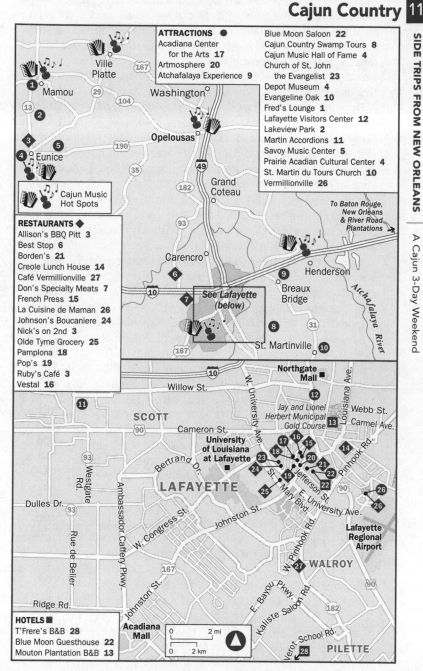

ATTRACTIONS ●
Acadiana Center
for the Arts **17**
Artmosphere **20**
Atchafalaya Experience **9**

Blue Moon Saloon **22**
Cajun Country Swamp Tours **8**
Cajun Music Hall of Fame **4**
Church of St. John
the Evangelist **23**
Depot Museum **4**
Evangeline Oak **10**
Fred's Lounge **1**
Lafayette Visitors Center **12**
Lakeview Park **2**
Martin Accordions **11**
Savoy Music Center **5**
Prairie Acadian Cultural Center **4**
St. Martin du Tours Church **10**
Vermillionville **26**

Cajun Music
Hot Spots

RESTAURANTS ◆
Allison's BBQ Pitt **3**
Best Stop **6**
Borden's **21**
Creole Lunch House **14**
Café Vermillionville **27**
Don's Specialty Meats **7**
French Press **15**
La Cuisine de Maman **26**
Johnson's Boucaniere **24**
Nick's on 2nd **3**
Olde Tyme Grocery **25**
Pamplona **18**
Pop's **19**
Ruby's Café **3**
Vestal **16**

HOTELS ■
T'Frere's B&B **28**
Blue Moon Guesthouse **22**
Mouton Plantation B&B **13**

music spectrum: a small-town bar that for half a century has hosted Saturday daytime dances starting in the early morn. Couples waltz and two-step around the mid-floor bandstand, while 80-something matriarch Tante Sue drinks shots and otherwise presides. It's pure dance-hall stuff (leaning toward the country-western side of Cajun, but much of it in French), where hardworking locals let loose. And we do mean loose (remember, they started with Coors while you were still on coffee).

Back in Eunice, lunch awaits. If it's the weekend, **Allison's BBQ Pitt** (501 W. Laurel Ave.; © **337/457-9218**) is your ticket to meaty nirvana. Some judge it the best barbecue in southern Louisiana. It's open Saturday and Sunday from 10am to 2pm for takeout plate lunch; you might have to stand in line (it's popular), but you can call ahead. Either way, you gotta sink your teeth into those smoky ribs, chicken, pork, or brisket with homemade sauce. (Thank us later.) Or for a lowkey lunch, try **Ruby's Café** (221 W. Walnut St.; © **337/550-7665**). Service is consistently warm and the menu, which changes daily, consistently comforting (think fried chicken, crawfish étouffée, smothered okra).

Stop by the **Prairie Acadian Cultural Center** (250 W. Park Ave.; www.nps.gov/jela/prairie-acadian-cultural-center-eunice.htm; © **337/457-8499;** Tues–Sat 10am–4pm) to see whether it's reopened after post-hurricane repairs—it has a terrific small collection of objects acquired from local families who had owned them for generations. Admission is free, with donations accepted. Or head around the corner to two side-by-side museums: the **Depot Museum** (220 S. C.C. Duson St.; cajuntravel.com/things/eunice-depot-museum; © **337/457-6540**), in the old train depot, with its sweet collection of memorabilia, toys, and tools, and the **Cajun Music Hall of Fame & Museum** (240 S. C.C. Duson St.; cajunfrenchmusic.org/hall-of-fame; © **337/457-6534**), where you can become an expert on the incredible music you've surely been surrounding yourself with. And speaking of music, on weekends from February until late November, **Lakeview Park & Beach** (www.lvpark.com) usually has fantastic live music in its barn—plus a motley array of other fun events, from candy bar bingo to karaoke contests and beef tongue cookoffs. (It has cute cottages, too, if you want to stay.)

Your dinner bell is probably ringing loudly. Stay in Eunice and head to **Nick's on 2nd** (123 S. 2nd St.; www.facebook.com/Nicks-on-2nd-379231635896583; © **337/466-3433**). Open since 1931, historic Nick's offers delicious, home-style dinners Tuesday to Saturday, and sweet courtyard ambiance (plus a drive-through). Or head back to Lafayette, where something a little different awaits you at **Pamplona** (631 Jefferson St., Lafayette; www.pamplonatapas.com; © **337/232-0070;** Sun–Thurs 5–10pm, Fri–Sat 5–11pm). The soothing wood-trimmed white-plaster-walled interior actually feels Spanish; the tapas are a mix of quasi-authentic and Americanized small plates. We never turn down bacon-wrapped dates or duck fat fries. And the paella? Worth the wait.

Still up for more? Check out what's on at the **Blue Moon Saloon** (215 E. Convent St., Lafayette; www.bluemoonpresents.com; ⏰ **337/234-2422;** cover free-$20), the city's premier live-music venue. Cajun, zydeco, and all forms of modern alternative roots music bring in the LSU student body and others. Cozy, funky **Artmosphere** often has local Cajun or indie bands or singer/songwriters and stays open late; (902 Johnston St.; check www.facebook.com/Artmosphere1 for updated listings).

Sunday, Day 3: Lafayette & St. Martinville ★★

After a relaxing breakfast at your B&B, visit **Vermilionville** ★★ (300 Fisher Rd., off Surrey St.; www.vermilionville.org; ⏰ **337/233-4077;** $10 adults, $8 seniors, $6 students, free for kids 5 and under; Tues–Sun 10am–4pm; admission desk closes 3pm), a Cajun-Creole settlement reconstructed on the bayou's banks, where costumed staff and crafts-people demonstrate activities of 18th- to 19th-century daily life and musicians jam. While it sounds like a kitschy "Cajunland" theme park, it's actually quite a good introduction to the culture and a thorough education about the region's Indigenous peoples, European settlers, and people of African descent. Our favorite part was meeting Sitting Bear, a retired chief and current tribal council member of the Avogel Tribe, who shared his vast knowledge. (He's there Tues–Fri until 2pm.) Live music is offered regularly; check the website for schedule. The food in on-site restaurant **La Cuisine de Maman,** is surprisingly good but for something more upscale, reserve at nearby **Café Vermillionville** ★★ in an historic inn (1304 W. Pinhook Ave.; www.cafev.com; ⏰ **337/237-0100**).

Or take an eco-conscious wildlife tour with **Atchafalaya Experience** (www.theatchafalayaexperience.com; ⏰ **337/766-1829;** $50 ages 13 and up, $25 kids under 12; daily 10am & 2pm), an outstanding 3-hour swamp excursion led by virtuoso naturalists who were raised on these bayous. If you have not yet taken to the waters of the Louisiana swamps, seeing this stunning, primeval, vital ecosystem is a must-do, and these guides are as good as it gets. Bring a hat, sunscreen, water, insect repellent, camera, and binoculars if you have them. Photography and private tours also available.

Another great choice is **Cajun Country Swamp Tours** (www.cajun countryswamptours.com; **337/319-0010;** $25 per seat), for a serene, 2-hour eco-conscious tour of Lake Martin in Breaux Bridge with a knowledgeable guide on an open boat. (Pack a hat and sunscreen!)

Lunch returns you to downtown Lafayette, to the **French Press** (214 E. Vermilion St.; www.thefrenchpresslafayette.com; ⏰ **337/233-9449;** Mon and Weds–Fri 7am–2pm, Sat–Sun 9am–2pm, closed Tues), a casual but refined spot on the higher end of the hipness scale. The biscuit sliders with boudin balls and sugarcane syrup are to die for; the chicken and waffles aren't far behind. If you're ready for lighter fare, the winning shrimp salad boasts a kicking remoulade.

To further experience the history, legend, and romance of this region, take a leisurely drive to the lovely historic burg of **St. Martinville.** Get there by taking U.S. 90 East heading south out of Lafayette, to the Louisiana 182 exit. Turn left onto East Main Street, and left again onto LA-96 East for 7⅓ miles to reach the peaceful town square. St. Martinville dates from 1765, when it was a military station. It was once known as "la Petite Paris" for the many French aristocrats who settled here after fleeing the French Revolution.

The town centers around **St. Martin du Tours Church,** constructed in 1836—the fourth-oldest Roman Catholic church in Louisiana—and poetry. Besides its natural and historic charm, the town is the home of Evangeline Emmeline, the (debatably) fictional heroine of Longfellow's tragic poem. A statue of her next to the church was donated to the town in 1929 by a movie company that shot the film version here; star Dolores del Rio supposedly posed for the sculptor. At Port Street and Bayou Teche is the ancient **Evangeline Oak** and commemorative mural, where self-proclaimed descendants claim Emmeline's boat landed after her arduous journey from Nova Scotia.

From St. Martinville, make your way to I-10 again to return to New Orleans, or alternately take U.S. 90 for a different view. It's slightly longer and moderately more interesting.

A Cajun Experience Day Trip

If you're not ready to delve deep—or you have only a day to spare—an alternative Cajun experience can be had in **Bayou/Lafourche Parish** (www.la cajunbayou.com), an hour west of New Orleans via US 90-W. There is a loose delineation between "prairie" Cajuns (those residing in the area where our 3-day tour takes you) and those of the Coast and bayous. This swath of South Louisiana, which hews to the latter, is known for its celebration of Cajun culture, extensive outdoor activities, and seafood-based fare.

Start with the **Acadian Wetlands Cultural Center** (314 St. Mary St., Thibodaux; www.nps.gov/jela/wetlands-acadian-cultural-center.htm; ✆ **985/ 448-1375**), one of six entries into Jean Lafitte National Park, which celebrates Cajun culture. The free museum also offers a free walking tour of the town of **Thibodaux** Tuesday through Thursday; and kid-friendly outside concert (BYO chair) **Music on the Bayou** at 2pm on Saturdays.

For sustenance, restaurants in this area mostly feature seafood—and it's what you should get. Try **Spahr's** (601 W. 4th St., Thibodaux; www.spahrs seafood.com; ✆ **985/448-0487;** Mon–Thurs 6am–9pm, Fri 6am–10pm, Sun 7am–9pm) for catfish, gumbo, and Bloody Marys.

Back toward New Orleans, get your hair blown back at **Arthur Matherne's Airboat Tours.** The six-passenger, customized experience goes deep into the swamps where big tour boats can't (4262 US 90, Des Allemands; www.air boattours.com; ✆ **800/975-9345;** $55–$70, book in advance). In late 2021, Hurricane Ida had forced them to temporarily shut down; if they're not back yet, book with **Ragin Cajun Airboat Tours** (10090 Hwy. 90, Luling; ragin cajunairboattours.com; ✆ **504/436-8000;** $60-$79, depending on size of boat).

PLANNING
YOUR TRIP

By Lavinia Spalding

N o matter what your idea of the perfect New Orleans trip is, this chapter will give you the information to make informed plans about getting here, getting around, and the essentials for an easy Big Easy vacation. We'll also point you toward additional resources, so you can let the *bons temps* begin even before you arrive.

GETTING THERE
By Plane

Most major domestic airlines serve the city's **Louis Armstrong New Orleans International Airport** (MSY; flymsy.com), along with several smaller regional lines. British Airways flies in from London, and Delta from Frankfurt. The dazzling Cesar Pelli–designed Louis Armstrong Airport is 15 miles west of New Orleans in the town of Kenner. Information booths are in the main terminal and in baggage claim. Private planes often use Lakefront Airport, 9 miles from downtown.

GETTING INTO TOWN FROM THE AIRPORT

Depending on the traffic and your mode of transportation, it takes approximately 30 to 45 minutes to get from the airport to the French Quarter or the Central Business District.

Most major **rental car** companies operate out of a unified facility that is accessed by a 24/7 shuttle bus. Follow the signs outside baggage claim. For $24 per person one-way (free for kids 5 and under), the official **Airport Shuttle New Orleans** van (www.airport shuttleneworleans.com; ✆ **866/596-2699** or 504/522-3500) will take you directly from the airport to your hotel in the French Quarter, Garden District, or Central Business District. The shuttle operates daily from 3:30am to 2am year-round; Airport Shuttle information ticket desks in the airport are staffed 9am to 10pm daily. *Tip:* If you plan to take the Airport Shuttle *to* the airport when you depart, book and pay for a round-trip ($44) in advance via phone or online. For the return, you must call 24 hours in advance to arrange a pickup time.

If two or more passengers are traveling, **taxis** and **ride shares** are a better, more direct deal than the shuttle. A taxi from the airport to most hotels costs $36 for one to two people; $15 per person for three or more passengers. Follow signs to taxi and ride share stands outside the baggage-claim area. **Uber** and **Lyft** rates run about $35 to $39 plus tip.

Limo service can be arranged via **Bonomolo Limousine Service** (www. bonolimo.com; ℂ **800/451-9258** or 504/522-0892). Airport transfers in a luxury sedan run about $85 plus gratuity; ask about in-town hourly rates.

The cheapest option is by **public bus.** The **New Orleans Regional Transit Authority (NORTA)** Airport Express line No. 202 runs directly from the airport to two different Central Business District stops on Loyola Avenue (Howard Ave. and Poydras St.) nine times daily between 3:45am and 7pm for $1.25. Another option is the **Jefferson Transit public bus No. E1** for $2, which runs daily into the city, starting at City Park Avenue and continuing down Canal St. to Tulane Ave. and Loyola Ave. in the Central Business District, stopping at major intersections along the way. Riders can transfer to Regional Transit Authority lines for an additional $1.25. Buses run from 5am to 8:13pm weekdays (6:39am-9:11pm Sat, 7:10am-8:40pm Sun; check schedule for return times). Follow signs outside baggage claim upstairs to the NORTA and RTA public bus stop, located on the outer curb outside departures (level 3). For more information, call **Jefferson Transit** (www.jeffersontransit. org) or the **Regional Transit Authority** (www.norta.com), both at ℂ **504/248-3900.**

By Car

You can drive to New Orleans via **I-10, I-55, U.S. 90, U.S. 61,** or across the Lake Pontchartrain Causeway (**U.S. 190**). If possible, drive in during daylight to allow time to enjoy the distinctive swampy scenery. U.S. 61 or the Causeway offer the best views, but the larger roads are considerably faster. Approximate drive time to New Orleans from Atlanta is almost 7 hours; from Houston it's over 5 hours; Chicago, 14 hours; Baton Rouge is an hour and a half away. For info on driving while you're in the city, see "Getting Around," p. 289.

By Bus

Greyhound buses serve New Orleans from **Union Passenger Terminal** (NOUPT) at 1001 Loyola Ave. (www.greyhound.com; ℂ **504/525-6075**), as do **Megabus** (us.megabus.com; ℂ **877/462-6342**) and **Flixbus** (www.flixbus. com; ℂ **855/626-8585**), both of which have cheap fares to/from select Southern cities where they connect to many others.

By Train

Passenger rail lines pass through some beautiful scenery. **Amtrak** (www. amtrak.com; ℂ **800/872-7245**) trains serve the city's **Union Passenger Terminal,** 1001 Loyola Ave., in the Central Business District. Though the station is on a streetcar line, at press time the route was being served by shuttle bus

#46 due to downtown construction. Alternately, call a taxi or ride share. Hotels in the French Quarter and the Central Business District are a short ride or a healthy walk away.

By Ship

Cruise passenger traffic to or from the Port of New Orleans is substantial, largely because passengers can add a Crescent City visit before or after their voyage. Cruise lines include **Carnival Cruises** (www.carnival.com; ✆ 800/764-7419), **Crystal Cruises** (www.crystalcruises.com; ✆ 888/722-0021), **Disney Cruise Line** (www.disneycruise.com; ✆ 800/951-3532), **Norwegian Cruise Line** (www.ncl.com; ✆ 866/234-7350), and **Royal Caribbean** (www.royalcaribbean.com; ✆ 866/562-7625). You can also explore the Mississippi River on **American Cruise Lines** (www.americancruiselines.com; ✆ 800/460-4518) or the **American Queen Steamboat Company** (www.americanqueensteamboatcompany.com; ✆ 888/749-5280). Taxi fare from the cruise terminal to most hotels is about $14, or $8 per person for two or more people. Parking at the terminal is about $22 per day.

GETTING AROUND

By Car

Unless you're planning to explore outside the major tourist zones (and, okay, this book does recommend a few outlying destinations), you really don't need to rent a car during your stay in New Orleans. The town is flat, ultra-picturesque, and made for daytime (nighttime, not so much) walking. Taxis are scarce these days (you can call one, but good luck hailing one from a corner), but **Uber, Lyft,** and **pedicabs** are available, and there's decent public transportation. Indeed, a streetcar ride is as much entertainment as a means of getting around. Driving and parking can be a hassle—many streets are narrow, potholed, crowded, and one-way, and outside the French Quarter, streets angle in logic-defying directions to accommodate the curvy Mississippi. Street parking is minimal in the Quarter and CBD (though parking enforcement is not) and parking lots, especially at hotels, are fiendishly expensive.

That said, all the major **car-rental agencies** have a presence in New Orleans, with offices at the airport and around town. Rates vary widely according to company and seasonal demand. Plan in advance, and shop around. Insurance and taxes are almost never included in quoted rental-car rates in the U.S., and they can be significant. You'll pay a premium to pick up a rental at the airport, but it may be worth the convenience. If your stay is lengthy, weigh the difference between renting from a lower-cost, in-town location vs. transfer costs to and from that cheaper locale.

To rent a car you need a valid driver's license and a major credit card. Foreign visitors will need a passport (foreign driver's licenses are usually recognized, but it's wise to get an international one if your home license is not in English). Some companies will accept a debit card with a cash deposit. The minimum age is usually 25, but Enterprise and Budget will rent to younger people for an added charge; they may also require proof of ability to pay (such as paycheck stubs or utility bills). It's a good idea to buy insurance coverage unless you're certain your own auto or credit card insurance is sufficient.

If you're in town for a while, download the **ParkMobile App.** Once you complete the annoying set-up, you can conveniently pay for many street meters via smartphone (and add meter time from afar—a huge plus). Some parking lots use other apps (couldn't they all decide on one?).

Generally, gas costs in New Orleans tends to be at or below the U.S. average (shockingly so, if you're from California or Hawaii). Gas stations are readily available on major streets, but there are none within the French Quarter. When driving in New Orleans, **right turns on a red light** are legal except where NO RIGHT TURN ON RED signs are posted. Sneaky red-light cameras abound (as do **speed cameras,** especially in school zones). Many major intersections restrict left turns. Drive past the intersection, make a U-turn at the next allowable place, then double back and turn right (a maneuver often called the "Louisiana left").

Streetcars run down the center of Canal Street and St. Charles, Rampart, Carrollton, and Loyola avenues, where drivers have to cross their paths frequently. **Look *both* ways for streetcars,** yield the right of way to them, and allow ample time to cross the tracks. They'll brake if you're in their way, of course, but it's best not to get stuck on the tracks and impede their progress.

It is illegal to have an open container of alcohol, including "go-cups," in a moving car, and, of course, driving while under the influence of alcohol is a serious offense. Keep car doors locked and never leave belongings, packages, or gadgets visible in parked cars.

By Taxi or Rideshare

Taxis used to be plentiful in New Orleans; these days, don't expect to hail one. The only recommended cab company in New Orleans at press time was **United Cabs;** book by phone or Curb app (www.unitedcabs.com; ℂ **504/522-9771**). The rate is $3.50 when you enter the taxi and $2.40 per mile thereafter. During special events, the rate is $7 per person (or the meter rate if it's greater) to the event site. From the French Quarter to an uptown restaurant or club, expect to spend $12 to $25 depending on traffic and distance; cash or credit cards accepted.

Uber and **Lyft** (available only by app) are usually readily available, but they can be slow to arrive in the midst of big events. Expect the fare to be slightly less than standard taxis until surge prices kick in (which is often).

On Foot

We can't stress this enough: Walking is by far the best way to see New Orleans in the daytime (besides, you need to walk off all those calories!). You'll miss the many unique and sometimes glorious sights if you whiz past them. Slow down, stroll, and take it in. Say hello to people you pass by, especially if they're sitting on their porches. If it's just too hot, humid, or rainy, seek the shelter of balconies and galleries, or pop into locally owned cafes and bars, and support the business by buying a cold one. Hydration, y'all. Roaming the streets at night isn't the best idea, however, unless you're with others in well-lit busy areas.

By Streetcar

Besides being a National Historic Landmark, the **St. Charles Avenue streetcar** is also a convenient, scenic, and fun way to get from downtown to uptown and back. Its iconic green cars click and clack for 6½ miles, 24 hours a day at frequent intervals, getting crowded at school and business rush hours. Board at Canal and Carondelet streets (directly across Canal from Bourbon St. in the French Quarter) or anywhere along the line. The tracks wind beyond the point where St. Charles Avenue bends into Carrollton Avenue, ending at Marsalis Harmony Park (Claiborne Ave.). The original cars used on the St. Charles line are not air-conditioned, and only three of the cars are wheelchair-accessible. All other lines have A/C and lifts.

The **Riverfront** line runs the length of the French Quarter, from the French Market near Esplanade (a great foot saver). Its spiffy bright-red cars turn onto Canal Street and transfer to the **Canal Street** line, serving two destinations (check the sign on the front of the car): CEMETERIES goes to several of the older cemeteries (daily 5am-4:12am); CITY PARK (5:08am-4:20am) goes along Carrollton Avenue through Mid-City to City Park/the New Orleans Museum of Art (and Jazz Fest, when streetcars will be jammed). *Note:* Due to major construction, at press time the Riverfront and Canal Street lines through downtown were being serviced by bus, and the Rampart Street/St. Claude line was closed (with the St. Claude/Jackson Barracks bus No. 88 filling in). They're expected to resume service in 2022–2023.

The **fare** for any streetcar line is $1.25; transfers are free. All streetcars take exact change in bills or coins only, or **JazzyPass** (see the box on p. 292).

By Bike & Scooter

Biking is also a great way to see the city. The terrain is flat, the breeze feels good, there are bike paths, and you can cover ground pretty swiftly on two wheels. Streets can be busy, bumpy, and potholed, however, so it's a plus if you're experienced in city riding. And while driver awareness has improved, this ain't Portland or Amsterdam: Stay aware at all times. Long-established **Bicycle Michael's,** 622 Frenchmen St. (www.bicyclemichaels.com; *⌀* **504/945-9505**) has good-quality, multi-gear hybrids and mountain bikes (most other rentals are cruisers) starting at $30 for a half-day (4 hr.), $40 per day. At the other end of the French Quarter, **American Bicycle Rentals,** 1025 Bienville St. (www.bikerentalneworleans.com; *⌀* **504/522-4368**), has super-sturdy, well-maintained, cushy-seated single-speed bikes with coaster brakes for $35 for 8 hours, $40 for 24 hours. If you're staying uptown, hit **Mike the Bike Guy,** $30 per day (4411 Magazine St.; www.mikethebikeguy.com;

☎ **504/899-1344**). Rates usually include a lock and optional helmet. All offer longer-term rentals; multi-day minimums may apply during Mardi Gras or Jazz Fest. Also see "Bicycle & Other Wheeled Tours," p. 199.

Launched in 2017, shut down during Covid, and re-launched through the nonprofit Blue Krewe, the convenient **Blue Bikes** bike-sharing system has 500 "pedal-assist e-bikes" available to rent, located in "hubs" around the city. After downloading the mobile app and choosing a plan and payment form, you can locate a bike nearby, scan the QR code, unlock for $1 and pay-as-you-go for 15¢ a minute (monthly plans available for frequent riders). Lock the bike back at a hub or at any rack (within the service area) for an extra $2, then snap and submit a photo to end the ride. Bikes have lights and a lock but no helmets (not required but recommended in NOLA). Maps and details are on the website and app (www.bluebikesnola.com).

Another fun, easy way to get around is on a Lance PCH50 motor scooter from **Avenue Scooters,** 1134 St. Charles Ave. (www.avenuescooters.com; ☎ **504/609-3838**). Rates start at $60 for 3 hours; $90 per full day including helmet. They get up to about 35 mph, so you ride in car lanes (and get no love from four-wheeled drivers). Follow all traffic rules, and watch those potholes!

By Pedicab

These rickshaw-like tricycles will get two people from point A to B via pedal power (a driver's, not yours). They're relatively easy to hail in the French Quarter and occasionally seen in other tourist parts, or you can call to request one from **Bike Taxi Unlimited** (☎ **504/891-3441**) or **Need a Ride Pedicabs** (☎ **504/488-6565**). City-set rates are $5 for the first 6 blocks, $1 per block per person after that (plus tip for your hard-riding driver, especially if they make you a deal for a longer ride). It's a great option for fatigued feet or short hops when you want a little breeze (or breezy conversation).

By Ferry

The **Canal Street/Algiers Point Ferry** (www.norta.com/Maps-Schedules/New-Orleans-Ferry; ☎ **504/248-3900**) is one of the city's great assets, for transportation to the old Algiers Point neighborhood (see p. 178) and views of

---

Discounted Rides with the JazzyPass

If you don't have a car in New Orleans, invest in a **JazzyPass,** which allows unlimited rides on all streetcar and bus lines. It's a bargain at $3 for 1 day, or $45 for a full month (31 days). Single-day passes can be purchased when boarding. Get passes on the **GoMobile** App, at numerous retail locations (like Walgreens), or at vending machines (1-day passes only) at the streetcar stops at Canal at Bourbon; N. Peters; White; or City Park streets. Mail order in advance is also an option. More info at **Regional Transit Authority** (www.norta. com; ☎ **504/248-3900**).

the city from the Mississippi River. It's a down-and-dirty, working ferry, but it's atmospheric at night when the city's glowing skyline reflects on the water. The 25-minute ride from the foot of Canal Street costs $2 each way cash, or purchase via RTA's GoMobile app. It's pedestrians and bikes only, no cars. The ferry leaves New Orleans every 15 minutes beginning at 6:15am Monday to Friday, with the last return ferry to downtown at 8:30pm Sunday to Thursday, and 10:30pm Saturday and Sunday. Check for schedule changes on holidays, events, and in general. At press time, the new terminal was under construction and RTA was providing shuttle service from Canal Street to an interim departure point not far downriver. It's a good idea to call first.

By City Bus

New Orleans has a good public bus system that many locals rely on—and the buses fill in when streetcars are down—so chances are there's a bus that runs exactly where you want to go. The single-ride fare is $1.25 (including transfer). You must have exact change in bills or coins to pay on-site, but you can buy fares via mobile phone using the **GoMobile** App. For all-day or multiple rides, invest in a **JazzyPass** (see box). For route information, contact the **RTA** (www.norta.com; © **504/248-3900**).

[FastFACTS] NEW ORLEANS

Area Codes The area code for New Orleans is **504.**

Business Hours Most stores don't open early in the morning—many open around 10am or noon and stay open until 5pm or 6pm. Bars tend to stay open until the wee hours, even 24/7, and restaurants' hours vary depending on the types of meals they serve. Expect breakfast to start around 8am, lunch around 11am, and dinner at 6pm.

Cellphones See "Mobile Phones," later in this section.

Crime See "Safety," later in this section.

Customs For U.S. Customs details and information on what you're allowed to bring home, consult your home country's customs

services agency. In the U.S., consult **U.S. Customs** at **U.S. Customs & Border Protection (CBP),** 1300 Pennsylvania Ave. NW, Washington, DC 20229 (www.cbp.gov; © **877/227-5511**).

Doctors See "Health," later in this section.

Drinking Laws The legal age for buying or consuming alcoholic beverages is 21; proof of age is required and often requested at bars, nightclubs, and restaurants, so bring ID when you go out. Due to recent crackdowns, nowadays pretty much everyone—even senior citizens—may get carded. Alcoholic beverages are available round-the-clock, 7 days a week. Bars can stay open all night in New

Orleans, and liquor is sold in grocery and liquor stores. You're allowed to drink in public, but not from a glass or bottle. Bars will provide a plastic "go-cup" into which you can transfer your drink as you leave (and some have walk-up windows for quick and easy refills).

Warning: Although New Orleans has a reputation for tolerance, public intoxication and "drunk and disorderly" are most definitely illegal, as many a jailed tourist can testify. Practice moderation and make smart decisions. And don't even think about driving (car, motorcycle, *or* bicycle) while intoxicated: This is a zero-tolerance crime. Do not carry open containers of alcohol in your car or any public area that isn't zoned for alcohol consumption.

Electricity   The United States uses 110 to 120 volts AC (60 cycles), compared to 220 to 240 volts AC (50 cycles) in most of Europe, Australia, and New Zealand. Converters that change 220–240 volts to 110–120 volts are difficult to find in the United States, so bring one with you.

Embassies & Consulates   All embassies are in the nation's capital, Washington, D.C. Some have consulate offices in major U.S. cities, including a few in New Orleans. To find a consulate for your home country, call for directory information in Washington, D.C. (© 202/555-1212), or check www.embassy.org/embassies. It's always a good idea to enter this information in your contacts before you leave your home country.

Emergencies   For fire, ambulance, and police, dial © 911 from any phone (it is a free call).

Family Travel   New Orleans offers plenty of activities and sights appropriate for children, who often get a real kick out of the city (and love Mardi Gras!). Summer months bring the heat but also the bargains, so weigh your family's tolerance levels for a visit during school vacation. See "Especially for Kids" in chapter 7 on p. 200.

Gyms   Most hotels have at least a nominal fitness center. Some offer day passes to local gyms. Otherwise, workout day passes

can be had at two **Downtown Fitness** locations (www.downtownfitnesscenter.com) convenient to the French Quarter and Bywater: at 365 Canal St., 3rd floor, © **504/525-2956;** or 2372 St. Claude Ave., © **504/754-1101.** The storied **New Orleans Athletic Club** has an indoor pool and track, a library, and (yup) a bar (222 N. Rampart St.; www.neworleansathleticclub.com; © **504/525-2375**). The enormous **Health Club at the Hilton New Orleans Riverside** has cardio machines, weights, two pools, and a sauna plus tennis, squash, and racquetball for additional costs. Day passes are $15 with local hotel key (2 Poydras St.; © **504/556-3742**). Members of the **Anytime Fitness** chain can find multiple locations around town. There are also lots of free or inexpensive drop-in workouts around town: **Move Ya Brass** (www.moveyabrass.com) gives stretch, bounce, hip-hop, and HIIT workouts in **Crescent Park and City Park;** the international workout group **November Project** (www.Facebook.com/NovProjectNO) has free 6am workouts Wednesdays at Champions Square and Fridays at NOMA in City Park; the **Cabildo** (p. 160) and **Besthoff Sculpture Garden** (p. 171) offer yoga classes.

Health   If you have a medical condition that may require care, make appropriate arrangements before traveling to New Orleans.

Pollen, sun, uneven sidewalks, overindulgence, and **mosquitoes** (especially near swamps and bayous) are the most common annoyances, so pack insect repellent, sunscreen, protective clothing, digestive aids, and antihistamines. For "Hospitals," see below. If you need a doctor for less urgent health concerns, try **Ochsner On Call** (www.ochsner.org/services/ochsner-on-call; © **504/842-3155** or 800/231-5257; daily 24 hr.) or visit an **Ochsner Urgent Care** clinic (www.ochsner.org/services/urgent-care-services): 4100 Canal St. in Mid-City (© **504/218-4853;** Mon–Fri 8am–7:30pm, Sat–Sun 9am–5:30pm); 900 Magazine St. in the Warehouse District (© **504/552-2433**); or 4605 Magazine St. in Uptown (© **504/891-7676**). The Louisiana Department of Health (www.ldh.la.gov; © **225/342-9500**) offers information on COVID-19 testing locations, as does Ochsner On Call. Also see "Pharmacies," later in this section.

Hospitals   In an emergency, dial © **911** from any phone to summon paramedics. Nearby emergency rooms are at **Ochsner Baptist Medical Center,** 2700 Napoleon Ave. (© **504/899-9311**); **Tulane Medical Center,** 1415 Tulane Ave. (© **504/988-5263**); and **Touro Infirmary,** 1401 Foucher St. (© **504/269-3943**).

Insurance   Travel insurance is a good safety net if you think for some reason you may need to cancel or postpone your trip (or even if you don't). Most medical insurance policies cover you if you are on vacation, but check your policy before you depart.

Internet, Wi-Fi & Computer Rentals
New Orleans is a pretty well-wired city. Nearly all major hotels have free Wi-Fi in their lobbies, as do many cafes, bars, and all Starbucks (there's one in the French Quarter in the Canal Place Mall, 333 Canal St.; ℂ 504/566-1223). The vast majority of hotels also offer some form of in-room Internet access, usually high-speed wireless. Many now include the cost in the room charge; some add a daily surcharge of $10 to $20. Barring that, the easiest option is simply to boot up and see what signals you get; or walk down any commercial street and look for "Free Wi-Fi" signs. Alternately, a concierge or front desk attendant should be able to direct you to nearby public Wi-Fi locations.

Most larger hotels have business centers with computers for rent. Also see "Mail & Shipping," below. **Louis Armstrong New Orleans International Airport** has free Wi-Fi coverage in all passenger areas.

Language English is spoken everywhere, while French and Spanish are heard occasionally in New Orleans.

Legal Aid If you are pulled over by the police for a minor infraction (such as

speeding), never attempt to pay the fine directly to an officer; this could be construed as attempted bribery, a much more serious crime. Pay fines by mail or directly into the hands of the clerk of the court. If accused of a more serious offense, say and do nothing before consulting a lawyer. Here in the U.S., the burden is on the state to prove a person's guilt beyond a reasonable doubt, and everyone has the right to remain silent, whether he or she is suspected of a crime or actually arrested. Once arrested, a person can make one telephone call to a party of his or her choice. The international visitor should call his or her embassy or consulate.

LGBTQIA Travelers
New Orleans is a very welcoming town with an extensive and active LGBTQIA community and many events specific to the community. The most fun you can have is to roll in during **Southern Decadence**, aka Gay Mardi Gras (p. 32) Otherwise, just hit the bars and clubs (p. 228) or go online and talk with people. For resources, try **Ambush Magazine**, 828-A Bourbon St. (www.ambushmag.com), and the **Gulf South LGBT Chamber** (www.gslgbt-chamber.org). The **Metropolitan Community Church of New Orleans**, 5401 S. Claiborne Ave. (www.MCCNewOrleans.org; ℂ 504/270-1622), serves a primarily gay and lesbian congregation. **Good**

Friends (p. 229) bar is a hub. The **AllWays Lounge & Cabaret** (p. 219) has fab drag and burlesque shows and also holds an amazing monthly queer storytelling event. Go to **Oz** (p. 230) to get your late-night dance on. The local **LGBT Community Center** (www.lgbtccneworleans.org) lists events and info on its website.

Mail & Shipping At press time, domestic postage rates were 40¢ for a postcard and 58¢ for a letter up to 1 ounce. For international mail, a first-class postcard or letter stamp costs $1.20. For more information, go to **www.usps.com**. Always include ZIP codes when mailing items in the U.S. Use the lookup tool at www.usps.com/zip4. Convenient **FedEx Office** locations with full shipping capabilities (and computer rental computer stations) are at 555 Canal St. (ℂ 504/654-1057) and 762 St. Charles Ave. (ℂ 504/581-2541).

If you aren't sure what your address will be while in the U.S., mail can be sent to you, in your name, c/o General Delivery at the main post office of the city or region where you expect to be. New Orleans' main post office is at 701 Loyola Ave. in the Warehouse District. The addressee must pick up mail in person, with proof of identity (such as driver's license, passport). Most post offices will hold mail for up to 30 days and are open weekdays 8am to 4pm (Sat 9am–noon).

Medical Care See "Health," earlier in this section.

Mobile Phones Mobile (cell) phone and texting service in New Orleans is generally good, with the larger carriers all getting excellent coverage. Some dead zones still exist around the city and inside old brick buildings. International mobile phone service can be hit-or-miss (despite what you may have been told before you began your trip). If you plan to use your phone a lot while in New Orleans, it may be worthwhile to purchase a prepaid, no-contract phone locally. You can get hooked up at most **CVS** or **Walgreens** drugstores or **Walmart** (1901 Tchoupitoulas St.; ℂ **504/522-4142**). Compare the plans' sign-on offers, roaming and data use charges, usage requirements, and limitations to make sure you're not purchasing more extensive or longer-term services than you need.

If you have a computer and internet service, consider using a broadband-based telephone service such as **Skype** (www.skype. com) or **Vonage** (www. vonage.com), which allows you to make free international calls from your computer. Neither service requires that the people you're calling also have the service (though you'll need an account and subscription to make a call if they do not).

Money & Costs Frommer's lists prices in U.S. dollars. The currency conversions quoted below were correct at press time. However, rates fluctuate, so before departing, consult a currency exchange website such as **www.xe.com**.

Costs in New Orleans are generally right in the middle of, and sometimes lower than, those in other midsize U.S. "destination" cities— less than New York, for example, but more than Phoenix. Prices have crept up over the last few years, so it's no longer the great value it once was, and costs vary greatly by season. In the heat of summer, you can often find good hotel and "Coolinary" restaurant deals, while prices can soar during big events. December's **prix-fixe Réveillon deals** can get you into restaurants for dinners that might otherwise be prohibitive.

With a few cash-only exceptions, **major credit cards** are accepted everywhere (some don't accept American Express, Discover, or Diner's Club). Cash is king anywhere, and ATMs are plentiful throughout the city (including inside many bars and souvenir shops). Expect a $2.50 to $4 charge to use an ATM outside your network. To avoid the fee, many grocery and convenience stores will allow you to get a small amount of cash back with your purchase (from $10–$100, depending on store policy).

Beware hidden credit-card fees while traveling. Check with your credit or debit card issuer to see what fees, if any, will be charged for overseas transactions, even if those charges were made in U.S. dollars. Check with your bank before departing to avoid surprise charges on your statement.

Newspapers & Magazines The city has one local paper, the Baton Rouge-based **Advocate** (www.theadvocate.com/ new_orleans), which bought the Pulitzer Prize–winning **Times-Picayune** in 2019, ending that paper's 182 years serving the city. **Offbeat** (www.offbeat.com) and **Where Y'at** (www.whereyat. com) are monthly entertainment guides with live music, art, and special-event listings. Both can usually be found in hotels and clubs and get scarce toward the end of the month. **Gambit Weekly** (www.theadvocate. com/gambit), which comes out every Sunday, is a free alternative paper with a mix of local news and entertainment.

THE VALUE OF THE U.S. DOLLAR VS. OTHER POPULAR CURRENCIES

US$	C$	£	€	A$	NZ$
1.00	1.26	0.73	0.88	1.40	1.50

WHAT THINGS COST IN NEW ORLEANS	US$
Ride share from airport to the Quarter	40.00 (for two people)
Shuttle from airport to the Quarter	24.00 (per person)
One-way ride on bus or streetcar	1.25
1-day JazzyPass for bus/streetcar	3.00
Double room at the Windsor Court Hotel	295.00–459.00
Double at The Antebellum Guest House	150.00–185.00
Dorm bed at The Quisby	23.00–100.00
Order of three beignets at Café du Monde	3.75
Dinner at Commander's Palace (three courses)	65.00 (per person)
Lunch Entrée at Dooky Chase	17.95 (per person)
Fried shrimp po'boy at Parkway Bakery & Tavern	8.99
Ticket to a show at Tipitina's (on average)	15.00–40.00
Cost of a Hurricane at Pat O' Brien's	11.50
Cost of a Pimm's Cup at Napoleon House	8.00

Packing   What to pack depends largely on when you'll be here and what you plan to do. Comfortable walking shoes are a must year-round. A compact umbrella will often be put to use, as will other rain gear during the wetter months (and a sun hat for much of the year). A light sweater or jacket is needed even in the hottest weather, when the indoor A/C can get frigid. Casual wear is the daytime norm, but cocktail wear is appropriate in nicer restaurants, and some of the old-liners require jackets for gentlemen. Also see the suggestions under "Health" and "Safety" in this section.

Passports   Every air traveler entering the U.S. is required to show a valid passport (including U.S. citizens). Those entering by land and sea must also present a passport or other appropriate documentation. See **www.dhs.gov/cross ing-us-borders** for details. For more on passport requirements, contact the Passport Office of your home country. If you need to obtain or renew a passport, do so at least 6 months before your departure.

Pharmacies   Pharmacies (aka chemists or druggists) are easily found. The large chain pharmacies **CVS** and **Walgreens** operate throughout the city, including several in the French Quarter.

Police   Dial 📞 **911** for emergencies. This is a free call from any phone.

Safety   Unfortunately, it's true that New Orleans has a high crime rate. Much (not all) of the serious crime is drug-related and confined to areas where tourists do not go. Still, we urge you to be very cautious about where you go, what you do, and with whom, particularly at night. Use the same street smarts you would in any big city: Travel in groups or pairs, take cabs or rideshares if you're not sure of an area, stay in well-lit areas with plenty of street and pedestrian traffic, don't hook up with strangers, and follow your instincts if something seems "off." Stay alert and walk with confidence; avoid looking distracted, confused, or (sorry) drunk. In fact, avoid *being* drunk—that's just a good general rule. One way to ensure that you will look like a tourist—and thus, a target—is to wear Mardi Gras beads at any time other than Mardi Gras.

iPhones have become a target of grab-and-run thieves, especially since users, like those who text while walking, are frequently distracted. If you must check something on your phone, stop into a hotel lobby, bar, or shop.

When it's not in use, put that expensive camera out of sight. Use camera cases and purses with a shoulder strap, carried diagonally over the shoulder. Consider using a money belt or other hidden travel wallet. For clubbing, invest in a cute little shoulder-strappy bag, one you can dance with rather than leave on your seat (better yet, go purse-free). Never leave valuables in the outside pocket of a backpack. Use those hotel safes, and if you must store belongings in a car, store them in the trunk. Leave expensive-looking jewelry and other conspicuous valuables at home. And by all means, don't look for or buy drugs or engage in any illegal activity.

On the **Bourbon Street** party blocks, be careful when socializing with strangers, and be alert to distractions by potential pickpocket teams. Use busy Bourbon Street or Decatur Street to walk from the French Quarter to Frenchmen Street (you may encounter unhoused people, but they're generally not dangerous). Better yet, call a cab, Uber, or Lyft. Also, never visit cemeteries at night, unless you're with a tour.

Sections of **Central City** and the **Seventh Ward** are transitional and may be considered sketchy; as are some bits of the **Tremé, Bywater, Marigny,** and the **Irish Channel** section of the Lower Garden District. This shouldn't dissuade you from visiting, but you should keep on your toes.

Single Travelers Single tourists and conventioneers are plentiful in New Orleans, and both male and female single travelers should feel comfortable here. People are generally friendly and many restaurants, including some of the city's finest, serve meals at the bar—a personal favorite spot when dining solo (Emeril's, Coquette, Cochon, Sylvain, Doris Metropolitan, and Acme come to mind). Still, single women travelers in particular should heed the warnings under "Safety," above.

Smoking The city council instituted a broad-reaching law in 2015, banning smoking indoors almost everywhere including hotels, restaurants, casinos, nightclubs, and bars (cigar and vape bars are excepted). Places with patios or courtyards can designate them as smoking areas, but not all do. It's okay to light up on the street a few feet from restaurant or shop entrances, and in most parks. Though **marijuana** was recently decriminalized in Louisiana it is still illegal to smoke it in public places. A new law in 2021 makes possession of up to 14 grams of marijuana—a half-ounce—a misdemeanor crime carrying a fine of no more than $100 (even for repeat offenses).

Taxes The United States has no value-added tax (VAT) or other indirect tax at the national level, but states, counties, and cities may levy their own taxes, which will not appear on price tags. The **sales tax** in New Orleans is 9.45%; **hotel room tax** is 16.35% plus US$1 to $2 per room per night.

International travelers who purchase goods in Louisiana to take back to their home countries can often get the sales tax refunded in full. When you make your purchase, keep your receipt and also request a "tax back" voucher (you'll be asked to show your passport). Before you leave the state, bring your receipts, vouchers, and travel ticket (of fewer than 90 days duration) to the **Refund Center** in the Outlet Collection at Riverwalk mall (p. 234) or the **Tax Free** counter at Louis Armstrong International Airport (Level 2, allow time before your flight). You'll be rebated in cash up to US$500. Larger rebates are mailed; see **www.louisianataxfree.com** for instructions and more information. Not all stores participate, so ask first.

Also, many original works of art purchased in New Orleans are tax-exempt. Do inquire, as this applies in designated cultural districts only.

Telephones Hotel costs for long-distance and local calls made from guest room phones vary widely, from complimentary to astronomically expensive—if you intend to use the room phone, definitely inquire about phone charges. You may be better off using a mobile phone or a prepaid calling card. Public payphones are rare, but some (for example, at airports) accept credit cards. Most long-distance and international calls can be dialed directly from any phone. Calls to area codes **800, 888, 877, 866, 855,** and **833** are free. **To make calls within the United States and to Canada,** dial **1** followed by the area code and the seven-digit number. **For other international calls,** dial **011** followed by the country code, city code, and the number you are calling. For **directory assistance** (help finding numbers, aka "Information") in the U.S. and Canada, dial **411.** For other phone services, dial **0** to reach an operator within the U.S.; dial **00** for assistance with international calls. Also see "Mobile Phones," p. 296.

Time New Orleans is in the Central Time Zone (CST), which is 6 hours earlier than Greenwich Mean Time. When it's noon in New Orleans, it's 10am in Los Angeles (PST); 1pm in New York City; 6pm in London (GMT); and 5am the next day in Sydney.

Daylight savings time (summer time) is in effect from 1am on the second Sunday in March to 1am on the first Sunday in November, except in Arizona, Hawaii, the U.S. Virgin Islands, and Puerto Rico.

Daylight saving time moves the clock 1 hour ahead of standard time.

Tipping In the U.S., tips are not a bonus but an essential part of certain workers' incomes. Even if service is poor, most people leave a smaller tip rather than none at all. Feeling generous? Tip more than amounts shown here. In hotels, tip **bellhops** $1 to $2 per bag ($3 if you have a lot of luggage) and tip the **chamber staff** $5 and up per night (more if you've been extra messy). Tip the **doorman** or **concierge** if he or she has provided you with some specific service (for example, calling a cab for you or obtaining tickets or reservations), $5 to $20 or more depending on complexity. Tip the **valet-parking attendant** $2 to $5 every time you get your car; more if you're driving something you need to protect.

In restaurants, bars, and nightclubs, tip **service staff** and **bartenders** 20% of the check, tip **checkroom attendants** $2 per garment, and tip **valet-parking attendants** $2 to $5 per vehicle. Some restaurants will automatically add a tip to the bill for larger parties (typically 18% for six or more guests). Check your bill or ask your server whether gratuity, sometimes labeled "service charge," has been included in your bill.

Tip **cab drivers** 15% to 20% of the fare, tip **skycaps** at airports at least $2 per bag (more if you have a lot of luggage), and tip

hairdressers and **barbers** 15% to 20%.

Toilets You won't find public toilets or "restrooms" on the streets in most U.S. cities, so scout them out in hotel lobbies, bars, restaurants, museums, department stores, railway and bus stations, and service stations. Large hotels are often the best bet for clean facilities. Restaurants and bars may restrict their restrooms to paying patrons, but it never hurts to ask.

Travelers with Disabilities Most disabilities shouldn't stop anyone from traveling in New Orleans. Most public places are required to comply with disability-friendly regulations. Almost all public establishments and at least some modes of public transportation provide accessible entrances and facilities. Still, some older properties, including some National Historic Landmarks, may be inaccessible, given exemptions due to their historic nature. Before you book a reservation, call and inquire based on your needs. The city's newer hotels, restaurants, and shops are fully accommodating, and many older ones have undergone retrofitting.

The city's bumpy and uneven sidewalks (and sometimes potholed or cobblestoned streets) can be challenging for those with mobility or visual differences, though most crossings have curb cuts. Three of the historic St. Charles streetcars are equipped with wheelchair lifts at the front and rear of each car. (Look for the universal accessibility icon on the front and side to determine if the car has lifts.) All other streetcar lines have wheelchair lifts. More accessibility information can be found at www.neworleans.com/plan/accessibility/faqs.

For paratransit information and reservations, contact **RTA Paratransit** (www.norta.com/Accessibility/Paratransit; ℂ **504/827-8345**).

Vaccinations & Inoculations At press time, anyone 12 and over in New Orleans had to provide proof of at least one dose of an approved COVID vaccine or negative PCR, molecular, or antigen test within 72 hours to enter restaurants, fitness centers, sports stadiums, entertainment venues, and large outdoor gatherings. Also check regulations if you're arriving from an area known to have rates of certain other illnesses (particularly cholera, yellow fever, measles, and Ebola).

Visas The U.S. State Department has a **Visa Waiver Program (VWP)** allowing citizens from a long list of countries to enter the United States without a visa for stays of up to 90 days. Even visitors from VWP countries (and others for whom a visa is not necessary) are required to have an e-passport, online registration through the Electronic System for Travel Authorization (ESTA), and an electronic application

before departing for the U.S. Travelers not eligible for VWP are required to get a visa. Some travelers may also be required to present a round-trip air or cruise ticket upon arrival in the U.S. Canadian citizens may enter the United States without visas but will need to show passports and proof of residence. Citizens of all other countries must have: (1) a valid passport that expires at least 6 months later than the scheduled end of their visit to the U.S., and (2) a tourist visa. All visa and passport information is subject to change. Check with the American Embassy in your home country at least 6 months before your planned departure and read up at travel.state.gov/content/travel/en/us-visas/tourism-visit/visa-waiver-program.html.

Visitor Information Even a seasoned traveler should consider writing or calling ahead to **New Orleans and Company,** 2020 St. Charles Ave., New Orleans, LA 70130 (www.neworleans.com; ℂ **800/672-6124** or 504/566-5011). The friendly staff can offer advice and help with decision-making; if you have a special interest, they'll help you plan your visit around it—this is definitely one of the most helpful tourist centers in any major city.

At the **Jean Lafitte National Park and Preserve's French Quarter Visitor Center,** 419 Decatur St., near Conti Street (www.

nps.gov/jela/french-quarter-site.htm; ℂ **504/589-2636**), super-cool National Park Service rangers are full of info and guidance. **Bonus:** They offer frequent free programs highlighting local culture, from musical performances to dance classes to lectures lead by local experts. The historical **Basin St. Station** building, 501 Basin St. (ℂ **504/544-0440;** daily 8:30am–5:30pm), in the Tremé neighborhood has a welcome center with maps; community exhibits; booklets on restaurants, accommodations, and sightseeing; and a walking tour kiosk.

Be aware: Many of the concierges, tour offices, and visitor centers scattered around the city (including the biggie at Basin Street Station) are for-profit offices operated by tourism businesses hawking their own wares. Rather than unbiased services that will recommend the best tour for you, these are commissioned sales offices. If you feel you're getting sold something that's not exactly right, you can always contact any tour company directly to buy tours. Or just use Frommer's most excellent, unbiased, carefully curated recommendations!

Water Tap water is safe to drink in New Orleans, although bottled water is still popular (though not eco-friendly). Treated water from the Mississippi River is the main source of tap water, as is true for most cities along the Mississippi.

Index

Map List

Photo Credits

p. i: Courtesy of New Orleans & Company/Chris Granger; p. ii: Courtesy of New Orleans & Company/Traveling Newlyweds; p. iii: © Andriy Blokhin; p. iv: Courtesy of New Orleans & Company/Zack Smith Photogrpahy; p. v, top: Courtesy of New Orleans & Company/Stephen Young; p. v, bottom: Courtesy of New Orleans & Company/Jeff Anding; p. vi, top: © Louisiana Travel; p. vi, bottom left: Courtesy of Bourbon Hotel/J.Stephen Young; p. vi, bottom right: © Jeremy Thompson; p. vii, top: © Michael Rosebrock/Shutterstock.com; p. vii, middle: © Dion Hinchcliffe; p. vii, bottom: Courtesy of New Orleans & Company/Stephen Young; p. viii, top left: Courtesy of New Orleans & Company/Zack Smith Photogrpahy; p. viii, top right: Courtesy of Arnuad's; p. viii, bottom left: Courtesy of New Orleans & Company/Zack Smith Photogrpahy; p. viii, bottom right: Courtesy of New Orleans & Company/Paul Broussard; p. ix, top: Courtesy of New Orleans & Company/Jeff Anding; p. ix, bottom left: Courtesy of New Orleans & Company/Pableaux Johnson; p. ix, bottom right: Courtesy of New Orleans & Company/Stephen Young; p. x, top: © cajunzydecophotos; p. x, middle: Courtesy of New Orleans & Company/Paul Broussard; p. x, bottom: Courtesy of New Orleans & Company/Paul Broussard; p. xi, top: Courtesy of New Orleans & Company/Paul Broussard; p. xi, bottom left: Courtesy of Audubon Park/Susan Poag; p. xi, bottom right: Courtesy of New Orleans & Company/Erika Goldring; p. xii, top: Courtesy of National WWII Museum; p. xii, middle: © Steven Depolo; p. xii, bottom: © William A. Morgan/Shutterstock.com; p. xiii, top left: © Pauline Frommer; p. xiii, top right: © travelview/Shutterstock.com; p. xiii, bottom left: © William A. Morgan/Shutterstock.com; p. xiii, bottom right: Courtesy of New Orleans & Company/Richard Nowitz New Orleans; p. xiv, top left: Courtesy of Ace Hotel/Fran Parente; p. xiv, top right: © Infrogmation of New Orleans; p. xiv, bottom: Courtesy of Compere Lapin; p. xv, top: Courtesy of Laura Plantation; p. xv, bottom left: © Sean Pavone/Shutterstock.com; p. xv, bottom right: © Malachi Jacobs/Shutterstock.com; p. xvi, top: © Karen Ambrose Hickey; p. xvi, middle: Courtesy of Lafayette Travel; p. xvi, bottom: Courtesy of Lafayette Travel

Frommer's EasyGuide to New Orleans, 8th Edition

Published by

FROMMER MEDIA LLC

Copyright © 2022 by Frommer Media LLC. All rights reserved. No part of this publication may be reproduced, stored in a retrieval system, or transmitted in any form or by any means, electronic, mechanical,
photocopying, recording, scanning or otherwise, except as permitted under Sections 107 or 108 of the
1976 United States Copyright Act, without the prior written permission of the Publisher. Requests to the
Publisher for permission should be addressed to support@frommermedia.com.

Frommer's is a registered trademark of Arthur Frommer. Frommer Media LLC is not associated with any
product or vendor mentioned in this book.

ISBN 978-1-62887-519-5 (paper), 978-1-62887-520-1 (e-book)

Editorial Director: Pauline Frommer
Editor: Holly Hughes
Production Editor: Heather Wilcox
Cartographer: Roberta Stockwell
Photo Editor: Meghan Lamb
Indexer: Kelly Henthorne
Cover Design: Dave Riedy

Front Cover: Jazz musicians perform in New Orleans' French Quarter. © Rainer Puster/iStock.com
Back Cover: New Orleans streetcars traveling on Canal Street. © CIS/Shutterstock

For information on our other products or services, see www.frommers.com.

FrommerMedia LLC also publishes its books in a variety of electronic formats. Some content that appears
in print may not be available in electronic formats.

Manufactured in the United States of America

5 4 3 2 1

ABOUT THE AUTHORS

Diana K. Schwam is a writer, strategic communications consultant, and a New Orleanian by choice from decades back. She can often be found in the city's music, food, and cultural havens and hovels or exploring its lesser-known and unfolding corners in Miss Gulch—her green, two-wheeled pothole-dodger. Diana has infinite love for New Orleans—its folks and its ghosts; its eccentric elegance and eternal mysteries; and its tellers of tales and truths: They are as warm and essential to her as its spring air. She's not much of a dancer but claps on the twos and fours. Usually.

Lavinia Spalding is series editor of *The Best Women's Travel Writing*, author of *Writing Away*, and co-author of *With a Measure of Grace* and *This Immeasurable Place*. Her work has appeared in the *New York Times*, *Tin House*, *Longreads*, and many other publications, and she co-hosts the podcast *There She Goes*. Since moving to New Orleans in 2016, Lavinia has been making her way through the city's extraordinary array of sights, sounds, scents, and tastes. But it's the feeling of New Orleans she loves most—a warmth and spirit unlike anything she's experienced in all her wanderings. She's here to stay.

ABOUT THE FROMMER TRAVEL GUIDES

For most of the past 50 years, Frommer's has been the leading series of travel guides in North America, accounting for as many as 24% of all guidebooks sold. I think I know why.

Though we hope our books are entertaining, we nevertheless deal with travel in a serious fashion. Our guidebooks have never looked on such journeys as a mere recreation, but as a far more important human function, a time of learning and introspection, an essential part of a civilized life. We stress the culture, lifestyle, history, and beliefs of the destinations we cover, and urge our readers to seek out people and new ideas as the chief rewards of travel.

We have never shied from controversy. We have, from the beginning, encouraged our authors to be intensely judgmental, critical—both pro and con—in their comments, and wholly independent. Our only clients are our readers, and we have triggered the ire of countless prominent sorts, from a tourist newspaper we called "practically worthless" (it unsuccessfully sued us) to the many rip-offs we've condemned.

And because we believe that travel should be available to everyone regardless of their incomes, we have always been cost-conscious at every level of expenditure. Though we have broadened our recommendations beyond the budget category, we insist that every lodging we include be sensibly priced. We use every form of media to assist our readers, and are particularly proud of our feisty daily website, the award-winning Frommers.com.

I have high hopes for the future of Frommer's. May these guidebooks, in all the years ahead, continue to reflect the joy of travel and the freedom that travel represents. May they always pursue a cost-conscious path, so that people of all incomes can enjoy the rewards of travel. And may they create, for both the traveler and the persons among whom we travel, a community of friends, where all human beings live in harmony and peace.

Arthur Frommer